A Practitioner's Guide to the Regulation of Insurance

Fourth Edition

A Practitioner's Guide to the Regulation of Insurance

Fourth Edition

Consultant Editor
John Young
Hogan Lovells

SWEET & MAXWELL

THOMSON REUTERS

First Edition	2002	by John Young
Second Edition	2004	by John Young
Third Edition	2008	by John Young

Published in 2011 by Sweet & Maxwell, 100 Avenue Road, London, NW3 3PF part of Thomson Reuters (Professional) UK Limited (Registered in England & Wales, Company No 1679046.
Registered Office and address for service: Aldgate House, 33 Aldgate High Street, London, EC3N 1DL)

Sweet & Maxwell ® is a registered trademark of Thomson Reuters (Professional) UK Limited.

For further information on our products and services, visit *www.sweetandmaxwell.co.uk*

Typeset by Letterpart Ltd, Reigate, Surrey

Printed and bound in Great Britain by CPI Group (UK) Ltd, Croydon, CR0 4YY

No natural forests were destroyed to make this product; only farmed timber was used and re-planted.

A CIP catalogue record of this book is available for the British Library.

ISBN: 978-0-414-04857-7

Thomson Reuters and the Thomson Reuters logo are trademarks of Thomson Reuters.

Crown copyright material is reproduced with the permission of the Controller of HMSO and the Queen's Printer for Scotland.

Biographies

John Young has been Co-Chair of international law firm, Hogan Lovells, since its formation in May 2010, having formerly been Senior Partner of Lovells since May 2004. He also heads the firm's highly-regarded corporate and regulatory insurance practice. He has for over 20 years been a respected adviser on the regulation of insurance business and corporate transactions within the insurance industry, both in the UK and internationally.

Katherine Coates has been a partner of the international law firm Clifford Chance since 1990, and heads the corporate financial institutions practice and the global insurance sector group. She has advised on the establishment of new insurance companies, mergers, acquisitions and joint ventures, portfolio transfers of both life and non-life portfolios, capital raising, demutualisations, distribution arrangements, a wide variety of regulatory issues, insurance securitisations and the development of insurance products and policy wordings.

Hilary Evenett is a partner within the corporate insurance practice of Clifford Chance, and has advised on the establishment of new insurance companies (life and non-life), mergers, acquisitions, joint ventures and portfolio transfers, together with a range of regulatory issues. The corporate insurance group specialises in providing regulatory, corporate and product development advice to life and non-life insurers, mutual insurers, insurance brokers and participants in the Lloyd's market.

Narind Singh is a partner of Clifford Chance and is part of the financial institutions group and corporate insurance practice. He specialises in financial services M&A and regulatory advice, including for insurers and reinsurers (both life and non-life) and brokers. His work in the insurance sector includes mergers, acquisitions and portfolio transfers, product and policy advice, regulatory advice, alternative risk transfer, joint ventures and distribution arrangements.

James Bateson is head of the Financial Institutions practice at Norton Rose. He specialises in the insurance and financial services sectors and has extensive experience in advising both domestic and international insurers in relation to corporate, regulatory and transactional matters. He is a regular public speaker and media commentator on insurance matters.

Laura Hodgson is a Professional Support Lawyer in charge of know-how and training in the insurance group at Norton Rose. She has contributed to a number of insurance and reinsurance law publications, with particular focus on regulatory issues.

John Philpott is a London-based Director in Ernst & Young's Financial Services Practice. He has worked for Ernst & Young and its predecessor firms throughout his career, specialising in insurance since he qualified as a chartered accountant in 1978. His particular area of expertise is the prudential regulation of insurance companies by the FSA: he has assisted many insurers with authorisations and other regulatory processes, and is the author of the firm's publication on the preparation of FSA returns.

Robert Stirling is a London based corporate partner in Freshfields Bruckhaus Deringer LLP. His experience includes both public and private M&A and a wide range of other corporate finance, securities and advisory work, with particular experience in the insurance sector.

James Smethurst is a London based corporate partner at Freshfields Bruckhaus Deringer LLP. He specialises in financial services regulation, advising a wide range of financial institutions, including investment banks, insurance companies and market infrastructure providers.

Geoffrey Maddock is a partner in the financial institutions group of the corporate department of Herbert Smith LLP. He works principally on corporate and finance transactions and regulatory advice in the insurance sector and has extensive experience of demutualisation of life assurance companies, acquisitions, disposals, joint ventures and the regulatory aspects of complex capital raising transactions in this sector. He also has considerable experience of transfers of insurance business under the Financial Services and Markets Act.

Laurence Elliott is a partner in Herbert Smith LLP's restructuring and insolvency group, with particular expertise in insurance insolvency, including solvent and insolvent schemes of arrangement. He also acts for insolvency practitioners in a wide range of formal insolvencies and provides advice to companies in financial difficulties.

Duncan Barber is a corporate partner at Linklaters who works primarily in the insurance sector, dealing with a wide range of corporate (share and portfolio acquisitions and disposals, demutualisations, takeovers, flotations, group reorganisations, regulatory problems), financing (equity, tier 1 and tier 2 debt securities, contingent loans, securitisations) and commercial (reinsurance, outsourcing and distribution arrangements) work both in the UK and on a cross-border basis. He advises a number of leading companies and banks on insurance sector and other financial services transactions, financings and regulation.

Ambereen Salamat is head of financial services regulation at Holman Fenwick Willan. She specialises in insurance regulation, distribution, policy wordings and products (including alternative risk transfer), corporate transactions and run-off. She has advised on most aspects of ongoing regulation of insurance and reinsurance companies, including restructurings, and has extensive experience of handling transfers of portfolios of life and non-life business, having advised on a substantial number of transfers under Part VII of the Financial Services and Markets Act 2000 and the predecessor legislation. Ambereen speaks extensively at industry events on insurance and regulatory issues (including Solvency II) and has been published regularly in the insurance press.

Charles Rix is a corporate partner at Hogan Lovells and a senior member of the firm's corporate and regulatory insurance team. Over the last 15 years, he has specialised in mergers and acquisitions, demutualisations, joint ventures, group restructurings, Part VII transfers and schemes of arrangement in the insurance sector as well as advice on the regulation of insurance businesses, in particular with-profits businesses. He recently advised on Paternoster's sale to Rothesay, Goldman Sachs' life assurance division, and on the restructuring and sale of the Phoenix Group to Liberty.

Steven McEwan is Of Counsel in Hogan Lovells' corporate and regulatory insurance team. He has advised on insurance law and regulation since 2002, specialising in matters involving long-term insurance, regulatory capital, reinsurance, insurance finance and Lloyd's. He has published articles on numerous topics, including recent articles on Solvency II, and regularly speaks at conferences.

Maria Ross has been a partner in the corporate insurance group at Norton Rose since 2000. Her experience includes mergers and acquisitions, joint ventures, portfolio transfers, outsourcing, flotations and product distribution in the insurance market. In addition to transactional work, Maria advises clients on regulatory issues, including solvency, compliance and policy wording. She has particular expertise in the life sector, having spent a year on secondment to a UK life assurer. In January 2011 Maria was named as one of the "Hot 100 Lawyers" by The Lawyer Magazine.

John Gilbert is a consultant with the international law firm, Hogan Lovells, following his retirement as a partner in the firm in 2005. He advises on the law and regulation of friendly societies and other mutual insurers and represents Hogan Lovells on various committees and working groups of the Association of Financial Mutuals. His clients include both incorporated and registered friendly societies and he has been involved in most of the major developments in the friendly societies movement over the last 15 years, including "Project Chrysalis", the industry's campaign to reform the regulation of with-profits funds operated by mutual insurers. He is also currently working on developing friendly societies as a vehicle for shariah-compliant insurance in the UK and European markets.

Preface to the 4th Edition

It is always wise for an author to consider the context in which he writes before making bold predictions. Rash statements made in a magazine article will almost certainly be forgotten, assuming the article is read by anyone at all. If not they can be attributed to a rush of blood to the head when meeting a deadline. Even more, those made on the internet. Those made in a printed book are frequently repented at leisure.

In the preface to the third (2008) edition of this publication I expressed the considered view that:

> "[I]t is time to acknowledge that the Financial Services Authority ('FSA') has now come of age. It has achieved both maturity and self-confidence in its approach to insurance, and the industry is largely getting used to that approach. . . . It is tempting to think that we may now be entering into the most settled period in the evolution of UK insurance regulation for a decade."

Sadly my crystal ball did not tell me that Lehman would collapse seven weeks after I wrote those words, nor that the Coalition Government that took office a year and half later would take a more jaundiced view of the FSA's track record than I took myself (and, in relation to the insurance industry, unrepentantly still take). As I write on this occasion the market is actively preparing for the abolition of the FSA and the transfer of its powers to the Bank of England.

Insurers will very shortly have to learn to deal with two separate bodies, both controlled by the Bank—a Prudential Regulatory Authority ("PRA") and a Financial Conduct Authority ("FCA"). And those bodies will barely have assumed their roles before the impact of Solvency II finally becomes a reality (after surely one of the longest gestation periods in history of any regulatory proposal). On this occasion I have little hesitation in predicting that we are now entering a period of swift evolution in our regulatory history. It is only to be hoped that it will be a productive one!

In broad terms, regulators around the world may be said to have used eight identifiable tools when supervising the activities of licensed insurance companies:

(a) restriction of ownership;
(b) review of managers and other controllers;
(c) prohibition of the placing of insurance or reinsurance with foreign insurance companies;
(d) solvency requirements;
(e) control of investments;
(f) control of premium rates;
(g) control of policy conditions;
(h) regulation of marketing practices.

The regulation of the insurance industry is usually explained in terms of consumer protection but has historically, in many jurisdictions, frequently had as much to do with national politics and economics. Many states now in the EU tradition-ally used all or most of the mechanisms listed above to regulate their insurance markets. Even if it has not always been the largest, the UK's insurance market has historically been, and remains, the most important in Europe and arguably (at least in the commercial arena) in the world. Yet the UK has traditionally avoided such excesses—not so much through positive action as through inaction.

Insurance was barely controlled by any UK governmental authority before the mid-1960s. Such regulation as then existed, and most of that created until the very recent past, was introduced as a reaction to a specific financial scandal. There was little systematic thought behind it other than that of minimal intervention—"freedom with disclosure". It was only after the passing of the Companies Act 1967 that a UK insurance company needed a licence to carry on business. That legislation was forced on the government of the day by the failure of Fire Auto & Marine, a company with a short but inglorious life founded by the infamous Emil Savundra, who took imaginative and lucrative advantage of the fact that even an insurance company did not legally have to file its first accounts for at least two years after it had commenced business. More detailed regulation was introduced in the Insurance Companies Amendment Act 1973, largely as a consequence of the insolvency of Vehicle & General, which held about 10 per cent of the UK motor market and borrowed heavily from a life assurance subsidiary in order to finance its loss-making activities.

UK insurance regulation first began to be influenced on a more considered basis when the UK joined the European Economic Community ("EEC") as it then was, subsequently the European Community ("EC"), in 1973. In the pursuit of the goals of "freedom of establishment" and the freedom to provide cross-border services the EC struggled to adopt a series of Directives which became, for a period, the dominant influence on the form and content of UK insurance legislation. However, and paradoxically, these Directives principally imposed on EC Member States a system that largely reflected the minimalist approach that had already evolved over the years in the UK.

Whilst non-life insurance intermediaries remained thinly regulated via the Insurance Brokers Registration Act, the marketing of life assurance products became regulated by statute from the late 1980s. Financial scandals in the investment industry gave rise to the Financial Services Act 1986 which, for the first time, recognised that most life assurance products were appropriately categorised as "investments" and regulated them accordingly. For a period of just over a decade the 1986 Act gave rise to a system of selective regulation of the financial services industries via "self-regulating organisations" recognised by the Securities and Investments Board ("SIB").

In the field of prudential regulation, no domestically-inspired legislation of any substance was passed in the UK between

1973 and 2000. However, 1997 saw the election of the UK's first Labour Government since 1979, and one of its stated priorities was the reform of the regulation and supervision of the UK's financial services industries. The Financial Services and Markets Act 2000 brought together the regulation of the UK's insurance, investment and banking activities under a single regulator, a renamed SIB now called the FSA. Unlike its predecessors, the FSA was tasked not only with the enforcement of specific rules but also with the formulation and evolution of those rules in the pursuit of its statutory regulatory objectives—market confidence, public awareness, the protection of consumers and the reduction of financial crime (see Chapter 1). The FSA made clear from the start that it would be more proactive than its predecessors in the adoption of UK-specific legislation that it perceived to be required in the context of the UK insurance market, scandals or none.

The initial consequence of the FSA's assumption of these powers was dramatic. On 1 December 2001, a UK insurance industry that had traditionally been governed by a few statutory requirements and a host of informal understandings woke to find itself buried under almost 10,000 pages of Principles, Rules and Guidance. In practice, the industry became used to the new Handbook reasonably quickly. It arguably reacted rather more nervously to the subsequent abbreviation of the Handbook in the context of the intensification by the FSA of "principles-based regulation" and "outcomes-focussed regulation", perhaps reflected most dramatically in the FSA's concept of "treating customers fairly" and its holistic approach to the regulation of solvency. Equally painful have been the FSA's increasingly pro-active approach to regulatory intervention, and its increasingly aggressive approach to enforcement.

At all times, UK regulatory development has continued to be impacted by further EC Insurance Directives. In recent years the Insurance Mediation Directive and the Reinsurance Directive have been welcome measures, plugging long-standing gaps in the EU insurance code (and, in the case of the marketing of non-life insurance, a notable gap in UK domestic legislation). The impact of Solvency II will of course be considerably more dramatic than either of these.

It will be for the next edition of this book to record the final details of the approach taken by the PRA and the FCA to the fulfilment of their respective responsibilities, as well as the ultimate fine detail of the Solvency II requirements. It is of some comfort that in many ways both the approach apparently intended to be taken by the new regulators and the general scheme of Solvency II will be less of the revolution that they are sometimes portrayed to be than a further iteration of the FSA's own constantly-evolving philosophy.

This Guide does not cover the FSA's involvement in Lloyd's, which is the subject of a companion volume. However, it does extend to the friendly societies movement.

It has been my privilege to be Consulting Editor of the first four editions of this book. I shall be retiring from Hogan Lovells, after 33 years with the firm and its predecessors, in the spring of 2012 and at that time shall also transfer my editing responsibilities to other hands. I shall do so in the knowledge that, in its first decade of existence, the book has become a highly respected resource among insurance industry executives and their advisers alike.

Before relinquishing my responsibilities I should like to put on record my gratitude to my colleagues in the Hogan Lovells insurance team who have generously assisted me in my task—in particular Kirsten Barber, who has been at my side throughout all four editions. It is also a fitting time to place on record what a pleasure it has been to work both with the publishers and with my fellow authors, who represent between them a substantial proportion of the leading legal advisers on the regulation of the insurance industry now practising in the UK. It was almost as great a pleasure working with them cooperatively as it has been over the years arguing with them across the negotiating table! I wish them all, and this publication, continuing success for many years and many further editions to come.

John Young

Co-Chair

Hogan Lovells

Contents

6   Portfolio Transfers and Solvent Schemes of Arrangement
Geoffrey Maddock and Laurence Elliott, Partners: Herbert Smith LLP

7   Sale and Administration of Non-Investment Insurance
Duncan Barber, Partner: Linklaters LLP

Chapter 1

Introduction

Katherine Coates,
Partner: Clifford Chance LLP

Narind Singh,
Partner: Clifford Chance LLP

1.1 An introduction to Financial Services Regulation in the UK

The introduction of the Financial Services and Markets Act 2000 ("FSMA") in December 2001 and the establishment of the Financial Services Authority ("FSA") as the United Kingdom ("UK") financial services industry's single statutory regulator represented a new modern era of regulation across the UK's insurance, investment and banking industries.

The insurance regulatory framework established under FSMA remains largely intact, although it has been subject to certain amendments and updates over the past ten years. It has survived the aftermath of two financial crises: the bursting of the dot-com bubble in 2000 and the ongoing financial crisis that began in 2007. The latter crisis has prompted a renewed debate around the appropriate level and nature of global financial regulation. While the FSA remains the insurance industry regulator at the time of writing, its role, and the FSMA regime more generally, will change in the coming years as a result of this debate.

The key proposed change to the regime was announced in 2010 by the newly elected coalition government. The proposal envisages splitting the UK supervisory structure into three bodies: the Prudential Regulation Authority ("PRA"), the Financial Conduct Authority ("FCA") and the Financial Policy Committee ("FPC"). The first two of these bodies will share responsibility for the regulation of the insurance industry, and each is discussed in greater detail below. At a high level, the PRA will be responsible for the stable and prudent operation of the financial system through the regulation of firms in a manner which is intended to minimise the disruption caused if they fail. The FCA's primary objective will be to ensure confidence in financial services and markets, with specific focus on protecting consumers and ensuring market integrity. At the time of writing, the details of the new arrangements are still being finalised, but the FSA is in the process of putting into place an internal shadow structure that reflects the new structure to some extent and is intended to smooth the transition. The government's current deadline for implementation of the new regime is at the end of 2012 or beginning of 2013. These proposals are examined in more detail in Section 1.3.4.1 below.

Whilst the subject of this book is the regulation of insurance in the UK, the vast majority of UK insurance regulation emanates from Europe. The European Community ("EC") Insurance Directives influence and seek to harmonise the regulation of insurance across the European Union ("EU") and the wider European Economic Area (the "EEA", comprising the 27 Member States of the EU plus Iceland, Liechtenstein and Norway). The degree of harmonisation across the EEA is intended to increase significantly under Solvency II, the most important current EU regulatory initiative for insurance in many years. The FSA has described the overarching objective of Solvency II as bringing about "a fundamental change to the solvency and risk management standards for the European insurance industry, with the intention of significantly strengthening the prudential standards to which European insurers adhere".

New pan-EEA authorities, such as the recently created European Insurance and Occupational Pensions Authority ("EIOPA"), will in future be able to issue binding rules which the FSA and the other EEA regulators will be tasked with implementing. For its part, the FSA has sought to establish itself as a key contributor to these initiatives, both in terms of proactively engaging with consultative processes and having representatives on the management and supervisory boards of the relevant bodies (including EIOPA). While many of the European regulatory initiatives relating to Solvency II technically pre-date the financial crisis, in practice almost all are now guided by its aftermath. The objectives, benefits and challenges of Solvency II are discussed in more detail below.

A further trend which is likely to become apparent in the coming years is for new European laws to be implemented through the use of Regulations, which have direct effect in member states, rather than through Directives, which have to be implemented through domestic legislation in member states. This should reduce the scope for variations in the implementation of European requirements and produce a more harmonised European market going forward.

1.1.1 Pre-FSMA

Before the introduction of the FSMA, the UK's banking, investment and insurance industries were not regulated under a single statutory framework. In contrast, the financial services industry was regulated through a variety of statutes, principally enacted in the 1980s following a series of crises and financial scandals in the 1970s and early 1980s which exposed the need for increased regulation and investor protection. In retrospect, the response was piecemeal and largely failed to provide the levels of investor protection in place today.

For the insurance sector, the Insurance Companies Act 1982 brought authorisation requirements to long term and general insurance and reinsurance firms but placed the responsibility of oversight and enforcement on the Department of Trade and Industry ("DTI"). However, business conducted through the Lloyd's insurance market was principally regulated by Lloyd's.

1.1.2 The introduction of FSMA

On 20 May 1997, the newly elected Labour government announced plans to bring the regulation of banking, securities and insurance together under one roof. FSMA received Royal Assent on 14 June 2000 and came into effect on 1 December 2001, creating the FSA in the process. The FSA now regulates 29,000 firms.

The FSMA brought an end to the previous fragmented approach to regulation of the industry, repealing (amongst other legislation) the Financial Services Act 1986, the Insurance Companies Act 1982 and parts of other legislation regulating specific sectors of the financial services industry, such as the Building Societies Act 1986 and the Friendly Societies Act 1992. The FSA assumed the regulatory responsibilities of the self-regulating organisations established under the Financial Services Act 1986, DTI, the Bank of England, the Friendly Societies Commission and the Building Societies Commission. Thus the UK financial services industry had for the first time in its history a single regulator, responsible for regulating the industry under a common statutory framework.

The FSMA was not enacted in response to any particular crisis or regulatory failure, but rather as a response to changing market conditions and a desire to rationalise the regulation of the financial services industry in the UK. Even the bursting of the dotcom bubble in 2000, and subsequent decline in global economic growth, did not result in wholesale changes to the FSA's regulation of the insurance industry.

1.1.3 The 2007 financial crisis and the UK insurance industry

Since early 2007, the financial crisis has spread from a relatively obscure corner of the United States mortgage-backed securities market to virtually every asset class, including those previously considered relatively "risk free". As with almost any financial crisis, at the most basic level it could be seen as the result of a failure of market participants to price risk accurately.

However, it could also be seen as a failure to *manage* these risks: investors failing to quantify the risks they faced, and regulators failing to manage the risks within the industries they regulated.

At the end of 2009, the global insurance industry held approximately US$23 trillion of investments, primarily in capital markets instruments. For an industry so reliant on its returns from investments, it is perhaps surprising that, with a few notable exceptions, insurers have so far survived the financial crisis as well as they have. Part of the reason for insurers' relative good health, at least in the UK, can be traced to their experiences in the aftermath of the dotcom bubble in 2000, and the resultant focus (both within insurers and at the then newly formed FSA) on risk management and the appropriateness of holding large portfolios of equities. Notwithstanding this relative outperformance, the regulatory transition that is underway will require insurers to further adapt their risk profile in a number of ways, particularly as a result of Solvency II.

The FSA is proactively preparing the UK insurance industry for the implementation of Solvency II, a new Directive which establishes a common set of capital requirements and risk management standards for insurance companies in the EEA. The Solvency II proposals are considered in more detail in Chapter 4.

1.2 The framework of legislation and regulation under FMSA

1.2.1 The FSMA and subordinate legislation

The FSMA is a large and significant piece of legislation. However, it does not operate in isolation. In order for the FSMA to achieve its objectives it was necessary for a plethora of secondary legislation to be enacted.

Central to the regulation of financial services under the FSMA is the requirement for all firms carrying on regulated activities by way of business to be authorised by the FSA to do so, unless they are otherwise exempt. This is known by practitioners as the "General Prohibition" and is discussed in detail in Chapter 2. The regulated activities that give rise to the need for authorisation are specified in one of the key pieces of secondary legislation made under the FSMA—the Financial Services and Markets Act 2000 (Regulated Activities) Order 2001 (the "RAO"). As the FSA's remit has widened since December 2001, the RAO has grown to include, for example, the regulation of the provision of mortgage advice and insurance broking and intermediation services.

In addition to the General Prohibition, a cornerstone of the FSMA is the so-called "financial promotions" regime which regulates the promotion of financial services in the UK. Under s.21 of the FSMA, a person must not, in the course of business, communicate an invitation or inducement to engage in investment activity unless that person is authorised under the FSMA, the content of the communication is approved by such an authorised person or an exemption applies. The activities and types of investment that fall within the financial promotions regime, together with the applicable exemptions, are set out in the Financial Services and Markets Act 2000 (Financial Promotion) Order 2005 ("FPO"). The FSA's high-level principles and conduct of business rules described below supplement the FPO, with the overall objective being that all financial promotions and communications with clients should be clear, fair and not misleading.

The FSMA also introduced the "approved persons" regime, under which those individuals carrying on certain "controlled functions" on behalf of a firm (broadly persons with managerial or customer responsibilities) need to be personally approved by the FSA as being fit and proper and having the appropriate qualifications to assume such responsibilities. The approved persons regime is considered in further detail in Chapter 3.

1.2.2 *The FSA's statutory objectives*

The FSMA sets out the regulatory objectives of the FSA and the supervisory principles to which the FSA must have regard when discharging its functions.

The FSA has four statutory objectives:

- Market confidence—maintaining confidence in the UK financial system.
- Financial stability—contributing to the protection and enhancement of stability of the UK financial system.
- Consumer protection—securing the appropriate degree of protection for consumers.
- The reduction of financial crime—reducing the extent to which it is possible for a regulated business to be used for a purpose connected with financial crime.

In pursuing its objectives, the FSA must have regard to the following "principles of good regulation":

- Efficiency and economy in the use of the FSA's resources.
- The responsibility of a firm's senior management for its activities and regulatory compliance, so that the affairs of the firm can be adequately monitored and controlled.
- Restrictions must be proportionate to their resulting benefits.
- Facilitating innovation in connection with regulated activities.
- The international character of financial services and markets and maintaining the competitive position of the UK.
- The desirability of enhancing the understanding and knowledge of members of the public of financial matters (including the UK financial system).

1.2.3   The FSA Handbook

Since becoming the single regulator of the financial services industry in 2001, in accordance with its rule-making powers under the FSMA, the FSA has issued and maintained a handbook of rules and guidance for regulated firms (the "FSA Handbook"). The FSA Handbook has changed and grown, in line with the FSA's developing remit and approach to regulation. The FSA Handbook as a whole is a large tome indeed. However, it is relatively user-friendly for practitioners as a result of its division into "blocks" and then "manuals" or "sourcebooks".

The two principal categories of the FSA Handbook provisions are rules and guidance. Rules create binding obligations and their contravention may result in enforcement action, while guidance is intended to explain the effect of the rules. Guidance provisions are not binding and their breach has no direct disciplinary implications, but the FSA will generally regard firms that follow guidance as having complied with the relevant aspects of the rule to which the guidance relates. As is explained in more detail later in this Chapter there has recently been a shift by the FSA towards principles-based regulation. This has resulted in a simplification of some parts of the FSA Handbook and a greater focus by the FSA on compliance with principles, which are in turn interpreted by reference to guidance in the FSA Handbook and elsewhere. Non-compliance with guidance may therefore give rise, in some cases, to disciplinary action in respect of breach of one or more high level principles.

Figure 1.1 shows the structure of the FSA Handbook, highlighting the sections most relevant to insurance firms. What follows is a high-level overview of the contents of the blocks and manuals.

1.2.3.1   High Level Standards

The High Level Standards block is a key part of the FSA Handbook that sets out overarching standards that apply to all authorised firms and their approved persons. It is comprised of seven manuals, which are central to the regulation of all firms and also provides an aid to general interpretation.

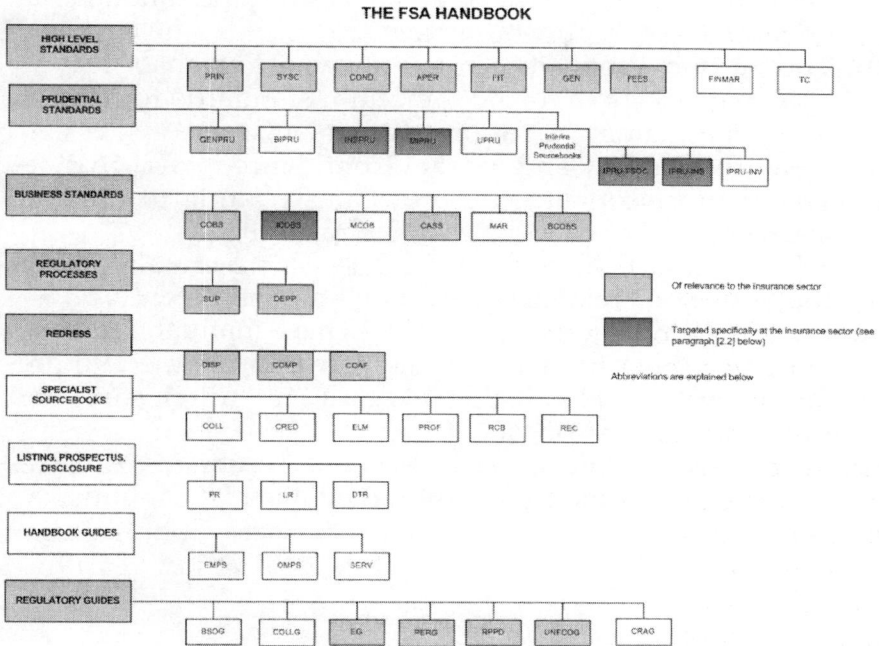

Figure 1.1: Structure of the FSA Handbook.

i.   Principles for Businesses ("PRIN")—This manual sets out the fundamental obligations of all FSA regulated firms, including eleven principles for business that all firms must adhere to in the conduct of their business. These principles have been of increasing significance as the FSA move towards a more principles-based approach to regulation. This is discussed further in Section 1.4.2.

ii.   Senior Management Arrangements, Systems and Controls ("SYSC")—This manual sets out the responsibilities of directors and senior management and certain high level organisational systems and controls requirements.

iii. Threshold Conditions ("COND")—This manual contains the minimum statutory conditions for a firm to become and remain FSA authorised.

iv. Statements of Principle and Code of Practice for Approved Persons ("APER")—This manual sets out the fundamental obligations of approved persons.

v. The Fit and Proper test for Approved Persons ("FIT")—This manual contains the minimum standards for becoming and remaining an approved person.

vi. Financial Stability and Market Confidence ("FINMAR")—This manual contains the provisions relating to financial stability, market confidence and short selling.

vii. Training and Competence ("TC")—This manual contains the provisions relating to training and competence.

viii. General Provisions ("GEN")—This manual contains (amongst other things) provisions relating to the interpretation of the Handbook, fees, status disclosure and insurance against fines.

ix. Fees Manual ("FEES")—This manual contains the fees provisions for funding the FSA, the Financial Ombudsman Service ("FOS") and the Financial Services Compensation Scheme ("FSCS").

1.2.3.2 *Prudential Standards*

The prudential standards block has undergone much change since its inception. Initially, the FSA issued prudential standards for banks, building societies, insurers, friendly societies and investment firms in separate sourcebooks. However, with effect from January 2007, the FSA has issued a single General Prudential Sourcebook ("GENPRU") for all banks, building societies, insurers and investment firms which primarily comprises rules and guidance on capital resource requirements and the management of prudential risks. GENPRU is then supplemented by more specific rules and guidance for each of the following sectors:

i. Prudential sourcebook for Banks, Building Societies and Investment Firms ("BIPRU").

ii. Prudential sourcebook for Insurers ("INSPRU").

iii.   Prudential sourcebook for Mortgage and Home Finance Firms and Insurance Intermediaries ("MIPRU").
iv.   Prudential sourcebook for UCITS Firms ("UPRU").

During the development of the FSA Handbook, "interim" sector-specific prudential sourcebooks were issued pending the consultation on and adoption of fuller sector-specific prudential sourcebooks. Certain of these interim prudential sourcebooks remain in place, although in many cases the majority of the content of such interim prudential sourcebooks has been deleted and is now dealt with in GENPRU or BIPRU, INSPRU, MIPRU or UPRU, as applicable. Until such time as the remaining provisions of these interim prudential sourcebooks are replaced in full, practitioners will need to continue to have regard to them. The interim prudential sourcebooks are:

i.   Interim Prudential sourcebook for Friendly Societies ("IPRU-FSOC").
ii.   Interim Prudential sourcebook for Insurers ("IPRU-INS").
iii.   Interim Prudential sourcebook for Investment Businesses ("IPRU-INV").

1.2.3.3   Business Standards

This block comprises detailed requirements relating to the conduct of a firm's day-to-day business. In line with the FSA's drive to implement a less prescriptive, more risk- and principles-based approach to regulation, the conduct of business rules for firms were significantly restructured and simplified in November 2007. The block contains the following manuals:

i.   Conduct of Business sourcebook ("COBS")—This manual sets out conduct of business requirements applying to all firms.
ii.   Insurance: Conduct of Business sourcebook ("ICOBS")—This manual sets out requirements applying to firms with non-investment insurance business customers.

iii. Mortgages and Home Finance: Conduct of Business sourcebook ("MCOB")—This manual sets out requirements applying to firms with mortgage business customers.
iv. Client Assets ("CASS")—This manual sets out the requirements relating to holding client assets and client money.
v. Banking: Conduct of Business Sourcebook ("BCOBS")—This manual applies to a firm with respect to the activity of accepting deposits from banking customers carried on from an establishment within the UK.
vi. Market Conduct ("MAR")—This manual contains the Code of Market Conduct, price stabilising rules, endorsement of the Takeover Code, Alternative Trading Systems and guidance on acceptable market conduct and what constitutes market abuse.

1.2.3.4 Regulatory processes

Previously, in addition to the two manuals referred to below, the regulatory processes block included the Authorisation Manual ("AUTH") which set out the procedures and guidance relating to obtaining authorisation from the FSA to conduct regulated activities. However, with effect from January 2007, in order to streamline the regulatory processes materials, the AUTH ceased to have effect and the relevant rules and guidance were moved to other sections of the FSA Handbook (for example PERG (see below) and SUP) or to the FSA's special publication on applying for authorisation. The block now therefore contains the following manuals:

i. Supervision ("SUP")—This manual applies to all firms and contains supervisory provisions including those relating to auditors, waivers, individual guidance, notifications and reporting. It also details, in SUP 11.1–11.9, the procedure for notifying the FSA regarding any change of control.
ii. Decision Procedure and Penalties Manual ("DEPP")—This manual describes the FSA's procedures for making statutory notice decisions, the FSA's policy on the imposition and amount of penalties and certain interview procedures.

1.2.3.5 Redress

This block is concerned with the processes for handling complaints and compensation and is comprised of three sourcebooks:

i. Dispute Resolution: Complaints ("DISP")—This manual contains detailed requirements for the handling of complaints and the FOS arrangements.
ii. Compensation ("COMP")—This manual contains the FSA's rules governing eligibility under, and levies for, the FSCS.
iii. Complaints against the FSA ("COAF")—This manual contains details of the scheme for the handling of complaints against the FSA.

1.2.3.6 Specialist sourcebooks

In addition to the prudential and business standards sourcebooks described above, there are six specialist sourcebooks that contain additional requirements applying to individual business sectors, namely, collective investment schemes, building societies, credit unions, firms issuing electronic money, professional firms, regulated covered bonds and recognised investment exchanges and clearing houses.

1.2.3.7 Listing, Prospectus and Disclosure

In May 2000, the FSA assumed primary responsibility for vetting public companies for listing on the London Stock Exchange ("LSE") from the LSE. Since that time, such responsibility has rested with a division of the FSA known as the UK Listing Authority ("UKLA"). With effect from July 2005, the UKLA Listing Rules ("LR"), together with the Prospectus Rules ("PR"), became part of the FSA Handbook. The current version of the Disclosure Rules and Transparency Rules ("DTR") came into effect in January 2007.

1.2.3.8   Handbook Guides

This block of the FSA Handbook contains guides for specific market participants, sectors and entities to assist them in understanding the FSA Handbook as it applies to them. The guides are for energy market participants ("EMPS"), oil market participants ("OMPS") and service companies ("SERV") and are unlikely to be of relevance to the insurance sector.

1.2.3.9   Regulatory Guides

This block contains guides to various regulatory topics as follows:

i.   The Building Societies Regulatory Guide ("BSOG").
ii.   The Collective Investment Scheme Information Guide ("COLLG").
iii.   The Enforcement Guide ("EG").
iv.   The Perimeter Guidance Manual ("PERG").
v.   The Responsibilities of Providers and Distributors for the Fair Treatment of Customers ("RPPD").
vi.   The Unfair Contract Terms Regulatory Guide ("UNFCOG").
vii.   The Credit Rating Agencies Guide ("CRAG").

See Section 1.3.2.3 below for further information on these.

1.2.4   European harmonisation

1.2.4.1   The Principal Insurance Directives

The EC Insurance Directives influence and seek to harmonise the regulation of insurance across the EU and the EEA. Understanding the EC legislation is important both as a background to the UK regulatory regime and as an indication of likely future developments.

Before the adoption of the Insurance Directives described below, the EEA Member States developed their own widely varied approaches to the regulation of the insurance industry and, to a degree, these disparate attitudes persist to this day. Fortunately, EC insurance legislation has been successful in achieving a degree of harmonisation, so that, at least to a certain extent, a single insurance market exists within the EEA.

The EC Treaty provides in very general terms for the creation of a common market in insurance, by requiring national businesses to be free to establish themselves (art.43), and provide services (art.49), in other Member States. Article 51(2) states that "the liberalisation of banking and insurance services connected with movement of capital shall be effected in step with the progressive liberalisation of movement of capital".

From this broad outline, three "generations" of directives fleshed out the details of the common insurance market as follows:

a) the first generation, being principally the Reinsurance Directive of 1964, the First Non-Life Directive of 1973 and the First Life Directive of 1979 (also called the Establishment Directives);
b) the second generation, being principally the Second Non-Life Directive of 1988 and the Second Life Directive of 1990 (also called the Services Directives); and
c) the third generation, being principally the Third Non-Life Directive of 1992, the Third Life Directive of 1992 (also called the Framework Directives) and the Accounts Directive of 1990.

The first generation directives allowed insurers incorporated in any Member State to establish branches or agencies in other Member States without having to provide a deposit or security. However, the host Member States were nonetheless required to authorise the establishment of such branches or agencies. Of enormous importance to the industry is that the directives also provided that an insurer established in multiple Member States need only demonstrate its solvency to a single regulator in the country of its head office on the basis of one test applied to its worldwide business.

The second generation directives enabled insurers incorporated in one Member State to cover risks situated in another Member State without having to establish a branch there.

The third generation directives provide that the carrying on of insurance business within the EU, whether by way of establishment or of the provision of cross-border services, should only be subject to a prior authorisation from the regulatory authority of the Member State in which the insurer has its head office (the "home Member State"). They also introduce some additional harmonisation in areas such as the establishment of technical provisions, matching and localisation of assets, calculation of margins of solvency and the regulation of control and management.

In 2002 the Life Directives were consolidated in a single Consolidated Life Directive.

1.2.4.2   More Specific Directives

Winding-Up

In 2001, a directive on "the reorganisation and winding-up of insurance undertakings" was adopted to harmonise the laws and procedures for insurers in the event of insolvency. It provided that supervision of the winding-up of an insurer was to be undertaken in the insurer's home Member State and contained provisions as to the priority of insurance claims in a winding-up. The directive was implemented in the UK in April 2003.

Groups

The Insurance Groups Directive of 1998 facilitated the assessment by insurance regulatory authorities of the solvency of corporate groups whose main business is insurance. It aimed to avoid "double gearing", where the same assets are used to support the solvency requirements of multiple insurers in the same group. Another directive, adopted in 2003 and implemented in the UK in August 2004, contains provisions to ensure that financial conglomerates (corporate groups with operations in the insurance, banking and securities sectors) have adequate capital. It introduces additional methods for monitoring the solvency position and intra-group transactions of such conglomerates. The impact of these two directives is discussed in Chapter 4.

Intermediation

The Insurance Mediation Directive of 2003 harmonised the hitherto varied approach of the Member States to insurance intermediaries. It was implemented in the UK in January 2005. The directive has had at least three important effects on insurance intermediaries:

i.   as with insurers, they are now able to operate throughout the EU using freedom of services and establishment;
ii.   they are subject to a common set of minimum professional and financial requirements throughout the EU; and
iii. they are required to provide extensive pre-contractual disclosure for most personal lines and certain commercial insurance business.

The impact of the Insurance Mediation Directive in the UK is described in further detail in Chapter 7.

Reinsurance

In December 2007 the Reinsurance Directive came into force, extending the EU insurance regime to insurers that only write reinsurance risks. Under the directive, a reinsurer authorised in one Member State has a right of establishment in all other Member States. Financial supervision can only be carried out by the reinsurer's home Member State and host Member States are prevented from imposing measures amounting to indirect supervision of EU authorised reinsurers.

In the UK, reinsurance was already regulated similarly to direct insurance and, furthermore, many of the technical rules in the Reinsurance Directive (such as those relating to solvency

17

margins and minimum capital requirements) had already been implemented through the FSA Handbook. As a result, implementation of the directive has required only limited changes to UK law. These changes have largely been effected by amendments to the FSA Handbook and some changes to the FSMA and related secondary legislation.

The FSA Handbook amendments, most of which took effect in December 2006, brought about the following principal changes and these include some relaxation of the previous regulations for pure reinsurers:

i.   replacing the restrictive rules on admissible assets with certain high level "prudent person" investment principles;

ii.   allowing pure reinsurance firms and mixed reinsurance firms that provide life reinsurance protection and permanent health insurance to use the non-life solvency tests to calculate their minimum capital requirements;

iii. reducing the margin of prudence applicable to the calculation of technical provisions of pure reinsurers;

iv.   widening the permitted activities of reinsurers to include reinsurance-related operations such as providing actuarial advice and claims management services;

v.   facilitating the use of insurance special purpose vehicles ("ISPVs"); and

vi.   introducing a single, high-level principle requiring effective transfer of risk before a firm can take credit for reinsurance.

The FSMA changes were effected using a number of statutory instruments which came into force in December 2007. They also extend the provisions on business transfers to cover the transfer of reinsurance business and enable EEA firms (including UK firms) to utilise the passporting rights contained in the Reinsurance Directive. See further Chapter 8.

Sector Specific Directives

A number of more sector-specific directives have been adopted over the years, dealing with topics such as co-insurance, tourist assistance insurance, credit and suretyship insurance, legal expenses insurance and motor insurance. See further Chapter 8.

1.3 Overview of the FSA regulation of insurance

1.3.1 *The FSMA*

Insurance and insurance mediation activities fall within the General Prohibition and are therefore within the remit of regulation by the FSMA and the FSA. Chapters 2 and 7 describe the regulated activities associated with insurance business and insurance mediation services in further detail.

1.3.2 *The FSA Handbook*

The rules and guidance in the High Level Standards, Regulatory Processes and Redress blocks apply to all authorised firms. The Prudential Standards and Business Standards blocks also apply to all authorised firms, except that these blocks have been tailored, to some extent, for the insurance industry.

1.3.2.1 *Prudential Standards*

GENPRU applies to insurance, banking and investment firms and includes rules and guidance on:

i.   the adequacy of financial resources and management of prudential risks;
ii.   the recognition and valuation of assets, liabilities, exposures, equity and income statement items;
iii. the calculation of capital resources requirements (and admissible assets in insurance); and
iv.   financial conglomerates and their capital adequacy requirements.

INSPRU supplements GENPRU for insurance firms and includes additional rules and guidance on:

i.   capital resources requirements and technical provisions for insurance business (including rules on mathematical reserves, the with-profits insurance capital component, equalisation provisions, internal-contagion risk and ISPVs);

ii. credit risk, market risk, liquidity risk, operational risk and group risk in insurance groups;

iii. individual capital assessments; and

iv. the application of INSPRU and GENPRU to Lloyd's.

In addition to GENPRU and INSPRU, insurance firms must continue to have regard to IPRU-INS, which currently contains rules and guidance on:

i.   the identification and application of assets and liabilities by long-term insurers, more specifically payment of dividends, allocation of established surplus to policyholders and arrangements to avoid unfairness between separate insurance funds;

ii. the appointment of a chief executive by overseas insurers with a UK branch; and

iii. financial reporting.

MIPRU contains the prudential rules and guidance and capital resources requirements for insurance intermediaries.

1.3.2.2   Business Standards

COBS applies to insurers and intermediaries in respect of long-term insurance business and includes rules and guidance on, amongst other things, communicating with clients (including financial promotions), distance marketing, provision of information about the firm and the product, suitability, cancellation rights and reporting requirements. It also contains specific Chapters on insurance mediation in respect of life policies, claims-handling for long-term care insurance, with-profits business and permitted links for linked long-term business. COBS is considered further in Chapter 10.

ICOBS applies to insurers and intermediaries in respect of non-investment insurance business and includes rules and guidance on topics that are broadly similar to those contained in COBS. ICOBS is considered further in Chapter 7.

CASS applies to firms that hold client money. It is of particular relevance to intermediaries and is considered further in Chapter 7.

1.3.2.3   *Handbook Guides and Regulatory Guides*

Of particular relevance to the insurance sector are EG (guidance on the FSA's approach to enforcement against authorised firms, its powers and the sanctions available), PERG (guidance on, among other things, the definition of insurance mediation activities and the identification of contracts of insurance), RPPD (guidance on fair treatment of customers) and UNFCOG (guidance on the regulations governing unfair contract terms).

1.3.3   **Thematic reviews**

The FSA takes a "risk-based" approach to supervision and we consider this further in the next section of this Chapter. As part of this approach the FSA monitors markets and authorised firms to identify areas of risk and conducts thematic reviews to further analyse those risks that it considers significant. Firms are often asked to change their practices or take specific actions as a result of these thematic reviews.

The FSA's key focus in its thematic reviews is the fair treatment of customers, a concept which features repeatedly in the FSA publications and which is discussed in further detail later in this Chapter. In the insurance sector, the FSA has recently undertaken, or is in the process of conducting, thematic reviews in the following areas, all of which relate to the fair treatment of customers:

1.3.3.1   Payment Protection Insurance ("PPI")

The FSA has identified poor PPI sales practices resulting in a failure to treat customers fairly when selling PPI. The focus is on improving sales practices, as well as improving consumer understanding of PPI. More detail on the FSA's action against firms for PPI mis-selling is set out in Section 4.3.

1.3.3.2   Quality of post-sale communications in the life sector

The FSA found instances of firms failing to treat customers fairly, for example by not mentioning valuable product features such as guaranteed annuity rates.

1.3.3.3   The availability of ongoing advice to with-profits policyholders

The FSA found that many advisers were not providing sufficient ongoing advice for with-profits policyholders about their policies.

1.3.3.4   With-profits governance arrangements

The FSA found that industry practice in respect of management of with-profits funds, specifically governance arrangements and run-off plans for closed funds, did not follow the FSA's rules and guidance in this area. The FSA has also found that with-profits business normally involves firms exercising significant discretion, which could potentially lead to conflicts of interest with the result that firms might not be treating policyholders fairly. In order to further review the COBS with-profits regime, the FSA conducted a thematic review of COBS called the "With-Profits Regime Review", with a particular focus on COBS 20, which was put in place with the protection of with-profits policyholders in mind. See Section 1.4.2.1(a) and Chapter 9 for further detail on COBS 20.

1.3.3.5 *Retail Distribution Review ("RDR")*

The purpose of the RDR was to increase market confidence in services offered by firms in the retail investment sector, by improving the manner in which firms describe the services that they offer to consumers, reducing the scope for these services to be distorted by the adviser's remuneration and improving professional standards.

Following a consultation by the FSA on the RDR, certain amendments are being made to COBS, which are due to take effect at the end of 2012. The new rules will require a higher level of transparency and disclosure in relation to the level of independence of advice given by advisers and, somewhat controversially, advisers will no longer be allowed to receive commissions from product providers. There will also be stricter requirements on training, qualification and supervision of advisers. Life insurance policies are among the types of investment to which the post-RDR regime will apply.

These changes will impact all advisers in the investment market, including advisers who work for banks, product providers, wealth managers and IFAs. See further Chapter 10.

1.3.3.6 *Platforms*

In August 2011, the FSA published rules on platforms regulation, following a review of the sector in light of the consumer protection objectives of the RDR. Platforms, in the context of the review, are internet based services that can be used by advisers to administer investments and suggest suitable products. The FSA's principal concern with platforms is the potential for offering unsuitable products or advice that is not in the best interests of consumers. The new rules seek to address these concerns.

The FSA has emphasised the requirement for investment advisers to act in a prudent manner when making recommendations to clients and offer independent unbiased advice. The rules specify, similarly to the rules to be included in COBS as a result of the RDR, that there must be disclosure of any commissions that platforms receive from third parties.

Following from the review, the FSA has imposed a penalty of £19,600 on a firm for failing to have the required compliance arrangements in place in relation to the advice that it offered to its clients using platforms. Two other firms have also been required to conduct reviews of their prior business operations and make improvements to their systems and processes.

It is evident that platforms advice will be a priority for the FSA in the future and the regulator will continue to monitor the implementation of these rules closely.

The FSA's thematic reviews do not always result in rule changes. Instead, the FSA often issues guidance as a result of its thematic work. Although the guidance is not legally binding, the FSA is likely to regard those firms that follow the guidance as having complied with the regulatory principles in question. A good example of this is the FSA's introduction of the Treating Customers Fairly ("TCF") initiative, where an emphasis on achieving a fair outcome for consumers, rather than reliance on prescriptive rules, is considered a more effective tool for promoting understanding of TCF. TCF and its importance to the insurance industry are discussed in Section 1.4.3.

1.3.4   The structure of regulatory oversight

At the time of writing the FSA is the sole statutory regulator of insurers and insurance intermediaries in the UK. It is responsible for authorising, regulating and supervising insurers and intermediaries and monitoring their compliance with the provisions of the FSMA and the FSA Handbook.

1.3.4.1   Reform of Regulatory Oversight Structure

In June 2011 the government presented to Parliament a draft Financial Services Bill which is intended to operate to dismantle the FSA and establish the Bank of England as one of two main regulators of the UK's financial services industry. This would result in a dramatic re-alignment of the regulatory landscape.

The proposed reforms have been prompted by the coalition government's belief that the existing tri-partite regulatory system of the Treasury, Bank of England and the FSA has to a certain extent failed to either foresee or adequately stem the effect of the financial crisis that began in 2007, with the result that some of the largest entities that the FSA regulates have effectively been nationalised as a result of the crisis.

In its introduction to the draft Bill the government states that it believes that the FSA has successfully monitored the compliance of individual firms with the regulations established in its handbook but has failed to ensure overall market stability. The government concludes that the reason for this failure lies, in part, with the current structure of the tri-partite system of regulation. It concludes that although the Bank of England has nominal responsibility for ensuring market stability it has been denuded of all real power to be able to do so. The FSA, on the other hand, has been granted extensive powers of supervision under the FSMA but has too wide a remit. In focusing on public awareness, financial crime and consumer protection, to name but a few of the FSA's responsibilities, its resources have been spread too thinly and its executives' focus has therefore been on micro-supervision (meaning supervision at the level of individual firms) at the expense of macro- supervision (meaning supervision of the financial markets as a whole).

The reforms outlined in the draft Bill are based on the premise that firm-specific supervision alone is not sufficient to deliver financial stability. The government suggests that it must be complemented by a macro-prudential regulatory regime. To that end the bill proposes establishing three new regulatory bodies: the Financial Policy Committee ("FPC"), the Prudential Regulatory Authority ("PRA") and the Financial Conduct Authority ("FCA").

The FPC will sit at the apex of the new system. Established as a committee of the Court of the Bank of England, the FPC will be charged with monitoring the stability of the sector as a whole. Below the FPC, the PRA and FCA will, between them, deal with the day-to-day regulatory workload presently shouldered by the FSA.

As an indicator of the importance that is being place on macro-prudential regulation, it is proposed that the FPC be chaired by the governor of the Bank of England and have among its members external experts, senior executives from within the Bank and the chief executives of the PRA and the FCA. It is intended for the committee to meet twice a quarter and to produce two market stability reports a year. Most significantly, it is intended that the FPC have formal powers of direction over the regulatory agencies that sit below it so that it can take action to address any perceived causes of market instability. It will have no direct regulatory power over any individual firms.

The FSA will be replaced by the PRA and the FCA. The split reflects the government's belief that the FSA's remit is too wide for one regulator and that the differing approaches required by prudential and conduct of business regulation do not fit easily into one body. The split is intended to allow for more focused supervision.

Under the proposed reforms, the PRA will be a subsidiary of the Bank of England and, as its name suggests, will be charged with prudential regulation and supervision of all banks, insurers and large investment firms. The FCA will regulate conduct of business and will be responsible for the prudential regulation of all firms not regulated by the PRA. Its primary focus will be to promote market confidence and safeguard consumers. The FCA will also take over the FSA's role of acting as the UK Listing Authority.

The government has placed a great emphasis on co-ordination between the three bodies to ensure that the link between macro-prudential regulation and the supervision of individual firms is effectively restored. A general duty of co-operation will feature in legislation and in agreements to be put in place between the PRA and the FCA. Co-operation will also be reflected in the membership of the boards of the FPC, PRA and FCA which will each include the chief executives of the FCA and the PRA (the latter also being the Bank of England's Deputy Governor for prudential regulation). Senior Bank of England executives will be on the board of each of the three bodies, which will allow them to have a general overview of the regulatory direction and its effect on the stability and soundness of the sector as a whole. With respect to the board of the FCA, independence will be provided by having a majority of non-executive members appointed by HM Treasury, with two being appointed jointly with the Department for Business, Innovation and Skills who it is intended will also provide relevant expertise in consumer and business experience.

1.3.4.2   *Proposed changes in Regulation of the Insurance Industry*

Much of the detail of the proposed new regulatory system is yet to be confirmed but following consultation with the industry the government has recognised that a tailored approach should be taken to insurance regulation given fundamental differences between insurance and banking activities and has added a specific statutory insurance objective to the PRA's proposed legislative framework.

At the time of writing it would appear that the PRA will provide prudential regulation of life insurers, general insurers and wholesale insurers (including reinsurers). These firms will be "dual-regulated", as the FCA will amongst other things be responsible for supervising the day-to-day conduct of insurance firms. The FCA will be the prudential (and conduct) regulator for all firms that are not dual-regulated, including insurance intermediaries.

It is expected that the PRA will lead most functions related to insurance but with significant involvement of the FCA. It is intended that the PRA will be the lead regulator for the Lloyd's market as a whole but that the Society of Lloyd's and Lloyd's managing agents be dual-regulated, whilst members' agents and advisers and Lloyd's brokers will be regulated by the FCA. The PRA is expected to be primarily responsible for the process of transfers of insurance business under Part VII of the FSMA, although both the PRA and FCA will be able to make representations to court during the transfer process. Responsibility for authorisation is not entirely clear but appears broadly to depend on whether the firm in question is dual-regulated or solely regulated by the FCA (dual-regulated firms will require the consent of both the PRA and FCA for authorisation). Authority to approve persons to undertake controlled functions will also depend on whether firms are dual-regulated or are solely regulated by the FCA. For the latter, it is proposed that the FCA will have all relevant powers in respect of firms of which it is the sole regulator, while it is proposed that responsibility for approving approved persons of dual-regulated firms will be split between the PRA and the FCA. Change of control applications are expected to be considered by the prudential supervisor of the relevant firm (i.e. the PRA for dual-regulated firms and the FCA for all other firms). However, where a firm is dual-regulated the PRA will be obliged to consult with the FCA and in some circumstances the FCA may be able to block a change of control. The passporting process is expected to be led by the FCA.

The focus on the link between micro and macro regulation has also informed the PRA's proposed approach to insurance in the context of systemic risk. The government has stated that the PRA will "seek to identify those insurance companies that pose a risk to the stability of the system and to supervise those firms in a way that reduces risk". It will pay particular attention to insurers that have exposures to banks and other financial institutions and who undertake banking type activities. The PRA's approach to supervision is intended to be "judgement based". All firms will still be subject to a baseline of supervision that will focus on capital adequacy standards, liquidity, asset valuation, provisioning and reserving. However, under judgement based supervision it is intended that the nature and intensity of the PRA's supervisory approach will be commensurate with the level of risk the firm poses to policyholders and the stability of the system, something that the FSA already does to some extent (see Section 1.4.1).

A greater emphasis is also being placed on the managed resolution of firms that pose a threat to the stability of the market as a whole. Firm failure is seen as a possibility and has even been recognised in the PRA's proposed statutory objectives. The PRA is to establish a "Proactive Intervention Framework" which will support the early identification of risks to a firm's viability and ensure that remedial action is taken to rectify the situation. If such action fails the framework will provide for the ordered resolution of the firm.

Efforts are being made by the government to reduce the disruption caused to firms by the reforms outlined above. The Bill is intended to amend the FSMA rather than repeal it and it is expected that much of the contents of the FSA Handbook will remain in place in some form or another (although it will also be affected by Solvency II for insurers and the Capital Requirements Directive IV for banks). At the time of writing the detail still remains uncertain. It is unclear exactly which of the three bodies will deal with certain aspects of the supervisory regime and what "judgement based supervision" will mean in practice. It can be expected that the details will emerge as the draft Bill makes its way through Parliament. It should be noted however, that an interim FPC was established in February 2011 and is already assessing the macro-prudential tools that should be placed at the disposal of the FPC. As noted at the outset of this Chapter, the implementation of the new regulatory system is expected (at the time of writing) to occur in January 2013. The FSA has meanwhile begun to separate its functions to ensure a smooth transition to the new unified regulatory approach, as described below.

1.3.4.3 *The FSA's shadow structure for the new regulatory system*

In a letter sent to firms in February 2011, the chief executive of the FSA confirmed that integrated supervision would continue for the time being and that the internal reorganisation is "the first step on the road to becoming two separate regulators".

The internal reorganisation has been referred to as a "shadow split" of the FSA. The concept is that, over time, the FSA's internal divisions will evolve to reflect where they will sit in the new structure. The FSA's expectation is that this will allow them to pilot new regulatory processes, train their staff, and assess the effectiveness of the proposed new structure, prior to the PRA and FCA formally commencing their functions. Therefore the structure of the FSA described below should be read in the context of this gradual transition.

1.3.4.4 *Supervision of Insurers under the shadow structure*

The shadow split has resulted, amongst other things, in the creation of a new Prudential Business Unit ("PBU") and a new Conduct of Business Unit ("CBU"). The PBU is responsible for prudential supervision of insurance. Wholesale and general insurance and life insurance sub divisions have been created within the supervision division of the CBU. At the time of writing, some aspects of the division between prudential and conduct supervision are unclear, such as those relating to systems and controls, and there are likely to be overlaps in certain areas. Other divisions of the shadow structure which have an impact on the supervision of insurance firms include the risk specialists and the policy divisions of the PBU. At the time of writing the authorisation function is unclear but the authorisations team appears to operate as part of both the PBU and CBU.

The main point of contact for insurance firms depends upon how much of a risk the firm is considered to pose to the FSA statutory objectives (assessed as part of the ARROW framework, see Section 1.4.1.2). Medium and high risk firms will be assigned a relationship manager who will carry out regular assessments of the firm and act as a point of contact between the firm and the relevant parts of the FSA. Low impact firms are referred to the general firm contact centre as a primary contact and are usually required to send regulatory reports only twice a year without separate risk assessments by the FSA.

1.3.4.5   Industry Focus

The specialist insurance sector team of the FSA is charged with identifying potential market risks and co-ordinating strategies for mitigating them. It works alongside the supervisory teams and its contacts in the insurance industry to gather intelligence in order to fulfil this function. It also acts as the FSA's insurance spokesperson in respect of external stakeholders such as professional bodies, trade associations, rating agencies, overseas regulators, the political community and the media. An important function of the insurance sector team is to ensure that the FSA maintains a coherent approach to the FSA's requirements and policies as they affect the insurance industry.

1.3.4.6   Think tank

The FSA has shown willingness to engage with industry participants by constituting the Insurance Standing Group ("ISG"). The ISG is composed of FSA insurance policy advisers and industry participants drawn from insurers (life and non-life), reinsurers, friendly societies, Lloyd's and trade associations. It serves as a pre-consultation forum that informs and assists the FSA in the formulation of FSA policy prior to consultation, although it is not a substitute for consultation. At the time of writing, the primary focus of the ISG is on Solvency II.

1.3.4.7   Enforcement

The FSA has an Enforcement and Financial Crime division which supports the FSA's statutory objectives and strategic aims through the use of its enforcement toolkit, further described at Section 1.5. The division carries out investigations into possible regulatory infringements by firms. If a matter appears to merit disciplinary action, the enforcement division refers it to a decision-making body in the FSA, usually the Regulatory Decisions Committee ("RDC"), whose members are independent from the investigating enforcement staff. The RDC then decides what disciplinary action, if any, the FSA should take.

If the firm is dissatisfied with the RDC's decision it may refer the matter to the Financial Services and Markets Tribunal ("Tribunal"), an independent body run by the Department of Constitutional Affairs, for determination.

The enforcement process is described in further detail in Section 1.5.2.

1.3.5 The Financial Ombudsman Service

The FOS is an informal dispute resolution service for financial services consumers, including individuals and small businesses. It provides a rapid means by which consumers can obtain impartial adjudication on disputes with financial services firms where they consider that the response by the firm to their complaint has been inadequate. The FOS was established to satisfy the FSMA's requirement for a scheme "under which certain disputes may be resolved quickly and with minimum formality by an independent person" (s.225(1)) and it is operated by a separate corporate entity, Financial Ombudsman Service Limited. The service is free for consumers. It is funded by a combination of a general levy on authorised firms and a fee per case payable by the firm involved.

The FOS only has jurisdiction over complaints relating to activities that are carried out from an establishment in the UK by FSA-authorised firms. Firms that carry on their business from an establishment elsewhere in the EEA can submit voluntarily to the FOS's jurisdiction in certain situations but otherwise are not subject to that jurisdiction.

The FOS uses an inquisitorial investigatory process, avoiding the need for consumers to be legally represented. It decides individual cases on the basis of what it considers to be fair and reasonable in the circumstances, taking into account relevant law, regulations, regulators' rules and guidance, industry standards, codes of practice and, where appropriate, good industry practice at the relevant time. Such a broad remit allows the FOS the flexibility to achieve what it considers to be a fair result, but means that its decisions can be somewhat unpredictable since it is not bound by legal precedent or the procedural rules of the courts.

The FOS can award compensation to the consumer of up to £100,000.

If the consumer accepts the FOS's decision, it is binding on both the consumer and the relevant firm. There is no right of appeal against the decision and the firm can only challenge it by way of judicial review, for example on grounds that the decision is illegal, irrational or improper. If the consumer rejects the decision it is not binding and the consumer remains free to pursue the case in the courts.

FOS decisions are widely influential because consumer bodies and the media expect firms to apply the same principles in other, similar, cases and, notwithstanding that the FOS is not bound by legal precedent, firms expect FOS to act consistently with its previous decisions and they will base their handling of future complaints based on how the FOS has reacted to similar cases.

1.3.6 The Financial Services Compensation Scheme

The FSCS provides compensation to eligible financial services consumers (mainly individuals and small businesses) with claims against firms that have ceased trading and have insufficient assets to meet the claim. The scheme covers claims relating to regulated activities carried out by FSA-authorised firms, including claims under insurance policies and in respect of insurance broking services. Claims relating to reinsurance contracts, Lloyd's policies and marine and aviation lines are not covered.

Like the FOS, the FSCS was established by the FSA pursuant to FSMA, but operates as an independent body. Compensation for claims arising out of each type of regulated activity is funded by levies charged to firms authorised to undertake that particular activity. The scheme is free for consumers.

A consumer will only be able to recover compensation from the FSCS if the relevant firm has been declared "in default", which typically occurs when it undergoes some kind of insolvency procedure. If the firm is able but unwilling to pay, the FOS and/or the courts are the appropriate channels.

The maximum compensation available under the FSCS varies according to the regulated activity giving rise to the claim. Compensation for insurance activities is not subject to any overall cap, but in some cases (as specified below) only a proportion of the value of the claim will be paid. For claims relating to compulsory general insurance (e.g. third party motor insurance), including the intermediation of such insurance, 100per cent of the claim is paid. For non-compulsory general insurance (e.g. home insurance) and the intermediation of such insurance, 90 per cent of the value of the claim is paid. For long term insurance contracts, and their intermediation, there are more complex provisions contained in the relevant FSA sourcebook but at least 90 per cent of the claim is payable. Compensation is only available for financial loss. The FSCS was extended to cover claims relating to general insurance intermediaries only in January 2005; compensation is not available for claims against such intermediaries in relation to policies arranged before that date.

1.4 FSA approach to the regulation of insurance business and key regulatory issues

1.4.1 A regulatory philosophy focusing on risk

The proposed reforms to the regulatory system referred to above, are not due to take effect until the end of 2012 at the earliest and therefore it is necessary to have an understanding of the current approach to regulation.

In pursuing its statutory objectives, the FSA has three principal aims—to promote efficient, fair and orderly markets, to help retail consumers achieve a fair deal and to improve its own business capability and effectiveness. To achieve these aims the

FSA has developed a risk-based approach to regulation, focusing its resources on areas that pose material risk to its objectives rather than striving to achieve a zero-failure regime. Indeed, a complete elimination of risk is not necessarily considered palatable. The financial markets operate on the basis that investment decisions involve an element of risk—the FSA recognises this and is reluctant to stifle innovation through disproportionate and overly burdensome regulation, although following the financial crisis the FSA has taken a more pro-active approach and has moved the goal posts in terms of what is considered an acceptable level of risk.

The FSA therefore concentrates its resources on identifying and mitigating those risks that pose the greatest threat to markets and consumers. The identification of risks in the insurance sector is achieved primarily through the monitoring of markets by the insurance sector team and supervision of individual firms.

1.4.1.1 *Monitoring insurance markets*

As discussed earlier in this Chapter, the insurance sector team regularly conducts thematic reviews in areas where market events and industry intelligence point to potential market or consumer detriment. Risks identified by thematic reviews are usually mitigated through industry guidance and, if individual firms have been examined as part of the review, through firm-specific programmes designed to rectify areas of weakness.

1.4.1.2 *Supervision of insurers and brokers*

An Advanced Risk Response Operating Framework ("ARROW") is used as a means to evaluate the level of risk that each firm poses to the FSA's statutory objectives. In addition to the supervisor allocated to each authorised firm, more complex groups that contain multiple authorised firms are allocated a lead supervisor to assess group-wide risk and co-ordinate supervision across the group. Where the authorised firm is part of a multinational group, the FSA also works closely with overseas regulators to ensure that risk is assessed at a group level.

As part of ARROW, the FSA conducts baseline monitoring through a review of the firm's regulatory returns and may make specific information requests, followed by onsite visits (commonly referred to as ARROW visits). Once the risks have been assessed against the FSA's statutory objectives, a risk mitigation plan is put in place and the FSA will monitor the firm's implementation of the plan.

The FSA's relationship with individual firms is risk-based and consequently it affords a lighter regulatory touch to those firms that have demonstrated prudent management of risk. Consistent or material regulatory breaches by a firm will lead to closer and more intrusive ongoing scrutiny. The failure by a firm to implement risk mitigation measures can also lead to enforcement action by the FSA against the firm or its approved persons.

1.4.2 *Principles-based regulation*

The FSA's approach to regulation has always been principles-based (albeit supplemented by extensive rules and guidance), as evidenced by the high-level principles set out in PRIN with which all authorised firms must comply. The high-level principles are:

- Principle 1: Integrity. A firm must conduct its business with integrity.
- Principle 2: Skill, care and diligence. A firm must conduct its business with due skill, care and diligence.
- Principle 3: Management and control. A firm must take reasonable care to organise and control its affairs responsibly and effectively, with adequate risk management systems.
- Principle 4: Financial prudence. A firm must maintain adequate financial resources.

- Principle 5: Market conduct. A firm must observe proper standards of market conduct.
- Principle 6: Customers' interests. A firm must pay due regard to the interests of its customers and treat them fairly.
- Principle 7: Communications with clients. A firm must pay due regard to the information needs of its clients, and communicate information to them in a way which is clear, fair and not misleading.
- Principle 8: Conflicts of interest. A firm must manage conflicts of interest fairly, both between itself and its customers and between a customer and another client.
- Principle 9: Customers: relationships of trust. A firm must take reasonable care to ensure the suitability of its advice and discretionary decisions for any customer who is entitled to rely upon its judgment.
- Principle 10: Clients' assets. A firm must arrange adequate protection for clients' assets when it is responsible for them.
- Principle 11: Relations with regulators. A firm must deal with its regulators in an open and cooperative way, and must disclose to the FSA appropriately anything relating to the firm of which the FSA would reasonably expect notice.

The FSA has encouraged corporate and individual behaviour which is consistent with its objectives to achieve better outcomes for consumers and markets rather than simply requiring compliance with prescriptive rules and guidance.

Accordingly, in addition to its powers in respect of breaches of the detailed rules set out elsewhere in the FSA Handbook (for example ICOBS or INSPRU), the FSA can and does take enforcement action for a breach of these high-level principles where no other specific rule breach can be identified.

Prior to the financial crisis, there had been a shift of emphasis from specific rules to the fundamental underlying principles as the FSA sought to engender a true compliance culture in firms with senior management fully engaged to ensure that the firms were making the right judgments consistent with the FSA's desired outcomes. This shift was accompanied by a simplification of the FSA Handbook with the intention that the regime comprised the high-level principles together with those rules that the FSA considers necessary to achieve a desired outcome.

A more robust approach to principles based regulation has evolved as a result of the financial crisis and has been described by the FSA as an approach of "direct and intrusive" supervision to prevent reckless actions. This indicates a more structured, outcomes-based form of supervision, such that the regulator will now seek to question business models and strategies with the aim of maintaining market confidence, protecting consumers and preventing financial crime.

1.4.2.1   What does principles-based regulation mean?

Various factors have driven the FSA to adopt its principles- and outcomes-based approach. Firstly, detailed rules, such as the old conduct of business rules, have not always resulted in a fair deal for consumers—witness the major mis-selling practices exposed in relation to the personal pensions, mortgage endowment, split-capital investment trusts, payment protection insurance and precipice bond products. Secondly, detailed rules often draw attention away from the desired outcomes and focus resources on strict compliance with the letter of the rules rather than on risk analysis and adherence to their underlying principles. This results in a poor deal for consumers and a heavy compliance burden on firms. Thirdly, prescriptive regulation can stifle innovation and competition (which ultimately leads to higher costs and less choice for the consumer) and does not necessarily keep pace with industry and product developments or, in principle, respond well in times of market turbulence. Finally, a principles-based approach to regulation ensures that senior management are more attuned to and involved in ensuring compliance with the regulatory requirements applicable to their business and should result in greater alignment of the regulatory and risk management objectives.

Mindful of the need to provide firms with certainty as to what is expected of them in order to comply with the Principles, the FSA issues guidance on particular subjects and publishes case studies and other documents showing examples of good and poor practice.

The FSA places responsibility squarely on senior management to engender a culture consistent with its Principles, an approach which can be seen, for example, in the context of the TCF regime, which is discussed in more detail below.

In addition to the thematic reviews referred to earlier in this Chapter, the following are examples of how the FSA has applied the principles-based approach in its regulation of the insurance sector.

COBS

The new conduct of business rules marked a significant step forward in the implementation of the principles-based regulatory regime. The COBS sourcebook has been shortened and simplified to focus on regulatory outcomes rather than procedures and to emphasise the responsibility of senior management in achieving those outcomes. The new provisions were designed to give firms more flexibility to decide what measures will best allow their particular business model to meet the regulatory requirements. See further Chapters 9 and 10.

The provisions of COBS relating to with-profits business are a good illustration of the principles-based approach. With-profits funds are of particular concern to the FSA because of a number of factors, including the degree of discretion retained by the firms in managing the funds, the investment risk profile of the funds, a lack of consumer understanding and the occurrence of mis-selling in the past. COBS 20 contains three sub-sections: treating with-profits policyholders fairly, principles and practices of financial management and communications with with-profits policyholders. Within each sub-section, previous detailed requirements have been compressed into a smaller number of high-level principles and rules. Notwithstanding this simplification, the amendments also sought to increase protection of with-profits policyholders resulting in changes in substance as well as form. The FSA remains concerned that COBS 20 still does not achieve all of its policyholder protection objectives and has issued a Consultation Paper (CP 11/05) which proposes further amendments.

Despite the FSA's preference to regulate through the use of principles and a streamlined rule book, it is sometimes frustrated in its efforts to do so by mandatory requirements of European law which require it to include prescriptive rules. For example, when the Markets in Financial Instruments Directive ("MiFID") was implemented in the UK in 2007, the FSA had to include in COBS a number of detailed rules required by MiFID in relation to investment products. The FSA decided that some of those rules would also apply to life insurance, with the result that the relevant sections of COBS contain a mixture of high level obligations and detailed requirements.

ICOBS

The ICOBS sourcebook is a good example of how the FSA has moved towards a less prescriptive approach in areas where the perceived risks are lower, whilst maintaining more detailed rules for high-risk products.

ICOBS represents a relaxation in the conduct of business rules relating to general insurance business (for example, household, motor or pet insurance) and a move to more high-level principles and rules.

For example, as part of the sales process firms are no longer required to produce policy summaries in the prescribed format provided that they give consumers appropriate information in good time to enable consumers to make informed decisions.

However, for protection products (critical illness, income protection, term assurance and PPI), ICOBS imposed certain additional rules that were designed to improve poor sales practices, particularly in respect of PPI. For example, firms are required to inform customers orally of the key features of the product (including benefits, exclusions, term and price) before the customer makes the decision to purchase. The recent investigation by the FSA into PPI mis-selling complaints procedures is described in Section 1.4.3 below.

ICOBS is considered in further detail in Chapter 7.

ICAS

As part of its prudential reforms, the FSA introduced the Individual Capital Adequacy Standards framework ("ICAS") in December 2004. The central tenet of ICAS is that, rather than following prescriptive rules to determine precise capital requirements, insurers must undertake their own regular assessment ("ICA") of the amount and quality of capital that is adequate for the nature and size of their business. Insurers were encouraged develop internal models to evaluate the impact on their business of various risks, such as market risk and insurance risk. The FSA reviews the ICA and issues individual capital guidance either confirming the adequacy of the assessment or adding capital where it perceives a shortfall.

The FSA believes that ICAS has not led to a significant decrease in capital in the industry overall but has enabled capital requirements to be better focused on the nature of the particular risks relating to specific businesses. It considers ICAS to have been successful in encouraging a greater risk-management culture within firms, with senior management now often using the ICA as a key decision-making tool. It sees the internal modelling processes now used by firms as a good example of how its principles-based rules promote market-led solutions and provide greater flexibility for the industry. The approach to capital adequacy under Solvency II is consistent with the ICA approach, though, further development and the ICA experience should assist UK insurers with the transition to Solvency II.

Permitted Links

In relation to linked long-term business (that is, broadly, insurance contracts in which the benefits are determined by reference to the value of certain property or assets), the rules have historically been quite restrictive about exactly what type of assets the insurer can invest in. However, in October 2007 the FSA introduced a new set of principles and widened the list of assets to which benefits could be linked, with a view to providing greater flexibility for firms undertaking this type of business. The principles are designed to give senior management greater responsibility for managing risks within the linked business. These principles and rules can be found in COBS. See further Chapter 9.

Insurance Special Purpose Vehicles ("ISPVs")

As part of the implementation of the Reinsurance Directive, the FSA introduced a special process for the authorisation of ISPVs. Recognising that the structure of these vehicles poses less threat to its regulatory objectives than traditional reinsurers, the FSA tailored its information requirements so that ISPVs need to provide less information than traditional insurers and reinsurers when seeking authorisation, imposed less stringent solvency requirements on ISPVs and supervises ISPVs on an ongoing basis through its supervision of the ceding insurer. The capital credit given to an insurer placing reinsurance with an ISPV is determined on a case by case basis. See further Chapter 8.

1.4.3   *Treating Customers Fairly*

Treating customers fairly is an example of principles-based regulation, yet it is of such central importance to the FSA's objectives that it merits separate discussion.

There are four main elements to the FSA's aim to promote the effective and efficient operation of retail markets in order to deliver benefits to consumers:

- Capable and confident consumers.
- Provision of simple and comprehensible information for use by consumers.
- Well managed and adequately capitalised firms that treat their customers fairly.
- Risk-based, principles-based and proportionate regulation that seeks to encourage market-led solutions.

Prior to implementing the TCF initiative, the FSA had found that the existing detailed rules were not delivering all of these benefits. To improve matters, the FSA required senior management to ensure that TCF is considered at every stage of the "product lifecycle" including product development and design, marketing, sales, advising, after sales information/ service, fund management (particularly with-profits) and complaints handling—with the objective of meeting six outcomes:

Outcome 1:	Consumers can be confident that they are dealing with firms where the fair treatment of customers is central to the corporate culture.
Outcome 2:	Products and services marketed and sold in the retail market are designed to meet the needs of identified consumer groups and are targeted accordingly.
Outcome 3:	Consumers are provided with clear information and are kept appropriately informed before, during and after the point of sale.
Outcome 4:	Where consumers receive advice, the advice is suitable and takes account of their circumstances.
Outcome 5:	Consumers are provided with products that perform as firms have led them to expect, and the associated service is of an acceptable standard and as they have been led to expect.

Outcome 6:   Consumers do not face unreasonable post-sale barriers imposed by firms to change product, switch provider, submit a claim or make a complaint.

Embedding a culture of TCF within the firm, in line with Outcome 1, is the responsibility of senior management, who must ensure that their TCF aspirations filter through to consumer experience. Leadership, controls, internal communications, training and competence of staff and sales commissions/rewards should be focused on TCF.

Senior management must also ensure that adequate management information is available in order for them to assess compliance with TCF, take action where necessary and demonstrate that the Outcomes are being achieved.

Delivery of TCF is monitored through thematic work and ARROW visits. The FSA takes TCF seriously. If firms are found deficient in this area, the FSA may take enforcement action against the firm and against senior management personnel that have failed in their responsibilities. In this regard, firms that follow the guidance issued by the FSA from time to time in relation to TCF (in the circumstances for which it is intended) are unlikely to face action.

1.4.3.1   Payment Protection Insurance

PPI was one of the principal TCF concerns for the FSA's insurance sector team. The FSA previously published the results of its thematic review on PPI and issued guidance to firms which, together with the amendments to the ICOBS rules, was aimed at ensuring that firms give consumers the opportunity to understand the features and costs of the product and their cancellation/refund rights.

PPI has been the subject of continued scrutiny and regulation following widespread complaints of mis-selling by policyholders. This has resulted in a series of consultations and a Policy

Statement by the FSA containing new provisions (to be included in DISP) for the handling of PPI complaints and an open letter to the PPI market participants. The open letter addressed many common failings in selling PPI which could lead to a breach of COBS.

The new DISP provisions provide guidance and evidential provisions for firms on how to assess complaints arising from the selling of PPI policies in order to establish whether the firm's conduct has failed to comply with the FSA's rules, or has otherwise breached the firm's duty of care or any other requirement of the general law. The new appendix to DISP provides specific guidance on handling PPI complaints, including the assessment of a complaint, the approach to considering evidence and the approach to redress. Importantly, the new DISP provisions contain guidance on the identification of recurring or systemic problems, obliging firms to undertake a root-cause analysis of complaints, taking into account several factors in the firm's assessment. Following identification of recurring or systemic problems, the new DISP provisions set out the guidance that a firm should follow in considering whether it ought to provide appropriate redress even to non-complainants who may have suffered detriment from the problems.

The Policy Statement, the new DISP provisions and the open letter, have been unsuccessfully challenged in a judicial review brought by the British Bankers' Association ("BBA"). The judgment emphasises the importance of the FSA's Principles, and the support of the judiciary for the FSA's wide discretion in tackling what it perceives to be common failures to protect customers in the market. Following the judgment a number of banks that had sold PPI to their customers announced that they had made provisions in anticipation of a wave of PPI mis-selling claims, in one case amounting to several billion pounds.

1.4.3.2   *With-profits*

As referred to above, the with-profits industry is another important area of focus in the context of TCF. Firms must ensure that their with-profits policyholders are treated fairly, for example by providing sufficient information about policies' investment and return characteristics and risks and managing the use, distribution or re-attribution of any inherited estate properly. The FSA has directed that effective governance arrangements, including some independent scrutiny of management's decisions, are implemented to oversee this outcome. It has also undertaken a number of thematic reviews of the issue and, as mentioned above, earlier this year it published Consultation Paper CP 11/05 which proposes further tightening of management discretion in the operation of with-profits funds.

1.4.3.3   *Product design and distribution*

Insurers should also have regard to their TCF obligations when designing products and dealing with distributors. This requires them, amongst other things, to identify their target market and stress test their products. They should also consider whether the information they provide to their distributors is sufficient, appropriate and comprehensible. Further detail on the obligations of product providers is contained in the FSA's Responsibilities of Providers and Distributors for the Fair Treatment of Customers ("RPPD") sourcebook.

1.5   Enforcement of insurance regulation

1.5.1   *Regulatory enforcement powers*

As the sole financial services industry regulator, the FSA is responsible for ensuring that firms comply with the regulatory regime. To make the FSA effective in this role, the FSMA confers upon the FSA wide powers of supervision, investigation, enforcement and discipline. The majority of these are exercisable only against firms authorised, and persons approved, under the FSMA. What follows is a brief overview of enforcement regime. For further details please see "A Practitioner's Guide to FSA Investigations and Enforcement".

1.5.1.1 *Investigation*

The FSA has considerable information-gathering and investigatory powers, both informal and formal. The FSA's high-level principles require individuals and firms to co-operate with the FSA, allowing it to obtain information by way of informal requests. There is also, under Principle 11, a positive duty on firms to disclose information likely to be of relevance to the FSA as regulator. The FSA rules also contain requirements for specific types of co-operation and assistance from firms. Under the FSMA, firms have formal obligations to provide information, or (on request) obtain a report from a skilled person (such as a lawyer or accountant), on any matter considered by the FSA to be relevant to the exercise of its statutory functions.

The FSA has wide-ranging powers to investigate the business, ownership and control of a firm and possible criminal and regulatory contraventions and offences by a firm. It also has sector-specific investigatory powers, for example to investigate listed companies and applicants for listing. HM Treasury and the Office of Fair Trading also have investigatory powers under the FSMA.

1.5.1.2 *Discipline*

The FSA has power to impose a fine (of any amount it considers appropriate) and/or publicly censure FSA-authorised firms for breach of the FSA rules, high level principles or FSMA itself. In certain circumstances it may issue informal private warnings rather than take formal disciplinary action. In some situations it can require a firm to pay compensation to consumers who have suffered losses as a result of the firm's regulatory breach. It can also apply to the court for a civil injunction to halt an ongoing regulatory breach or to freeze a firm's assets. A civil injunction would usually be used against firms not authorised by the FSMA, since the FSA's other powers are normally sufficient as against authorised firms.

1.5.1.3 Direct intervention

The FSA also has so-called "own-initiative" powers to intervene directly in the business of firms in pursuance of its regulatory objectives. These powers are used rarely, for example to restrict the business a firm can undertake or require it to maintain particular assets. In serious cases, the FSA can cancel a firm's FSMA authorisation.

1.5.1.4 Criminal offences

The most serious breaches of regulatory provisions constitute criminal offences under the FSMA which can give rise to fines and imprisonment. Offences relevant to insurance include falsely claiming to be an authorised or exempt person, unlawful financial promotions, breach of a prohibition order, breach of the asset identification rules in the insurance business regulations, breaches in connection with changes in control over authorised persons and certain breaches committed by directors of long term insurers. The FSA is empowered by the FSMA to act as a criminal prosecutor in relation to these offences.

Enforcement of the regulatory regime as it applies to Lloyd's is somewhat different to the system described above. For further information please see "A Practitioner's Guide to the FSA Regulation of Lloyd's".

1.5.2 The enforcement process

When a firm is alleged to have breached its regulatory obligations, the FSA's enforcement division may carry out an initial fact-finding investigation and then refer the matter to the RDC for consideration. The RDC issues a "warning notice" to the relevant firm, commencing the enforcement process proper. It then hears representations from, and enters into settlement negotiations with, the firm before making a final determination and issuing a "decision notice" to that effect.

If the firm is unhappy with the decision of the RDC, it may refer the matter to the Tribunal. The Tribunal acts as a tribunal of first instance, examining all the available evidence before deciding what disciplinary action, if any, the FSA is to take. There is a limited right of appeal to the courts against decisions of the Tribunal on points of law.

After a final decision has been reached and the appeals process exhausted, the FSA issues a "final notice" and the enforcement action takes effect.

1.5.3 The FSA's approach to enforcement

The FSA conducts its enforcement activities in pursuance of its four statutory objectives and in accordance with its supervisory principles. It adopts a risk-based approach, concentrating its available resources on issues that it considers pose the greatest threat to consumers and the financial system and using enforcement strategically as a tool to change behaviour in the industry. Accordingly, it will often address minor regulatory breaches informally, with a private warning or even no action at all, particularly when the breach has been rapidly rectified by the offending firm. In contrast, where a breach is serious or concerns an area that the FSA considers is of particular importance, such as the protection of consumers or the orderliness of markets, it takes the view that strong and public enforcement action is the best means of maintaining market confidence and sending an effective message of deterrence.

Importantly, the FSA follows a principles-based approach to enforcement, meaning it will look for breaches not merely of detailed rules but also of their underlying principles, including those set out in PRIN (see Section 1.4.2). Where it believes a firm has acted improperly but there is no clear breach of a specific rule, the FSA may take action for breach of a principle alone and the FSA has indicated that it is likely that in the future there will be more enforcement cases where principles rather than specific rules have been breached. Recent examples of such cases include a substantial penalty on a financial institution for mishandling complaints about retail investment products amounting to £3,500,000, and a penalty of £1,127,559 on another financial institution for failure to segregate client money.

The FSA recently also imposed a fine of £17.5 million on a major financial institution for inadequate controls resulting in it failing to provide the FSA with certain information about a regulatory investigation being brought against it overseas which constituted a breach of FSA Principles 2 and 3.

The FSA is also showing an increasing tendency to take enforcement proceedings against individuals within author-ised firms. Anyone who is an approved person (see Chapter 3 for more details) is personally subject to the FSA's jurisdiction and potentially subject to FSA sanctions. There have been a number of examples of the FSA imposing fines against members of senior management within a firm in circumstances where they can be considered personally responsible for a regulatory failure.

For example, in relation to PPI mis-selling, the FSA has relatively recently imposed financial penalties on employees of firms for breaches of Principle 7 of the FSA's Statements of Principles for Approved Persons, in addition to imposing penalties on the relevant firms.

1.6   Solvency II

The Solvency II proposals are considered in more detail in Chapter 4 but the background and certain challenges are briefly set out below.

1.6.1 Background

The implementation of the Solvency II Directive represents one of the most significant changes to the regulation of insurance and will establish a common set of capital requirements and risk management standards to replace the current Solvency I system.

Solvency II will effect sweeping reform of the current EU capital adequacy regime to bring it into line with modern standards of risk management, addressing a number of widely recognised deficiencies in the existing system. The reforms are intended to enhance competition by making it easier for insurers to operate across Member States and to increase consumer protection by closely aligning insurers' capital requirements with their risk profiles.

The framework directive implementing Solvency II aims to consolidate the relevant provisions of the existing Insurance Directives into a single directive. Significant differences have arisen between the regimes of Member States as a result of their differing approaches to the implementation of the Insurance Directives. This has impeded the development of a single, EU-wide, insurance market and resulted in "regulatory arbitrage" where, for example, insurers have established head offices in Member States perceived to have lighter regimes but carry on most of their business in another Member State, or where financial services products are structured so as to fall within the more lightly regulated jurisdictions.

Another problem under the current rules is that they permit inappropriate methods for valuing insurers' liabilities and assets, resulting in inflexible capital adequacy requirements that can be too strict in some cases and too lax in others. Some existing capital adequacy rules are considered in any event to be set too low, which has led certain Member State regulators to impose their own (stricter) standards, which in turn has led to regulatory arbitrage.

At the time of writing the implementation date for Solvency II has been set at 1 January 2013 although a delay might now be necessary as the timetable for finalising the European Commission's detailed implementing measures has slipped and it appears that although the Directive is intended to be transposed into UK law by 1 January 2013, the Solvency II requirements will only apply to firms from 1 January 2014. It also appears that initially there may be significant transitional provisions.

The Omnibus II Directive is expected to make a number of important changes to Solvency II. Apart from formally postponing the implementation date of Solvency II the Commission is likely to be given the power to implement transitional provisions in a number of areas and EIOPA will be required to develop binding technical standards for adoption by the Commission (in addition to its responsibility to issue non-binding supervisory guidelines).

1.6.2   Challenges

The implementation date for Solvency II is looming. The ICAS regime has put UK firms in good stead. Nonetheless, firms should have by now identified and as far as possible activated the changes they will need to make to comply with the proposed new regime. For example, larger firms wishing to use their own internal models rather than the standard formula to calculate their capital requirements should have already been liaising with the FSA to obtain the necessary regulatory approval for internal models.

At the time of writing, it is not clear exactly what the European Commission's detailed implementing measures or transitional provisions will contain, nor precisely what impact they will have on implementation. Further, the lack of clarity on the implementation date, the content of most of EIOPA's non-binding supervisory guidelines and the content of EIOPA's binding technical standards has caused some uncertainty in the industry. However, most of the Commission's detailed implementing measures are not expected to differ significantly from those reflected in the Commission's technical specifications for its fifth quantitative impact study for industry participants and its subsequent consultation papers on key issues. Insurers are therefore starting to implement changes to their structure and business risk to reflect the Solvency II regime.

Chapter 2

Authorisation of UK, EEA and Overseas Insurance Companies

James Bateson,
Partner: Head of Insurance Group

Laura Hodgson,
Insurance Group,
Norton Rose LLP

2.1 Introduction

The purpose of this chapter is to give general guidance about the circumstances in which authorisation is required in order to carry on insurance business (other than at Lloyd's) pursuant to the Financial Services and Markets Act 2000 ("FSMA 2000"), the procedures applicable to applicants and the FSA's powers in relation to authorisation. It is not and should not be taken as a substitute for detailed professional advice and indeed the Financial Services Authority ("FSA") encourages all applicants to seek and obtain such advice in relation to their application for authorisation to carry out a regulated activity. The authorisation of insurance intermediaries is considered separately in Chapter 7.

The FSMA 2000, the secondary legislation made under the FSMA 2000 and the FSA Handbook of rules and guidance are complex. For convenience, certain provisions of the legislation have been summarised in this chapter. In addition, the regulatory framework makes considerable use of definitions, the meaning of which is not always obvious from the defined term. For precise details of the legislation, reference should be made to the relevant source materials and to the glossary of definitions in the FSA Handbook. Cross-references have been provided where appropriate.

The principal statutory sources for the authorisation of insurers are the FSMA 2000 and the Financial Services and Markets Act (Regulated Activities) Order 2001 ("RAO"). The FSA Handbook contains much of the detail which determines exactly what will be required of an authorised firm. Much of the authorisation process is set out in the Perimeter Guidance Manual ("PERG"). Other information relevant to the authorisation process can be found in the Statements of Principle and Code of Practice for Approved Persons ("APER") and the Fit and Proper Test for Approved Persons ("FIT"), Threshold Conditions ("COND"), Principles for Businesses ("PRIN"), and in Senior Management Arrangements Systems and Controls ("SYSC"). Materials of continuing relevance after authorisation can generally be found in the Supervision Manual ("SUP") as well as in the New Insurance Conduct of Business Sourcebook ("ICOBS") and the Prudential Sourcebooks relevant to insurers, the General Prudential Sourcebook ("GENPRU"), the Prudential Sourcebook for Insurers ("INSPRU") and the remaining sections of the Interim Prudential Sourcebook for Insurers ("IPRU(INS)"). The Decision Procedure and Penalties Manual ("DEPP") sets out the FSA's procedures for decisions that involve the giving of warning notices, decision notices or supervisory notices. The current fee rates can be found in the Fees Manual ("FEES"). The FSA's website (www.fsa.gov.uk) contains additional information and guidance on how to submit an application for authorisation.

This chapter addresses the two main routes for authorisation to carry on a regulated activity under the FSMA 2000. They are:

(a) through an application to the FSA for permission under Part IV of the FSMA 2000 (a "Part IV Permission"); or
(b) by a person authorised in another EEA state exercising an EEA passport right or Treaty right.

Any person who is not otherwise exempt but who wishes to effect or carry out insurance contracts in the UK needs the prior authorisation of the FSA to do so. Under the FSMA 2000 there is a single process for authorisation, which covers the whole of the financial services community. Because the scope of the information required to be submitted to the FSA as part of the authorisation process will vary depending on the nature and complexity of the activities undertaken, in accordance with the principle of proportionality set out in s.2 of the FSMA 2000, it is important that a person contemplating carrying out a regulated activity in the UK determines at the outset which type of authorisation is required.

Broadly, to become authorised an applicant must satisfy certain threshold conditions and the FSA's risk assessment process, which involves an assessment of the risks posed by an applicant against a number of probability and impact factors. These are discussed later in this chapter. In reaching a decision on whether an applicant satisfies these conditions, the FSA will consider whether the applicant is ready, willing and organised enough to comply with its regulatory obligations that will apply if permission is given.

Readers should be aware that the process of authorisation will change following the reform of Financial Services regulation in the UK. The draft Financial Services Bill envisages the replacement of the FSA as single regulator with a Prudential Regulatory Authority ("PRA") with primary responsibility for regulation of deposit taking institutions, banks and insurers and a Financial Conduct Authority ("FCA") which will have responsibility for all conduct of business matters in firms and will regulate insurance intermediaries.

As a result of the proposed changes, the authorisation process will reflect the roles played by the two new regulatory authorities. For insurers, the Government has proposed that both the PRA and FCA work together to consider the suitability of applications for authorisation to conduct insurance business. The PRA will have responsibility for assessing whether the firm will be capable of running its business prudently whilst the FCA will need to ensure that all new entrants to financial services markets meet conduct of business and consumer protection standards. In order for a firm to receive final permission to conduct insurance business both the PRA and FCA will need to give their consent to the application. The details of the new regime remain subject to Parliamentary scrutiny and therefore will not be discussed in this edition.

2.2   The general prohibition

The FSMA 2000 is the primary statute which regulates the carrying on of certain activities known as "regulated activities". Section 19 of the FSMA 2000 contains the general prohibition against carrying on a regulated activity in the UK without being authorised to do so. The purpose of the general prohibition is to ensure only persons who satisfy the necessary conditions engage in a regulated activity, and that only fit and proper persons perform key functions in the financial services industry.

Section 19(1) of the FSMA 2000 provides that:

"No person may carry on a regulated activity in the UK, or

purport to do so, unless he is -

(a)   an authorised person; or
(b)   an exempt person."

The prohibition is referred to as the general prohibition.

An authorised person is defined by reference to s.31 of the FSMA 2000 and it includes the following:

(a)   a person who has a Part IV Permission to carry out one or more regulated activities, including the Society of Lloyd's;
(b)   an incoming EEA firm; and
(c)   an incoming Treaty firm.

The first category covers those persons who have obtained permission under the FSMA 2000, and the second and third categories permit the exercise of passport rights and Treaty rights by EEA firms. An EEA firm is entitled to exercise its passport right to set up a branch or provide services in the UK in accordance with one of the single-market directives. In contrast, a Treaty firm exercises a right contained in the EC Treaty but not specifically reflected in a directive.

Exempt persons are defined in s.417(1) of the FSMA 2000 as being persons falling within the following groups:

(a) a person or class of persons specified in an Exemption Order;
(b) an appointed representative;
(c) a recognised investment exchange or a recognised clearing house as specified in s.285 of the FSMA 2000.

In granting a permission to carry out a regulated activity, the FSA is required by s.42(2) of the FSMA 2000 to specify the regulated activities for which permission has been granted. An authorised person who carries on a regulated activity other-wise than in accordance with its permission, or who purports to do so, will be taken to have contravened a requirement imposed on him by the FSA under the FSMA 2000. However, s.20 of the FSMA 2000 provides that such a contravention does not make the person concerned guilty of an offence, or make the transaction void or unenforceable, or give rise to any right of action for breach of statutory duty. In certain prescribed cases the contravention is actionable at the suit of a person who suffers loss as a result of the contravention. Contravention of s.20 may also lead to the exercise by the FSA of its regulatory powers of intervention or to closer monitoring and supervision from the regulator.

Section 23 of the FSMA 2000 provides that a person who contravenes the general prohibition is guilty of an offence and is liable:

(a) on summary conviction to imprisonment for a term not exceeding six months or a fine not exceeding the statutory maximum, or both;
(b) on conviction on indictment, to imprisonment for a term not exceeding two years or a fine or both.

It is a defence for the accused to show that he took all reasonable precautions and exercised all due diligence to avoid committing an offence.

In addition to the commission of a criminal offence, s.26 of the FSMA 2000 provides that an agreement entered into by a person in contravention of the general prohibition will be unenforceable against the other party, who will be able to recover any money or other property paid or transferred by him under the relevant agreement. Compensation will also be payable for any loss suffered as a result of having transferred the property concerned. Section 27 of the FSMA 2000 extends the scope of the restriction to contracts entered into by an authorised person through the intermediaryship of a person who is carrying on a regulated activity without authorisation.

2.3 Regulated activities

The list of regulated activities requiring authorisation is contained in the Regulated Activities Order 2001. They include effecting contracts of insurance (art.10(1)), and carrying out contracts of insurance (art.10(2)). It is important to note that "effecting" and "carrying out" are regarded as separate activities under the RAO and that a separate authorisation is required for each. Furthermore, since the implementation of the Insurance Mediation Directive, through various amendments to the RAO, it has become necessary for insurers to ensure that the scope of their authorisation is extended to cover certain insurance mediation activities that are routinely carried on as part of the insurance process (*see* Chapter 7).

The first stage in the application process is to establish whether the proposed activities will constitute the carrying on of regulated activities requiring Part IV Permission. Section 22 of the FSMA 2000 provides that authorisation is necessary where it is proposed to carry on a regulated activity:

(a)   by way of business;
(b)   in the UK;
(c)   which relates to an investment of a specified kind.

These three elements which must be taken into account are discussed below. Before looking at the specified investments themselves, it is necessary to examine the business element and geographical scope of the section.

2.3.1   The business element

For an activity to be a regulated activity under s.22 of the FSMA 2000, it must be carried on "by way of business"—the so-called "business element". The Treasury has power under s.419 of the FSMA 2000 to alter the scope of the business element so that different requirements will apply in respect of different activities. This in part reflects differences in the nature of each activity and the broad scope of the legislation governing the financial services industry.

Although in many cases it will be clearly apparent whether an activity is being carried on "by way of business", there are cases where this is more difficult to determine. The FSA has issued guidance on what activities will meet what is known as the "business test". PERG 2.3.3 states that whether an activity is carried on by way of business is "ultimately a question of judgment that takes account of several factors (none of which is likely to be conclusive)". The following should be considered:

(a)   the degree of continuity;
(b)   whether there is a commercial element in the transaction;
(c)   the scale of the activity;
(d)   the proportion of the given activity in relation to other unregulated activities; and
(e)   the nature of the activity itself.

2.3.2   Link between the activities and the UK

The need to be authorised only arises if the activities are carried on in the UK. In most cases it is likely to be obvious where this is so. However, there will be occasions where the answer is not so apparent. This may be the case, for example, where services are carried out cross-border or where the transaction is multi-jurisdictional. Furthermore, s.418 of the FSMA 2000 sets out five circumstances where a person who would not otherwise be regarded as carrying on a regulated activity in the UK is deemed to do so. In each of the five cases, for insurers it is irrelevant where the policyholder is situated.

The first case is where the registered or head office of the person concerned is in the UK, the person is entitled to exercise rights under a single market directive as a UK firm and he is carrying on in another EEA state a regulated activity to which that directive applies. This would catch, for example, a UK firm exercising a passport right to carry on insurance business in France irrespective of whether the firm is carrying on insurance business in the UK as well.

The second case arises where the registered or head office of the person concerned is in the UK, he is the manager of a scheme which is entitled to enjoy the rights conferred by an instrument which is a relevant community instrument for the purposes of s.264 of the FSMA 2000, and persons in another EEA state are invited to become participants in the scheme. This would apply to a collective investment scheme managed from the UK where the scheme is only promoted abroad and is not likely to be relevant to insurance business.

The third case is where the registered or head office is in the UK, and the day-to-day management of the carrying on of the regulated activity is the responsibility of the head or registered office or another establishment maintained by the person concerned in the UK. This case would catch a UK firm carrying on insurance business overseas where the international business is managed from the UK, irrespective of whether any insurance business is also being carried on in the UK. This can be quite problematic, as it may not always be clear to what extent the day-to-day management of the regulated activity is being carried on from the UK where the management functions are split between several locations. In addition, it is important to note that there are two regulated activities: "effecting" and "carrying out" contracts of insurance. It will be necessary to assess s.418 in the context of both regulated activities, and whilst the regulated activity of effecting contracts of insurance might be carried on outside the UK it may be that the separate activity of carrying them out is undertaken from the UK, triggering the requirement for authorisation.

The fourth case is where the head or registered office is not in the UK, but the activity is carried on from an establishment maintained in the UK. This case is also likely to cause practical difficulties, as it would catch the activities of any insurer where the activity is being carried on from an establishment maintained in the UK wherever the underlying risks are being written. Again, the question of whether the activity is being carried on from one location or another is likely to be a matter of fine judgment in many cases, especially where the activity is carried on partly from one location and partly from another.

The fifth case is where the activity consists of the provision of an information society service to a person in one of the EEA states and is carried on from an establishment maintained in the UK.

A person may also be carrying on an activity in the UK even if there is no permanent establishment there. For example, the activities could constitute the carrying on of regulated activities where carried out during occasional visits to the UK from overseas (*see* PERG 2 for details of the link between activities and the UK). To be a regulated activity the requirement for the business element to be met will still apply and the activity taking place in the UK will need to form a significant and regular part of the relevant regulated activity. Further, it will be important in such scenarios to consider whether the overseas persons exclusion under art.72 of the RAO might be applicable.

2.3.3   Specified investments

A person needs an authorisation to carry out a regulated activity only if the activity relates to one of the specified investments laid down by the RAO. It is a requirement of the FSMA 2000 that both the investments themselves and the activities carried out in relation to those investments are caught within the regulatory net. Both the investments and the activities are defined in the RAO. This chapter focuses only on those specified investments and regulated activities likely to be relevant to insurance business.

2.3.3.1   Rights under a contract of insurance

Rights under contracts of insurance are specified investments by virtue of art.75 of the RAO. Article 3 of the RAO defines a contract of insurance as: "any contract of insurance which is a contract of long-term insurance or a contact of general insurance", and the definition goes on to give examples of types of contract that are included as contracts of insurance, notwithstanding that they may not ordinarily be regarded as being so. Examples given include:

(a)   fidelity bonds;
(b)   performance bonds;
(c)   administration bonds;
(d)   bail bonds;
(e)   customs bonds or similar contracts of guarantee;
(f)   tontines;
(g)   capital redemption contracts or pension fund management contracts;
(h)   contracts to pay annuities on human life; and
(i)   collective insurance contracts and social insurance contracts.

For more information about the circumstances in which these contracts are to be treated as insurance contracts, reference should be made to art.3 of the RAO as well as PERG 6.

The expressions "contract of general insurance" and "contract of long-term insurance" are defined by reference to the various different classes of insurance contract. These are set out in Sch.1 to the RAO.

PERG 6 contains general guidance on the identification of contracts of insurance. The RAO itself does not set out a detailed definition of contract of insurance, and reliance is still placed on the common law in determining whether a particular contract is a contract of insurance or whether a particular activity amounts to carrying on insurance business. What constitutes an insurance contract is outside the scope of this chapter, but in July 2004 the FSA published a policy statement (PS 04/19) on the identification of contracts of insurance. The FSA cites the established description found in the case of *Prudential* v *Commissioners of the Inland Revenue*[1904] 2 K.B. 658 as the starting point for any determination. However, each case will be treated on its own merits and the guidance provided by the FSA is not intended to be exhaustive.

The insurance directives (the first, second and third non-life insurance directives and the life assurance consolidated directive) impose certain limitations on the combinations of regulated activities for which authorisation can be given. In particular, it is not generally possible to obtain authorisation to undertake regulated activities in respect of both contracts of general insurance and contracts of long-term insurance save in certain limited circumstances where accident and health may be written alongside life contracts (*see* below).

The RAO (art.3) also provides that certain rights, under qualifying contracts of insurance, are treated as contractually based investments. In order to be a "qualifying contract of insurance" (and subject to additional levels of regulation—*see* Chapter 8) the contract concerned must be in respect of long-term insurance, other than a reinsurance contract, and other than a contract in respect of which certain specified conditions are met. The specified conditions are that:

(a) the benefits must be payable only on death or in respect of incapacity due to injury, sickness or infirmity;

(b) the contract has no surrender value, or the consideration consists of a single premium and the surrender value does not exceed that premium; and

(c) the contract makes no provision for its conversion or extension in a manner which would result in it ceasing to comply with any of the foregoing provisions.

2.3.3.2   Rights under a pension scheme

Rights under pension schemes are specified investments for the purpose of the RAO. A personal pension scheme means a scheme or arrangement which is neither an occupational pension scheme or a stakeholder pension scheme.

2.3.3.3   Lloyd's investments

There are two types of specified investment in relation to Lloyd's: the underwriting capacity of a Lloyd's syndicate, and a person's membership (or prospective membership) of a Lloyd's syndicate. Generally Lloyd's business falls outside the scope of this chapter (*see A Practitioner's Guide to The FSA Regulation of Lloyds (Second edition),* City & Financial, 2005).

2.3.3.4   Rights under funeral plans

Rights under a funeral plan are the rights to a funeral obtained by a person before the death of a person whose funeral it will be.

2.3.3.5   Rights to or interests in investments

Rights to, or interests in, all of the specified investments are themselves treated as specified investments. This means that an activity carried on in relation to rights or interests derived from any specified investments is also a regulated activity if the activity would be regulated if carried on in relation to the investment itself.

2.3.4 *Regulated activities*

As referred to above, there are two elements to be taken into account when looking at regulated activities. The first concerns the specified investments, which are outlined above in so far as they relate to insurance. The second element concerns the activities that are undertaken in relation to the specified investments. These activities are referred to as regulated activities. A regulated activity is an activity specified in Part II of the RAO and carried on in relation to one or more specified investments. The RAO sets out a wide range of regulated activities and describes any exclusion that is applicable to the regulated activity concerned. This chapter concentrates on those activities and exclusions that are relevant to insurance.

2.3.4.1 *Effecting or carrying out contracts of insurance as a principal*

Article 10 of the RAO provides that both *effecting* and *carrying out* contracts of insurance as a principal are regulated activities for the purposes of the FSMA 2000. The activities of effecting and carrying out a contract of insurance are separate activities, each requiring their own authorisation. This means that an insurance company in run-off, for example, would not need to be authorised to *effect* new contracts of insurance, but would need authorisation to *carry out* those contracts of insurance already written.

Generally an insurer must be authorised to effect and carry out contracts of insurance by reference to the various classes of insurance contract specified in the RAO. However, the permission to effect or carry out certain classes of insurance includes permission to both effect or carry out certain classes of general insurance contracts on an *ancillary* or *supplementary* basis. This right derives from the insurance directives. Accordingly, in determining which classes to apply for, an applicant should have regard to whether the contracts he wishes to carry out would qualify to be effected or carried out on an ancillary basis. For example, permission relating to life and annuity contracts includes permission to effect or carry out accident or sickness contracts on a supplementary basis and permission to effect or carry out any class of general insurance contract includes permission to carry out any other class of general insurance contract, other than credit, suretyship and (except in certain circumstances) legal expenses contracts on an ancillary basis. For this reason, applicants seeking to carry on insurance business will also need to consider whether the class of specified investments qualifies to be carried on in an ancillary or supplementary capacity.

A contract of insurance will qualify to be effected or carried out on an ancillary basis if:

(a) the business in question is to be the subject of the same contract as the principal business and concerns the same object; and
(b) the risks covered are connected to the principal risk.

Two activities, which might otherwise constitute the effecting or carrying out of contracts of insurance, are expressly excluded from the need for Part IV Permission:

(a) in circumstances specified in art.11 of the RAO, the activities of an EEA firm where participating in a community co-insurance operation (*see* Chapter 8) other than as leading insurer; and
(b) in circumstances specified in art.12 of the RAO, activities that are carried out in connection with the provision of on-the-spot accident or breakdown assistance for cars and other vehicles.

Although this chapter is concerned largely with effecting and carrying out contracts of insurance as "a principal", the activities of brokers, agents and all those arranging contracts of insurance (collectively known as intermediaries) also require authorisation. Since 14 January 2005 the FSA has regulated all insurance mediation activities (*see* Chapter 1). As a consequence FSA authorisation is required for people or firms who carry out a mediation activity. An insurance mediation activity is defined as any of the following activities specified in the

RAO which is carried on in relation to a contract of insurance or rights to, or interests in, a life policy:

(a)   dealing in investments as agent;
(b)   arranging (bringing about) deals in investments;
(c)   making arrangements with a view to transactions in investments;
(d)   assisting in the administration of and performance of a contract of insurance;
(e)   advising on investments; and
(f)   agreeing to carry on a regulated activity in (a)–(e).

Further, a number of activities conducted in relation to specified investments will require FSA permission to be carried on, where the following should be considered.

Dealing in investments (as a principal or an agent)

The activity of dealing in investments is a regulated activity by virtue of arts 14 and 21 of the RAO. It is defined in terms of "buying, selling, subscribing for, or underwriting securities or contractually based investments".

However, the scope of the activity of dealing in investments as a principal is reduced by further exclusions. In relation to life policies, for example, dealing as a principal is only a regulated activity if the person holds himself out as making a market in the relevant specified investments, or as being in the business of dealing with them, or he must regularly solicit members of the public with the purpose of inducing them into the deal.

Arranging deals in investments

Arranging deals in investments may be of relevance to insurers to the extent that it applies to arrangements that relate to contractually based investments, or the underwriting capacity of a Lloyd's syndicate or membership of a Lloyd's syndicate. Arranging is made up of two distinct regulated activities:

(a) Making arrangements with a view to transactions in investments—this activity is described as "making arrangements for another person to buy, sell, subscribe for, or underwrite a particular investment". It is aimed at arrangements that would have the direct effect that a transaction is concluded.

(b) Arranging (bringing about) deals in investments—this second activity is described as "making arrangements with a view to a person who participates in the arrangements buying, selling, subscribing for, or underwriting investments". It is aimed at cases where it may be said that the transaction is "brought about" directly by the parties to it, but where this happens in a context set up by a third party specifically with a view to the conclusion by others of transactions through the use of that third party's facilities. A person may therefore be carrying on this activity even if it is only providing part of the facilities necessary before a transaction is brought about.

Safeguarding and administering investments

Safeguarding and administering investments covers the circumstances where a person undertakes to arrange on a continuing basis for others actually to carry out the safeguarding and administering. In each case, both elements of safeguarding and administering must be present before a person will be deemed to carry on such an activity. The property that is safeguarded and administered must belong beneficially to another person and consist of contractually based investments.

Establishing a pension scheme

The regulated activities carried on in relation to pension schemes are their establishment, operation or winding up. Managers of such schemes will require authorisation to operate the scheme.

Advising on investments

Advising on investments only applies to contractually based investments and does not include giving advice about rights under general insurance contracts or generally about things that are not specified investments in the RAO. Additionally, the advice must be given to someone who holds specified investments or is a prospective investor.

Entering into funeral plan contracts

Entering as a provider into a funeral plan contract is a regulated activity, the provider being the person to whom the prepayments are made and who undertakes to provide the funeral.

Lloyd's activities

The RAO expressly lays down three regulated activities in relation to Lloyd's:

(a) Advising on syndicate participation at Lloyd's (i.e. advising a person to become, continue or cease to be a member of a particular syndicate) is a regulated activity. Giving advice about the syndicate participation (how to use capital within the Lloyd's market and arranging syndicate participation) is a separate regulated activity to that of providing advice in relation to securities and contractually based investments.

(b) Managing the underwriting capacity of a Lloyd's syndicate as a managing agent.

(c) Arranging deals in contracts of insurance written at Lloyd's.

The Society of Lloyd's is authorised for (c) under s.315 of the FSMA 2000. Section 316 provides that Lloyd's members do not breach the general prohibition (and consequently do not require authorisation for effecting and carrying out contracts of insurance) unless the FSA directs otherwise. Lloyd's is generally outside the scope of this chapter.

2.4 Persons who do not need authorisation to carry on regulated activities

The scope of the general prohibition against carrying on regulated activities without permission has been addressed above, as have the regulated activities themselves. Before moving on to look at the authorisation process, it is necessary to address certain persons who do not need authorisation to undertake regulated activities. Although there is no general provision allowing persons to apply for exemption, certain specific persons may be exempted from the general prohibition in relation to one or more regulated activities. The FSMA 2000 provides that appointed representatives, recognised exchanges or clearing houses, members of the professions under particular conditions (laid down in s.326 of the FSMA 2000), and other particular exempt persons by order made by the Treasury (under s.38 of the FSMA 2000) are exempted persons. None of these exemptions will be applicable to the regulated activities of effecting or carrying out contracts of insurance as a principal, but reference is made to them here for the sake of completeness.

2.4.1 Authorisation and regulated activities

PERG 2 contains some helpful diagrams which show whether or not permission is required under the FSMA 2000 to carry on a regulated activity. Reproduced in Figure 2.1 is the diagram relating to Authorisation and Regulated Activities (found in PERG 2 Annex 1).

2.5 Part IV Permission

As shown above, subject to certain exceptions (particularly in respect of EEA firms or those wishing to exercise EU passporting rights), a person wishing to carry out regulated activities in the UK by way of business must apply to the FSA under s.40 of the FSMA 2000 for permission under Part IV of the FSMA 2000 before commencing those activities. A permission under Part IV is referred to as a Part IV Permission. An

```
NO ─────────── Will you be carrying on in any activities ──── YES        Consult the Business Order
               by way of business?

NO ─────────── Are you, or will you be, involved with ──── YES          Consult Part III of the RAO
               specified investments of any kind or
               establishing etc a CIS or stakeholder
               pension scheme?

NO ─────────── Are you, or will you be, carrying on a ──── YES          Consult Part II of the RAO
               regulated activity?

NO ─────────── Are you, or will you be, carrying on a ──── YES          Consult section 418 of the Act
               regulated activity in the United
               Kingdom?

YES ────────── Are your activities excluded in full under ──── NO       Consult Part II of the RAO and,
               the RAO?                                                 if an investment firm, article 4
                                                                        of the RAO

YES ────────── Do you conduct regulated activities only ──── NO        Consult Part XIX of the Act
               as a member or former underwriting
               member of Lloyd's?

YES ────────── Are you a member of the professions ──── NO             Consult Part XX of the Act and
               whose activities are exempt under Part                  the Non-Exempt Activities
               XX of the Act?                                          Order and Part XIX of the Act

YES ────────── Are you an exempt person under ──── NO                  Consult the Exemption Order
               section 38 or 39 of the Act?                            and the Appointed
                                                                       Representatives Regulations.

               Will you be managing the assets of an ──── YES
               OPS (e.g. as a trustee)?

                            NO

Authorisation   YES ──── Will you be delegating decisions or be a ──── NO
not                      trustee of a qualifying SSAS as
required                 provided for in the Business Order?

               YES ──── Are you an EEA firm, a Treaty firm or a ──── Authorisation
                        UCITS qualifier in relation to the          required
                        regulated activity?

                            NO

Contact the Home State        Apply for Part IV          Obtain exemption under the Act as
regulator, and the FSA, to    permission from the FSA    an appointed representative
obtain authorisation under    under Part IV of the Act.  (section 39) or recognised
Schedule 3, 4 or 5 of the                                investment exchange or
Act (see PERG 5).                                        recognised clearing house (Part
                                                         XVIII).
```

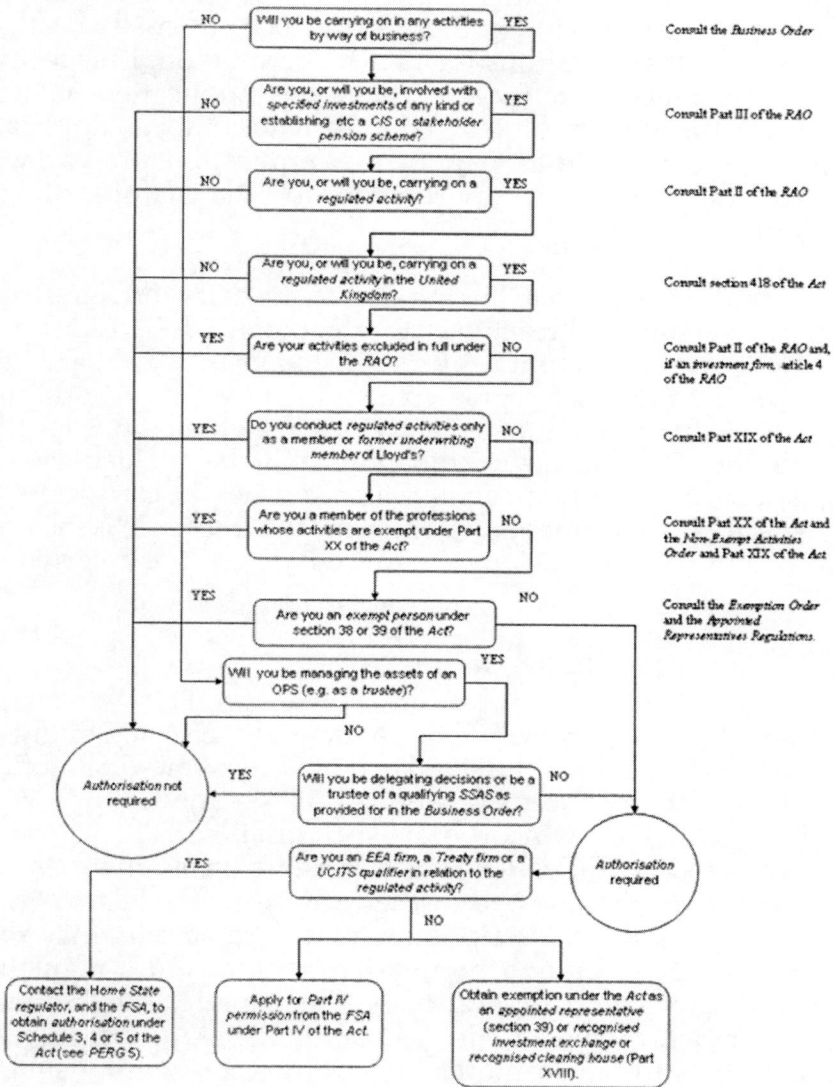

Figure 2.1 Authorisation and regulated activities

73

applicant who is in receipt of such a permission will become an authorised person. Under the FSMA 2000, there is a single process for all applications for Part IV Permission, irrespective of the regulated activity to which the application relates. However, the amount of detailed information that an applicant will have to provide as part of the application process will depend on, and be proportionate to, the nature of the application.

Authorisation gives a firm the ability to carry on regulated activities without breaching the general prohibition and incurring criminal liability. A firm must have the necessary Part IV Permission for each regulated activity it carries on and must carry on only those regulated activities for which it has Part IV Permission. The first step, therefore, will be to identify the regulated activities that the applicant wishes to carry on and the specified investments associated with those activities for which Part IV Permission is required. These are referred to above.

2.5.1 Content of the permission

Section 42(6) of the FSMA 2000 requires the FSA to set out in the Part IV Permission the regulated activities for which a firm is given authorisation. Section 42(7) of the FSMA 2000 empowers the FSA to incorporate such limitations in respect of the regulated activities for which permission is given as the FSA deems appropriate and further empowers the FSA to grant a narrower or wider description of regulated activity than that applied for, or to grant a permission to carry out a regulated activity for which no application has been made. The FSA may also exercise its powers under s.43 of the FSMA 2000 to include requirements to which the Part IV Permission will be subject where the FSA considers it appropriate.

Accordingly, a Part IV Permission will specify:

(a) a description of the activities the firm can carry on, including any limitations to the scope of the permission;
(b) the specified investments involved; and

(c) if appropriate, any requirements imposed in relation to the Part IV Permission.

The specified investments and the regulated activities have already been discussed.

2.5.2 *Limitations*

Under s.42(7) of the FSMA 2000, the FSA may impose limitations on the scope of the regulated activities for which Part IV Permission is given if it decides it is appropriate to do so. Generally, a limitation is imposed to limit in some way the scope of the regulated activities in respect of which permission is given. Each limitation is specific to a particular regulated activity, either in relation to the regulated activity, the specified investments or both. For this reason the limitation is actually incorporated in the definition of the regulated activity itself rather than being separately listed. An applicant may wish to apply for certain limitations to be imposed on the scope of its regulated activities at the outset, or alternatively the FSA may impose the limitation using its own initiative powers under s.45 of the FSMA 2000. Examples of limitations include:

(a) a limit on the types of clients with whom the applicant may deal;
(b) a limit on the number of clients with whom the applicant may deal;
(c) a limit on the types of specified investments with which the applicant may deal;
(d) a limit on the type of insurance business that the applicant may carry on, for example limiting it to reinsurance only.

Where the FSA intends to impose a limitation the applicant will be advised formally and given the opportunity to make representations before a final decision is made. Once a Part IV Permission has been given, a firm can apply at any time under s.44 of the FSMA 2000 to have a limitation or requirement varied or removed.

2.5.3   Requirements

Section 43 of the FSMA 2000 gives the FSA power to include any requirement in a Part IV Permission that it considers appropriate. This may be a requirement on a firm to either take or refrain from particular action.

A requirement can apply to unregulated activities as well as to regulated activities and accordingly can be used to control the performance of certain business activities that are not themselves regulated. The requirements can extend to the group of which the applicant is a member and to any member of such group. The FSA may set time limits on the imposition of a requirement.

Requirements can also be used to define the scope of a number of regulated activities carried out by a firm so that a particular differentiated regulatory regime applies.

If after reviewing an application the FSA proposes to impose a requirement, the applicant will be advised formally and given the opportunity to make representations before the FSA reaches its final decision. After being given permission, a firm can apply under s.44 of the FSMA 2000 at any time to have a limitation or a requirement varied or removed following the procedures in Section 6 of the Supervision Manual.

As part of its application process, an applicant may wish to apply for certain requirements to be imposed, or alternatively, the FSA may impose the requirement using its own initiative powers under s.45 of the FSMA 2000. One of the advantages of applying for certain requirements is that, by reducing the scope of the permission requested, the firm will only be required to demonstrate that it will be able to satisfy the threshold conditions in respect of this reduced scope.

2.5.4   Prudential categories

The structure of financial services regulation is divided into prudential categories, with different rule books applying dependent on the relevant prudential category. For insurers the current structure includes GENPRU, INSPRU and parts of the original prudential sourcebook IPRU(INS). MIPRU will be applicable to firms with permission to carry on insurance business and use the services of an insurance intermediary. When applying for Part IV Permission it is necessary for a firm to identify the relevant prudential category that it will fit into. Appendix 1 to SUP gives guidance as to the determination of the relevant prudential category. As a consequence of falling within the prudential category of insurer, certain restrictions are imposed in INSPRU 1.5.13 on the other commercial business that the firm may wish to carry on in addition to an insurance business.

The assessment of a firm's prudential category can be made according to Figure 2.2, prepared by the FSA.

2.5.5   Risk assessment

In considering whether to impose limitations and require-ments, the FSA will adopt a risk-based approach in order to concentrate the FSA's regulatory resources in the areas that most need attention. According to s.1 of SUP, the approach to risk assessment is based on the extent to which a firm poses risks to the FSA in meeting its regulatory objectives. This involves an analysis of the impact of a risk materialising and the likelihood of it doing so. The probability of a risk materialising will depend on several factors including the inherent risks run by firms, the environment in which they operate and the firm's internal systems and controls.

The impact of a firm is assessed by reference to a range of factors derived from the regulatory objectives including:

(a)   the degree to which risks related to the firm, if they were to materialise, would damage market confidence;

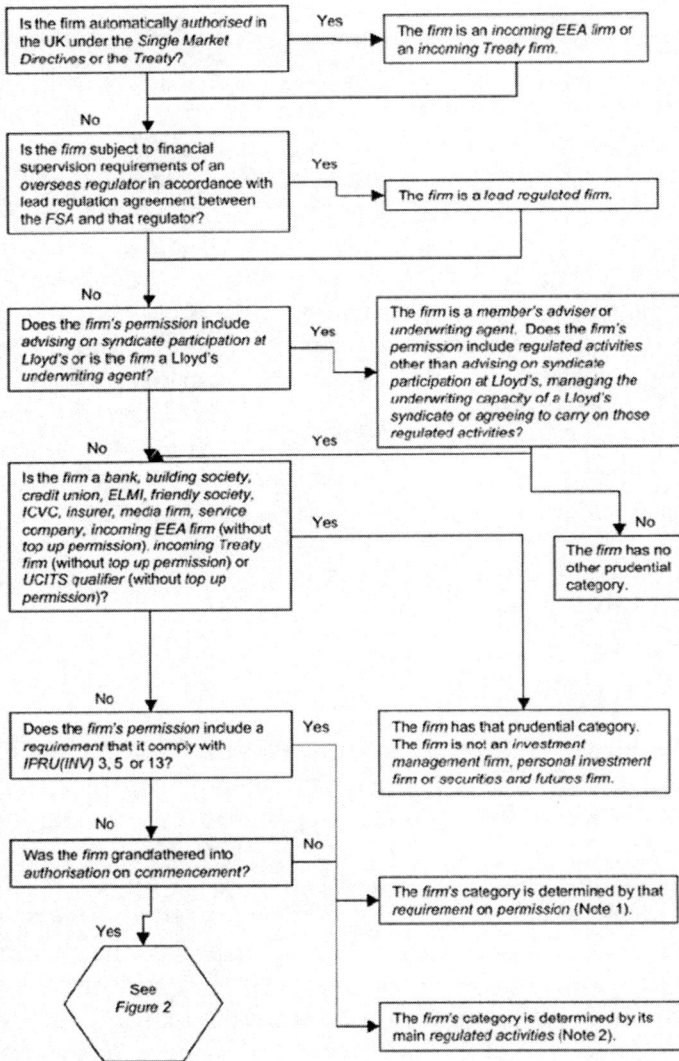

```
                    ╭───────────╮
                   ╱             ╲
                  ╱   Figure 1    ╲
                  ╲               ╱
                   ╲             ╱
                    ╰─────┬─────╯
                          │
    ┌──────────────────────┐        Yes      ┌──────────────────────┐
    │ Is the firm an ex-section 43 ├─────────────→│ The firm is a securities and │
    │ lead regulated firm?  │                 │      futures firm.     │
    └──────────┬───────────┘                 └──────────────────────┘
               │ No
    ┌──────────┴───────────┐        Yes      ┌──────────────────────┐
    │ Was the firm a member of a ├───────────→│ The firm's category is │
    │ single SRO immediately │                 │ determined by that SRO │
    │ before commencement?  │                 │ membership (Note 2).   │
    └──────────┬───────────┘                 └──────────────────────┘
               │ No
    ┌──────────┴───────────┐                 ┌──────────────────────┐
    │ Was the firm a member of │             │ The firm's category is │
    │ more than one SRO,    │      Yes       │ determined by the financial │
    │ immediately before    ├───────────────→│ supervision requirements to │
    │ commencement?         │                 │ which the firm was subject │
    └──────────┬───────────┘                 │ immediately before     │
               │ No                          │ commencement (Note 4). │
                                             └──────────────────────┘
    ┌──────────┴───────────┐                 ┌──────────────────────┐
    │ Was the firm authorised under │         │ The firm's category is │
    │ section 25 of the Financial │   Yes    │ determined by its main │
    │ Services Act 1986 immediately ├────────→│ regulated activities (Note 3). │
    │ before commencement but not │           │                        │
    │ a member of an SRO (Note │               └──────────────────────┘
    │ 5)?                   │
    └──────────┬───────────┘
               │ No                Yes
    ┌──────────┴───────────┐                 ┌──────────────────────┐
    │ Is the firm an ex-section 43 ├──────────→│ The firm is a securities and │
    │ firm?                 │                 │      futures firm.     │
    └──────────────────────┘                 └──────────────────────┘
```

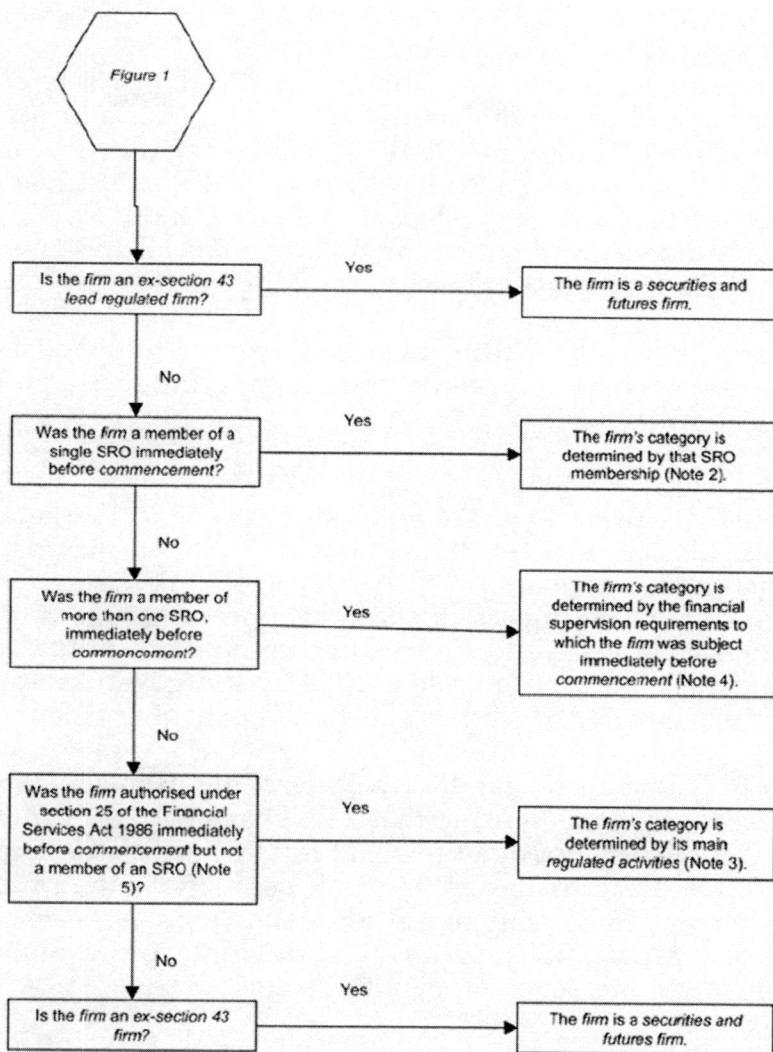

Figure 2.2 Prudential categories

(b) the extent to which the firm may pose risks to the stability of the UK financial system;

(c) the extent to which consumers may be adversely affected either directly or indirectly by the firm as a result of prudential failure, misconduct, market malfunction, market manipulation or the need to contribute to the financial reconstitution of compensation schemes; and

(d) the incidence and materiality of any financial crime which may be perpetrated through or by the firm.

The probability of a firm posing a risk to the regulatory objectives is, where applicable, assessed in terms of risk groups arising from the firm's:

(a) strategy;

(b) business risk (i.e., those risks, such as credit, market and operational risk) which are inherent in the business;

(c) financial soundness;

(d) customers and the products and services offered;

(e) internal systems and controls and compliance culture; and

(f) organisation and the role played by the governing body, management and staff in effectively managing risk.

The FSA will take an overall view in reaching its assessment of the nature of the relationship that it will have with the firm and will take into account other relevant factors such as the level of confidence the FSA has in the risk assessment information available to it, the quality of the home state regulator (for firms with their head office overseas) and any anticipated material change in the impact or probability factors.

The risk assessment process will be applied to all firms although the details may vary from firm to firm. The FSA will communicate its risk assessment to firms and will also outline a programme intended to address any significant concerns. The FSA emphasises that the assessment is provided for specific regulatory purposes and as such encourages firms to keep its regulatory grading confidential.

2.6 The threshold conditions

Under s.41(2) of the FSMA 2000, the FSA is required, in giving Part IV Permission or in imposing any requirement, to ensure that the applicant satisfies and will continue to satisfy the threshold conditions in relation to all the regulated activities for which it has permission. The threshold conditions are set out in Sch.6 to the FSMA 2000 and represent the minimum conditions that a firm is required to satisfy in order to become authorised. The statutory provisions are supplemented by a guidance section of the Handbook entitled Threshold Conditions ("COND"). In considering whether an applicant meets the threshold conditions, the FSA is empowered to take such steps as are necessary for the preservation of the regulatory objective of protecting consumers. Once authorised, the obligation to meet these conditions is an ongoing one and if the FSA is concerned that a firm is not meeting one of these conditions, it may vary or even withdraw a firm's permission to carry out its regulated activities.

There are five threshold conditions specified in Sch.6 to the FSMA 2000, relating to the applicant's:

(a) legal status;
(b) location of office;
(c) appointment of claims representatives;
(d) close links;
(e) adequacy of resources; and
(f) suitability.

Each of the last three threshold conditions (close links, resources and suitability) will be viewed in the context of the regulated activities which the applicant wishes to carry on and in the light of the FSA's statutory objectives. The threshold conditions are applied in relation to each of the activities in respect of which Part IV Permission is sought, and it is not necessarily the case that the applicant will satisfy all of the threshold conditions in relation to each. Where the FSA is not satisfied that an applicant will satisfy a threshold condition, the application will be denied in respect of that regulated activity.

In making its determination, the FSA will consider whether the applicant can demonstrate that it is ready, willing and organised so as to enable it to comply with the specific regulatory obligations that will apply to the applicant if Part IV Permission is granted.

2.6.1 Legal status

If an applicant is seeking permission to effect or carry out contracts of insurance it must be a body corporate (other than a limited liability partnership), a registered friendly society or a member of Lloyd's. This reflects the requirements of art.8(1) of the first life and non-life directives.

2.6.2 Location of offices

Where the applicant is a body corporate constituted under the law of any part of the UK, its head office and registered office must be in the UK. If an applicant is not a body corporate but has its head office in the UK, it must also carry on business in the UK. However, where a body corporate constituted in the UK carries on insurance mediation activities, the registered office (or where there is no registered office, the head office) must be in the UK. Individuals who carry on insurance mediation activities are treated as having their head office in the UK if they are residents. The expression "head office" is not defined in the FSMA 2000 or the insurance directives. The FSA has indicated that it regards the head office as the location at which the central management and control of the firm is undertaken. Whilst in some cases this will not be clear, the FSA guidance indicates that it will look at the location of the directors and senior management and the principal administrative functions in reaching its determination.

2.6.3   *Appointment of claims representatives*

Any person carrying on motor vehicle liability insurance must have a claims representative in each EEA state other than the UK. A claims representative has responsibility for handling and settling claims arising from certain types of motor accidents.

2.6.4   *Close links*

Close links must not prevent the FSA's supervision of the applicant. Close links are defined in para.3(2) of Sch.6 to the FSMA 2000. Essentially the definition extends to links between the applicant and its parent undertaking, subsidiary undertaking and fellow subsidiary undertakings of the parent undertaking. It also extends to 20 per cent controllers.

In assessing whether this threshold condition is satisfied, the FSA will be primarily concerned to ensure that the information flow between the applicant and members of its group and those persons with whom the applicant has close links will be such as to enable the FSA to be satisfied that the applicant will be fulfilling its regulatory requirements and that the impact on the FSA's regulatory objectives is capable of being accurately assessed. The FSA will look at the structure and geographical spread of the group and will be especially concerned where the group has subsidiaries or branches located in jurisdictions which restrict the free flow of information. The FSA will also investigate how confident it can be that it can assess the overall financial position of the group at any particular time and will take into account factors such as whether the group prepares audited consolidated accounts, whether different members of the group have different financial periods or whether they share common auditors. The FSA must be satisfied that where the applicant has close links with a party which is not subject to the jurisdiction of a country in the EEA, the local regulatory regime, and its application, will not prevent the effective supervision of the applicant by the FSA.

Whilst the FSA will take into account these matters only in so far as they are significant in the context of the applicant viewed in the light of the FSA's regulatory objectives, the FSA will look at these issues as a package, so that although certain provisions may not be significant taken individually, when combined and taken together they may nevertheless prove to be significant.

2.6.5 Adequacy of resources

The resources of the applicant must, in the opinion of the FSA, be adequate with regard to the regulated activities it seeks to carry on. This requirement is not limited to financial resources and the FSA will look at all of the resources available to the applicant. The FSA will look at the adequacy of the firm's resources in terms of quantity, quality and availability and will also be concerned to understand the means by which the firm is to manage its resources. The section of the Handbook entitled Senior Management Arrangements, Systems and Controls ("SYSC") supplements this threshold condition and is described in more detail below.

The FSA will consider whether the firm is ready, willing and organised to comply with these requirements in assessing whether this threshold condition is satisfied. In reaching its opinion, the FSA may take into account the applicant's membership of a group and any effect which that membership may have on the applicant's resources. This reflects the provisions of s.49 of the FSMA 2000, which provides:

> "In considering –
>
> (a) an application for a Part IV Permission ... the [FSA] may have regard to any person appearing to be or likely to be in a relationship with the applicant ... which is relevant."

This section also gives the FSA very wide powers to investigate the firm's controllers, directors and persons who have close links with the firm. It could also extend to other persons who are in a position to exert influence over the firm.

In assessing the adequacy of resources, the FSA will act in accordance with the regulatory principle of proportionality but will look at the resources taken as a whole. Matters may not be of significance taken individually, but may nevertheless be significant when combined with one or more matters in relation to the applicant.

2.6.6 *Financial adequacy*

The detailed financial requirements for insurers are set out in the relevant prudential sourcebooks for insurers (GENPRU, INSPRU and IPRU(INS) and *see*Chapter 4). An applicant will be required to demonstrate that it has adequate financial resources to meet the financial resources requirement for its prudential category of being an insurance company. The Single Market and the Capital Adequacy Directives set out minimum financial requirements for insurance businesses which are reflected in the prudential sourcebooks. When an applicant wishes to become an insurer the FSA will give it individual guidance (e.g. on its margin of solvency) during the preliminary application phase.

The FSA must also have regard to the provisions made by the applicant, or where relevant the group, in respect of liabilities including future or contingent liabilities. The FSA will also take into account the applicant's procedures, and where relevant the applicant's group procedures for managing risk.

The FSA will be concerned to ensure the business plans are well drawn up and robustly tested against a number of scenarios. The level of detail contained in the business plan will depend on the complexity of the business concerned.

Other relevant matters may include:

(a) the firm's ability to comply with the FSA's prudential rules;

(b) any indications that the firm may not be able to meet its debts as they fall due;

(c) any implications that may be drawn from the firm's history;

(d) the steps taken to identify and measure risks that may be of regulatory concern, including the systems and controls in place and the human resources available to manage and control them; and

(e) the steps taken to investigate the sector in which the firm is to carry on business and that its resources are sufficient in terms of capital adequacy and consumer protection.

2.6.7 Suitability

The applicant must satisfy the FSA that it is a fit and proper person to perform the regulated activities for which application is made. In assessing whether the applicant is "fit and proper", the FSA will have regard to:

(a) the applicant's connection with any person;

(b) the nature of any activity which the applicant carries on or seeks to carry on; and

(c) the need to ensure that the applicant's affairs are conducted soundly and prudently.

Whilst the emphasis of this threshold condition is on the suitability of the firm itself, the suitability of the persons performing certain functions (known as "controlled functions", *see* below) may also be relevant because where there are concerns raised about the suitability of an individual or management collectively, the FSA may determine that the candidate is not suitable for authorisation.

In assessing the suitability of a firm, the FSA is not confined geographically and the provisions of s.49 of the FSMA 2000 confer on the FSA broad powers to investigate and take into account any person who appears or is likely to be relevant.

Matters that the FSA is likely to take into account in assessing the suitability of a candidate for authorisation include:

(a) the integrity and standards with which the firm will conduct its business;
(b) the competence and prudence of management; and
(c) the extent to which the firm is able to demonstrate that it will conduct its affairs with due skill, care and diligence.

In determining whether the firm satisfies this threshold condition in so far as it relates to the firm's integrity and standards, the Handbook contains guidance as to the matters that the FSA will take into account. These matters include:

(a) the extent to which the firm has been open and cooperative in its dealings with the FSA and has demonstrated that it is ready, willing and organised to comply with the applicable standards and requirements of the regulatory system and other legal and professional obligations;
(b) whether the firm or any person connected with it has been convicted of any unspent criminal offence, including offences relating to consumer credit, consumer protection or significant tax offences;
(c) whether the firm has been the subject of any regulatory investigation or enforcement proceedings by the FSA or any other relevant regulatory body;
(d) whether the firm or any connected person has contravened the FSMA 2000 or any preceding legislation or the regulatory system or any other applicable rules and regulations of a regulatory nature;
(e) whether the firm or any person connected with it has been refused registration, or any similar authorisation or permission to carry out any trade or business, or whether any such authorisation or permission has been withdrawn or terminated, or whether the firm or any person connected with it has been expelled from any relevant regulatory or governmental body;
(f) the systems and controls that the firm has in place in order to ensure regulatory compliance;
(g) the firm's procedures for ensuring that its employees, approved persons and subcontractors are aware of and comply with their regulatory obligations;

(h) whether the firm or any person connected with the firm has ever been dismissed from employment or a position of trust or fiduciary or similar relationship, or has ever been asked to resign from such an appointment; and

(i) whether the firm or any person connected with it has ever been disqualified from being a director.

In determining whether the firm satisfies the suitability threshold condition with respect to the competence and prudence of management, and the exercise of due skill, care and diligence of management, the Handbook gives guidance as to the matters that the FSA will take into account as follows:

(a) whether there is a sufficient range of skills and experience on the firm's governing body to understand, operate and manage the firm's regulated activities;

(b) whether the firm has sufficient non-executive directors and whether those non-executives are given appropriate responsibilities;

(c) whether the systems and controls in place with regard to the governing body enable it to assess and control the firm's regulated activities;

(d) the extent to which the persons performing controlled functions act with due skill and diligence in performing those functions;

(e) the extent to which the firm has in place systems and controls to enable it to comply with SYSC;

(f) whether the firm has approached financial control and other risks in a prudent manner and has taken reasonable steps to ensure that robust information and reporting systems have been developed, tested and installed;

(g) whether the firm or any person connected with it has been concerned in the management of a company or other organisation that has become insolvent;

(h) whether the firm has developed human resources policies and procedures that are designed to ensure that the firm only employs individuals who are honest and committed to high standards of integrity in the conduct of their activities;

(i)   the extent to which the firm has conducted enquiries that are sufficient to give it reasonable assurance that it will not be posing unacceptable risks to consumers or the financial system;

(j)   the firm's procedures for dealing with money laundering;

(k)   the suitability of the firm's actuaries and auditors; and

(l)   in the case of a firm carrying out insurance mediation activities, a reasonable proportion of the firm's management in addition to those people directly involved in insurance mediation activities should be of good repute and demonstrate relevant knowledge and ability to perform their duties adequately.

2.6.8   Principles for businesses

The fit and proper test is supplemented by the principles for businesses which form part of the Handbook (*see* Chapter 1). The principles for businesses apply to every firm, but are modified in respect of incoming EEA firms and treaty firms. Compliance with the principles is therefore important in determining whether an applicant is ready, willing and organised to carry on regulated activities, and will be a crucial factor in assessing whether the firm satisfies the suitability condition.

2.6.9   Systems and controls

The threshold condition relating to adequacy of resources is supplemented by a section of the Handbook dealing with Senior Management Arrangements, Systems and Controls ("SYSC") (*see* Chapter 3), which amplifies the areas that the FSA will be examining in determining whether this threshold condition is satisfied. SYSC applies to every firm that carries on regulated activities in the UK but is modified in relation to incoming EEA firms and incoming Treaty firms. SYSC does not apply where services are provided cross-border only. The principal purpose of SYSC is to encourage management of regulated firms to take practical responsibility for their firm's arrangements for compliance with the regulatory system, and to amplify Principle 3 of the Principles for Businesses whereby a firm must take "reasonable care to organise and control its affairs responsibly and effectively with adequate risk management systems and to encourage firms to vest responsibility for effective and responsible organisation in specific managers and directors."

The principal requirement of SYSC is set out in art.2.1.1, which provides:

> "A firm must take reasonable care to maintain a clear and appropriate apportionment of significant responsibilities among its directors and senior managers in such a way
>
> that:
>
> (a) it is clear who has which of those responsibilities; and
> (b) the business and affairs of the firm can be adequately monitored and controlled by the directors, relevant senior managers and governing body of the firm."

The firm is required to nominate one or more individuals to assume overall responsibility for ensuring compliance with the rule set out above in what is generally referred to as the "apportionment and oversight function". SYSC specifies the individuals who may be appointed to perform this function, which will usually be undertaken by the chief executive.

Record keeping is an important part of SYSC. The firm is required to record and update regularly the arrangements that it has made for complying with the requirements of the regulatory system. The name of the person or persons appointed to perform the compliance and oversight functions must be recorded and, where responsibilities are shared, the division of responsibility should be clearly identified. Firms are required to take reasonable care to make and retain adequate records of matters and dealings. The length of time that records should be maintained for will depend upon the type of information concerned. Records relating to management decisions, for example, should be maintained for six years. Guidance on how long records should be kept can be found in the Handbook.

Article 3.1.1 of SYSC provides that: "A firm must take reasonable care to establish and maintain such systems and controls as are appropriate to its business." The nature and extent of the systems and controls that a firm is required to have in place will depend on the nature and complexity of the firm's business and its geographical spread. The volume of transactions undertaken and the degree of risk associated with its areas of operation will be relevant considerations. The FSA will expect a firm to review its systems and controls regularly and to update them as appropriate.

SYSC gives guidance as to the main areas that the FSA expects firms to consider in establishing appropriate systems and controls, and investigation of these issues will form part of the authorisation process in determining whether the threshold condition relating to the adequacy of resources has been satisfied.

With regard to the organisation of its affairs, SYSC requires a firm to delegate and segregate the duties of individuals and departments responsibly. A firm's reporting lines should be clear and appropriate having regard to the nature, scale and complexity of its business. These reporting lines together with clear management responsibilities should be communicated throughout the firm and should be properly documented.

An insurance firm is likely to delegate many functions and tasks to more junior members of staff for the purpose of carrying on its business. When functions and tasks are delegated, appropriate safeguards should be put in place. For example, the firm should assess whether the person to whom the task has been delegated is suitably qualified to perform it, taking into account the degree of skill or responsibility concerned. Where appropriate, limits should be placed on the extent to which authority has been delegated and the scope of delegation should be made clear.

Where tasks are delegated outside the firm to independent contractors, such as actuaries or accountants, similar issues will arise. In addition, it will be necessary for the firm to obtain sufficient information from its external contractor to enable it to assess the impact of outsourcing on its systems and controls.

Compliance plays an important part in the regulatory system and in appropriate circumstances the FSA may require the firm to have a separate compliance function. It is a requirement of SYSC that:

> "a firm must take reasonable care to establish and maintain effective systems and controls for compliance with applicable requirements and standards under the regulatory system for countering the risk that the firm might be used to further financial crime."

This is consistent with the regulatory objectives set out in s.2 of the FSMA 2000.

With regard to risk assessment, it may be necessary in large or complex firms to have a person or persons who have responsibility for assessing a firm's risk and advising management on risk. The organisation and responsibilities of the risk assessment function should be properly documented and the function should be adequately resourced by an appropriate number of suitably trained and competent staff who are sufficiently independent to perform their duties effectively. There should be regular reporting to line management and onwards to the board.

The FSA requires firms to determine and document policies for dealing with risk including credit, market group, operational, liquidity and insurance technical risks, together with matching and aggregating of risks between insurance and investment functions. Firms are also required to demonstrate how combinations of these risks have been aggregated and mitigated; in particular, firms are required to have written risk management plans that document the policies, methods and assumptions used. This would include, for example, a statement of how much risk the firm is prepared to accept and to what extent this is mitigated by reinsurance, hedging or other means.

SYSC 17 provides specific guidance on insurance risk systems and controls. Insurance risk concerns the frequency, fluctuations and severity of insured events, relative to the expectations of the firm at the time of underwriting. Where the firm is a general insurer such risk may include the variation in the amount or frequency of claims or the amount of claims arising out of a single occurrence. Long-term business insurance risks might include taking into consideration variations in mortality and persistency rates of policyholders. The appropriate systems and controls that a firm should have in place to manage insurance risks will depend upon the scale, nature and complexity of the firm's business. High-level requirements for prudential systems and controls for managing insurance risk include:

(a) requiring a firm to take reasonable steps to establish and maintain a business plan and suitable risk management systems;
(b) requiring a firm to document its policy for insurance risk; and
(c) requiring firms to establish and maintain adequate internal controls to assess and monitor the effectiveness of their business plan and prudential risk management systems.

SYSC outlines matters that a firm should include in its insurance risk policy. Although not exhaustive, such matters include the firm's underwriting criteria, its approach to limiting significant aggregations of insurance risk, the firm's policy for identifying and managing risk when it has delegated underwriting authority to another party, and the firm's use of reinsurance. The full list of matters that an insurance firm should consider can be found in SYSC 17.1.9G. Guidance is also given to insurers on risk identification, risk measurement, risk monitoring, risk control and reinsurance as a means of risk transfer.

With regard to management information, the FSA will expect the firm to ensure that the information flow to the governing body is sufficient to enable it to identify, measure, manage and control risk. It will be important that the systems that are put in place enable the board to consider all relevant information in a timely manner and that the information provided to the board is reliable. Again, the FSA would expect to see a greater level of documentation of these procedures and, where tasks have been delegated, the competence of the delegate should be appropriate for the task allocated.

Larger or complex firms may need an audit committee or an internal audit function to examine the process implemented by management for ensuring that there are appropriate and effective systems and controls. The audit committee will also be responsible for overseeing any internal audit function and will provide the interface between the management and the external auditors. Where established, the committees should have formal terms of reference and should include non-executive directors.

It will be important that the internal audit function is independent of the day-to-day activities of the firm and that members of internal audit have access to the firm's records. Again the internal audit committee should have formal terms of reference and the individuals charged with the internal audit function should be suitably trained and be able to operate with independence. To ensure that this is the case it may be appropriate for the internal audit function to have a direct reporting line to one of the non-executive directors in addition to reporting lines to executive management and the audit committee function.

Business strategy, remuneration and business continuity will be areas of key importance to a firm's compliance with SYSC and hence the threshold condition relating to the adequacy of the firm's resources. Firms should have in place arrangements to ensure that they can continue to function in the event of interruption. Disaster recovery plans will obviously be key to the fulfilment of this, but there will be other less obvious steps that the firm can incorporate in its culture that will assist in ensuring business continuity. An example of this would be ensuring that knowledge is appropriately spread and documented throughout the organisation, to ensure that systems and controls impacting on solvency are not harmed by the loss of a single individual.

The need for the employees and agents of insurance firms to be competent to perform the tasks allocated to them has been mentioned several times already and the systems and controls put in place by a firm should enable the firm to satisfy itself that such is the case. The detailed requirements with respect to training and competence are set out in the Training and Competence section of the Handbook.

Once proper systems have been established, these need to be reviewed regularly and the firm will need to ensure that it maintains adequate records of its matters and dealings.

2.6.10   Approved persons

The obligation to satisfy the threshold conditions is primarily an obligation of the firm. As mentioned above, in considering the suitability of the firm for Part IV Permission, the FSA will take into account the question of whether the persons performing certain specified functions in relation to the firm are fit and proper to perform those functions. The approved persons regime is derived from s.59 of the FSMA 2000 which provides that firms must take reasonable care to ensure that certain individuals within authorised firms are approved by the FSA as being fit and proper to perform certain functions that they carry out. These people are known as approved persons and the functions they carry out are referred to as controlled functions. It is a requirement of SYSC that one or more individuals must be appointed to the "apportionment and oversight function" and must be individually approved by the FSA as being fit and proper for this role. Other controlled functions are divided into five categories:

(a) governing functions including both executive and non-executive directors, as well as the chief executive;
(b) required functions including the apportionment and oversight function, compliance oversight function and actuarial functions (where appropriate);
(c) the systems and control function;
(d) the significant management function; and
(e) customer function.

All the above functions with the exception of the customer function are known as 'significant influence functions' (commonly termed SIFs) as persons performing these functions exercise a significant influence over the conduct of the firm's regulatory affairs. The full list of the controlled functions, which appears in SUP 10.4.5, is set out in Chapter 3, together with a commentary on the FSA's statements of principle and Code of Practice for Approved Persons.

Each governing function (except non-executive director) includes systems and controls functions and significant management functions. A person with approval for a governing function will not need to seek additional approval for the systems and controls or significant management function but will need approval for a required or customer function.

The people approved to carry out these functions must comply with seven Statements of Principle for Approved Persons set out in the Code of Practice for Approved Persons ("APER") which is found in the Handbook. The application procedure for candidates is set out in SUP 10.

Applicants must complete Form A and submit it to the FSA using the Online Notifications and Applications System ("ONA") on the FSA website. Following criticism of the rigor of its supervisory approach to firm management after the collapse of Northern Rock, the FSA has implemented a number of changes to the approved person regime. The detail of the changes are beyond the scope of this chapter but include: changes to Form A requiring supplementary information from the candidate about their competence and capability to perform the relevant function and details as to how the appointment complements the firm's business strategy; the introduction of FSA SIF candidate interviews at larger firms; and a shift in enforcement emphasis which aims to hold individuals accountable for poor conduct. In addition, new controlled functions were expected to be introduced on 1 May 2011, but at the time of writing have not yet come into force (*see* Chapter 3).

In assessing whether or not a person (referred to as a candidate) is fit and proper to perform a controlled function, the FSA will have regard to the section of the Handbook entitled the Fit and Proper Test for Approved Persons ("FIT"). FIT applies to every approved person and candidate and reflects the requirements of s.61 of the FSMA 2000 which provides that the FSA may only grant an application for approval if it is satisfied that the candidate is a fit and proper person to perform the relevant function. In dealing with that question, s.61(2) provides that the FSA may have regard to whether the candidate or any person who may perform a function on his behalf has:

(a)   obtained a qualification;
(b)   undergone or is undergoing any training; or
(c)   possesses a level of competence,

required by the rules relevant to the application. This list is not exhaustive and the FSA may have regard to other additional factors.

The guidance issued by the FSA and reflected in FIT indicates that the FSA will take into account several additional factors in assessing the suitability of a candidate for a controlled function. The most important are the candidate's:

(a)   honesty integrity and reputation;
(b)   competence and capability; and

(c) financial soundness.

The FSA will look at the context in which the controlled functions are to be performed and will normally view any matter that comes to its attention in the light of its relevance and importance to the activities of the firm and the performance of the controlled function. As part of the application process the FSA would expect to discuss with the firm any matters giving rise to concern.

FIT gives further examples of the matters the FSA will take into account in assessing the honesty, integrity and reputation of a candidate as follows:

(a) whether the person has been convicted of any criminal offence; this may include where relevant any spent convictions under the Rehabilitation of Offenders Act 1974. Particular consideration will be given to offences involving dishonesty, fraud, financial crime or other offences under legislation relating to banking and financial services, companies, insurance and consumer protection;

(b) whether the person has been subject to adverse findings or any settlements in civil proceedings particularly in connection with investment or other financial business misconduct, fraud or the formation or management of a body corporate;

(c) whether the person has been the subject of or interviewed in the course of any existing or previous investigation or disciplinary proceedings by the FSA or by any other regulatory authorities (including any previous regulator), clearing houses and exchanges, professional bodies or governmental bodies or agencies;

(d) whether the person is or has been the subject of any proceedings of a disciplinary or criminal nature or has been notified of any potential proceedings or of any investigation that might lead to those proceedings;

(e) whether the person has contravened any of the requirements and standards of the regulatory system or the equivalent standards and requirements of other regulatory authorities (including any previous regulator), clearing houses and exchanges, professional bodies or government bodies or agencies;

(f) whether the person has been the subject of any justified complaint relating to regulated activities;

(g) whether the person has been involved with a company, partnership or other organisation that has been refused registration, authorisation, membership or a licence to carry out a trade, business or profession or has had that registration, authorisation, membership or licence revoked, withdrawn or terminated or has been expelled by a regulatory or governmental body;

(h) whether as a result of the removal of the relevant licence, registration or other authority the person has been refused the right to carry on a trade, business or profession requiring a licence, registration or other authority;

(i) whether the person has been a director, partner or concerned in the management of a business that has gone into insolvency, liquidation or administration while a person has been connected with that organisation or within one year of that connection;

(j) whether the person or any business with which the person has been involved has been investigated, disciplined, censured, suspended or criticised by a regulatory or professional body, a court or tribunal whether publicly or privately;

(k) whether the person has been dismissed or asked to resign and has resigned from employment or a position of trust, fiduciary appointment or similar;

(l) whether the person has ever been disqualified from acting as a director or disqualified from acting in any managerial capacity;

(m) whether in the past the person has been candid and truthful in all his dealings with any regulatory body and whether the person demonstrates a readiness and willingness to comply with the requirements and standards of the regulatory system and with other legal regulatory and professional requirements and standards.

It is important to bear in mind that the FSA will not necessarily reject a person's application where one of the above matters is disclosed. The FSA will treat each candidate's application on a case-by-case basis. The circumstances of, for example, the offence or insolvency, would be taken into consideration.

In assessing the competence and capability of a candidate, the FSA will consider a variety of factors including the extent to which the candidate has complied with the FSA's Training and Competence Sourcebook and the extent to which the candidate is able to demonstrate by experience and training that he is competent to perform the controlled function to which he is to be appointed.

The financial soundness of a candidate will be determined by reference to whether the candidate is the subject of any unsatisfied judgment or award, or has been the subject of bankruptcy proceedings in each case on a global basis. The FSA will not normally require a statement of assets.

2.6.11   Controllers

As has been mentioned above in considering an application for Part IV Permission, the FSA must be satisfied that close links will not prevent the effective supervision of the applicant and that certain persons appointed to perform specified functions are fit and proper to perform those functions. The suitability of an applicant to receive authorisation to carry out regulated activities will also be viewed in the light of its controllers. The threshold conditions requiring the FSA to take account of an insurer's controllers are supplemented by Chapter 11 of SUP and by Part XII of the FSMA 2000 which requires the FSA's approval before a person can become a controller of an insurer (*see* Chapter 3). Where a controller is not an authorised person, an applicant will be required to provide the information required in the relevant controllers form. The controllers forms can be found on the FSA website.

2.7   The application procedure

Firms seeking permission will find the information needed, including how to build an application, from the FSA's online resources available on the "How do I get authorised" pages. Additional guidance on authorisation is contained in PERG.

As described above, any applicant must satisfy the FSA that they will meet the minimum standards required in the threshold conditions and that all persons involved in running the firm meet the fit and proper criteria. Before commencing any application firms should conduct a thorough review of how they meet these fundamental criteria.

The FSA will expect applicants to have done preparatory work prior to filling in their application pack. In its guidance on the process entitled "Applying for authorisation", the FSA sets out the main steps that it will expect firms to have completed prior to submitting the application form:

(a) firms should determine what type of business they will be carrying on. PERG 2 Annex 2 provides a complete list of the activities for which you can apply;

(b) the FSA recommends that firms familiarise themselves with the Principles for Businesses which are found in the Handbook;

(c) a business plan should be prepared by all firms which sets out the planned activities (and related risks), budget and resources (including human, systems and capital);

(d) firms should decide which rules in the Handbook apply to the activities that they will carry on and should ensure that they are ready and organised to comply with those rules;

(e) firms should ensure that they determine the applicable minimum regulatory financial requirements for their business. Reference should be made to GENPRU and INSPRU;

(f) firms should determine the systems and controls that are necessary to support their activities and have plans to implement the required systems and controls;

(g) firms should determine what qualifications will be required by staff to ensure that the FSA's qualification and training requirements are met in accordance with the FSA's Training and Competence Manual;

(h) firms will need to determine who should fall under the approved persons regime and the appropriate approval for these persons should be sought. The requirements for approved persons are set out in SUP.

Section 51(3) of the FSMA 2000 sets out the authority for the FSA authorisation process. All applicants for Part IV Permission will follow roughly the same authorisation process. However, depending on what type of business is to be carried on, the application pack will be tailored to meet the particular demands of that business. For example, the amount of information required by a firm seeking to carry on business as an insurer will be significantly greater than the amount of information required for a high-street insurance intermediary.

Before the application is submitted, it is usually sensible for firms to approach the FSA about the proposed application and, where necessary, meet FSA officials to discuss the application.

An applicant for authorisation will be required to submit an application pack, comprising a number of completed forms and supporting documentation. A case officer will be allocated to the applicant who will be tasked with reviewing the application and may contact the candidate for additional information where required. An application fee will be payable, the size of which will depend on the complexity of the application. The application will not be deemed to be complete until the fee is paid.

In some instances a firm seeking authorisation will not be able to have everything required for approval in place at the time that their application form is submitted. For example it may be that capital will only be injected on receipt of FSA authorisation. In such circumstances the FSA may advise that it is "minded to grant" its approval so long as certain conditions will be met.

The application pack which must be submitted comprises several different elements depending upon the type of firm seeking authorisation and the permission being sought. An application form, effectively a covering document to the application, must be signed by two authorised signatories of the firm and confirm the accuracy of information in the application. In addition to a core details form there are supplementary forms to be completed depending on the nature of the application. There are specific forms required for firms seeking authorisation as insurers. Forms covering applications to become approved persons and forms detailing the applicants controllers will be included in the package of documents required for the application.

2.7.1 Application pack information

The core details form requires the applicant to provide certain information about the application, including:

(a) the name and contact details of the applicant;
(b) the name and details of any professional advisers;
(c) the legal status of the applicant;
(d) details of auditors;
(e) the applicant's history;
(f) details of any close links.
(g) details of firm personnel; and
(h) information on systems and controls including IT, business transaction recording, accounting, disaster recover and business continuity systems.

In addition to the relevant forms which applicants must complete, certain supporting documents must be included with the application. These include:

(a) a staff organisational chart which outlines the firm's management structure and reporting lines;
(b) the regulatory business plan;
(c) compliance procedures;
(d) details of professional advisers;
(e) an opening balance sheet;

(f) a forecast closing balance sheet after 12-months' trading or the first year's trading; and

(g) Companies House Form 88(2) showing share allotment.

The applicant will be requested to provide a regulatory business plan which describes the regulated activities that the applicant proposes to carry on, the management and organisational structure of the applicant, and details of any proposed outsourcing agreements. The level of detail required will depend on the risks to consumers arising from those activities. The plan must also specify whether the firm intends to passport its activities into another EEA state.

For an applicant seeking to carry on insurance business, the business plan should include a scheme of operations prepared in accordance with Appendix 2.12 of SUP. The plan should cover a minimum of three years from the date of authorisation (five years for long-tail business). The scheme of operations will describe the applicant's business strategy and include financial projections of the applicant's profit and loss account, a summary balance sheet and a solvency forecast, describing the assumptions underlying the forecasts and identifying any material transactions proposed to be entered into with any associate.

The regulatory business plan must describe the applicant's business strategy and include financial projections of the applicant's profit and loss account, a summary balance sheet and a solvency forecast, describing the assumptions underlying the forecasts and identifying any material transactions proposed to be entered into with any associate. The FSA is seeking to understand the source and level of capital requirements, as well as liabilities. The notes accompanying the supplementary form provide extensive detail of the type of information required about the firm's financial resources.

Applicants must describe the insurance activities in sufficient detail to enable the FSA to understand the business that the firm will undertake. This may require details of proposed insurance products, the nature and location of risk as well as details of risks written on a supplementary basis. The business plan should also describe how insurance products will be sold and present details of how reinsurance will be used to protect business underwritten. In addition to information about underwriting the business plan should also include details of the firm's non financial resources, including board composition, underwriters' qualifications, details of material outsourcing arrangements and information about firm systems.

The supplementary form for insurers also requires the applicant to ensure that the scope of permission it requests accurately reflects its business plan. The scope of permission requested on application must match its needs and cover every aspect of the regulated business that it intends to carry on.

In addition to the business plan a firm seeking authorisation as an insurer will be required to supply the FSA with details of personnel including the names of all those individuals who will perform a controlled function. "Form A" must be completed for each individual seeking approval to perform a controlled function.

Although the applicant is not required to produce compliance procedures with its application form it must be able to produce a copy of its procedures at any time while its application is being processed by the FSA (or in the future). Compliance procedures must address the firm's obligations contained in the FSA Handbook. Applicants will often wish to discuss applications with the FSA Authorisation Department during the application process; similarly, the FSA will often need to discuss and clarify information that has been submitted within the application pack. The exchange of information during the application process is viewed as important by the FSA, since the final decision about an application needs to be based on as complete a picture of the application as possible.

2.7.2   Reports from third parties

Section 51(6) of the FSMA 2000 empowers the FSA to require the applicant to verify information provided in such a way as the FSA directs. Thus, as part of the application process, the FSA may require the applicant to provide, at its own expense, a report by an auditor, reporting accountant, actuary or other qualified person approved by the FSA. The report may be on such aspects of the information provided, or to be provided, by the applicant as the FSA may specify.

Applicants seeking to carry on long-term insurance business are also required to provide a certificate from an actuary confirming the appropriateness of the projections for the long-term insurance business and, in particular, the adequacy of premium rates, technical provisions, margin of solvency and how quickly capital strains from effecting new business will be overcome.

If an applicant appoints a reporting accountant other than its own auditor or an actuary other than its own actuary to report on an application for Part IV Permission, the applicant is required to take reasonable steps to ensure that the reporting accountant or actuary satisfies the qualification and independence tests specified in SUP.

Occasionally, the FSA may identify a need for an independent report on specific areas of an application; for example where the applicant's business plan is innovative, complex or raises concerns as a result of matrix management. Such reports will usually be discussed and agreed with the applicant as part of the pre-application meeting.

2.7.3   Connected persons

As has been mentioned above, under s.49 of the FSMA 2000 (persons connected with an application), in considering an application for Part IV Permission, the FSA may have regard to any person appearing to it to be, or likely to be, in a relationship with the applicant which is relevant.

A person in, or likely to be in, a relationship with an applicant that is relevant is known as a connected person. The FSA will assess whether a particular relationship is relevant in the light of the particular circumstances of each application. Examples of persons who might be considered connected with an applicant include, but are not limited to:

(a) a controller of the applicant; or
(b) an applicant's directors, partners or members of its governing body; or
(c) a company in the same group as the applicant; or
(d) a person with whom the applicant intends to enter into a material outsourcing agreement; or
(e) any other person who may exert influence on the applicant, which might pose a risk to the applicant satisfying or continuing to satisfy the threshold conditions.

As a result, in addition to the specific information required to be submitted in respect of controllers, authorised persons and appointed representatives as part of the application process, the FSA may request information about any other person whom the FSA determines is in a relevant relationship with an applicant. The FSA may request information from the applicant or persons who are connected persons or are likely to become connected persons under any proposed transactions or relationships.

2.7.4 *Applicants seeking to passport into another EEA state*

If an applicant wants to exert an EEA right shortly after acquiring Part IV Permission, it should contact the Authorisation Department at the FSA to discuss its plans. The notice of intention to passport (*see* Chapter 5) will be reviewed alongside the application for authorisation. The business plans, financial projections and scheme of operations submitted with its application should in that case always reflect any passported activity that the firm plans to commence.

2.7.5   The authorisation fee

The FSA operates a scale of fees depending upon the complexity of the application. The current rates are £1,800 for a straightforward application, £5,000 for a moderately complex application, and £25,000 for complex applications. Applications to carry out either general or long term insurance business will be considered complex by the FSA. The current fee rates can be found in the Fees Manual ("FEES").

2.7.6   How long will an applicant have to wait?

Once the completed application has been received, the FSA has six months from the date of receipt to make its determination. This is a requirement of the FSMA 2000 specified in s.52(1). However, the length of the process may vary with the complexity of the application. If the FSA receives an incomplete application, it has to determine it within 12 months of the initial receipt of the application. If material remains outstanding at the expiry of 12 months from the date of receipt of an incomplete application, the FSA must decline the application.

2.7.7   Commencing regulated activities

If Part IV Permission is given, the FSA will expect a firm to commence its regulated activity in line with its current business plan and the FSA may exercise its own initiative powers to vary or cancel a Part IV Permission once granted if it is redundant for 12 months from the date the permission was given or for a period of at least 12 months (irrespective of the date of the grant of permission).

If the FSA considers that it may be appropriate to exercise its own initiative powers to vary or cancel a firm's Part IV Permission, FSA staff will discuss the proposed action with the firm and ascertain the firm's reasons for not commencing or carrying on the regulated activities concerned.

Finally, an applicant seeking to carry on insurance business should be aware that specific reporting requirements apply during its first three years of operation.

2.7.8 The FSA Register

The FSA is required to maintain a register containing details of all firms and the regulated activities for which they have Part IV Permission. The FSA register is open to public inspection and is available on the FSA website at www.fsa.gov.uk.

2.8 Applications to vary and cancel Part IV Permission and end authorisation

Sections 44 and 45 of the FSMA 2000 and Chapter 6 of SUP specify the circumstances in which a Part IV Permission can be varied or cancelled at the initiative of the firm concerned or by the FSA on its own initiative.

Variation will occur where the regulated activities carried on in the UK under a Part IV Permission are varied either by adding new regulated activities to the permission, or by removing certain categories from it. Cancellation will occur where a firm has ceased to carry on all of the regulated activities for which it has a Part IV Permission or expects to cease carrying on such activities. For insurers the cancellation of a Part IV Permission is not altogether straightforward because of the long-tail nature of some of the liabilities under insurance contracts that may have been written.

A firm which is seeking to vary or cancel its Part IV Permission, should, before applying to do so, discuss its plans with its supervision team at the FSA as the FSA has wide powers to apply different or additional prudential rules even where the varied or additional business proposed does not per se require a variation to its existing Part IV Permissions.

2.8.1 *Variation of permission*

There are a number of scenarios in which a firm may wish to vary its permission. Where a firm decides to develop a new line of business, undertake a new regulated activity or extend the scope of its business it will need to consider whether an application to vary its existing permission should be made to the FSA.

Under s.44 of the FSMA 2000, a firm may apply to the FSA to vary its Part IV Permission in order to:

(a) allow it to carry on further regulated activities; or
(b) reduce the number of regulated activities it is permitted to carry on; or
(c) vary the FSA's description of its regulated activities (including by the removal or variation of any limitation); or
(d) cancel any requirement imposed by the FSA; or
(e) vary any requirement imposed by the FSA.

An application for variation may include any one or more of the above. In dealing with any application to vary, the FSA can impose new limitations and requirements as well as vary existing ones. It will consider the application against the threshold conditions and the FSA's regulatory objectives in much the same way as it would consider a new application for authorisation, but with due regard to the principle of proportionality. A firm awaiting a grant of permission or a variation must wait until the permission is granted before undertaking any regulated activities including in the application.

A firm that wishes to apply for variation of its Part IV Permission must apply to do so online using the FSA's ONA system. There is an ongoing duty to update the information submitted in connection with an application to vary a Part IV Permission in accordance with Principle 11 referred to earlier in this chapter. It is advisable that firm's discuss any plans to vary their Part IV Permission with their contacts at the FSA before submitting an application.

To apply to vary a Part IV Permission firms should complete a Variation of Permission ("VoP") form. There are specific application forms tailored to particular businesses. For example, there are different forms for insurance intermediaries and insurance companies wishing to vary their Part IV Permission. For certain types of variation an application fee may be charged. The FSA may at any time during the approval process require the applicant to provide additional information or documents. Information that may be requested includes business plans, financial projections, future regulatory compliance proposals and details of any changes in the persons performing controlled functions or in the functions they perform. Where an insurer is applying to add categories of insurance business to its Part IV Permission, it will also need to provide details of its existing business by submitting a scheme of operations in the format specified in SUP. Care will also need to be taken to ensure that the application for variation encompasses all of the ancillary activities that may now need to be carried on. It will be necessary to make considerations similar to those specified in relation to a new authorisation.

Where the FSA considers that the variation constitutes a significant change in the firm's business or risk profile, it may require the firm to submit an application pack or certain sections of it.

Where a variation involves a change in the controlled functions of existing personnel or the appointment of new personnel to perform controlled functions, the firm should, at the same time as applying for variation, apply to the FSA for approval or transfer of its approved persons or notify the FSA of any approved person who has ceased to perform a controlled function.

In relation to a firm which is applying to vary its Part IV Permission by removing certain categories of specified investments in relation to insurance business, the application, if approved will mean that the applicant is no longer authorised to *effect* contracts of insurance in the relevant class, but will continue to be authorised to *carry out* contracts of insurance in the relevant class. This will enable the firm concerned to run-off those contracts written in the former class. When the business has been run-off completely, the firm should apply for removal of the permission to carry out the relevant regulated activity.

Under s.52(1) of the FSMA 2000, the FSA has six months to consider a completed application. Where the FSA receives an application that is incomplete, s.52(2) of the FSMA 2000 requires the FSA to determine that incomplete application within 12 months of the initial receipt of the application. Similar issues concerning the point at which an application for variation of a permission is complete arise in respect of an original authorisation referred to above.

2.8.2 Cancellation of permission

A firm carrying on insurance business which, ultimately, intends to cease insurance business completely, will first need to apply for a variation of its Part IV Permission while it is running-off its business. The firm should apply to remove the activity of effecting contracts of insurance from its Part IV Permission, thereby restricting its activities to carrying out insurance contracts to enable it to run-off its business. Where an application is made for cancellation prior to the firm ceasing to carry on its regulated activities, the FSA will expect to review formal plans for the wind-down of the firm's activities in the period from the date of application.

If a firm wishes to cancel its Part IV Permission it must submit a cancellation of permission application form through the ONA system. Until the application to cancel permission has been determined the firm must inform the FSA of any significant change to the information given in the application. Cancellation applies to a firm's entire Part IV Permission and not to the individual elements such as specified investments, changes to which constitute a variation.

The information concerning the circumstances of the application for cancellation and the confirmation that a firm is required to give to the FSA will differ according to the nature of the firm and the activities that it has a Part IV Permission to carry on. For insurers, the FSA will expect to see:

(a) an audited closing balance sheet which demonstrates that the firm has no liabilities to policyholders;
(b) a report from the auditors or reporting accountants; and
(c) in some cases, an opinion as to the likelihood of any remaining liabilities to policyholders.

If a firm is transferring business, the FSA may also require a professional opinion in respect of the transfer. The FSA may at any time during the cancellation process require the applicant to provide additional information or documents. The FSA will also expect to receive a copy of the board resolution of the applicant resolving to cancel the Part IV Permission.

At the same time as it applies for cancellation of its Part IV Permission the firm should notify the FSA of the persons ceasing to perform controlled functions.

Furthermore, the firm will be expected to be able to demonstrate that it has ceased or transferred all regulated activities under that permission. For example, the firm may be asked to provide evidence that a transfer of business is complete.

Where the FSA has granted an application for cancellation of a Part IV Permission and withdrawn a firm's status as an authorised person it will still retain certain investigative and enforcement powers in relation to the firm as a former authorised person.

2.8.3   Ending authorisation

Section 33 of the FSMA 2000 requires that where a firm's authorisation is cancelled, and as a result there are no regulated activities carried on by the firm in question, the FSA is required to give a direction withdrawing the firm's status as an authorised person. It must also update the firm's entry in the register to show that it has ceased to be authorised.

2.9 Applicants with a head office outside the EEA seeking to establish a branch in the UK

So far, this chapter has addressed the provisions applicable to a UK entity applying for authorisation under the FSMA 2000. It is permissible for an entity that is not incorporated in the UK or in the EEA to apply for authorisation under the FSMA 2000 by establishing a branch. This section looks at the provisions of the regulatory system applicable to such applicants.

The first and most important point to note is that in considering a branch application, the FSA will assess the applicant's application having regard to its situation as a whole (and not just to the circumstances of the proposed branch). This means that the regulatory requirements will apply to a firm in full and worldwide, and where necessary waivers, limitations and requirements will be used to ensure that appropriate prudential requirements apply to the branch. In making this assessment of the applicant for Part IV Permission as a whole, the FSA will take into account all relevant matters, including the extent to which the applicant is regulated in its home state. The FSA will seek to liaise with any home state regulator and will take into account information from it with respect to, for example, the adequacy of the applicant's resources and the applicant's suitability, having regard to the need to ensure that the applicant's affairs are conducted soundly and prudently. Information with respect to the conduct of the applicant's affairs would extend in particular to the adequacy of the internal control systems under SYSC.

The Financial Services and Markets Act 2000 (Variation of Threshold Conditions) Order 2001 (SI 2001/2507) makes certain amendments to the applicable threshold conditions for non-EEA applicants. Under the order such an applicant must:

(a) have a representative who is resident in the UK and who has authority to bind the applicant in its relations with third parties and to represent it in its relations with the authority and in the courts of the UK;

(b) be a body corporate entitled under the laws of the place where its head office is situated to effect and carry out contracts of insurance;

(c) have assets of such value as may be specified located in the UK;

(d) have made a deposit (of money or securities as may be specified) of such an amount and with such a person as may be specified and on such terms and subject to such other provisions as may be specified (unless the regulated activity in question relates solely to reinsurance). The deposit will be subject to provisions in INSPRU 1.5.

The order makes certain additional amendments in relation to Swiss general insurance companies, which are not generally covered in this chapter.

The FSA's regulatory requirements, including both prudential and conduct of business rules will apply to a branch applicant unless otherwise stated.

The approved persons regime will be applicable to an overseas branch to the extent that regulated activities are carried on by that branch in the UK. The following controlled functions will apply:

(a) both the director and non-executive director functions where the person performing either function has responsibility for regulated activities of the branch which are likely to enable them to exercise significant influence over the branch or whose decisions are regularly taken into account by the governing body of the UK branch;

(b) the chief executive function;

(c) the required functions;

(d) the systems and controls function;

(e) the significant management function; and

(f) customer function.

While all the above functions may apply to the branch, they will only be applicable where relevant. For example, the FSA will not require approval for all directors, only those whose role means that they will have a significant influence over the UK operations. There are three additional positions that for insurers will require notification to the FSA rather than approval. These are:

(a) the firm's worldwide chief executive where the person holding the position is situated outside the UK;
(b) the person, if not the worldwide chief executive, within the overseas firm with a purely strategic responsibility for UK operations;
(c) for a UK branch of an insurer, the authorised UK representative.

If the FSA considers that the applicant may be unable to satisfy the threshold conditions and that this cannot be addressed by the use of limitations and requirements, the FSA would have to conclude that a branch presence in the UK would be inappropriate. In such circumstances, the applicant may wish to consider forming a UK incorporated subsidiary as an alternative method of obtaining a presence in the UK.

2.10   Passporting of EEA and Treaty firms

Much of the foregoing provisions of this chapter relate to the first method of authorisation under the FSMA 2000, namely by way of a Part IV Permission. The following sections of this chapter relate to the second principal method of authorisation, which is by way of exercise of a passport right by an EEA firm. Specific provisions concerning the provision of services cross-border are dealt with in Chapter 5. Schedule 3 to the FSMA 2000 deals with EEA firms qualifying for authorisation and Sch.4 to the FSMA 2000 deals with Treaty firms.

2.10.1   EEA Firms

Schedule 3, Part 1 applies to EEA firms seeking to exercise rights under the single market directives. Included within the definition of the single market directives are the Insurance Mediation Directive, the first, second and third non-life directives, the Consolidated Life Directive and the Reinsurance Directive. An EEA firm is defined in Schedule 3. The first requirement is that the firm must not have its head office in the UK. The definition includes:

> "an undertaking pursuing the Activity of direct insurance .... which has received authorisation (within the meaning of the life assurance consolidation directive or the first non-life insurance directive) from its home state regulator."

The basic principle is set out in para.12 of Schedule 3. Once a firm which is seeking to establish a branch in the UK in exercise of an EEA right satisfies the establishment conditions it qualifies for authorisation.

The establishment conditions are set out in para.13(1) of Sch.3. It provides:

> "The establishment conditions are -
>
> (a) the Authority has received notice ('a consent notice') from the firm's home state regulator that it has given the firm consent to establish a branch in the UK;
> (b)
>
>   the consent notice -
>   (i)   is given in accordance with the relevant single market directive;
>   (ii) identifies the activities to which the consent relates; and
>   (iii) includes such other conditions as may be pre-scribed; and
> (c) the firm has been informed of the applicable provi-sions or two months have elapsed beginning with the date on which the Authority received the consent notice."

If the firm is an insurance intermediary the establishment conditions are that:

"(a) the firm has given its home state regulator notice of its intention to establish a branch in the UK;

(b) the Authority has received notice ('a regulator's notice') from the firm's home state regulator that the firm intends to establish a branch in the UK;

(c) the firm's home state regulator has informed the firm that the regulator's notice has been sent to the Authority; and

(d) one month has elapsed beginning with the date on which the firm's home state regulator informed the firm that the regulator's notice has been sent to the Authority."

Where it has received a consent notice, the FSA is required to prepare for the firm's supervision, notify the firm of any applicable provisions and (because the firm will be an insurance firm) notify the home state regulator of any applicable provisions. Such a notification must be given within two months of the receipt of the consent notice. Applicable provisions mean in this context the host state rules with which the firm is required to comply when carrying on a permitted activity identified in the consent notice. The host state rules will mean the rules made in accordance with the applicable single market directive and which are the responsibility of the UK both as to implementation and supervision of compliance in accordance with that directive (for example, conduct of business rules – *see* Chapters 7 and 10).

Where an EEA firm has satisfied the requirements with regard to qualification, it is permitted to carry out the regulated activities referred to in the consent notice on terms equivalent to those contained in the consent notice. Where an EEA firm carries out a regulated activity for which it has not qualified for authorisation, ss.26, 27 and 29 of the FSMA 2000, relating to the enforceability of contracts entered into in breach of the general prohibition (*see* above), do not apply to agreements entered into by the firm.

2.10.2 Treaty firms

A Treaty firm is defined in Sch.4 to the FSMA 2000. It means:

"a person -

(a) Whose head office is situated in an EEA state (its 'home state') other than the UK; and

(b) Which is recognised under the law of that state as its national."

Home state regulator is defined in relation to a Treaty firm as "the competent authority of the firm's home state for the purpose of its home state authorisation".

Once a Treaty firm has received authorisation under the law of its home state to carry on the regulated activity in question, it qualifies for authorisation provided:

(a) the laws of the firm's home state provide equivalent protection or satisfy certain conditions laid down by a Community instrument for the coordination or approximation of laws, regulations or administrative provisions of Member States relating to the carrying on of that activity; and

(b) the firm has no EEA right to carry on the activity concerned.

The home state regulator must inform the FSA that the firm has home state authorisation in order to qualify.

For the purposes of this requirement, provisions afford equivalent protection if, in relation to the firm's carrying on of the permitted activity they afford consumers protection which is at least equivalent to that afforded by or under the FSMA 2000 in relation to that activity. A certificate issued by the Treasury that the provisions of a law of a particular EEA state afford equivalent protection in relation to the activities specified in the certificate is conclusive evidence of that fact.

On qualifying in this manner, a firm has permission to carry on each permitted activity through its UK branch or by providing cross-border services on terms equivalent to those to which the firm's home state is subject.

The application of Sch.4 is extremely rare as it is designed to cover cases where a firm has a right under the EC treaty that has not been given effect by a specific directive. It was formerly applicable in certain cases to reinsurance companies based elsewhere in the EEA; following the implementation of the Reinsurance Directive (*see* Chapter 8) it is questionable whether it has any remaining application to the industry at all.

Chapter 3

Ownership and management of insurance companies

Katherine Coates and Hilary Evenett,

Partners: Financial Institutions Group,

Clifford Chance LLP

3.1   Ownership of insurance companies

3.1.1   *Introduction to the provisions of the Financial Services and Markets Act 2000*

In relation to the acquisition of ownership and control of insurance companies, the key requirement under the Financial Services and Markets Act 2000 (the "Act") is for a person to obtain prior approval before becoming a controller of an insurer. Very broadly, a controller is a person who holds 10 per cent or more of the shares in an insurance company or one of its parents.

This regime, which was largely carried over from the previous regime under the Insurance Companies Act 1982, now reflects the changes introduced on the implementation of EC Directive 2007/44/EC (the "Directive") which was implemented in 2009.

The Directive resulted from the Commission's concerns that member states might impose unreasonable requirements on overseas acquisitions of financial services firms in their jurisdictions, contrary to the spirit of the single market.

3.1.2 Requirements imposed on controllers and proposed controllers

3.1.2.1 Notification to the Financial Services Authority ("FSA")

The provisions of Part XII of the Act establish the framework under which persons are obliged to notify the FSA of intended acquisitions, and increases and reductions, of control over authorised persons. Sections 178(1) and 191D(1) of the Act provide as follows:

> "178(1) A person who decides to acquire or increase control over a UK authorised person must give the Authority notice in writing before making the acquisition."

> "191D(1) a person who decides to reduce or cease to have control over a UK authorised person must give the Authority notice in writing before making the disposition."

What is control, in this context?

Section 181 provides that a person acquires control over a firm where he:

(a) holds 10 per cent or more of the shares of the firm or its parent (where "parent" is defined in s.420 of the Act); or
(b) holds 10 per cent or more of the voting power in the firm or its parent; or
(c) is able to exercise significant influence over the management of the firm by virtue of his shareholding or voting power in the firm or its parent respectively.

Section 182 provides that a person increases control over a firm whenever:

(a) the percentage of shares which such person holds in the firm or its parent increases by any of the steps mentioned below; or

(b) the percentage of voting power such person holds in the firm or its parent increases by any of the relevant steps; or

(c) such person becomes a parent undertaking of the firm.

The steps which will trigger the notification requirements are:

(a) from below 20 per cent to 20 per cent or more;
(b) from below 30 per cent to 30 per cent or more;
(c) from less than 50 per cent to 50 per cent or more

Correspondingly for a reduction of control, the steps are from:

(a) 50 per cent or more to less than 50 per cent;
(b) 30 per cent or more to less than 30 per cent; or
(c) 20 per cent or more to less than 20 per cent.

If a person's holding of shares or voting power reduces below 10 per cent or if his shareholding or voting power in the firm or its parent no longer enables him to exercise significant influence over its management, then he will cease to be a controller of the firm.[1]

Article 4 of the Financial Services and Markets Act 2000 (Controllers) (Exemption) Order 2009/774 provides for a single 20 per cent threshold for control of a UK insurance intermediary instead of the incremental thresholds that apply in respect of other authorised persons.

For the purpose of calculating whether a person has acquired control, the holding of shares or voting rights by any person includes any shares or voting power held by another person if they are acting in concert. The interpretation of the phrase "acting in concert" therefore becomes crucial in determining whether a person has become a controller. The phrase is not defined in the Directive, or in the Act.

The FSA has however issued guidance at SUP 11 Annex 6G, which considers the circumstances when one person's holding of shares or voting power must be aggregated with that of

---

[1] FIN: s.183(2) and FIN s.183(3)

another person for the purposes of determining whether they have decided to acquire or increase control over a UK authorised person. This may happen in two situations, firstly where the shares or voting power are held by persons "acting in concert" and secondly where a person is deemed to hold not only his own voting power in a firm but that of another person as well.

As regards "acting in concert", the FSA guidance explains that level 3 guidelines issued under the Directive require that for persons to be acting in concert they must: (i) hold shares and/or voting power in the firm or its parent's undertaking; and (ii) reach a decision to exercise the rights linked to those shares in accordance with an agreement (in writing or otherwise) between them.

Although the phrase "acting in concert" is also used in the UK Takeover Code, the FSA guidance makes clear that the definition of acting in concert in the Takeover Code should not be taken as guidance to the interpretation of s.181 and 182, and conversely the FSA guidance has no relevance as to how "acting in concert" is to be interpreted in the context of the Takeover Code.

Deemed voting power arises where one person's holding of voting power is attributed to another. Section 422(5) provides that in the following circumstances voting power held by one person is aggregated with another's voting power:

(a) voting power held by a third party with whom that person has concluded an agreement, which obliges that person and a third party to adopt, by concerted exercise of the voting power they hold, a lasting common policy towards the management of the firm;

(b) voting power held by a third party under an agreement concluded with that person providing for the temporary transfer for consideration of the voting power in question;

(c)   voting power attaching to shares which are lodged as collateral with that person, provided that that person controls the voting power and declares an intention to exercise it;

(d)   voting power attaching to shares in which that person has a life interest;

(e)   voting power which is held or may be exercised within the meaning of sub-paras (a)–(d) above by a subsidiary undertaking of that person;

(f)   voting power attaching to shares deposited with that person which he has discretion to exercise in the absence of specific instructions from shareholders;

(g)   voting power held in the name of a third party on behalf of that person; and

(h)   voting power which that person may exercise as a proxy where that person has discretion about the exercise of the voting power in the absence of specific instructions from the shareholders.

Part XII of the Act relates only to control over a UK-authorised person, which is defined in s.191G (subject to certain exceptions) as a body incorporated in (or an unincorporated association formed under the law of) any part of the UK. Accordingly, controllers or proposed controllers of entities which are not registered or formed in the UK do not require pre-approval from the FSA under the Act even though such entities may be doing business in the UK. They may of course require to be approved by the supervisory authority of the entity's jurisdiction of incorporation. They may also be required by the FSA Rules to notify the FSA of changes to their controllers, so as to enable the FSA to monitor the firm's controllers.

Section 184 sets out certain exemptions from the controller requirements. For the purposes of ss.181–183 the following shares and voting power held by a person in a firm are to be disregarded:

(a)   shares held only for the purposes of clearing and settling within a short settlement cycle;

(b)   shares held by a custodian or its nominee in a custodian capacity, provided that the custodian or nominee is only able to exercise voting power represented by the shares in accordance with instructions given to it in writing;

(c)   shares representing no more than 5 per cent of the total voting power in the firm or its parents if they are held by a market maker which is an authorised entity in its home state and which does not intervene in the management of the firm or exert any influence on the firm to buy the shares or back the share price;

(d)   shares held by a bank or investment firm in its trading book, providing that the shares represent no more than 5 per cent of the total voting power in the firm or its parent and the bank or investment firm ensures that the voting power is not used to intervene in the management of the firm;

(e)   shares held by a bank or investment firm as a result of underwriting a share issue or conducting a firm placing of shares, provided that the bank or investment firm does not exercise voting power represented by the shares or otherwise intervene in the management of the issue and retains the holding for a period of less than one year; and

(f)   where an investment manager, or a UCITS management company and its parent undertaking each hold shares or voting power in an entity, each may disregard holdings of the other provided that they exercise their voting power independently of each other,

or if the information provided by the proposed controller is incomplete.

In relation to acquisition of control (but not reductions in control), the requirement is not only for notification to be made to the FSA, but for FSA approval to be given, in advance of the actual acquisition of control. The consequences of the acquisition of control without such approval are dealt with at Section 3.1.4.

3.1.2.2   FSA Approval process

Following notification of a proposed acquisition of control, under s.189(1) of the Act, the FSA then has a period of up to 60 working days from the date on which it acknowledges receipt of the notice of control either to approve the proposal or to issue a warning notice notifying the proposed controller that it intends to issue a notice of objection to the proposals or that it intends to impose conditions on the proposed controller. During the assessment period, if the FSA determines that it requires further information in order to complete its assessment, it may request the proposed controller to provide such information. Under s.190 such a request must be made no later than the 50th working day of the assessment period, and stops the clock running on the assessment for a maximum period of 20 working days (or 30 if the proposed controller is situated or regulated outside the EU or is not regulated by the insurance or reinsurance directives). In effect, the FSA is able to "re-set" the timetable by requesting additional information if it is not satisfied that the applicant's notification includes all of the information the FSA requires.

The clock may, however, only be stopped once.

In carrying out its assessment of a proposed change of control, s.185(2) provides that the authority must consider the suitability of the proposed controller and the financial soundness of the acquisition in order to ensure the sound and prudent management of the firm, must have regard to the likely influence that the proposed controller will have on the UK authorised person and must disregard the economic needs of the market. The authority may only object to an acquisition on the basis of certain specified criteria, which are:

(a)   the reputation of the proposed controller;
(b)   the reputation and experience of any person who will direct the business of the firm going forward;
(c)   the financial soundness of the proposed controller;

(d) the ability of the firm to comply on an ongoing basis with applicable prudential requirements in relation to its regulated activities;

(e) whether as a result of the acquisition the UK authorised person will be part of a group whose structure will enable the authority to effectively supervise the firm; and

(f) whether there are reasonable grounds to suspect that, in connection with the proposed acquisition, money laundering or terrorist financing is being, or has been committed or attempted, or that the proposed acquisition could increase the risk of this occurring.

These criteria represent a change from the previous position whereby the FSA, for instance, had power to object to a proposed acquisition on the grounds that the interests of consumers would be threatened; there is no equivalent in the new assessment criteria, although the Commission has power to adjust the assessment criteria to take account of future market developments.

If the FSA fails to determine whether to approve or issue a warning notice in respect of a particular proposal within the assessment period then, under s.189(6) of the Act, the FSA will be deemed to have approved the proposal.

Once approval has been given, it only remains effective provided that the proposed controller actually effects the relevant change of control within the period specified in the approval notice (if any) or, if no period is specified, within one year of the date on which approval was granted or deemed to have been granted.

3.1.2.3   Improperly acquired shares

If a controller has acquired or continues to hold shares in contravention of a notice of objection issued by the FSA or a condition imposed on the FSA's approval, or the FSA believes that there are grounds for objecting to control on the basis of the criteria set out at Section 3.1.2.2, the FSA may issue a restriction notice to such controller restricting those shares in accordance with s.191B of the Act. Furthermore, the FSA may apply to court for an order for the sale of the shares concerned or disposition of the voting power.

3.1.2.4 Reductions in control

Where a controller's control over a firm is reduced by one of the steps mentioned above, the FSA must be notified in accordance with s.191D of the Act. However, the FSA's formal approval is not required prior to the reduction taking place.

3.1.2.5 Acquisitions or disposals by Fund Managers

The FSA recognises that investment managers may have difficulty complying with the prior notification and approval requirements of the Act, and has therefore made provision for fund managers to give a blanket notification and obtain pre-approval in relation to any acquisition of control of any firm whose shares (or those of its parent) are listed, provided that such acquisition occurs only in the course of the applicant's business as an investment manager, and that the level of control acquired at all times remains less than 20 per cent. Such pre-approval may be valid for a period lasting up to one year.[2] The applicant remains subject to the requirement to notify the FSA when a change in control actually occurs and such notifications should be made no later than five business days after the end of each month, setting out all changes to the control position during that month.[3]

3.1.3 Requirements imposed on the controlled firm

UK domestic insurers and overseas firms are required to notify the FSA where a person is acquiring or ceasing to have control over them.[4] The firm's written notification must be in the prescribed form and must be made as soon as the firm becomes aware that a person has decided to acquire or increase or

---

[2] SUP 11.3.5AG.
[3] SUP 11.3.5CG
[4] SUP 11.4.2R(1) and (4); SUP 11.4.4.R(1) and (2).

relieve control or, where the event takes place without the knowledge of the firm, within 14 days of the firm becoming aware of the event.[5]

A firm must also notify the FSA if it becomes aware of certain changes in the circumstances of its controller, namely:

(a) if there is a significant deterioration in the financial position of the controller; or
(b) if there is a substantial change to the controller's governing body; or
(c) if the controller is involved in legal proceedings or an investigation which may bring into question the integrity of the controller; or
(d) if a controller, who is authorised under the Insurance Directives or as A MiFID investment firm or BCD credit institution or is registered under the Insurance Mediation Directive ("IMD"), ceases to be so authorised or registered.[6]

The FSA's view (as set out in SUP 11.4.8G) is that firms should discuss at the earliest opportunity any prospective changes in controllers' or proposed controllers' shareholdings or voting power if such change is material:

"As a minimum ... such discussions should take place

before a person:

(i) enters into any formal agreement in respect of the purchase of shares or a proposed acquisition or merger which would result in a change in control (whether or not the agreement is conditional upon any matter, including the FSA's approval); or
(ii) purchases any share options, warrants or other financial instruments, the exercise of which would result in the person acquiring control or any other change in control."

---

[5] SUP 11.4.7R.
[6] SUP 11.8.1R.

This Guidance codifies what has, in any event, always been regarded as good practice.

The FSA requires firms to "take reasonable steps" to keep themselves informed about the identity of their controllers, and requires them to submit an annual report (within four months of their accounting reference date) as to who their controllers were on that date.[7]

SUP 11 Annex 1G provides a useful summary of notifications required to be made by both controllers and the firms regulated by the FSA.

3.1.4 *Offences*

Section 191F of the Act provides that, *inter alia*, failure to notify the FSA in relation to an acquisition or increase or decrease in control is an offence, as is completion of a proposed acquisition of control before the FSA has completed its consideration of the proposal and notified the proposed controller of the outcome (or the proposal has been deemed to be approved). Guilty persons will be liable on conviction to a fine which in the case of a conviction on indictment is not subject to a maximum amount.

If a person to whom a warning notice or a notice of objection has been given acquires the control to which the notice applies, he will be guilty of an offence and will be liable on summary conviction to a fine (subject to the specified maximum) or on conviction on indictment to an unlimited fine or imprisonment for a term not exceeding two years or both.

In September 2009 the FSA brought its first ever criminal prosecution for failing to notify a proposed change of control in a regulated entity. Mr V.K. Sharma was fined £3,000 for acquiring a controlling interest in a regulated firm without giving the FSA prior notice and a further £3,000 for making false and misleading statements to the FSA.

---

[7]   SUP 16.4.5R.

In February 2010 a further prosecution was brought against Semperian PPP Investment Partners Limited Partnership, for acquiring an authorised firm before it had received the approval of the FSA. The defendant notified the FSA in mid-December 2008 that it proposed to acquire the authorised firm in question but failed to wait for FSA approval before completing the deal three weeks later.

These cases have been used by the FSA to signal that "the FSA is taking a much tougher line with those that seek to avoid or ride rough-shod over the change in control regime" and that they should operate as:

> "a clear warning to other potential controllers that the FSA will prosecute change in control offences in appropriate cases".

3.1.5   Proposals for change

Following the establishment of the PRA and the FCA, it is proposed that the relevant prudential regulator will be responsible for considering change of control applications, in consultation with its counterpart where the alternative authority has an interest. Thus for insurers, the PRA will have the principal role, subject to consultation with the FCA. It remains to be seen if this will be a workable proposal, as there may be some situations where there is a risk of overlap or duplication, for instance, around applications for change of control of a group which contains both insurers and intermediaries.[8]

3.2   Management of insurance companies

3.2.1   Introduction to the "approved persons" regime

The formal regulation of the management of insurance companies (and, more recently, insurance intermediaries) was developed significantly by the Act, which introduced an

---

[8]   HM Treasury White Paper, para.2.180.

entirely new system compared with the previous regime under the Insurance Companies Act 1982. Under this new system, those who carry out what the FSA refers to as "controlled functions" for an authorised person need to be approved individually by the FSA. This new system is generally referred to as the "approved persons" regime (the "AP regime"). The approval requirements apply both to those in managerial positions (e.g. directors, service managers and compliance heads) and to those with customer responsibilities (e.g. advisers). Insurance firms regulated by the FSA (which now include general insurance intermediaries) are required to take a proactive approach in considering both the controlled functions performed within the firm and who will perform those functions. The pre-approval AP regime necessitates the establishment and maintenance by authorised insurance firms of appropriate internal controls which facilitate both organisational structuring and ongoing compliance with the provisions and rules contained in the Act and the Handbook respectively. Firms need to map the categories of controlled functions onto their existing organisational structures and document the division of responsibilities and job descriptions. It is important that firms consider adequately the actual functions undertaken by an individual, as the mere allocation of a job title will not be sufficient to satisfy the requirements under the AP regime. In particular, they have to decide how to address the FSA's requirements relating to how certain of the managerial functions are allocated within the firm.

Prior to its implementation, there were concerns that the AP regime could lead to increased levels of bureaucracy, external interference in the management of firms and generally an increase in the regulatory requirements to be complied with by the industry which is already subject to a relatively high level of regulation. Accordingly, in setting out the requirements of the AP regime, the FSA was attempting to strike a balance:

"between relying on those who manage the firm's affairs to employ appropriate staff, without intervention from the

FSA, and seeking to ensure that such staff are fit and proper, in the interest of customers and potential customers."[9]

3.2.1.1 The purpose of the AP regime

The AP regime provides for the direct regulation of individuals (and in certain circumstances bodies corporate). The main aim is to ensure that fit and proper persons with the appropriate qualifications undertake those functions within an insurance firm which are likely to have an impact on the integrity of the firm and the industry as a whole and are likely to affect customers and potential customers.

SUP 10.3–10.10 of the Handbook specify, under s.59 of the Act, descriptions of the controlled functions. The underlying purpose is to establish, and mark the boundaries of, the AP regime.[10]

3.2.1.2 The provisions of the Act

Section 59 of the Act requires an authorised person to take "reasonable care to ensure" that no person performs a controlled function under an arrangement entered into by the authorised person (or a contractor of the authorised person) unless approval for the performance of that function has been obtained from the FSA. Accordingly, the authorised person must ensure that personnel are not performing controlled functions without the FSA's approval and should apply for approval of an individual who will be performing a controlled function prior to that function being assumed by the relevant individual. The person performing the function may not necessarily be an employee of the firm. For example, in a group there may be staff employed by one firm who carry out certain functions within other group firms. Those staff require approval in relation to each firm for which they carry out the functions.

---

[9] Consultation Paper 53: The Regulation of Approved Persons: Controlled Functions, June 2000, p.8.
[10] SUP 10.2.1G.

Under s.61 of the Act the FSA has three months to consider an application for approval. This could cause practical problems for firms needing to make appointments in a timely fashion, and it is often necessary when announcing new appointments to make it clear that the appointment is conditional upon FSA approval. For routine cases, however, the FSA is able to process the appointment within a matter of days. There are also provisions which allow persons to carry out controlled functions for up to 12 weeks within a 12-month period without having to obtain the FSA's approval. This allows for emergency cover for sickness or holidays for example.[11]

3.2.1.3 Notification of changes

If a person who has been approved to perform one particular function within a firm wishes to carry out another, different function, the firm must apply to the FSA for approval in relation to the second, new function, and the approved person must not carry out the second function before approval has been obtained. If there are any changes to the information previously submitted in respect of an approved person then the FSA must be notified. Lastly, the FSA must be notified within seven days of a person ceasing to perform a controlled function.[12]

3.2.1.4 Fit and proper test for approved persons ("FIT")

FIT, which forms part of the Handbook, is the standard used by the FSA to assess whether or not to grant approval to a person to perform a controlled function. Once the FSA has approved an individual, that person must remain fit and proper to carry out his functions in addition to observing the standards of conduct set out in the Statements of Principle and Code of Practice for Approved Persons ("APER") which also forms part of the Handbook. Failure to do so could, *inter alia*, result in the FSA withdrawing its approval.

---

[11] SUP 10.5.5R.
[12] SUP 10.13.6R.

The FSA has regard to a number of factors when assessing the fitness and propriety of a person to perform a particular controlled function. The most important factors are the person's honesty, integrity and reputation; competency and capability; and financial soundness.[13] Further guidance in relation to the FSA's methods of assessing these factors is to be found at FIT 2.1.3G, 2.2 and 2.3. The FSA will also take into account the activities of the firm for which the controlled function is or is to be performed, the permission held by that firm and the markets within which it operates.[14]

3.2.2 Application of the AP regime

3.2.2.1 To which firms does the AP regime apply?

The notes contained in Chapter 10 of the Supervision Manual of the Handbook set out the boundaries of application of the AP regime. The general rule is that the AP regime applies to every firm, although there are certain exceptions.[15]

Chapter 10 does not apply to overseas firms (i.e. firms which have their registered office or head office outside the UK) unless the overseas firm concerned carries on regulated activities from an "establishment maintained by it or its appointed representative" in the UK.[16] Where an overseas firm does have a UK establishment, the AP regime applies in a slightly restricted form and so the members of governing bodies of such firms, other than the chief executives, do not fall within the AP regime.[17]

Likewise, in relation to EEA firms, where the FSA is not responsible for prudential supervision, the AP regime does not apply to their governing bodies.[18]

---

[13] FIT 1.3.1G.
[14] FIT 1.3.2G.
[15] SUP 10.1.1R.
[16] SUP 10.1.6R.
[17] SUP 10.1.7R.
[18] SUP 10.1.9R.

Another case where the AP regime applies to a more limited extent is where there is only an appointed representative of an EEA firm in the UK, in which case only the governing functions and customer functions are relevant.[19] Where the scope of the appointment of the appointed representative includes non-investment insurance mediation only, or the principal purpose of the appointed representative is to carry on activities other than regulated activities, the requirements of the AP regime are limited to just one of the governing functions.[20]

3.2.2.2   To which persons does the AP regime apply?

The AP regime applies to those persons who perform controlled functions within an authorised insurance firm. The focus is on the functions actually performed by an individual as opposed to his job title. Accordingly, it is possible for an individual to be performing a director function without formally being appointed to the board, as the regime applies to a person "acting in the capacity of a director".[21]

The AP regime is essentially directed at the governing body and senior management of an authorised firm. Once approval has been obtained for the particular person to perform the controlled functions, and the relevant individual has been designated as an "approved person" by the FSA, personal culpability will attach to that person in certain circumstances if his conduct falls short of that required of approved persons.[22]

In addition, however, the AP regime can apply to persons who are directors, partners, officers or members, senior managers or employees of parent companies of authorised firms if their directions or actions are regularly taken into account by the firm's governing body.

---

[19]   SUP 10.1.16R.
[20]   SUP 10.1.16AR.
[21]   SUP 10.6.4R.
[22]   Section 66 of the Act and APER 3.1.4G.

3.2.3 Controlled functions

3.2.3.1 Specification of the controlled functions

The Act does not specify the controlled functions central to the AP regime but rather leaves it to the FSA to determine which functions are to be controlled functions necessitating prior approval for their performance.[23] This approach is clearly adopted to allow the FSA flexibility in the specification process which is necessary in light of the range of financial service industries regulated by it and the changing commercial and organisational structures of the firms authorised by it.

As explained above, individuals are required to be approved by the FSA in order to carry out a controlled function. There are 16 controlled functions specified and they are grouped into five categories: the governing functions, the required functions, the systems and control functions, the significant management functions, and the customer functions. They are set out at SUP 10.4.5R and are detailed in Table 3.1.

Table 3.1 Controlled functions

Type	*CF*	*Description of controlled function*
Governing functions*	1	Director function
	2	Non-executive director function
	3	Chief executive function
	4	Partner function
	5	Director of unincorporated association function
	6	Small friendly society function
Required functions*	8	Apportionment and oversight function
	10	Compliance oversight function

---

[23] Section 59(4) of the Act.

Type	CF	Description of controlled function
	11	Money laundering reporting function
	12	Actuarial function
	12A	With-profits actuary function
	12B	Lloyd's actuary function
Systems and controls function*	28	Systems and controls function
Significant management function*	29	Significant management function
Customer functions	30	Customer function

*significant influence functions

Significant influence functions

The significant influence functions comprise the governing functions, the required functions, the systems and controls function and the significant management function. As their title suggests, each significant influence function is one which is likely to result in the person responsible for its performance exercising a significant influence on the conduct of a firm's affairs as far as they relate to a regulated activity of the firm.[24]

As far as the directors are concerned, they will require approval to perform the governing function and, depending on the division of responsibility within the entity, they may also perform (and hence require approval for) certain of the other significant influence functions. In relation to the governing function, every director (both executive and non-executive) of a body corporate will perform the governing function, that is, he will be responsible for directing a firm's affairs and will therefore be required to be approved by the FSA.[25] A person

---

[24] SUP 10.5.2R.
[25] SUP 10.6.1G.

who is approved to perform a governing function (other than the non-executive function) will not have to be specifically approved to perform any of the systems and controls functions or the significant management functions, although additional approval will need to be obtained before he can perform any of the required functions or customer functions.[26]

The scope of the governing functions has been widened with the extension of regulation to cover insurance mediation activity to include a requirement for any insurance intermediary other than a sole trader to allocate to a director or senior manager the responsibility for the firm's insurance mediation activities.[27]

3.2.4   High-level standards

3.2.4.1   Senior management arrangements, systems and controls ("SYSC")

Purpose of SYSC

SYSC is a body of rules contained in the High Level Standards Manual of the Handbook. The stated purpose of the rules include:

(a)   to encourage firms' directors and senior managers to take practical responsibility for a firm's arrangements on matters which are likely to be of interest to the FSA because they impact on the FSA's functions under the Act;

(b)   to increase certainty by amplifying Principle 3, under which a firm is required to take reasonable care to organise and control its affairs responsibly, effectively and with adequate risk management systems;

(c)   to encourage firms to vest responsibility for effective and responsible organisation in specific directors and senior managers; and

---

[26]   SUP 10.6.3G.
[27]   SUP 10.6.3AG and SUP 10.7.4AG.

(d) to create a common platform of organisational and systems and control requirements for firms.[28]

The FSA emphasised in the consultation process which occurred prior to the implementation of these rules that, in its view, the rules contained in SYSC do not go beyond "accepted standards of good business practice".[29]

Senior management arrangements: apportionment and allocation

Firms are required to take reasonable care to maintain clear and appropriate apportionment of significant responsibilities among both directors and senior managers. The apportionment must be effected such that "it is clear who has which of those responsibilities"[30] and "the business and affairs of the firm can be adequately monitored and controlled by the directors, relevant senior managers and governing body of the firm".[31] In order to monitor the apportionment of responsibilities, firms are required to appropriately allocate to one or more individuals (usually the firm's chief executive(s) or a director or senior manager responsible for the overall management of the group or a group division)[32] the functions of dealing with the apportionment of responsibilities and overseeing the establishment and maintenance of systems and controls. Furthermore, authorised firms are required by SYSC 2.2.1R(1) to ensure that they have adequate record-keeping controls in place recording the arrangements made to satisfy the rules in relation to appropriation and allocation.

Guidance on the practical implications of the dual concepts of reasonableness and appropriateness is given in the FSA's

---

[28] SYSC 1.2.1G.
[29] Consultation Paper 35: Senior management arrangements, systems and controls, p.8.
[30] SYSC 2.1.1R(1).
[31] SYSC 2.1.1R(2).
[32] Firms must refer to the Allocation of Functions table at SYSC 2.1.4R to determine who in their organisation these functions must be allocated to.

guidance note[33] in relation to the record-keeping requirement. The FSA is of the view that appropriate records may include:

(a) organisational charts and diagrams;
(b) project management documents;
(c) job descriptions;
(d) committee constitutions; and
(e) terms of reference, provided they show a clear description of the firm's major functions.

One of the FSA's key aims has been to enhance and enforce compliance culture within the firms it regulates. Central to this culture will be the requirement that firms establish and keep up-to-date adequate records reflecting their internal compliance controls.

Systems and controls

SYSC 3.1.1R states that "a firm must take reasonable care to establish and maintain such systems and controls as are appropriate to its business". The FSA gives guidance[34] as to the factors which should be taken into account when determining the nature and extent of the systems and controls which a firm will need to maintain. These factors include the nature, scale and complexity of its business; the diversity of its operations, including geographical diversity; the volume and size of its transactions; and the degree of risk associated with each area of its operation.

In determining which systems and controls are to be established in order to satisfy the FSA's requirements an insurance company will need to start by considering the areas listed and discussed by the FSA in para.3.2 of SYSC in the High Level Standards Manual.

---

[33] SYSC 2.2.2G(1).
[34] SYSC 3.1.2G.

3.2.4.2 *Statements of principle and code of practice for approved persons*

APER sets out Statements of Principle for approved persons, and in accordance with s.64(2) of the Act it also includes a code of practice in order to facilitate the FSA's determination of whether or not a person's conduct complies with the Statements of Principle.

Those approved persons who perform a significant influence function will be under a duty to comply with Statements of Principle 1–7; other approved persons will need to comply only with Statements of Principle 1–4.

Statements of Principle

(1) An approved person must act with integrity in carrying out his controlled function.
(2) An approved person must act with due skill, care and diligence in carrying out his controlled function.
(3) An approved person must observe proper standards of market conduct in carrying out his controlled function.
(4) An approved person must deal with the FSA and with other regulators in an open and cooperative way and must disclose appropriately any information of which the FSA would reasonably expect notice.
(5) An approved person performing a significant influence function must take reasonable steps to ensure that the business of the firm for which he is responsible in his controlled function is organised so that it can be controlled effectively.
(6) An approved person performing a significant influence function must exercise due skill, care and diligence in managing the business of the firm for which he is responsible in his controlled function.
(7) An approved person performing a significant influence function must take reasonable steps to ensure that the business of the firm for which he is responsible in his controlled function complies with the relevant requirements and standards of the regulatory system.

The FSA considers[35] the following factors to be relevant when determining whether or not an approved person's conduct in relation to a controlled function complies with:

(a) Statements of Principle 1, 2, 3 and 4:
   (i)   whether the conduct relates to activities that are subject to other provisions of the Handbook; and
   (ii) whether that conduct is consistent with the requirements and standards of the regulatory system relevant to the particular firm.
(b) Statements of Principle 5–7:
   (i)   whether he exercised reasonable care when considering the information available to him;
   (ii)   whether he reached a reasonable conclusion which he acted on;
   (iii) the nature, scale and complexity of the firm's business;
   (iv)   his role and responsibility as an approved person performing a significant influence function; and
   (v)   the knowledge he had, or should have had, of regulatory concerns, if any, arising in the business under his control.

As would be expected, the principles to be complied with by an approved person performing a significant influence function are far wider in scope than those relating to other approved persons. In relation to the first two factors discussed under Statements of Principle 5–7, the concept of reasonableness once again emerges. In so far as practicable, it is advisable for approved persons to adequately document their consideration and consequent conclusions reached in relation to the controlled functions which they perform so that, if called upon to do so, they would be in a position to defend their decisions and actions on the basis of reasonableness. The last factor listed under Statements of Principle 5–7 is interesting in that it highlights once again the level of compliance culture which the FSA is aiming for and, in particular, the need for approved persons to ensure that they understand the regulatory regime within which their controlled function is to be performed.

---

[35] APER 3.2.1E and 3.3.1E.

The Code of Practice for Approved Persons (the "Code")

The Code is framed in the negative, in that it describes conduct which would be regarded by the FSA to be a breach of a Statement of Principle.[36] An approved person will only be in breach of a Statement of Principle where he is personally culpable.[37] The Code is not exhaustive of the kinds of conduct that may contravene the Statements of Principle.[38]

3.2.5 *Enforcement of the AP regime*

In addition to the power of the FSA to withdraw its approval from an individual to perform a controlled function in the event that the standards of conduct set out in APER are not complied with, the FSA may take action against an approved person if he is found to be guilty of misconduct. An approved person will be guilty of misconduct if he fails to comply with a Statement of Principle or if he has been knowingly involved in a contravention of a requirement imposed by the Act on the authorised person for whom he performs the controlled function.[39] If the FSA takes disciplinary action against an approved person guilty of misconduct it may impose a penalty on him in such amount as it considers appropriate or it may publish a statement of his misconduct.[40] In extreme cases the FSA may seek a prohibition order which will effectively ban the individual from holding a post involving responsibility for regulated activities.[41]

It is important to note that the FSA will only take disciplinary action against an approved person where there is evidence of personal culpability on the part of that approved person. Personal culpability only arises where the FSA considers the approved person's behaviour to be deliberate or where the

---

[36] APER 4.1–4.7.
[37] APER 3.1.4G.
[38] APER 3.1.6G.
[39] Section 66 of the Act.
[40] Section 66 of the Act.
[41] EG 9.1.

approved person's standard of behaviour was below that which would be reasonable in all the circumstances.[42]

The FSA's approach to the AP regime has changed since the financial crisis, and in particular there has been increased focus those approved for Significant Influence Functions.

The approval process has become much more rigorous, with candidates being subject to searching interviews by the FSA, and with ongoing compliance with the Statements of Principles expected. In a speech on June 18, 2008 Margaret Cole, Director of FSA Enforcement, made it clear that:

> "you can expect to see more supervision and enforcement focus on individuals, especially SIF holders ... Previously ... we tended to focus on cases of dishonesty or lack of integrity, where prohibition or withdrawal of approval was the most appropriate outcome. In the future we will also consider the competence of SIF holders and won't shy away from pursuing SIF holders who breach our Principles or Code. In these cases, fines may be more appropriate than prohibitions. We've made a strategic decision to investigate more individuals."

3.2.5.1 *Proposals for change*

Following the establishment of the PRA and the FCA, it is proposed that the PRA will have primary responsibility for designating Significant Influence Functions, but where the PRA has not designated a SIF and the FCA would like to, the FCA will be able to do so. The FCA will be able to make and enforce its own codes on all approved persons, and will ultimately be able to remove approved individuals for egregious conduct or consumer protection breaches.

---

[42] DEPP 6.2.4G.

In practice, one may anticipate that the line between the roles of the two authorities may not be easy to draw, and the authorities will need to consult each other to minimise the risk of overlap.[43]

---

[43] FIN HM Treasury White Paper 2.158 et seq.

Chapter 4

Financial Supervision

John Philpott,
Director: Ernst & Young LLP

4.1 Introduction

The financial requirements in the FSA Handbook are to a large extent driven by the FSA's statutory objective laid down by s.5 of the Financial Services and Markets Act 2000 ("FSMA") to secure the appropriate degree of protection for consumers by making it unlikely (although not impossible, as the FSA does not set out to operate a zero-failure regime) that an insurance company will fail to the detriment of its policyholders. However, the rules need to be consistent with the requirements of a series of EU Insurance Directives relating to life and non-life insurance. The present Directive requirements will be superseded by the Solvency II Directive, which is currently due to be implemented with effect from 1 January 2013 (although slippage in the timetable would not be a completely unexpected outcome). However, there is a period during which insurers will need to continue to operate (while pursuing the preparations for Solvency II), under the existing rules, and this chapter therefore concentrates on the present position, with the concluding s.4.7 identifying the principal differences that will arise under Solvency II.

The detailed financial supervision rules are underpinned by high level principles, firstly in threshold condition 4 set out in Sch.6 to FSMA, which requires the resources of an FSA-regulated firm to be adequate, in the opinion of the FSA, in relation to the regulated activities carried on. This condition is broad-ranging as it is relevant to non-financial as well as financial resources. More specifically, principle 4 of the FSA Principles for Businesses requires a firm to maintain adequate financial resources.

The significance of principle 4 is that the FSA could take action against a firm for having inadequate financial resources even if that firm satisfied the mathematical requirements set out in the detailed rules. The requirements derived from the EU Directives are to a large extent formulaic and generally recognised to be insufficiently risk sensitive. However, the Handbook as it is now drafted contains not only the formulaic requirements, but the non-formulaic requirement for an insurer to perform an individual capital assessment which recognises the insurer's unique risk profile.

Any set of financial rules will have two primary elements: an articulation of what is required of a firm by way of resources, and a basis for measuring the actual resources of a firm to determine whether the requirement has been satisfied or not. Section 4.2 of this Chapter will consider the requirements and sections 4.3 and 4.4 the measurement of the actual resources. Section 4.5 then provides an overview of the way in which information about requirements and resources is reported to the FSA. These sections concentrate on the rules for an insurer as a standalone entity: the implications of that insurer being a member of a group are picked up in Section 4.6. Section 4.7 then provides a preview of the changes under Solvency II.

The principal rules relating to the financial supervision of insurers, to which many references will be made in this chapter, are split between three modules of the FSA Handbook:

- The General Prudential Sourcebook ("GENPRU") which contains prudential requirements relevant to insurers, banks, building societies and certain investment firms.
- The Prudential Sourcebook for Insurers ("INSPRU") which contains prudential requirements specific to insurers.
- The Interim Prudential Sourcebook for Insurers ("IPRU-(INS)") which contains the reporting requirements.

4.2 Capital requirements—Pillar one and pillar two

There are two types of capital requirements in the FSA Handbook, which are commonly referred to as pillar one and pillar two. (Solvency II also features a concept of pillars, but as will be seen there is a slightly different distinction there.) Pillar one is to a large extent formula-driven, in terms of the way in which the requirements are defined, whereas pillar two is much more risk-based, and sensitive to the individual circumstances of an insurer.

4.2.1 Pillar one

The key pillar one rule is GENPRU 2.1.13R(1) which states that "an insurer must at all times maintain capital resources equal to or in excess of its capital resources requirement (CRR)". Although routine financial information is, as will be seen, submitted to the FSA annually (or in some cases quarterly), the "at all times" requirement means that an insurer's systems must continuously monitor compliance with the rule: if an insurer's capital resources at any time fall below the CRR, it is required by SUP Appendix 2 to inform the FSA of this fact and submit a scheme of operations.

The two elements of the rule are the measurement of the capital resources and the calculation of the CRR. The former will be considered in the next section: to a large extent the latter is determined by formulae prescribed by EU Directives.

The CRR is the higher of (a) the capital requirement derived by applying the formulae described in this section to determine a minimum or enhanced capital requirement and (b) an absolute yardstick expressed in Euros known as the base capital resources requirement ("BCRR"). For the majority of insurers the BCRR is currently €3.5 million (although lower rates apply in some cases such as mutuals and general insurers not writing liability business), and is therefore only of practical relevance to a small insurer, a newly authorised insurer or a life insurer

151

writing predominantly linked business (for which the formulae normally produce a low requirement).

There are otherwise three types of requirement, depending upon the type of business that an insurer carries on.

4.2.1.1 *General insurer*

The minimum capital requirement for a general insurer is (subject to the BCRR) the general insurance capital requirement ("GICR"), arrived at by applying the formulae prescribed by INSPRU 1.1.44G–1.1.71R: the calculation is documented on Forms 11 and 12 of the annual return submitted to the FSA (see Section 4.5). Three separate calculations are performed, with the GICR being the highest of the three results.

(a) The "premiums amount", which is arrived at by taking 18 per cent of the higher of gross premiums written and gross premiums earned (with a 2 per cent reduction for premiums in excess of €57.5 million) and reducing the calculated figure by the ratio of net claims incurred divided by gross claims incurred for the last three financial years (subject to a minimum ratio of ½ and a maximum ratio of 1). There is a 50 per cent loading on the aviation liability, marine liability and general liability gross premiums brought into the calculation, and a reduction of two-thirds for gross premiums brought into the calculation in respect of actuarial health insurance satisfying prescribed conditions.

(b) The "claims amount", which is arrived at by taking 26 per cent of annualised gross claims incurred over a three (or in exceptional circumstances seven) year reference period (with a 3 per cent reduction for annualised gross claims incurred in excess of €40.3 million) and reducing the calculated figure by the same ratio of net claims incurred to gross claims incurred as is used in (a). There is again a 50 per cent loading for aviation liability, marine liability and general liability gross claims incurred and a reduction of two thirds for gross claims incurred in respect of actuarial health insurance.

(c) The "brought forward amount" , which can have the effect of limiting the extent by which the GICR can fall from one year to the next, by reference to the movement in net outstanding claims. If net outstanding claims have increased, the GICR must be at least as large as the previous GICR. If net outstanding claims have reduced, the GICR must be at least as large as the previous year's GICR multiplied by the fraction of closing net outstanding claims divided by opening net outstanding claims. Where an insurer is fully reinsured, and both the opening and closing net outstanding claims are therefore nil, a fraction based on gross outstanding claims is used instead. The brought forward method was introduced to prevent the minimum capital requirement falling away too rapidly for an insurer in run-off, but does in practice determine the requirement for a number of insurers that are still writing new business.

The rules also define an enhanced capital requirement ("ECR") for general insurers, arrived at by applying prescribed factors to net premiums written and to net technical provisions by category of business, and to assets by type. The ECR methodology involves more sophisticated formulae than those underpinning the GICR, and the FSA's original intention had been that where the ECR produced a higher result than the GICR, this would serve to define the CRR. However, in the light of reservations expressed about the granularity of the ECR calculation, the FSA decided not to make this a hard capital requirement, although an insurer needs to calculate the ECR and submit it to the FSA annually on a Form prescribed by Appendix 9.10 of IPRU(INS). It also provides an input to the pillar two calculations.

4.2.1.2 *Regulatory basis only life insurer*

With the exception of large with-profits life offices applying realistic reporting (see Section 4.2.1.3), a life insurer's capital resources requirement will be the higher of (a) the BCRR and (b) the sum of its long term insurance capital requirement ("LTICR") and its resilience capital requirement.

The LTICR (which is the subject of INSPRU 1.1.80G–1.1.92G) has four distinct components, not all of which will necessarily apply to any given insurer, with the computations being documented on Form 60 in the annual return. These four components are as follows:

(1) The "insurance death risk capital component", arrived at by applying a factor of between 0.1 and 0.3 per cent to "capital at risk" (which is the present value of the aggregate benefits payable as a result of death, where the contract provides for periodic or deferred payments, or if it does not the amount payable as a result of death, less in either case the mathematical reserves for the contract).

(2) The "insurance health risk and life protection reinsurance capital component", arrived at by applying the general insurance capital formulae described in the Section 4.2.1.1 to the relevant long-term business. This applies to permanent health insurance business, to accident and sickness general insurance business written incidentally as part of a life contract, and to life protection reinsurance business written by a mixed insurer or pure reinsurer.

(3) The "insurance expense risk capital component", which is 25 per cent of the net administrative expenses for linked business and 1 per cent of adjusted mathematical reserves otherwise.

(4) The "insurance market risk capital component", which is 3 per cent of adjusted mathematical reserves.

A direct life office writing non-linked business will be subject to (1), (3) and (4), and will only need to consider (2) to the extent that it is writing permanent health insurance business or incidental general insurance business. "Mathematical reserves" represent the provision made by a life insurer to cover liabilities arising under or in connection with long-term insurance contracts (but excluding liabilities that have fallen due and liabilities arising from deposit-back arrangements). Adjusted mathematical reserves are arrived at by taking gross mathematical reserves and reducing these for outward reinsurance, subject to a maximum reduction of 15 per cent.

A linked insurer will be primarily concerned with the 25 per cent of net administrative expenses criterion of (3), provided that it bears no investment risk and the allocation to cover mathematical reserves in the contract does not have a fixed upper limit which is effective as a limit for a period exceeding five years from the commencement of the contract.

A pure reinsurer will be subject to (2) in respect of its life protection and permanent health reinsurance and is exempt from (1), (3) and (4) in respect of such business.

In addition to the LTICR, a resilience capital requirement has to be calculated. This is a complex calculation dealt with in INSPRU 3.1.10R–3.1.26R, and is intended to cover adverse deviation from:

(1) the value of long-term insurance liabilities;
(2) the value of assets held to cover long-term insurance liabilities; and
(3) the value of assets held to cover the resilience capital requirement,

arising from the effect of market risk for equities, real estate and fixed interest securities. The determination of the resilience capital requirement is explained in Appendix 9.4 of the annual return.

4.2.1.3 *Realistic basis life insurer*

A life insurer writing with-profits business is a "realistic basis" firm unless its with-profits liabilities are, and at all times since 31 December 2004 have remained, less than £500 million. An insurer with a smaller with-profits fund can make a written election to be treated as a realistic basis life firm. The differences in the treatment of a realistic-basis life firm are as follows.

(1) It is necessary to calculate a "with-profits insurance capital component" ("WPICC"). The WPICC is added to the LTICR to produce an enhanced capital requirement, which

will define the CRR for such an insurer. The FSA's intention in introducing the concept of the WPICC was to ensure that a with-profits office adequately recognised policyholders' reasonable expectations that discretionary bonuses would increase in certain circumstances.

(2) Although the LTICR needs to be calculated, there is no resilience capital requirement.

(3) There are relaxations in the rules relating to the computation of mathematical reserves.

A realistic basis life insurer is required by INSPRU 1.3.7R to calculate a separate WPICC for each with-profits fund that it maintains: the calculations are documented on Forms 18 and 19 in the annual return. These separate WPICCs (where positive) are aggregated to determine the overall WPICC for the firm. To calculate a WPICC, the firm must arrive at two values for the fund.

(1) "Regulatory excess capital", defined by INSPRU 1.3.23R as the excess of the regulatory value of the assets of the fund under INSPRU 1.3.24R over the sum of:
   • the regulatory value of the liabilities of the fund under INSPRU 1.3.29R; and
   • the LTICR in respect of the fund's with-profits insurance contracts.

(2) "Realistic excess capital", defined by INSPRU 1.3.32R as the excess of the realistic value of assets of the fund under INSPRU 1.3.33R over the sum of:
   • the realistic value of liabilities of the fund under INSPRU 1.3.40R; and
   • the risk capital margin for the fund under INSPRU 1.3.43R.

A WPICC arises where (1) exceeds (2).

One slightly counter-intuitive aspect of the WPICC is that the difference between regulatory and realistic excess capital is dealt with as a capital requirement for regulatory purposes, whereas a provision to recognise realistic liabilities is instead made in the balance sheet of Companies Act accounts. An insurer with a WPICC will therefore normally have a positive valuation difference reported in its return to reflect the elimination of the extra balance sheet liability.

4.2.1.4 Non-EEA direct insurers

A non-EEA direct insurer is subject to the requirements described above in respect of the company globally. In addition, such an insurer is required by INSPRU 1.5.42R to calculate a UK minimum capital requirement by applying the relevant formulae to the business carried on in the United Kingdom, and to hold admissible assets to cover this requirement. Localisation requirements also apply: the assets covering the UK branch's technical provisions and "guarantee fund" (one third of the UK minimum capital requirement) must be held in the United Kingdom, and the assets covering the balance of the requirement in any EEA State. Special rules apply for the purpose of determining where an asset is deemed to be localised.

4.2.2 Pillar two

The key pillar two requirement appears in GENPRU 1.2.26R which states that a firm must maintain overall financial resources, including capital resources and liquidity resources, which are adequate, both as to amount and quality, to ensure that there is no significant risk that its liabilities cannot be met as they fall due. An insurer is required to carry out regular assessments of the adequacy of its financial resources using processes and systems which are commensurate to the nature, scale and complexity of its activities. The processes and systems must enable the firm to identify the major sources of risk to its ability to meet its liabilities as they fall due, including the major sources of credit risk, market risk, liquidity risk, operational risk and insurance risk and to carry out an assessment of how it intends to deal with each of the major sources of risk so identified.

A formal process is required to be performed under GENPRU 1.2.42R to carry out stress tests (shifting the value of individual parameters) and scenario analysis (varying a wider range of parameters at the same time) to identify an appropriate range of realistic adverse circumstances and events in which each risk identified crystallises, and to estimate the financial resources which the firm would need in each of the circumstances and events considered in order to be able to meet its liabilities as they fall due. The results of the exercise need to be documented. An insurer is required for the purposes of this review to provide the FSA with an assessment (its "individual capital assessment" or ICA) comparable to a 99.5 per cent confidence level over a one year timeframe that the value of assets exceeds the value of liabilities, whether or not this is the confidence level otherwise used in the firm's own assessments (INSPRU 7.1.42R). Revised guidance on the ICA was introduced by legal instrument 2006/62, and this is complemented by guidance issued by the ABI.

The FSA will periodically review an insurer's ICA, and in the light of its review will normally issue Individual Capital Guidance ("ICG") setting out the level of capital that the FSA considers that an insurer needs to maintain. Although it is referred to as "guidance", breach of the ICG could well lead the FSA to conclude that the insurer was not complying with threshold condition 4 and principle 4.

4.3   Capital resources

The insurer's capital resources with which the CRR is compared take as the starting point capital and reserves per the accounts (either Companies Act accounts or IFRS accounts are acceptable for this purpose). A series of regulatory adjustments to the GAAP numbers are then applied in order to arrive at the regulatory capital figures. Many of these adjustments relate to the application of specific valuation rules that have the result of a different value being ascribed to particular assets or liabilities than appeared in the accounts: such adjustments are described in section 4.4. However, there are also specific rules in GENPRU 2.2 which define the types of capital that qualify for regulatory purposes, and place limits on the extent to which particular types of capital can be recognised. The rules introduce the concept of tiers of capital, with capital qualifying as tier one being regarded as of a higher quality than capital falling into tier two.

The key characteristics of capital that would qualify for tier one are described by GENPRU 2.2.9G as follows.

(1) It is able to absorb losses.
(2) It is permanent.
(3) It ranks for repayment upon winding-up, administration or similar procedure after all other debts and liabilities.
(4) It has no fixed costs, that is there is no inescapable obligation to pay dividends and interest.

There are distinctions within tier one. The optimal type of capital is referred to as "core tier one" and can be held without restriction, whereas there are limits on the proportion of regulatory capital that can be made up of all other types. To qualify as core tier one, a capital instrument must fall within the GENPRU 2.2.83R definition of "permanent share capital":

• It must be an ordinary share, a members' contribution or part of the initial fund of a mutual;
• Any coupon must be non-cumulative, the firm must be under no obligation to pay a coupon in any circumstances and the firm must have the right to choose the amount of any coupon that it pays; and
• The terms upon which it is issued must not permit redemption and it is otherwise incapable of being redeemed at least to the same extent as an ordinary share issued under the Companies Act.

Core tier one also includes profit and loss account and other reserves, share premium account, externally verified interim net profits, positive valuation differences and the fund for future appropriations.

Also qualifying as tier one, but not as core tier one, are perpetual non-cumulative preference shares and "innovative tier one instruments". As these are not core tier one, restrictions apply, but these are far more generous than those for tier two. An instrument is deemed to be an innovative tier one instrument if it satisfies the general tier one conditions, but is redeemable and a reasonable person would think that the insurer is likely to redeem it or to have an economic incentive to redeem it (e.g. because there will be a step-up in the coupon rate after a specified date).

Tier two instruments are instruments such as cumulative preference shares and subordinated debt that combine features of debt and equity in that they are structured like debt, but exhibit some of the loss absorption and funding flexibility features of equity. There are detailed conditions to be satisfied for an instrument to qualify for tier two: the most important feature is that the claims of the creditors under the instrument must rank behind the claims of all unsubordinated creditors.

Tier two capital resources are also split into upper and lower tiers. The major distinction is that only perpetual instruments can be included in upper tier two, whereas dated instruments such as fixed term preference shares and dated subordinated debt can qualify for lower tier two. "Perpetual" does not mean that an instrument cannot be redeemed: rather it must have no fixed maturity date, and any redemption or repayment must be at the option of the firm. To qualify as lower tier two, an instrument must either have an original maturity of at least five years or, if redeemable on notice from the holder, require five or more years' notice of repayment. Over the final five years to repayment, the value of the instrument that qualifies for regulatory capital treatment has to be amortised on a straight line basis.

The restrictions on the extent to which credit can be taken for non-core tier one capital are referred to as the capital resources gearing rules. The key features of the gearing rules are as follows.

(1) Total tier two cannot exceed tier one capital resources after deductions.

(2) Lower tier two cannot exceed 50 per cent of tier one capital resources after deductions.

(3) At least 50 per cent of tier one capital after deductions must be represented by core tier one capital.

(4) No more than 15 per cent of tier one capital after deductions can be represented by innovative tier one capital.

(5) Instruments that do not qualify as tier one as a result of (3) and (4) may be included in tier two (provided the tier two conditions are satisfied) to the extent that these do not lead to the limits in (1) and (2) being breached.

These rules in effect introduce a "multiplier": an additional injection of core tier one capital will increase an insurer's capacity to take credit for other tier one and for tier two instruments. However, it is extremely unwise for an insurer to seek to push the gearing rules to the limit by introducing the maximum in terms of other types of capital that the current core tier one capital will support. The multiplier can work in reverse: any reduction in the profit and loss account balance as a result of a bad trading year will reduce core tier one capital and therefore *also* reduce the amount of other capital that can be recognised.

4.4 Valuation of assets and determination of liabilities

GENPRU 1.3.4R provides what is sometimes referred to as "the general GAAP presumption". This specifies that, unless there is a regulatory rule in GENPRU or INSPRU to the contrary, any asset, liability, exposure, equity or income statement item must be recognised and have its value determined in accordance with GAAP. GAAP for this purpose can represent either the insurance accounts rules made under the Companies Act 2006, which are currently set out in Sch.3 to the Large and Medium-sized Companies (Accounts and Reports) Regulations 2008, or international accounting standards where these are applicable to an insurer's external financial reporting: the definition also extends to Financial Reporting Standards and

Statements of Standard Accounting Practice issued or adopted by the Accounting Standards Board ("ASB") and Statements of Recommended Practice ("SORPs") issued by industry or sectoral bodies recognised for this purpose by the ASB. The most relevant example of the latter for an insurer is the SORP on accounting for insurance business issued by the ABI.

Needless to say, there are a significant number of rules in GENPRU and INSPRU that do provide to the contrary and override the general GAAP presumption: a feature of the regulatory returns is the explicit presentation of the differences between GAAP values and regulatory values both in the derivation of capital resources on Form 3 and in the reconciliations back from regulatory values to GAAP values at the foot of Forms 13, 14 and 15. The principal rules giving rise to differences are the following.

(1)   GENPRU 2.2.155R requires the deduction from tier one capital of any intangible assets.
(2)   The table in GENPRU 2 Annex 1R requires the deduction from tier one capital of any investment by an insurer in its own shares.
(3)   GENPRU 2.2.107R requires, with certain exceptions, a general insurer that discounts its technical provisions in its GAAP accounts to deduct from tier one capital the difference between the discounted and the undiscounted provisions (i.e. reverse out the benefit of discounting).
(4)   GENPRU 2.2.250R requires an insurer that is not a pure reinsurer to deduct from its total capital resources the value of any asset that does not appear in the list of admissible assets in GENPRU 2 Annex 7R. The Annex includes the majority of assets that will routinely feature in an insurer's balance sheet (although there is a curious omission of "other debtors"). Circumstances in which an asset may need to be deducted under this rule include:
      (a)   Premium debtors more than three months overdue.
      (b)   Derivatives, quasi-derivatives and stock-lending transactions that fail to satisfy the conditions in INSPRU 3.2 to be approved.

(c)   Deferred tax assets.

The list of admissible assets does not apply to a pure reinsurer, which is subject instead to the "prudent person" principles of INSPRU 3.1.61A R in respect of the assets in which it is permitted to invest. Prudent person principles are likely to be a feature of Solvency II.

(5)   Where an insurer operates a defined benefit occupational pension scheme, GENPRU 1.3.9R requires it to derecognise any defined benefit asset, but permits it to substitute for the GAAP defined benefit liability a "deficit reduction amount", based on the sum determined in conjunction with the scheme's actuaries or trustees of the additional funding (net of tax) that the insurer will need to pay into the scheme over the following five years period for the purpose of reducing the defined benefit liability.

(6)   GENPRU 1.3 requires investments, and both assets and liabilities arising from derivatives and quasi-derivatives, to be valued where possible on a mark to market basis (taking the more prudent side of the bid/offer spread), or failing that on a mark to model basis. While this will most of the time produce a value corresponding to GAAP, there is no provision within the regulatory rules to allow investments to be valued at amortised cost. Valuation differences may also arise as a result of the requirement of GENPRU 1.3.30R for an insurer to establish and maintain procedures for establishing valuation adjustments and reserves: for example, GENPRU 1.3.32R requires the consideration of reserves for less liquid positions.

(7)   Special rules apply to investments in other group undertakings. These will be considered in Section 4.6.

(8)   Detailed rules for the establishment of mathematical reserves are set out in INSPRU 1.2, and will often give rise to differences from the insurance technical liabilities reported in the accounts. The INSPRU 1.2 rules are grounded on a prospective actuarial valuation on prudent assumptions of all future cash flows expected to arise under or in respect of each of its contracts of long-term insurance. The rules allow reinsurance cashflows not to be valued where they are unambiguously linked to the emergence of surplus and certain other conditions are

satisfied: the extension of these rules by INSPRU 1.2.77A R(1) to analogous non-reinsurance financing arrangements, means that certain types of contingent loan that an insurer has received need not be treated as a regulatory liability.

(9) INSPRU 2.1.22R defines a series of mathematical limits for counterparty and asset exposures, which seek to reinforce the high level principle of INSPRU 2.1.8R that taking into account relevant risks, a firm must restrict its counterparty exposures and asset exposures to prudent levels and ensure that those exposures are adequately diversified. The limits are expressed as percentages of a yardstick figure known as the "business amount", based on gross liabilities plus capital resources, and are graded so that higher percentages apply to higher quality exposures (e.g. an approved counterparty has a higher limit than a non-approved corporate counterparty which has a higher limit than an individual). Some exposures, such as Zone A Governments, UCITS schemes, premium debtors and amounts due from reinsurers are excluded from the limits. Where an exposure does exceed the limit, the excess is deducted from total capital resources. Exposures can be mitigated by collateral.

(10) INSPRU 1.4 requires the establishment of an equalisation provision (which represents a regulatory liability) by a general insurer writing credit business, or business falling into one of the defined insurance business groupings defined by INSPRU 1.4.12R. An insurer preparing accounts under Sch.3 will be required to include the equalisation provision calculated under the regulatory rules as a technical provision in those accounts even though it does not represent an actual liability. However, equalisation provisions do not feature in IFRS accounts, and can therefore give rise to a valuation difference between the accounts and the regulatory return.

The term "valuation difference" is used as a sweep up by GENPRU 2.2.105R for all differences between accounts and regulatory values that are not specifically dealt with elsewhere in the table of capital resources in GENRPU 2 Annex 7R. The items referred to in (5), (6), (8) and (10) above all represent valuation differences. Such differences are aggregated: if the total is positive, it is added to core tier one capital; if the total is negative it is deducted in arriving at total tier one capital after deductions.

4.5   The regulatory return

A considerable amount of information needs to be filed by an insurer with the FSA, either as a matter of routine or on an ad hoc basis. This section will concentrate on the annual return submitted under IPRU(INS) on a pillar 1 basis, where the requirements are extremely prescriptive, and will also touch on the quarterly return required by SUP Appendix 2 of an insurer that has submitted a scheme of operations and the documentation required in respect of pillar 2. The next section will cover the group capital adequacy report.

4.5.1   *The annual return under IPRU(INS)*

Chapter 9 of IPRU(INS) requires an insurer to prepare an annual return in a prescribed format and to submit this to the FSA within three months of the end of a financial year provided that in addition to a signed hard copy the return is provided in an approved electronic format: a reduced filing period of 2 months and 15 days applies to the minority of insurers that continue to file in paper form only.

Much of the return consists of Forms designed for computer processing which are set out in the Appendices to IPRU(INS): most insurers use one of the commercially available software packages to generate these Forms. In addition to the Forms there is a significant "words" part of the return, including supplementary notes and statements and other documents required by rules within Chapter 9. In preparing the return, the requirements of IPRU(INS) need to be read in conjunction with the text of GENPRU and INSPRU, as these set out underlying rules relevant to the determination of the figures that are reported on the Forms.

The following Appendices to IPRU(INS) prescribe reporting information for the annual return:

Appendix 9.1: Balance sheet and profit and loss account (Forms 1–3 and 10–19)
Appendix 9.2: General insurance business: revenue account and other information (Forms 20A and 20–39)
Appendix 9.3: Long-term insurance business: revenue account and other information (Forms 40–60)
Appendix 9.4: Abstract of valuation report
Appendix 9.4A: Abstract of valuation report for realistic valuation
Appendix 9.5: General insurance business: additional information on reinsurance ceded:
Appendix 9.6: Directors' certificate and report of the auditor

The following statements also feature in the annual return:

Rule 9.25—major treaty reinsurers
Rule 9.26—major facultative reinsurers
Rule 9.27—major reinsurance cedants
Rule 9.29—additional information on derivative contracts
Rule 9.30—additional information on controllers
Rule 9.32A—additional information on financial reinsurance and financing arrangements
Rule 9.36—information on the actuary who has been appointed to perform the with-profits actuary function.

4.5.1.1 *Appendix 9.1—Balance sheet and profit and loss account*

Most of this Appendix deals with the build up to the comparison on Forms 1 and 2 of the return between the insurer's capital resources and its capital resources requirement: Form 16, which provides the non-technical part of the profit and loss account is included but seems slightly out of place. The following diagrams shows separately for general and life insurers the Forms and their inter-relationship: Forms relating to resources are on the left of the page and Forms relating to requirements are on the right.

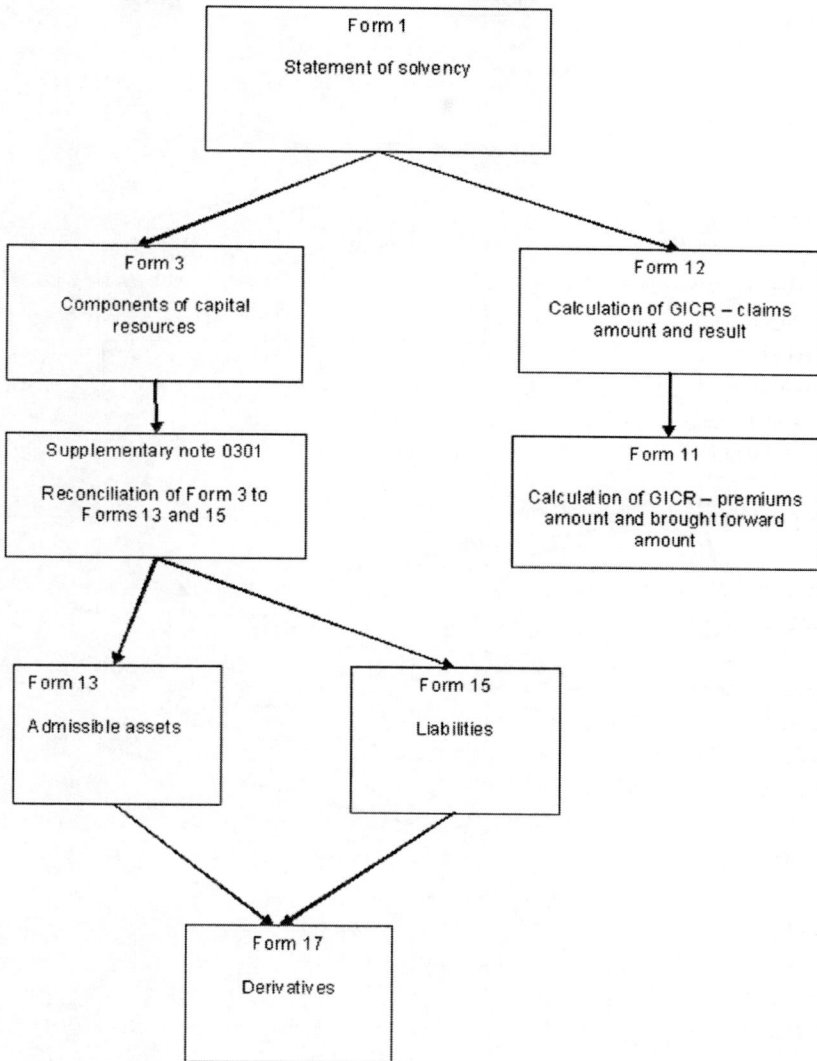

Figure 4.1. General Insurer

The diagram for life insurers is slightly more complicated because, apart from the separate sources for the LTICR and the WPICC there are additional balance sheet Forms resulting from

```
                    ┌─────────────────────────┐
                    │         Form 2          │
                    │                         │
                    │   Statement of solvency │
                    └─────────────────────────┘
```

Form 3	Form 60	Form 18
Components of capital resources	LTICR	WPICC (realistic basis life firms only)

Supplementary note 0301	Form 19
Reconciliation of Form 3 to Forms 13, 14 and 15	Realistic balance sheet

Form 13 category 1	Form 13 category 10	Form 14	Form 15
Admissible assets (other than long term business)	Admissible assets (long term business)	Long term business liabilities and margins	Other than long term liabilities

Form 17
Derivatives

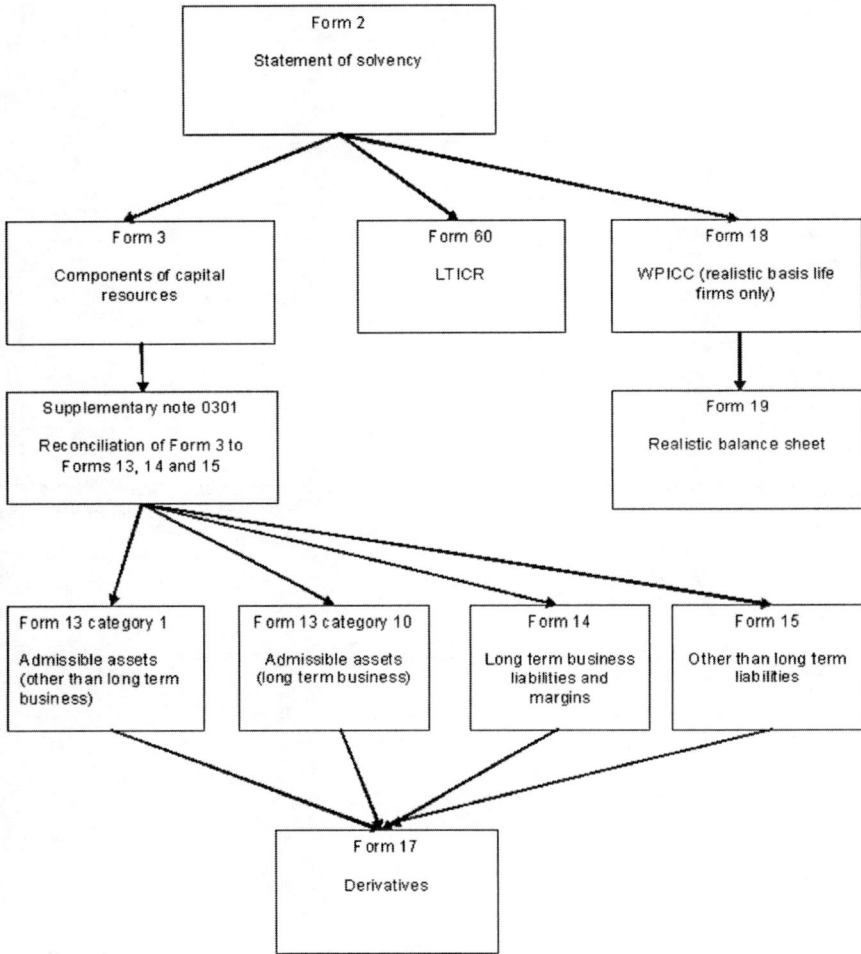

Figure 4.2. Life Insurer

the requirement of INSPRU 1.5.18R for a life insurer to identify separately and maintain the assets relating to its long term insurance business (*see* Chapter 9). In effect these assets are ring-fenced to form a life fund, and can only be used for the purposes of the long term insurance business until there has been an actuarial valuation demonstrating the existence of surplus in the fund. A proportion of surplus in a fund may need to be allocated to with-profits policyholders by way of bonuses in line with the policyholders' contractual entitlement or reasonable expectations: surplus not so utilised can be transferred to become available to the shareholders (in which case the assets corresponding to the surplus will move from the category 10 to the category 1 Form 13, with the transfer being shown on Forms 40 and 16), or carried forward unappropriated in the fund.

4.5.1.2 *Appendix 9.2—General insurance business revenue account and other information*

In the Companies Act accounts, a single technical account is provided for general insurance business, with a limited amount of segmental information being provided in the notes to the return. One key feature of Appendix 9.2 is the sub-division of the accounts information into reporting categories prescribed by the FSA, so that the information can be reviewed on a granular basis and meaningful comparisons be made between insurers. The other particularly important aspect is the analysis of information by accident or underwriting year, to enable claims development statistics to be prepared from the return (and previous returns submitted) so that an appropriate challenge can be made to the adequacy of claims provisions.

There are a relatively large number of prescribed Forms in this Appendix for a number of reasons.

- The rules are flexible as to whether business is accounted for on an accident year basis (whereby claims are classified according to the date on which the incident giving rise to the claim occurred) or an underwriting year basis (whereby incidents are classified by reference to the date on which the policy under which the claim is being made incepted). Except for Forms 20 and 20A, different Forms are used to report accident year and underwriting year business.

- In some cases different Forms are used to report (1) direct insurance and facultative reinsurance business and (2) treaty reinsurance business.

- There are two levels of detail required, with one set of Forms relating to relatively broad groupings of business (mainly referred to as "combined categories") prepared exclusively in sterling and a second set relating to more detailed groupings (referred to as "risk categories") prepared by currency and by reporting territory. De minimis limits apply, but whereas at the combined category level, de minimis categories are reported in aggregate on a set of balancing category Forms, at the risk category level only the categories above the limits are reported.

The following diagram sets out the structure of the primary Forms in this Appendix.

In addition, the Appendix includes a Form 30 providing information where technical provisions are discounted (which seems relatively pointless as the benefit of any discounting adjustment is normally reversed out on Form 3), a Form 36 specifying the exchange rates used when any Form has been completed in a currency other than sterling, and Forms 37–39 which document the calculation of the equalisation provision.

4.5.1.3 *Appendix 9.3—Long-term business revenue account and other information*

This Appendix is rather different in character to Appendix 9.2, as the contents are largely "other information" of various types and the Forms break down into a number of distinct groups, most of which have no connection with the revenue account.

(1) The actual revenue account, which appears on Form 40, and which is supported by Form 41 (providing additional analysis of premiums), Form 42 (providing additional information on claims) and Form 43 (providing additional information on expenses). There is no concept equivalent to the reporting categories which the FSA prescribe for

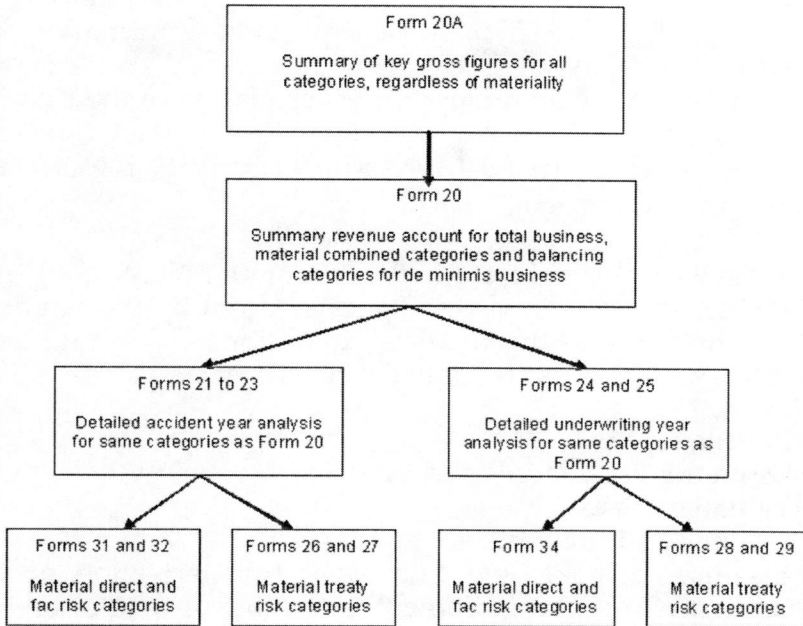

```
┌─────────────────────────────────────────┐
│              Form 20A                     │
│                                           │
│   Summary of key gross figures for all    │
│   categories, regardless of materiality   │
└─────────────────────────────────────────┘
                    │
┌─────────────────────────────────────────┐
│              Form 20                      │
│                                           │
│   Summary revenue account for total       │
│   business, material combined categories   │
│   and balancing categories for de         │
│   minimis business                        │
└─────────────────────────────────────────┘
```

Forms 21 to 23 — Detailed accident year analysis for same categories as Form 20

Forms 24 and 25 — Detailed underwriting year analysis for same categories as Form 20

Forms 31 and 32 — Material direct and fac risk categories

Forms 26 and 27 — Material treaty risk categories

Form 34 — Material direct and fac risk categories

Forms 28 and 29 — Material treaty risk categories

Figure 4.3

general business. Forms are prepared for each separate long-term business fund (with summary Forms where there is more than one fund), and Forms 41–43 provide inter alia a breakdown into UK life, UK pension and overseas business.

(2) Forms 44, 45, 55 and 56, which provide information specifically relating to linked business.

(3) Forms 46 and 47, which provides an analysis of new business.

(4) Forms 48 and 49, which provide information on yields to support interest rate assumptions in the actuarial valuation.

(5) Forms 50–54, which summarise mathematical reserves, and are supported by Form 57 which analyses the valuation interest rate.

(6) Form 58, which analyses the composition and distribution of surplus.
(7) Forms 59A and 59B, which provide information on with-profits payouts.
(8) Form 60, which summarises the calculation of the LTICR.

4.5.1.4 *Appendix 9.4 and 9.4A—Abstract of valuation report and realistic valuation report*

Appendix 9.4 will be present in the return for any life company as the abstract of the investigation carried out by the actuarial function holder into the financial condition of the long-term insurance business. Its contents cover:

• Product range.
• Discretionary charges and benefits.
• Valuation basis.
• Options and guarantees.
• Expense, mismatching (including the derivation of the resilience capital requirement) and other special reserves.
• Reinsurance.
• Reversionary bonuses.

A realistic basis life insurer will need to provide an Appendix 9.4A realistic report, explaining the methods and assumptions underpinning the calculation of the WPICC. It is also necessary for such a firm to make a half yearly submission to the FSA under r.9.3A of IPRU(INS), setting out any changes to the methods and assumptions since the previous realistic valuation report, and providing Forms 2, 18 and 19.

4.5.1.5 *Appendix 9.5—Additional information on general insurance business reinsurance ceded*

Appendix 9.5 provides information on all non-facultative contracts of reinsurance ceded entered into or modified during the financial year, and also includes maximum net probable loss information. It is complemented by the identification of major treaty and facultative reinsurers by the rr.9.25 and 9.26 statements respectively, and by the information on financial reinsurance and other financing arrangements on the r.9.32A statement. An arrangement is disclosable under r.9.32A where the value placed on the future payments under a contract of reinsurance ceded (or analogous arrangement) is not commensurate with the economic value provided by that contract, after taking account of the level of risk transferred, or where there are terms or foreseeable contingencies (other than the insured event) that have the potential to affect materially the future value of the contract.

4.5.1.6   *Appendix 9.6—Directors' certificate and report of the auditor*

The annual return has to be signed off by two directors and the chief executive (or, if there is no chief executive, by the company secretary). In addition, the same individuals are required to sign off a certificate which is annexed to the return. For all insurers, the certificate is required to state:

(1) That the return has been prepared in accordance with the requirements of IPRU(INS), INSPRU and GENPRU; and
(2) That the insurer has, throughout the financial year, complied in all material respects with the requirements of SYSC and PRIN as well as the provisions of IPRU(INS), GENPRU and INSPRU, and that it is reasonable to believe that the insurer has continued so to comply subsequently and will continue so to comply in future.

While the first of these statements simply provides confirmation that the return has been drawn up in accordance with the rules, the latter is extremely wide ranging and would need to be qualified if there had been any breaches during the year. Additional statements are required in the certificate for a life insurer, dealing with the sufficiency of premiums, the adequacy of the mathematical reserves, the management of the with-profits fund and the obtaining of actuarial advice.

The annual return is subject to audit, with the exception of Appendix 9.5, the rr.9.30 and 9.32A statements and certain of the Appendix 9.3 Forms. The primary statement that the auditor is required to make is whether, in his opinion, the Forms and other documents subject to audit have been properly prepared in accordance with the rules. In the case of a life insurer, the auditor is also required to state whether in his opinion the method and assumptions used by the insurer to perform the actuarial valuation as set out in the valuation reports appropriately reflect the requirements of INSPRU 1.2 (and where applicable INSPRU 1.3), and to confirm that advice has been taken from an appropriately qualified actuary independent of the insurer.

4.5.2 Quarterly reporting

Although annual reporting is the norm, a significant number of insurers are currently subject to a requirement under SUP Appendix 2 to submit quarterly information, a feature that will apply across the market under Solvency II. The trigger for quarterly reporting is the submission of a "scheme of operations": once a scheme has been submitted, quarterly information is required to be submitted to the FSA for the duration of the scheme.

SUP Appendix 2 requires the submission of a scheme of operations when an insurer breaches capital requirements or decides to cease accepting new contracts of insurance. The application pack submitted by an insurer applying for Part IV permission is deemed to include a scheme of operations: the FSA may also require a scheme of operations from a firm that is applying to vary its Part IV permission or which is under the control of a new parent undertaking.

There are no Forms prescribed by the FSA for quarterly reporting: rather the minimum information to be provided is prescribed, but it is up to the individual insurer as to how this is presented. The required elements of a quarterly report are:

(a) A summary profit and loss account, indicating gross and net premiums and claims analysed by class, investment return, expenses, other charges and income, taxation and dividends paid and accrued.

(b) A summary balance sheet indicating investments analysed by class, assets held to cover linked liabilities, other assets and liabilities, capital and reserves, subordinated liabilities, the fund for future appropriations, technical provisions gross and net analysed by class and other liabilities and credits.

(c) A statement of capital resources.

In practice many insurers choose to report using slightly adapted versions of the annual return forms.

4.5.3 *Pillar 2 reporting*

Pillar two does not give rise to formal regulatory reporting, in the form of a submission to the FSA, in the same way as pillar one. When the FSA plans to review an insurer's ICA, it will provide a detailed list of the information that it needs to see. However, an insurer is required by GENPRU 1.2.60R to make a written record of its pillar two assessments and to retain this record for at least three years. The record must include:

- The major sources of risk identified.
- How the insurer intends to deal with those risks.
- Details of the stress tests and scenario analysis carried out, including any assumptions made in relation to scenario design, and the resulting financial resources estimated to be required.

4.6 Group Supervision

Insurance supervision has historically concentrated on the individual entities conducting insurance business, although regard has been had to the identity of those who are controllers of an insurance company, and prior regulatory approval has been required before control can be obtained or increased beyond certain benchmarks (*see* Chapter 3). Since the Insurance Groups Directive was implemented in 2001 there has been an increased focus on the group to which an insurer belongs, although this represents supplementary supervision and does not in any sense replace the established solo supervision approach. There are essentially three aspects to group supervision:

(a) The treatment of investments by an insurer in other group undertakings.
(b) The requirement for an insurer to calculate and report group solvency at the level of an insurance parent undertaking of which it is a subsidiary.
(c) The disclosure of intra-group transactions.

Each of these will be considered in turn.

4.6.1 Investments in other group undertakings

The normal market to market/mark to model rules of GENPRU 1.3 are overridden in the case of certain investments in group undertakings, generally in favour of what will be referred to in this section as a "look through" valuation, which has regard to the underlying balance sheet of the other group company. There are three situations that need to be distinguished.

(a) Where the other group undertaking falls into the definition of a "regulated related undertaking", a look through approach is mandatory.
(b) Where the other group undertaking is a subsidiary of the insurer, but not a regulated related undertaking, the use of a look through approach is optional, failing which mark to market/model applies.
(c) Where the other group undertaking represents an ancillary services undertaking, it is (somewhat illogically) in effect valued at zero.

The term "regulated related undertaking" has a technical definition and can exclude some companies that are FSA regulated (e.g. insurance intermediaries) and include others that are not regulated by anybody. The definition encompasses a regulated entity (a credit institution, a regulated insurance entity or an investment firm), an insurance undertaking that is not a regulated insurance entity, an asset management company, a financial institution, a financial holding company and an insurance holding company. The word "related" means either that the undertaking is a subsidiary of the insurer or that the insurer has a participation (in effect 20 per cent or more of the voting rights or capital) in the undertaking.

For the purpose of valuing and reporting on Form 13 in the regulatory return shares in a regulated related undertaking (or a non-regulated subsidiary for which the insurer has elected to apply the look through basis), the insurer's proportionate share of the regulatory surplus value of the undertaking is used. The regulatory surplus value represents that undertaking's total capital after deductions, with certain adjustments, less its individual capital resources requirement. The proportionate share principle means that the proportion of the regulatory surplus value that is recognised is based on the proportion of the number of shares issued by the undertaking that is held directly or indirectly by the insurer. Where, however, the undertaking is in deficit and is a subsidiary undertaking of the insurer, the full amount of the deficit must be recognised regardless of the proportion of shares held.

Where one or more of the regulated related undertakings of the insurer is itself an insurance undertaking, special rules (analogous to those relating to the group capital adequacy report considered in Section 4.6.2) apply, and the insurer, which would then represent "a participating insurance undertaking", has to prepare what is referred to as an "adjusted solo solvency calculation". In these circumstances, the normal pillar one rule of GENPRU 2.1.13R is overridden by the requirement of INSPRU 6.1.9R for the insurer to maintain at all times tier one capital resources and tier two capital resources of such an amount that its group capital resources are equal to or exceed its group capital resources requirement.

The group capital resources requirement ("GCRR") represents the aggregate of the insurer's own solo capital requirement and its proportionate share of the individual capital resources requirement of each of its regulated related undertakings.

Group capital resources are based on the insurer's own resources but adjusting these for the difference between the book value of its investment in a regulated related undertaking, and its proportionate share of the underlying capital resources of that undertaking. Adjustments are made for inadmissible assets and assets in excess of the market risk and counterparty exposure limits within the regulated related undertaking.

In the annual return, a participating insurance undertaking will prepare Forms 1, 2 and 3 on an adjusted solo basis. There will consequently be a difference in approach between Form 13 (where the investment in a regulated related undertaking is reported net of that undertaking's individual capital resources requirement) and Form 3, where the figures are "grossed up" for that undertaking's capital resources requirement as that is treated as part of the GCRR on Form 1 or 2 rather than as a deduction in arriving at the resources. This will give rise to an adjustment in the reconciliation between net admissible assets per Forms 13, 14 and 15 and capital resources after deductions per Form 3, which has to be included in the return as supplementary note 0301.

4.6.2   Insurance parent undertakings

The Insurance Groups Directive in principle requires a calculation to be performed at the level of each parent undertaking above an insurer in the group structure, but allows a member State to dispense with calculations at the intermediate holding company level, and is not specific as to the action to be taken if the calculation produces a deficit. The FSA decided at the time that the Directive was implemented to require the calculation at the level only of the ultimate "insurance parent undertaking" and (where different) the ultimate EEA insurance parent undertaking, and subsequently made the test at the level of an ultimate EEA insurance parent undertaking a hard one The parent undertaking as such is not regulated: rather, the obligation is on the FSA-regulated insurer to ensure that its capital resources are of such an amount that the group capital resources of the parent undertaking exceed that undertaking's group capital resources requirement.

An insurance parent undertaking can be itself an insurance undertaking which has a subsidiary that is an insurer, or an insurance holding company—defined as a parent undertaking, the main business of which is to acquire and hold participations in subsidiary undertakings, where such subsidiary undertakings are either exclusively or mainly insurance undertakings. The "exclusively or mainly" test means that a holding company which has subsidiaries in a variety of sectors, and where the insurance subsidiaries are dwarfed by the non-insurance subsidiaries, will not be regarded as an insurance holding company and will fall outside the scope of the group capital requirements.

The methodology of calculating group capital resources and the GCRR is similar to that referred to in relation to the adjusted solo calculation. An insurance holding company will have an individual capital requirement of nil, as it is not performing regulated activities, so the GCRR will represent the sum of its proportionate share of the individual capital resources requirement of each of its regulated related undertakings. The methodology of arriving at group capital resources by adjusting for the difference between the book value of the group's investment in the capital resources of a subsidiary, and those capital resources also normally holds good. Particular points to note are:

(a) In the case of a non-EEA ultimate insurance parent undertaking, the insurer can make an election to apply an accounting consolidation approach, rather than the methodology described.

(b) For a regulated related undertaking located in a designated state or territory (which includes inter alia all other EEA States, North America, Australasia, South Africa and Singapore) it is possible to apply local rules rather than FSA rules in determining the capital resources and requirement for that undertaking.

(c) In performing the calculation for a parent undertaking, there is no requirement to make deductions for assets in excess of market risk and counterparty exposure limits.

(d) Gearing rules, analogous to those applying to an insurer under GENPRU 2.2, are applied to group capital resources.

INSPRU 6.1.8R requires the regular calculation of group capital resources and the GCRR. Formal reporting to the FSA is required annually by Part V of Chapter 9 of IPRU(INS) within four months of the end of the relevant financial year (which can be either that of the insurer or of the relevant parent undertaking). The rules require the submission of:

(1) The name, location of the head office and principal activity of the parent undertaking.

(2) The group capital resources.

(3) The group capital resources requirement.

(4) The difference between (2) and (3).

(5) For an ultimate EEA insurance parent undertaking that prepares consolidated accounts, a reconciliation between group capital resources and shareholders' funds, subordinated liabilities and other relevant amounts published in those consolidated accounts.

(6) For an ultimate EEA insurance parent undertaking that publishes a capital statement under FRS 27, an explanation of differences between the amounts included in that capital statement and group capital resources.

(7) Details of deficits in regulated related undertakings.

(8) An auditor's statement, which falls some way short of a full scope audit report.

4.6.3 Intra-group transactions

There have always been a number of specific disclosures required in the regulatory return of connected party transactions—for example information about connected reinsurers and cedants in the rr.9.25, 9.26 and 9.27 statements. To address the Directive requirement for the supervision by the competent authorities of intra-group transactions, the existing

specific disclosures were complemented by the general requirement of r.9.39 of IPRU(INS) to disclose material connected
party transactions in the supplementary notes to the annual
return.

The concept of "connection" goes beyond parent/subsidiary/
fellow-subsidiary relationships and includes participations
(>20 per cent interest in or by the insurer) and natural persons.
A transaction is "material" and therefore disclosable if the price
actually paid for the transfer of assets or liabilities or the
provision of services, or the price that would have been paid or
received had that transaction been notified at arm's length
between unconnected parties exceeds a benchmark based on 5
per cent of non-linked insurance liabilities net of reinsurance.

The prescribed disclosure comprises the names of the transact-
ing parties, a description of the relationship between the
parties, a description of the transaction, the amounts involved,
any other elements of the transaction necessary for a proper
understanding of its effect upon the financial standing or
performance of the insurer and amounts written off in the
period in respect of debts due to or from connected parties.

4.7   Solvency II

The Solvency II Directive was adopted by the European
Parliament on 22 April 2009 and endorsed by the Council of
Ministers on May 5, 2009. The Directive provides a framework
for future regulation, with the detail appearing elsewhere. EU
financial services legislation is subject to the Lamfalussy
approach which comprises a four-level procedure intended to
speed up the legislative process.

Level 1—the development of framework legislation voted on
by the Parliament and Council, with implementing powers for
level 2 measures.

Level 2—more detailed implementing measures to operational-
ise the level 1 framework, prepared by the Commission

following advice from the European Insurance and Occupational Pensions Authority ("EIOPA"), or its predecessor the Committee of European Insurance and Occupational Pensions Supervisors ("CEIOPS").

Level 3—guidance developed by EIOPA to provide joint interpretation recommendations, consistent guidelines and common standards.

Level 4—enforcement of all EU measures, led by the Commission, but underpinned by enhanced cooperation between member States, regulators and the private sector.

At the date of publication of this chapter, level 2 advice exists in the form of recommendations submitted by CEIOPS to the Commission, but the definitive measures had not been published. Although the general shape is known, there is therefore a degree of uncertainty over some of the detail. The framework Directive will need to be transposed into UK law, and will give rise to amendments to GENPRU and INSPRU that will have to be consulted upon by the FSA before they are introduced. However, level 2 measures apply directly in member States without the need for transposition. Although the FSA's practice is to incorporate the text of level 2 measures into the Handbook with a UK flag, there is in effect nothing to consult upon as the text is a given once it has been finalised at European level.

Solvency II is based on a "three pillar" approach. The pillars, which are analogous to those that apply to banks under Basel, are not referred to as such in the Directive, but are defined by EIOPA as a convenient way of grouping Solvency II requirements.

- Pillar 1—this contains the basic financial requirements, and aims to ensure that insurers are adequately capitalised with sufficient risk-based capital. It provides for the use of internal models by firms.
- Pillar 2—this is concerned with imposing higher standards of risk management and governance within a firm's

organisation. The pillar also gives supervisors greater powers to challenge firms on risk management issues. The Own Risk and Solvency Assessment ("ORSA") requires a firm to undertake its own forward looking assessment of its risk, corresponding capital requirements and adequacy of capital resources.

- Pillar 3—this aims to achieve greater levels of transparency in the information provided to supervisors and the public.

Under pillar 1, each insurance or reinsurance undertaking is required to hold eligible own funds (equivalent to capital resources—a tiering methodology applies under Solvency II) to cover its Solvency Capital Requirement ("SCR"). The SCR is analogous in some respects to the ICA, as it is intended to correspond to the value at risk of the basic own funds of the firm subject to a confidence level of 99.5 per cent over a one year period. It is accompanied by a Minimum Capital Requirement, based on an 85 per cent confidence level, and subject to an absolute floor in Euros similar to the BCRR. The SCR is required to cover at least:

- non-life underwriting risk
- life underwriting risk
- health underwriting risk
- market risk
- credit risk
- operational risk

This classification is somewhat reminiscent of the current structuring of INSPRU.

The SCR can be calculated in accordance with the European standard formula prescribed under the Directive. A number of quantitative impact studies ("QISs"), in which many UK insurers have participated, have been carried out by CEIOPS in order to refine the calibration of the formula. However, there is an option under art.119 of the Solvency II Directive to use an internal model to calculate the SCR, or relevant risk modules thereof, where the risk profile of the firm deviates significantly from the assumptions underpinning the standard formula. A number of requirements need to be satisfied, including a use test under art.120 (in effect that the model will be widely used and play an important role in the firm's system of governance, and does not exist purely to calculate a regulatory capital requirement). Any use of an internal model is subject to prior regulatory approval: the process and timeline for this was initially set out by the FSA in DP 08/4: *Insurance risk management: the path to Solvency II*, but there have been worrying indications that the FSA may only have the resources to review the internal models of the larger insurers in sufficient time if Solvency II is implemented according to its present timeline.

CEIOPS published consultation paper 58 dealing with Supervisory Reporting and Disclosure in June 2009. After consideration of the responses received, this led in October 2009 to advice from CEIOPS to the European Commission on level two measures in this area. Key elements of the advice provided were:

- The Solvency and Financial Condition Report ("SFCR"), providing the information to be publicly disclosed.
- The Report to Supervisors ("RTS"), which provides information that to be reported regularly to the regulatory authorities but not publicly disclosed.
- Quantitative reporting templates, which would be incorporated into the Solvency Financial and Condition Report when the level 3 guidance was issued.

CEIOPS considered that it was appropriate to subject some of the supervisory reporting and public disclosure requirements to external audit, but had not at the time of the advice reached firm conclusions as to which documents should be subject to audit and what the level of assurance would be.

The SFCR is intended to be published and submitted electronically to the supervisor within 14 weeks of the end of the financial year, which is marginally longer than the three months currently allowed for the filing of an electronic FSA return. Public disclosure will be achieved through publication on the website, and by sending a copy to any stakeholder who requests one within five business days. The structure of the SFCR will be as follows:

- Executive summary.
- Business and performance
- System of governance
- Risk profile
- Regulatory balance sheet
- Capital management
- Information for undertakings with an approved internal model
- Quantitative templates

The RTS is intended to be a standalone document which will incorporate the information in the SFCR and adopt the same general structure. The same 14 week filing deadline will apply. On the first financial year end after the Directive comes into force, all undertakings will be required to complete a full qualitative RTS. Thereafter, unless an undertaking is notified by its supervisor that a full qualitative RTS will have to be completed annually, only material changes will have to be reported, although it will be necessary to report annually all the information within the SFCR. A periodic full qualitative RTS will be required at a frequency set by the supervisor, which CEIOPS recommends should not exceed five years.

Chapter 5

The Establishment of Branches and Cross-border Provision of Services

Robert Stirling and James Smethurst,
Partners: Freshfields Bruckhaus Deringer LLP[1]

5.1 Overview

5.1.1 Concept of the insurance, reinsurance and insurance mediation passport

European legislation establishes a common system for the authorisation and prudential supervision of insurance and reinsurance undertakings. Such an undertaking is supervised by the Member State in which it has its head office. This is its "home Member State" (or "home state"). That authorisation, in turn, enables that insurer or reinsurer to carry on insurance or reinsurance business anywhere in the European Union ("EU")[2] without the need for further authorisation. This is referred to as the "insurance passport".

The insurance passport originally only applied to insurers carrying on direct insurance business, or a combination of direct and reinsurance (including retrocession) business. These undertakings are referred to in the remainder of this Chapter as "insurers" or "direct insurers". Their passport only applies to their direct insurance business. Their reinsurance business is

---

[1]   The authors are grateful to Jonathan Goodliffe, solicitor at Freshfields Bruckhaus Deringer LLP, for his help in producing this chapter.
[2]   By virtue of the EEA Agreement, the single passport regime extends to all EEA states (*see* Section 5.1.6).

separately addressed (*see* Section 5.8 below). The passport was extended to "pure reinsurers" on 10 December 2007. Pure reinsurers are undertakings that carry on reinsurance business but not direct insurance business. They are referred to as "reinsurers" in the remainder of this Chapter.

A passporting regime for insurance intermediaries came into force on 14 January 2005. It is described separately at Section 5.10.

The rights of insurers, reinsurers and insurance intermediaries to carry on business throughout Europe derive, at a general level, from the Treaty on the Functioning of the European Union ("the Treaty"). It was amended by the Treaty of Amsterdam, the Treaty of Nice and the Treaty of Lisbon. In addition, a framework for the operation of the passport is contained in distinct EU directives which apply separately to direct insurers, reinsurers and insurance intermediaries. These directives have been transposed (or should have been transposed) into Member States' domestic law (*see* Sections 5.2 and 5.10). The Directives applying to direct insurers and reinsurers are due to be amended (with no significant changes so far as this chapter is concerned) and consolidated into the Solvency II Directive 2009/138/EC from 1 January 2014. There are also proposals by the Commission to amend the directive affecting insurance intermediaries.

5.1.2 *Origins of the concept of the insurance and reinsurance passport: the Treaty*

The basic goals of the Treaty include establishing "an internal market . . . without internal frontiers in which the free movement of goods, persons, services and capital is ensured in accordance with the provisions of the Treaties" (art.26). In addition, art.49[3] embodies the principle of the right of establishment. This is the right of an undertaking in any Member State to set up a branch or agency in another Member State. Article 56 of the Treaty[4] establishes the right of an

---

[3]   Article 52 of the Treaty before amendment by the Treaty of Amsterdam.
[4]   Article 59 of the Treaty before amendment by the Treaty of Amsterdam.

undertaking in one Member State to provide services to customers in other Member States. This distinction between "branch" business and "services" business is an important one. It is discussed further at Section 5.6.

5.1.3 *Origins of the insurance and reinsurance passport: the directives*

Based on the above provisions of the Treaty, the framework for the single insurance market was established in seven stages. There were three directives in relation to life and non-life insurance respectively and one in relation to reinsurance.

The First Non-Life Directive (73/239/EEC) and the First Life Directive (79/267/EEC) (the "First Insurance Directives") introduced a single set of standards for authorisation of insurers. They applied to direct insurers only. These directives also introduced some coordination of regulation compatible with art.49 of the Treaty.

The Second Non-Life Directive (88/357/EEC) and the Second Life Directive (90/619/EEC) (the "Second Insurance Directives") removed some of the barriers to the cross-border supply of services.

The Third Non-Life Directive (92/49/EC) and the Third Life Directive (92/96/EEC) (the "Third Insurance Directives") established the passport in its current form. They were introduced as part of the single market initiative in 1992. The Third Life Directive was modelled closely on the Third Non-Life Directive. However, it contained certain more onerous provisions specific to the regulation of life insurance.

With effect from 19 December 2002, the First, Second and Third Life Directives were replaced by the consolidated text contained in Directive 2002/83/EC on life assurance (the "Life Directive"). A similar exercise has not been effected in relation to non-life insurance.

189

The Insurance Mediation Directive (2002/92/EC) was adopted by the European Council in December 2002. It was due to be transposed by Member States by 14 January 2005. The Directive establishes a harmonised framework for the sale and administration of insurance throughout the EU. It catches brokers and other insurance intermediaries. Other persons may be caught even when they carry out insurance mediation activities incidentally to their main business. Under the regime, intermediaries are registered in their home state to sell insurance or carry out certain acts in relation to the administration of insurance contracts. With the benefit of that registration they are then able to passport those activities throughout the EU, in much the same way as under the insurance passport described above. The general requirements of the Insurance Mediation Directive are considered further in Chapter 7. The passporting rules applying to insurance intermediaries are covered at Section 5.10.

The Reinsurance Directive (2005/68/EC) was adopted in November 2005. It was due to be transposed into the laws of EU Member States on 10 December 2007. It extended the passport to reinsurers on a different basis to that applying to direct insurers (*see* Section 5.5).

UK implementation was achieved first by amendments to the Financial Services and Markets Act 2000 ("FSMA 2000"). Secondly, changes were made to the Handbook of Rules and Guidance and to rules made by the Financial Services Authority ("FSA") under FSMA 2000.

These directives are, however, consolidated, without significant changes so far as the subject matter of this chapter is concerned, under the Solvency II Directive (2009/138/EC) with effect from 1 January 2014 (*see* Chapter 4). Solvency II will also effect a major reform of the rules relating to the prudential regulation of insurers and reinsurers.

5.1.4 Mutual recognition

Insurance is a regulated industry. Direct insurance is more heavily regulated than reinsurance. Therefore, the single market is based on a system of mutual recognition. This has been achieved by harmonisation of national laws according to the requirements of the relevant EU directives. The home state has responsibility for prudential regulation of the activity of an insurance or reinsurance undertaking, wherever that undertaking carries on business.

Under the Insurance and Reinsurance Directives, the home state has responsibility for authorisation and the financial supervision of an insurer or reinsurer. In turn, a (re)insurer's right to provide services into, or establish a branch in, another Member State (the "host Member State" or "host state") derives from its home state authorisation. This must be recognised as sufficient authorisation by the host state authorities.

5.1.5 Summary of the procedure applying to direct insurers

To establish a branch in, or provide services into, another Member State, a direct insurer must follow certain notification procedures prescribed by the Insurance Directives. Broadly, these involve providing the relevant home state regulator with certain information. That authority, in turn, passes the information on to the competent regulatory authority of the host state. The host state regulator may impose conditions on business carried on in its territory (whether through a branch or by way of services). However, it may do so only if those conditions are in the interests of the "general good", as discussed further at Section 5.7.

5.1.6 The procedure applying to reinsurers

By contrast reinsurers are not required to adhere to any formalities before carrying on business in the host state, whether they do so through an establishment or by way of services. *See* Section 5.5.

5.1.7 Application of the insurance and reinsurance passport

The insurance and reinsurance passport applies throughout the Member States of the EU. Before May 2004 the Member States were Germany, France, Italy, Spain, Belgium, Luxembourg, the Netherlands, Portugal, Greece, Denmark, the UK, Ireland, Finland, Austria and Sweden. From 1 May 2004 the passport was extended to Cyprus, the Czech Republic, Estonia, Hungary, Latvia, Lithuania, Malta, Poland, Slovakia and Slovenia (each being required to implement the insurance passport into domestic law by that date). The passport was further extended to Bulgaria and Romania on 1 January 2007 under equivalent conditions.

Under the EEA Agreement[5] the passport also extends to Iceland, Norway and Liechtenstein. These states are the remaining states of the European Free Trade Association ("EFTA") with the exception of Switzerland, which did not become a party to the EEA Agreement.

Under the law of the UK the insurance passport further extends to Gibraltar as if it were an EEA state.[6] The FSMA 2000, which implements the insurance passport in the UK, reflects this position.

5.1.8 The special position of Switzerland

As permitted by the First Non-Life Directive, the EU and Switzerland (which is not a member of the EEA) entered into an agreement in 1991.[7] This provided insurance companies in

---

5 The agreement on the European Economic Area signed at Oporto on 2 May 1992. SI 2001/2511.
6 The Financial Services and Markets Act 2000 (Gibraltar) Order 2001 (SI 2001/3084), which has been amended in pursuance of the Reinsurance Directive, treats Gibraltar as if it were an EEA state with regard to the use of the insurance passport by Gibraltar insurers/reinsurers and UK insurers/reinsurers *(see* Articles 2 and 4). But note that where an EEA direct insurer (other than a UK insurer) has already established a branch or provides services in the UK and wishes to do so in Gibraltar, it needs only to comply with the requirements for changing the details of its activities in the UK as if Gibraltar were part of the UK *(see* art.3).
7 [1991] OJ L 205, pp.3–27.

the EU and Switzerland with reciprocal rights to establish branches to carry on non-life business.

The agreement, which entered into force on 1 January 1993, does not apply to life business. It does not confer an automatic passporting right or a right to provide cross-border services. EU Insurers who wish to establish an agency or branch in Switzerland must still apply separately to the Swiss regulator (and vice versa). They must meet the requirements provided for under the agreement in respect of a minimum guarantee fund or minimum solvency margin. Their home state regulator must also certify that they have met the minimum requirements.

The special requirements for Swiss general insurers seeking a UK authorisation are set out in para.8 of Sch.6 to the FSMA 2000. They are exempted from certain requirements that otherwise apply to non-EEA insurers seeking to establish a branch in the UK. These requirements cover the maintenance of assets in the UK and the lodging of security.

The arrangements between the EEA and Switzerland described above are unaffected by the Solvency II Directive.

5.2 How EU legislation has been implemented in the UK

From 1 December 2001, the passporting requirements of the Insurance Directives were transposed in the UK by the FSMA 2000. This was supplemented by the Financial Services and Markets Act 2000 (EEA Passport Rights) Regulations 2001 (SI 2001/2511) ("the Regulations"). The Insurance Companies Act 1982, which formerly implemented the regime, was repealed from that date. Various sections of the Handbook issued by the FSA provide further guidance on the application of the passport under the FSMA 2000 regime. This is indicated where relevant below. Amendments to the FSMA 2000 were effected from 10 December 2007 to extend the passport to reinsurers. The UK Government proposed in June 2011 major changes to the FSMA 2000 regime. These include splitting the FSA's current functions between the Financial Conduct Authority ("FCA") and the Prudential Regulation Authority ("PRA") (*see* Chapter 1). The FSA's functions in relation to the authorisation of insurers and reinsurers and European passporting regime will, under these proposals, be taken over by the PRA. In relation to insurance intermediaries those functions will be exercised by the FCA. The new UK regulatory regime is expected to come into force at the beginning of 2013[8].

Generally, by virtue of s.19 of the FSMA 2000 an insurer or reinsurer may not carry on its business in the UK without first obtaining authorisation from the FSA. This provision catches insurers/reinsurers that have their head office in the UK. The position of non-UK EEA insurers/reinsurers is different.

Direct insurers that comply with certain conditions in Sch.3 to FSMA 2000 are entitled to the insurance passport. They are then granted automatic authorisation under the FSMA 2000 without any need to apply to the FSA.[9] However, the position is different in relation to reinsurers authorised in other EEA states. They qualify for a UK authorisation as soon as they carry on business in the UK, without being subject to any prior notification requirements.

Schedule 3 reflects the notification requirements applying under the Insurance and Reinsurance Directives to firms wishing to passport their business activities into an EEA state. It covers both EEA insurers/reinsurers passporting into the UK and UK direct insurers passporting out.

Schedule 3 is not specific to insurance and reinsurance. It also applies as appropriate to investment firms, credit institutions and financial institutions. There are some differences between the rules as they apply to each sector. These differences are beyond the scope of this chapter.

---

[8]   See "A new approach to financial regulation: the bluprint for reform" HM Treasury, June 2011, CM 8083.

[9]   *See* s.31 and Sch.3, para.12 of the FSMA 2000. NB Sch.3 has been amended by the Financial Services and Markets Act 2000 (EEA Passport Rights) Regulations 2001 (SI 2001/2511).

Section 31 of the FSMA 2000 also confers authorisation under the Act on so-called "Treaty firms". These qualify for authorisation under Sch.4 to that Act. The application of Sch.4 to reinsurance business carried on by direct insurers is considered briefly at Section 5.8. However, this Chapter does not aim to describe in detail the exercise by firms of Treaty rights under that Schedule.

5.3 Procedure for establishment of a branch or provision of services by direct insurers

5.3.1 Overview

Notification requirements that a direct insurer must follow in order to take advantage of the insurance passport are different in the following cases, each of which is considered separately below:

(a) establishment of a branch in the UK by an EEA firm (as defined—see Section 5.3.2);
(b) provision of services into the UK by an EEA firm;
(c) establishment of a branch in an EEA state other than the UK by a UK firm (as defined—see Section 5.3.5); and
(d) provision of services into an EEA state other than the UK by a UK firm.

The terms "EEA firm" and "UK firm" each have a technical meaning.[10] This reflects the fact that not all insurers are entitled to the rights conferred by the Insurance Directives.

In particular, under the Life Directive and the First Non-Life Directive some mutual insurers (including friendly societies (*see* Chapter 11)) are below the financial threshold at which the directives apply. A modified version of this threshold, extending to firms other than mutuals, will apply when the Solvency II Directive comes into force on 1 January 2013, although this may change to 1 January 2014. Or the firms concerned may

---

[10] *See* Sch.3, paras 5 and 10 of the FSMA 2000.

only carry on insurance business to which the directives do not apply. They are referred to as "non-directive insurers or friendly societies" and do not have passporting rights. Moreover the notification requirements in Schedule 3 do not apply to reinsurers. *See* Section 5.5.

5.3.2   General requirements—EEA firms

To qualify for the right to establish a branch in, or provide services into, the UK (the "inward passport") an insurer or reinsurer must:

(a)   have its head office in an EEA state other than the UK;
(b)   carry on insurance business, or in the case of a reinsurer, reinsurance and/or retrocession business; and
(c)   have received authorisation under art.6 of either of the First Insurance Directives or under art.3 of the Reinsurance Directive from its home state regulator,[11]

in which case it is an "EEA firm" (*see* Sch.3, para.5 of the FSMA 2000). An EEA firm which is a direct insurer must also satisfy certain conditions summarised below. Additional guidance for EEA firms wishing to establish a branch in the UK or provide services into the UK is contained in Chapter 13A of the FSA's Supervision Manual. This includes guidance for EEA firms qualifying for authorisation under Sch.3 to the FSMA 2000. It describes how direct insurers wishing to carry on extra activities for which they do not have an EEA right (broadly, the right to passport under the relevant directive) may apply for a "top-up" permission.

5.3.3   Procedure for the establishment of a branch of an EEA direct insurer in the UK

An EEA direct insurer which is seeking to establish a branch in the UK qualifies for authorisation under s.31 of the FSMA 2000 once it satisfies certain "establishment conditions" (Sch.3, paras 12(1) and 13 of the FSMA 2000). The insurer's home state

---

[11]   Article 4 of the Life Directive.

regulator must give the FSA notice that it has given the insurer its consent to establish a branch in the UK (a "consent notice"). The FSA must, in turn, have informed both the insurer and its home state regulator of any host state rules imposed in the "general good" (*see* Section 5.7). The insurer must comply with these rules when carrying on its branch activities. They must be notified to the firm within two months of the date that the FSA received the consent notice.

The consent notice must:

(a) be given in accordance with the relevant insurance directive;
(b) identify the activities to which the consent relates; and
(c) include such other information as is prescribed by the Regulations,[12] being (see reg.2(5)):
   (i) a scheme of operations prepared in accordance with such requirements as may be imposed by the insurer's home state regulator setting out, amongst other things, the types of business to be carried on and the structural organisation of the branch;
   (ii) the name of the insurer's authorised agent;
   (iii) the address in the UK from which information about the business may be obtained and a statement that this is the address for service on the firm's authorised agent;
   (iv) a declaration of membership of the Motor Insurers' Bureau if the insurer intends to cover relevant motor vehicle risks; and
   (v) a statement by the home state regulator attesting that the insurer has the minimum margin of solvency calculated in accordance with the relevant provisions of the First Non-Life or the First Life Directive, as the case may be (when the Solvency II Directive comes

---

[12] Information prescribed in the Regulations reflects the requirements of the Insurance Directives.

into force a certificate of compliance with the Minimum Capital Requirement ("MCR") and the Solvency Capital Requirement ("SCR") under that Directive will be required).[13]

Once a firm has satisfied each of the establishment conditions, it has permission pursuant to its branch authorisation to carry on each activity identified in the consent notice through its UK branch. The permission will be on terms equivalent to those appearing in the notice (*see* Sch.3, para.15(1) and (2) of the FSMA 2000). In practice the permissions granted to passporting direct insurers will cover not just insurance business as such but also other regulated activities incidental to that business[14].

5.3.4 Procedure for notifying provision of services by an EEA direct insurer into the UK

An EEA direct insurer which is seeking to provide services into the UK qualifies for authorisation under s.31 of the FSMA 2000 once it satisfies certain "service conditions" (*see* Sch.3, paras 12(2) and 14 of the FSMA 2000).

The insurer must have given its home state regulator notice of its intention to provide services into the UK (a "notice of intention"). In turn, the FSA must have received notice from the home state regulator (a "regulator's notice") containing the information prescribed in the Regulations. The home state regulator must have informed the insurer that notice has been sent to the FSA. The FSA must then notify the firm of any host state rules imposed in the "general good" within two months of receipt of the regulator's notice.

The regulator's notice must contain the following (*see* reg.3(3)):

---

[13] *See* arts 16 and 17 of the First Non-Life Directive, arts 18–20 of the First Life Directive (arts 27–29 of the Life Directive) and arts 145 and 146 of the Solvency II Directive)
[14] See SUP App.3.10.11.

(a) a statement of the classes of business which the firm is authorised to carry on in accordance with art.6 of the First Non-Life or First Life Directive;[15]

(b) the name and address of the firm;

(c) the nature of the risks or commitments which the firm proposes to cover in the UK;

(d) in the case of an insurer which intends to cover relevant motor vehicle risks:

    (i) the name and address of the claims representative; and

    (ii) a declaration by the insurer that it has become a member of the Motor Insurers' Bureau; and

(e) a statement (in the same terms as in Section 5.3.3 above) in relation to the EEA firm's minimum margin of solvency.

Once a firm has satisfied the service conditions, it has permission to provide the services identified in the regulator's notice into the UK. This will be on terms equivalent to those appearing in the notice (*see* Sch.3, para.15(1) and (2) of the FSMA 2000). In practice the permissions granted to passporting direct insurers will cover not just insurance business as such but also other regulated activities incidental to that business.[16]

5.3.5 General requirements—UK firms

To qualify for the right to establish a branch in, or provide services into, an EEA state other than the UK (the so-called "outward passport"), a UK insurer or reinsurer must:

(a) have its head office in the UK; and

(b) have an "EEA right" to establish a branch in EEA states other than the UK (i.e. it must be an insurer or reinsurer which is entitled to the passport under the terms of the Insurance and Reinsurance Directives),[17]

---

[15] Article 4 of the Life Directive.

[16] *See* SUP App.3.10.11

[17] *See* Sch.3, para.7 of the FSMA 2000.

in which case it will satisfy the definition of "UK firm" for the purposes of the FSMA 2000.[18]

Most UK-authorised insurers and reinsurers should, therefore, be entitled to passport their activities subject to limited exceptions (e.g. in the case of small mutuals, and, once Solvency II comes into force, some other small firms).[19]

Chapter 13 of the FSA's Supervision Manual ("SUP") provides guidance on the exercise of passport rights by UK firms. It also gives guidance on the provisions in the Regulations that govern changes in the details of a UK firm's branches or cross-border services (*see* below).

It is a criminal offence for a UK firm which is not an authorised person to establish a branch in, or provide services into, another EEA state without first complying with the requirements as set out at Sections 5.3.6 and 5.3.7 (Sch.3, para.21 of the FSMA 2000).

5.3.6 *Procedure for establishment of a branch of a UK direct insurer in an EEA state*

For a UK direct insurer to establish a branch in an EEA state other than the UK, the following three conditions must be satisfied:[20]

(a) the UK insurer must have given the FSA notice, in the specified way, of its intention to establish a branch (a "notice of intention"), which:
    (i)   identifies the activities which it seeks to carry on through that branch (para.19(3) specifically provides that unregulated activities may be included); and
    (ii) includes other specified information (see reg.14 and SUP Chapter 13);

---

[18] *See* Sch.3, para.10 of the FSMA 2000.
[19] *See* Section 5.3.1.
[20] *See* Sch.3, para.19 of the FSMA 2000.

(b) the FSA must have given notice in specified terms (a "consent notice") to the host state regulator (and it must give written notice to the firm that it has given the notice); and

(c) either the host state regulator must have notified the FSA of any host state rules that will apply to the branch business (*see* Section 5.7 on the "general good") or two months must have elapsed from the date the FSA gave the consent notice. In turn, the FSA must notify the insurer of those rules (but no time limit is provided for such notification).

The FSA has discretion to refuse to send a consent notice to the host state regulator if it has reason:

(a) to doubt the adequacy of the firm's resources or its administrative structure; or

(b) to question the reputation, qualifications or experience of the directors or managers of the firm or its proposed authorised agent in relation to the business that the firm intends to conduct through the branch (see Sch.3, para.19(7) of the FSMA 2000).

The FSA may in particular ask the firm for more information or require a report from a skilled person.

If the FSA proposes to refuse its consent it must issue a warning notice to the firm (*see* Sch.3, para.19(8) of the FSMA 2000). Subsequently, if the FSA decides to refuse to give a consent notice it must give the person who sent the notice of intention a decision notice to that effect within three months of receipt of the notice of intention (*see* Sch.3, para.19(12)(a) of the FSMA 2000).

Matters required to be "specified" for these purposes have been left under the relevant provisions of the FSMA 2000 for the FSA to prescribe in rules. These rules are contained in Chapter 13 of SUP. The effect is that, for example, SUP 13.5.1R specifies the information to be included in a notice of intention (*see* SUP 13 Ann 1R). SUP 13.5.3R in turn sets out the required manner for delivery of such a notice, including the various methods of delivery that may be used.

It is worth noting that the Regulations provide that where:

(a) the activities identified in a notice of intention under Sch.3, para.19 of the FSMA 2000 include any activity which is not a regulated activity;[21] and

(b) that activity is one which the UK firm in question is able to carry on in the EEA state in question without contravening any provision of the law of (any part of) the UK,

the UK firm is to be treated, for the purposes of its passported activities, as being authorised to carry on that activity.[22] This provision applies equally to services business.

5.3.7 Procedure for notifying the provision of services by UK direct insurer into an EEA state

For a UK direct insurer to provide services into another EEA state it must have given the FSA notice, in the specified way, of its intention to provide services (a "notice of intention")[23] which:

(a) identifies the activities that it seeks to carry out (para.20(2) specifically provides that unregulated activities may be included); and

(b) includes such other information as may be specified.

Within one month of receiving the notice of intention, the FSA must:[24]

(a) give notice in specified terms (a "consent notice") to the host state regulator (and inform the UK firm in writing that it has done so); or

(b) give written notice to the firm of:

---

[21] That is, regulated under the FSMA 2000.
[22] *See* reg.19.
[23] *See* Sch.3, para.20 of the FSMA 2000.
[24] *See* Sch.3, para.20(3A) of the FSMA 2000.

    (i)   its refusal to give a consent notice; and

    (ii) its reasons for that refusal.

Again, "specified" requirements are contained in Chapter 13 of SUP (*see*, in particular, SUP 13.5.2R and SUP 13 Ann 3R on the contents of a notice of intention and, again, SUP 13.5.3R for requirements as to delivery).

At SUP 13.4.4G the FSA provides guidance on the exercise of its powers to issue or refuse to give consent notices. In particular, in contrast to the position for branches (*see* Section 5.3.6), it notes that the consent notice in para.(a) above is not a statutory notice for the purpose of Section 395 of the FSMA 2000. However, if the FSA refuses to give a consent notice the firm may refer the matter to the Financial Services and Markets Tribunal (the "FSMA tribunal").

5.3.8 *Validity of policies*

The European Commission regards the purpose of the notification procedures (both for branch and services business) described above to be the exchange of information between supervisory authorities. They are not consumer protection measures. As such, they should not be construed as conditions affecting the validity of insurance policies.

This position is reinforced by FSMA 2000. Under s.26, agreements made by unauthorised persons are generally unenforceable against the other party. However, Sch.3, para.16 of the FSMA 2000 provides express derogation from this provision and its consequential provisions for an EEA firm that does not qualify for authorisation under para.12 of that Schedule.

5.3.9 *Cancellation of qualification for authorisation*

Section 34 of the FSMA 2000 provides that an EEA firm ceases to qualify for authorisation under Part II of Sch.3 to that Act if, broadly, it ceases to be an EEA firm because its EEA

authorisation has been withdrawn. In addition, s.34(2) provides that, on request by an EEA firm, the FSA may give a
direction cancelling its authorisation under Part II of Sch.3.
Regulation 8 of the Regulations provides that where an EEA
firm that is qualified for authorisation under Sch.3:

(a)   has ceased, or is to cease, to carry on regulated activities in
      the UK; and
(b)   gives notice of that fact to the FSA,

the notice is to be treated as a request for cancellation of the
firm's qualification for authorisation under Sch.3 (and hence as
a request under s.34(2)). Among other things, Chapter 14 of
SUP provides for cancellation of EEA firms' qualification for
authorisation (*see* SUP 14.6).

5.4   Changes in details relating to EEA direct insurers

5.4.1   *General*

As stated above, an EEA firm that qualifies for authorisation to
carry on insurance activities in the UK by satisfying the
requirements of Sch.3 of the FSMA 2000 becomes an authorised
person by virtue of s.31 of that Act. For direct insurers,
authorisation is treated as being on terms equivalent to those
appearing on the consent notice or regulator's notice. Authorisation is withdrawn, by virtue of s.34, if, broadly, the firm
ceases to be authorised by its home state regulator.

If, therefore, the firm passports activities into the UK which
exceed the scope of its authorisation, it will still be an
authorised person but will be acting outside the terms of its
permission for the purposes of s.20 of the FSMA 2000. Sections
194–199 of the FSMA 2000 set out the FSA's powers of
intervention if it appears that an incoming firm has contravened a requirement of the Act.

Because of this, if an EEA direct insurer intends to conduct business or provide services that are supplementary to those originally notified, it should consider whether it should notify the FSA of those changes. The Regulations set out detailed requirements in this respect and Chapter 14 of SUP provides additional guidance. Similarly, UK direct insurers are required to notify certain changes in details described below (Chapter 13 of SUP is also relevant here). Failure to notify is a criminal offence.

5.4.2 Changes relating to EEA direct insurers

The requirement to notify changes relating to a UK branch of an EEA firm arises if any of the details described in Section 5.3.3(c)(i)–(iii) are to change.[25] Procedural requirements for giving effect to such a change are similar to the original notification procedures for establishment of that branch. Where the relevant requirements are complied with, the firm's permission is to be treated as varied accordingly. Broadly, except where the change is outside the insurer's control[26] the requirements are that:

(a) the firm has given notice of the change to the FSA and to its home state regulator;

(b) the FSA has received from the home state regulator a notice stating that it has approved the proposed change;

(c) a period of one month beginning with the day on which the insurer gave the FSA the notice mentioned in subpara.(a) has elapsed; and

(d) either:

    (i) a further month has elapsed; or

    (ii) the FSA has informed the home state regulator of any consequential changes in the rules with which the insurer must comply when carrying on its branch activities in the UK.

---

[25] *See* reg.6(1).

[26] In this case, the Regulations provide for notice to be given to the FSA and the firm's home state regulator as soon as practicable (whether before or after the change).

In the case of services business, changes to any of the details described in Section 5.3.4(b), (c) or (d) must be notified to the firm's home state regulator as soon as practicable and then passed on by the home state regulator to the FSA for the permission to be treated as altered.[27]

5.4.3 Changes relating to UK direct insurers

A UK firm must notify the FSA of any change to the "EEA details" with respect to a branch.[28]These details are, in summary:

(a) the address of the branch;
(b) the name of the firm's authorised agent;
(c) the classes or parts of classes of business carried on, or to be carried on, and the nature of the risks or commitments covered, or to be covered;
(d) details of the structural organisation of the branch;
(e) the guiding principles as to reinsurance of business carried on, or to be carried on;
(f) estimates of the costs of installing administrative services and the organisation for securing business and the resources available to cover those costs; and
(g) for each of the first three years following the establishment of the branch:
　(i) estimates of the firm's margin of solvency and the margin of solvency required, and the method of calculation; and
　(ii) various other information and estimates, according to whether the firm carries on, or intends to carry on, general or long-term business through the branch.

A UK firm must also notify the FSA of any changes to the details that it is required to provide to the FSA by or under Sch.3, para.19(2) of the FSMA 2000 (*see* Chapter 13 of SUP).

Notification procedures for changes of details in relation to the provision of services are similar to those in relation to

---

[27] *See* reg.7(1).
[28] *See* reg.13.

branches. However, the procedures are triggered by changes to a list of details much less comprehensive than the EEA details. These include:

(a)   the EEA state in which the activities are carried on;
(b)   the nature of the risks or commitments covered; and
(c)   certain details in relation to motor vehicle or health risks.

5.5   Passporting arrangements applying to reinsurers

5.5.1   *The reinsurance passport*

Article 4 of the Reinsurance Directive (which as mentioned above is due ultimately to be consolidated into the Solvency II Directive) provides that authorisation pursuant to the Directive "shall be valid for the entire Community. It shall permit a reinsurance undertaking to carry on business there, under either the right of establishment or the freedom to provide services." Unlike the position in relation to direct insurers, the Reinsurance Directive does not envisage any formalities applying to the exercise of the right of establishment or the freedom to provide services.

Article 4 of the Directive has been transposed in the UK by para.12(5) of Sch.3 to the FSMA 2000 (as amended). This provides that a reinsurer authorised in another EEA state "has in respect of each permitted activity which is a regulated activity, permission to carry it on through its United Kingdom branch or by providing services in the UK". As with direct insurers it can be expected that the permitted activities will include regulated activities, other than reinsurance, which are related to the reinsurance business. Indeed, the scope of those activities may be wider than for direct insurers. Both direct insurers and reinsurers are required to restrict their business to insurance and reinsurance respectively. However, this restriction applies more strictly to direct insurers than to reinsurers.[29]

The question arises as to how the FSA is to be informed that the EEA reinsurer qualifies for authorisation, so as, among other things, to update its register of authorised firms (*see* Chapter 2). The Directive, FSMA 2000 and the FSA Handbook are silent on this point. However, the Committee of European Insurance and Occupational Pensions Authority ("EIOPA", formerly the Committee of European Insurance and Occupational Pensions Supervisors ("CEIOPS") has published a "General Protocol relating to the Collaboration of the Insurance Supervisory Authorities of the Member States of the European Union".[30] This makes provision for the home state supervisor of a reinsurer to provide information, as far as possible, to the host state supervisor where the reinsurer proposes to set up a branch in the host state. Provision is also made for changes in that information to be notified.

No equivalent provision is made for EEA reinsurers operating in other Member States under the freedom to provide services. However, before the Reinsurance Directive was implemented in the UK, an EEA reinsurer providing services in the UK without a local branch was unlikely to have been carrying out any regulated activity in the UK. For that reason it would not normally have required a UK authorisation. In other Member States, however, an authorisation requirement was triggered by the reinsurer covering risks treated as located in the host state. In such cases the services passport under the Reinsurance Directive will provide a more tangible benefit to passporting reinsurers.

Article 47 of the Reinsurance Directive requires passporting reinsurers to comply with legal provisions applicable to them in the host state and provides for the appropriate sanctions where they do not. However, there is no requirement for the host state to notify the passporting reinsurer what those legal

---

[29] *See* rr.1.5.13R and 1.5.13AR of the FSA's Prudential Sourcebook for Insurers ("INSPRU").

[30] Accessible on the EIOPA website www.ceiops.eu under Publications—Protocols.

provisions are. In the UK most rules relating specifically to reinsurance are, in any event, applied as prudential rules to the ceding direct insurer and not to the reinsurer.[31]

5.6   Right of establishment versus freedom to provide services

5.6.1   Interaction and analysis

As stated above, EU law makes an important distinction between the freedom of establishment and the freedom to provide services, which is reflected in arts 49 and 56 of the Treaty. As the distinction is not specific to insurance, it is not dealt with in detail in the directives or the FSMA, although art.1(b) of the Life Directive provides:

> "Any permanent presence of an undertaking in the territory of a Member State shall be treated in the same way as an agency or branch, even if that presence does not take the form of a branch or agency, but consists merely of an office managed by the undertaking's own staff or by a person who is independent but has permanent authority to act for the undertaking as an agency would."

There is a provision to the same effect in art.3 of the Second Non-Life Directive.

As the original Treaty provisions suggest, the concept of provision of services is basically distinguished from that of establishment by its temporary character. This is assessed in the light of duration, regularity and continuity. However, this does not mean that the provider of services may not provide himself with some form of infrastructure without coming under the right of establishment.

In 2000, the European Commission published an interpretative communication, "Freedom to provide services and the general

---

[31] See, in particular, Chapter 9 of the FSA's Interim Prudential Sourcebook for Insurers.

good in the insurance sector" (222/C43/03) (the "Interpretative Communication"), containing guidance on the difference between a branch and the provision of services. The FSA has published its own guidance in SUP Appendix 3 which comments on and supplements the Interpretative Communication on a number of points.

Grey areas in relation to the division between branch and service business (and, therefore, which notification procedure should apply) may arise. An example is where an insurer has recourse to independent persons established in the host Member State or where it uses electronic machines to carry out insurance business. Based on case law, the Commission has determined that if an independent person meets all the following conditions he falls within the scope of the rules governing the right of establishment, rather than those covering the provision of services:

(a) he must be subject to the direction and control of the insurance undertaking he represents;
(b) he must be able to commit the insurance undertaking; and
(c) he must have received a permanent brief.

If an insurer's only presence in a Member State is through automatic telling machines ("ATMs") capable of performing insurance activities covered by the Insurance Directives, the Commission thinks they can only be considered an establishment of that insurer if the same three criteria are satisfied.

5.6.2 *Meaning of the provision of services under the Insurance Directives*

The cross-border provision of services has a special meaning under the Insurance Directives. It will usually cover operations in the host state without a branch or establishment there. More precisely, however, it extends to insurance activities which result in contracts covering risks (in the case of general insurance) or commitments (in the case of long-term insurance) treated as located in the host state. These operations may in some cases be carried out entirely within the territory of the home state. It is the coverage of those risks or commitments by the insurer which triggers the requirement to passport on a services basis.

Under art.2 of the Second Non-Life Directive and Article 1 of the Life Directive the risk or commitment is usually treated as located either:

(a)   in the Member State where the policyholder has his habitual residence; or
(b)   if the policyholder is a legal person, in the Member State where the latter's establishment, to which the contract relates, is situated.

However, the member state of the risk in non-life insurance is identified as follows[32] for specific types of insurance:

(a)   in buildings or buildings and contents insurance by the member state where the property is situated,
(b)   in motor insurance by the member state where the vehicle is registered (although where a vehicle is dispatched from one member state to another, the member state of the risk is the member state of destination, immediately upon acceptance of delivery by the purchaser, for a period of 30 days, even though the vehicle has not yet formally been registered in that state[33]),
(c)   in the case of policies covering travel or holiday risks for a duration of four months or less the state where the policy was taken out.

5.6.3   Consequences of setting up a branch or providing services

Key reasons why it is important to identify accurately whether particular activities fall to be treated as services or branch business are as follows:

---

[32]   Second Non-Life Directive 88/357/EEC, art.2(d)
[33]   Consolidated Motor Insurance Directive 2009/103/EC, art.15(1).

(a) the procedure to establish a branch, while similar, is more onerous than for the provision of services. For example, a consent notice in respect of a UK branch will have to include a scheme of operations;

(b) timing: it takes considerably longer to comply with notification provisions for branch business than to comply with the relevant requirements for services business;

(c) an undertaking that establishes a branch should comply with branch registration requirements under Part 34 of the Companies Act 2006;

(d) taxation: the holder of an EEA passport who can provide services in another EEA state without the use of a local branch may not be taxable locally owing to the operation of double tax treaties. However, it should be noted that the test for determining the existence of a "permanent establishment" for income and corporation tax purposes is different from that applying under the Treaty;[34]

(e) cost: the administrative costs of setting up a branch may be marginally higher, but there is no difference in the solvency margin required for services or branch business;

(f) regulation: most of the FSA's conduct of business rules only apply to insurers or insurance intermediaries who have a UK establishment or who have an appointed person with a UK establishment.

The Third Insurance Directives permitted an insurer to carry on both services and branch business simultaneously, but it should be able to relate a particular activity to one or the other. This was originally prohibited (in certain cases) under the Second Insurance Directives.

---

[34] *See* Part 7 of the Finance Act 2003 and the Model Tax Convention of the Organisation for Economic Co-operation and Development ("OECD").

5.7 Conditions imposed by host Member State in the "general good"

5.7.1 Background to the concept of the "general good"

Direct insurers operating under the single passport must comply with host state rules imposed in the interest of the "general good". The Insurance Directives refer to the "general good" in the following places:

(a) under the procedure for establishing a branch, a host Member State has two months from receipt of notice from the home Member State to notify the passporting insurer of any conditions imposed on the activities of the proposed branch in the "general good". There is no corresponding express provision relating to services (art.10 of the First Non-Life Directive and art.40 of the Life Directive);

(b) the host state should not prevent policyholders from concluding a contract with an insurer authorised under the Insurance Directives, provided that to do so does not conflict with legal provisions protecting the general good in the host state (art.28 of the Third Non-Life Directive and art.33 of the Life Directive);

(c) Recital 20 to the Third Non-Life Directive and Recital 47 to the Life Directive refer to the "general good" in relation to both the establishment of branches and the provision of services as follows:

"Whereas the Member States must be able to ensure that the assurance products and contract documents used, under *the right of establishment or the freedom to provide services*, to cover commitments within their territories comply with such specific legal provisions protecting the general good as are applicable" (emphasis added);

(d) Recital 24 to the Third Non-Life Directive refers to health insurance taken out as an alternative cover to that provided by a statutory system of social security. In that context it also refers to Member State rules adopted to protect the general good;

213

(e)   Recital 19 to the Third Non-Life Directive and Recital 46 to the Life Directive explicitly mention advertising or marketing of insurance policies. Article 41 and art.47 respectively state:

> "Nothing in this Directive shall prevent insurance undertakings with head offices in Member States from advertising their services, through all available means of communication, in the Member State of the branch or the Member State of the provision of services, subject to any rules governing the form and content of such advertising adopted in the interest of the general good."

This Article, taken with the Recitals, suggests that the ability of the host state to regulate marketing and promotion is one of the key reasons for introducing the "general good" concept into EU legislation.

5.7.2   *"General good" under the FSMA 2000*

As noted above, the First Insurance Directives only expressly conferred authority on the host state to impose "general good" conditions in relation to branch business. However, the recitals to those directives extended the concept to the provision of services. In addition, art.28 of the Third Non-Life Directive and art.33 of the Life Directive are not specific to establishment or services business. Unlike the earlier Insurance Companies Act 1982 regime, the FSMA 2000 regime gives the FSA explicit power to impose provisions in the interest of the "general good" on EEA firms wishing to provide services into the UK (as well as establishing a branch). Arguably, it does so, therefore, on the basis of these provisions.

Article 40 of the Third Non-Life Directive and art.46 of the Life Directive give the host state regulator power to remedy the situation if a passporting firm is not complying with legal provisions applicable to it in that state. After informing the home state competent authority, the regulator may, in certain circumstances, take steps to prevent or penalise further infringements. Under the FSMA 2000 the FSA has powers of intervention in respect of passported EEA firms, which it may exercise if it appears that:[35]

(a) the firm has contravened, or is likely to contravene, a requirement imposed on it by or under the FSMA 2000; or
(b) the firm has, in purported compliance with a requirement under the FSMA 2000, knowingly or recklessly given the FSA false or misleading information; or
(c) it is desirable to exercise the power in order to protect the interests of actual or potential customers; or
(d) there have been certain contraventions of the Consumer Credit Act 1974.

The FSA may also exercise its powers of intervention at the request of, or for the purpose of assisting, an overseas regulator. This primarily means a home state regulator, although it can also cover other regulators in certain specified circumstances.

The power of intervention is a power to impose any requirement in relation to the firm that the FSA could impose if the firm had permissions under the FSMA 2000 and if the FSA were entitled to exercise its power to impose requirements in relation to UK regulated insurers. This means that the FSA can impose on incoming firms the same types of requirements as it can impose on UK regulated insurers.[36]

5.7.3 Interpretation/case law

Recital 19 to the Third Non-Life Directive and Recital 46 to the Life Directive provide that conditions imposed in the interest of the general good should only be applied:

---

[35] Section 194.
[36] In relation to such a firm it cannot add, remove or vary the description of a regulated activity.

> "in so far as the general good *is not safeguarded by the rules of the home Member State,*[37] provided that such provisions must be applied *without discrimination* to all undertakings operating in that Member State and *be objectively necessary* and in *proportion* to the objective pursued."(Emphasis added).

The concept of the general good has been subjected to further qualification by European case law. In particular, the European Court of Justice and the Court of the European Free Trade Association require that a national provision must satisfy the following requirements:

(a)　it must come within a field that has not been harmonised;
(b)　it must pursue an objective of the general good;
(c)　it must be non-discriminatory;
(d)　it must be objectively necessary;
(e)　it must be proportionate to the objective pursued;
(f)　it is also necessary for the "general good" objective not to be safeguarded by rules to which the provider of services is already subject in its home state.

These conditions are analysed in more detail in the Interpretative Communication.

5.7.4　Examples

The Interpretative Communication sets out the following possible problem areas:

(a)　prior notification of policy conditions;
(b)　capital redemption operations of insurance undertakings;
(c)　uniform no-claims bonus systems;
(d)　language of the policy;
(e)　professional codes of conduct;
(f)　maximum technical interest rates for life insurance;
(g)　imposition of standard clauses or minimum insurance conditions;

37　It could be argued that this statement is only relevant when the home country has rules governing the provision of cross-border insurance.

(h) clauses imposing mandatory levels of excess in insurance policies;

(i) compulsory stipulation of a surrender value in life assurance policies;

(j) prohibition of cold calling;

(k) arrangements for charging indirect taxes on insurance premiums for policies concluded under the freedom to provide services; and

(l) appointment of a tax representative of the insurer.

The Commission has expressed views on these problem areas. It considers that the requirement to appoint a tax representative of an insurer doing business under the freedom to provide services pursues an objective that is justified under community law. However, the host state may not reject a notification on the ground that no tax representative has been appointed. The tax representative should be appointed only once the activities have effectively begun.

Of the other possible "general good" conditions, the Interpretative Communication concludes, for the most part, that there is no justification for their imposition. This is either because the area has already been harmonised or because the host Member State has no competence for financial supervision of an insurer authorised in, and supervised by, its home Member State.

5.7.5 *Recent cases on general good requirements*

The judgment in 2006 of the EFTA Court in *EFTA Surveillance Authority* v *Kingdom of Norway*, Case E-1/05, concerned "general good" rules applying in Norway. These provided that costs incurred by a policyholder when life assurance was taken out must be charged and paid at the latest at the same time as the first premium. One of the purposes of the rule was to make policyholders more aware of the costs that they were incurring.

The Court accepted that this was a legitimate objective. However, it considered that it could also be achieved by less restrictive means. For instance, full information could be required to be provided about costs spread over the life of the contract. The Court held, therefore, that the rules were incompatible with art.33 of the Life Directive.

By contrast in *Commission v Italian Republic* Case C-518/06 the Court of Justice of the European Communities made a ruling with respect to Italian rules requiring incoming motor insurers to offer cover to the entire market and to adhere to prescriptive rules relating to the calculation of motor insurance premiums. The Court accepted that these rules restricted the right of establishment and the freedom to provide services. It held, however, that they were justified by the objective of ensuring that victims of road traffic accidents were appropriately compensated.

5.7.6   Typical FSA conditions

The UK's approach to the imposition of conditions on incoming firms in the "general good" has not been entirely straightforward. Its usual approach to insurance notifications under the former Insurance Companies Act 1982 regime seemed to be merely to send out a notice incorporating a list of insurance legislation applying in the UK (headed "Measures imposed in the interest of the general good and other provisions applicable to insurers authorised in other EEA states which propose to offer insurance in the United Kingdom").

The notice was carefully worded, stressing that applicants should take their own legal advice as to what rules and regulations should be followed, and stating that the interpretation of the law is a matter for the courts. However, the FSA's approach in this respect seemed to be at odds with the narrow meaning given to the "general good" in the Interpretative Communication. The position under the FSMA 2000 regime remains unclear. The FSA originally issued some guidance in s.5.6 of its Authorisation Manual, but most of this guidance has since been removed and what remains transferred to Chapter 13A and Appendix 3 of SUP. In addition to including a table (at SUP 13A Annex 1) summarising the application of the Handbook to incoming EEA firms, the FSA states, at SUP

13A.6.2.G, that such a firm must comply with the "applicable provisions" (i.e. host state rules which are notified to it by the FSA).

Confusingly though, the FSA then states that incoming firms must also comply with "other relevant UK legislation" (e.g. where relevant, the requirement to become a member of the Motor Insurers' Bureau). The basis for requiring firms to comply with UK legislation other than that which has been notified to them by the FSA (i.e. "applicable provisions") is not clear.

5.8 Reinsurance activities of direct insurers

5.8.1 Reinsurance and Retrocession Directive of 1964 (64/225/EEC)

This Directive pre-dates the Insurance and Reinsurance Directives. It applies to insurers and reinsurers carrying on reinsurance business in the EU. It provides for the abolition of restrictions on their right to establish themselves in other Member States. It goes no further than this. In its application to reinsurers it has now been effectively superseded by the Reinsurance Directive.

5.8.2 Limited application of Insurance Directives to reinsurance

The Insurance Directives do not apply to reinsurers. The need for the regime established under those Directives to extend to reinsurers was ultimately met by the adoption of the Reinsurance Directive in 2005. The Reinsurance Directive was due for transposition by Member States on 10 December 2007 (*see* Section 5.1.3).

However, many of the prudential requirements under the Insurance Directives apply to the "entire business" of the direct insurer. Many direct insurers carry on some reinsurance and/or retrocession business. In the case of some insurers that business may be significant. The Lloyd's market, for instance, is treated as a single direct insurer under the Insurance Directives, although it is also a major player in the reinsurance and retrocession market.

FSMA 2000 contains provisions allowing EEA firms to passport into the UK using "Treaty rights"[38] (broadly, rights deriving directly from the Treaty rather than from a specific single-market directive). In order to take advantage of Treaty rights, the following conditions apply:

(a) a firm must be authorised in its home state for the particular activity;
(b) the relevant provisions of the law of the firm's home state must either:
 (i) afford equivalent protection to that provided to consumers under the FSMA 2000; or
 (ii) satisfy conditions laid down in an EU instrument for the coordination of laws, regulations or administrative provisions applying to the particular activity;
(c) there must be no single-market directive which applies to the particular activity.

In relation to the "equivalent protection" condition, a certificate from the Treasury may be obtained. It is conclusive (but not necessary) evidence of the fact that the home state laws provide equivalent protection. For mixed direct and reinsurance business Treaty rights form the basis of the ability to passport the reinsurance business element. The FSA has indicated that it regards the equivalent protection requirement as satisfied for a mixed direct and reinsurance business. This is because, by virtue of the insurance directives, the reinsurance element would be subject to the same solvency requirements in the home state as the direct business.

The FSA mentions that UK direct insurers may wish to take advantage of the equivalent of Treaty rights in other EEA states in relation to reinsurance (*see* SUP 13.2.3.G). In that event they are invited to consult with the FSA on their particular

---

[38] Schedule 4 of the FSMA 2000.

circumstances. Such direct insurers' rights to carry on reinsurance business may or may not be recognised in the EEA jurisdiction concerned.

The Solvency II Directive will make no significant changes to the passporting rights of direct insurers in relation to their reinsurance business (if any). Recital (9) says that "it is for the Member States to decide to lay down any rules in that regard". Under art.310 Directive 64/225/EEC will be repealed on the basis that it is obsolete.

5.9   Approved Persons regime

The Approved Persons regime under the FSMA 2000 (*see* Chapter 3) has a "controlled function" test (s.59), requiring prior approval by the FSA of persons performing specified functions. Under the proposed reforms to the UK regulatory regime (see Chapter 1) the task of granting such approvals will be split between the PRA and the FCA depending on the nature of the firm and function concerned. This would apply to key people of a UK branch of an EEA firm. Section 59(8) exempts this requirement where the question of whether a person is fit and proper is reserved under any of the single market directives to an authority in a country or territory outside the UK.

Section 10 of the Regulations explicitly subjects EEA firms seeking an inward passport to the Approved Persons regime, although some controlled functions do not apply to such firms (*see* SUP 10.1.7R).

It is questionable whether these provisions are consistent with the framework of the Insurance and Reinsurance Directives. Under the directives, prudential matters (which include the fitness of the undertaking's senior management) are a home state responsibility. Under art.42 of the Solvency II Directive fitness and properness requirements will be extended to "persons who effectively run the undertaking or have other key functions" and are the responsibility of the home state supervisor. The FSA's approved persons regime may need to be adapted to comply with this.

5.10 Passporting arrangements for insurance intermediaries

The Insurance Mediation Directive ("IMD") came into force on 14 January 2005. Its requirements are referred to in more detail in Chapter 7.

5.10.1 Authorisation and registration of insurance intermediaries

The IMD only requires that insurance intermediaries who do not benefit from an exemption should be registered in their home state. It does not apply a full authorisation requirement to them. Insurance intermediaries whose head office is in the UK may apply for a full UK authorisation. Alternatively they may operate as an appointed representative of an authorised person.[39] In either event, the requirement that they are registered is met by the fact that their details are included on the FSA Register.[40] Under the proposed reforms to the UK regulatory structure the FSA's functions in relation to the supervision and regulation of isnurance intermediaries will be carried out by the FCA.[41]

5.10.2 Insurers and reinsurers carrying on insurance mediation activities

In the UK it is not only insurance intermediaries who require permission for insurance mediation activities. To the extent that those activities are carried out by insurers and reinsurers (where, for instance, the insurer/reinsurer sells its products directly and not just through intermediaries) their permissions must cover those activities and they are subject to some of the

---

[39] As to appointed representatives see Section 7.3.5.5 of Chapter 7.
[40] See Chapter 2.
[41] See fn. 8.

regulatory requirements that also apply to insurance intermediaries. An EEA insurer/reinsurer passporting into the UK may therefore be treated as having permissions for insurance mediation activities as well as for insurance business as such.[42] Under proposed reforms to the IMD, on which the Commission has consulted,[43] many of the requirements under that directive will extend to direct sales in line with the current UK approach.

5.10.3   The IMD passporting rules

Like insurers and reinsurers, insurance intermediaries authorised in one Member State may wish to carry on business in another state under the right of establishment or the freedom to provide services. In that event, like direct insurers, they are usually required by art.6 of the IMD to notify the home state supervisor.

The home state supervisor must normally notify the host state supervisor within a month of receiving that notice. The intermediary may then start business within a further month. However, these procedures need not be followed if the host state has indicated that it does not wish to receive notification.[44] Schedule 3 of the FSMA 2000 makes clear that the UK does wish to receive such notifications, since the passporting procedures cover EEA firms, which include EEA insurance intermediaries. The Commission's consultation on reforms to the IMD has reported that the notification requirements are in any event viewed as highly burdensome. Improvements and modernisation may be introduced in due course.

Under s.31 of the FSMA 2000 an EEA insurance intermediary registered in another EEA state passports into a UK authorisation—there is no provision for it to passport into a mere registration.

---

[42] *See* Sections 5.3.3 and 5.3.4 and SUP App. 3.10.11. The permissions of the passporting insurer derive from para.15 of Sch.3 to the FSMA.

[43] Consultation document on the Review of the Insurance Mediation Directive (IMD) Commission Staff Working Paper, 26 November 2010.

[44] *See* SUP 13 and 13A for the UK transposition of these requirements.

There is no specific requirement in the IMD that the host state should notify "general good" rules to the passporting intermediary. However, art.6(3) of the IMD provides that Member States may arrange for the publication of their general good rules. The FSA has effectively done this in SUP 13A.6. This explains how its Handbook applies to passporting firms.

The Commission's proposals for reform of the IMD also consider the position of natural persons fully qualified as insurance intermediaries in a EU Member State wishing to take up the same profession in another EU Member State on the basis of permanent establishment, without keeping their original registration or authorisation. It is proposed that such persons should also be able to benefit from rights equivalent to those applying under the IMD. Such persons would also rely on Directive 2005/36/EC on the recognition of professional qualifications.

5.10.4   Establishment and services under the IMD

Under the IMD the question whether a passporting intermediary has acquired an establishment in the host state will be determined by similar considerations to those applying to insurers and reinsurers.[45] If the intermediary has acquired such an establishment, depending on the circumstances it may also create an establishment for one or more insurers in whose products it deals. An insurance intermediary registered in another EEA state proposing to acquire an establishment in the UK must follow the passporting formalities described in SUP 13A.

By contrast, the IMD does not, as do the insurance directives, define what amounts to the "provision of services" in a host state by an insurance intermediary. As far as concerns EEA insurance intermediaries operating in the UK, the question is in any event largely academic. Most of the FSA Handbook does not apply to firms without a UK establishment. The main exception, the FSA's financial promotion rules,[46] applies to

---

[45] *See* Section 5.6.
[46] *See* Chapter 7 as to the FSA's financial promotion rules. Even the financial

promotions "capable of having an effect in the UK", regardless of the existence of an establishment or the territoriality of the provision of services.[47]

However, this issue may have more importance in relation to the application of the rules of other Member States. These may more often be triggered by the provision of services in the host state, as well as by the existence there of an establishment.

However, the issue has been addressed in the "Luxembourg Protocol" to the IMD. Under this protocol an insurance intermediary is treated as operating in the host state under the freedom to provide services:

(a) if it intends to supply a policyholder; and
(b) the policyholder is established in a Member State different from the one where the insurance intermediary is established; and
(c) the intermediary is supplying an insurance contract relating to a risk situated in a Member State different from the Member State where the insurance intermediary is established.

One of the options discussed by the Commission in its consultation on reforms to the IMD is that this protocol defining how the freedom to provide services operates should be incorporated into the directive itself with a view to creating legal certainty.

---

promotion rules will not apply to an EEA insurance intermediary without a UK establishment to the extent that the application of those rules is removed by the E-Commerce Directive (2000/31/EC) (*see* paras 5.12.15G to 5.12.17G of the FSA's Perimeter Guidance Manual ("PERG")).

[47] *See* also the overseas persons exclusion in art.72 of the Financial Services and Markets (Regulated Activities) Order 2001 (SI 2001/544).

Chapter 6

Portfolio Transfers and Solvent Schemes of Arrangement

Geoffrey Maddock and Laurence Elliott,
Partners: Herbert Smith LLP

6.1 Portfolio transfers

6.1.1 *Introduction*

Part VII of the Financial Services and Markets Act 2000 ("FSMA 2000") deals with the control of transfers of long-term and general insurance business and banking business.[1] Rules relating to insurance extend to reinsurance and are intended to meet the requirements of the Consolidated Life Directive (2002/83/EC), the Third Non-Life Directive (92/49/EC) and the Reinsurance Directive (2005/68/EC) (together, the "Directives"). The Directives require EU Member States to provide a method for transferring insurance and reinsurance business, based on the principle that the transferring (re)insurer's home state regime will apply to all EEA policies being transferred without the need also to meet host state requirements.

The main sources of the rules are Part VII of, and Sch.12 to, the FSMA 2000, the Financial Services and Markets Act 2000 (Control of Business Transfers) (Requirements on Applicants) Regulations 2001 (SI 2001/3625) (the "Regulations") and guidance from the Financial Services Authority ("FSA") in

---

[1] Since March 2009, Part VII of the FSMA 2000 has also covered transfers of business carried on by a "reclaim fund" (as defined by section 5(1) of the Dormant Bank and Building Society Accounts Act 2008), which are outside the scope of this chapter.

Chapter 18 of the Supervision Manual (the "Guidance").[2] The Treasury may make further regulations under s.108 and/or s.117 of the FSMA 2000. Sections 115 and 116 of, and Part III of Sch.12 to, the FSMA 2000 deal with insurance business transfers ("IBTs" or "transfers") which take place outside the UK.

Except as expressly noted below, the terms "insurance" and "insurer" should be taken to include "reinsurance" and "reinsurer" respectively. The term "direct insurer" refers to a firm authorised under either art.4 of the Consolidated Life Directive or art.6 of the First Non-Life Directive (73/239/EEC) and "pure reinsurer" refers to a firm authorised under art.3 of the Reinsurance Directive.

6.1.2 Scope of insurance business transfer provisions

6.1.2.1 Meaning of insurance business transfer scheme

The expression for an IBT that is used in s.105 of the FSMA 2000 is "insurance business transfer scheme". Under s.104, no transfer is to have effect unless an order of the court has been made in relation to it under s.111. With the exception of the five excluded cases referred to below (*see*Section 6.1.2.5), the expression covers any IBT to transfer the whole or part of the insurance business carried on by an authorised person, including a member of Lloyd's, if:

(a) the transferor is a "UK authorised person" (i.e. an authorised person which is incorporated in the UK or is an unincorporated association formed under the law of any

---

[2] Part VII of the FSMA 2000 and the Regulations were amended with effect from 30 June 2008 by the Financial Services and Markets Act 2000 (Amendments to Part 7) Regulations 2008 (SI 2008/1468); the Financial Services and Markets Act 2000 (Control of Business Transfers) (Requirements on Applicants) (Amendment) Regulations 2008 (SI 2008/1467); and the Financial Services and Markets Act 2000 (Amendment of Section 323) Regulations 2008 (SI 2008/1469). The Guidance has not been updated at the date of publication to reflect these changes, despite the amount of time that has now elapsed.

part of the UK) and the insurance business is being carried on in one or more EEA states;[3] or

(b)　the business is reinsurance carried on in the UK by a direct insurer (but not a pure reinsurer) authorised in an EEA state other than the UK; or

(c)　the insurance business is carried on in the UK and the transferor is neither a UK authorised person nor an EEA firm (a term defined in Sch.3 to the FSMA 2000 to mean, for these purposes, either a direct insurer or pure reinsurer); and

in each case, the transferred business will be carried on by the transferee from an establishment in an EEA state.

It was held in *Re Eagle Star Insurance Co Ltd and Eagle Star Life Assurance Co Ltd* (1990) *The Times*, 7 December that where a single IBT proposed the transfer of all insurance business wherever carried on, the court could sanction the transfer only so far as it related to insurance business which it had jurisdiction to transfer, notwithstanding that the same document also proposed a transfer of business which was outside the court's jurisdiction. However, it is more normal to document the IBT so that it covers only business which the court has jurisdiction to transfer and propose a separate transfer for other jurisdictions.

Although this is not apparent from the legislation, it is clear from established practice that a single transfer, court application and court hearing can be used to transfer the insurance business of one or more transferors to one or more transferees. A limited exception to this is where a transfer requires more than one independent expert's report—in practice, this is only likely to happen if both long-term and general business are being transferred.

---

[3]　Section 105(2)(a), FSMA 2000 refers to "business carried on in one or more Member States", not EEA states. The reference to "Member States" is unfortunate as the term is not defined in the Act or used elsewhere in Part VII. The term appears to have been mistakenly carried over from earlier legislation covering insurance business transfers (the Insurance Companies Act 1982 (now repealed) where it is defined in Section 2(7)). It is unlikely that the scope of Section 105(2)(a) does not extend to EEA states.

6.1.2.2   The transferee

Section 111(2) of the FSMA 2000 provides that the transferee must have the authorisation required (if any) to enable the business which is to be transferred to be carried on in the place to which it is to be transferred not later than the date on which the transfer is to take effect. Subject to this requirement and to the additional requirement to obtain certificates of solvency and consent (Part I of Sch.12), there is no express restriction on the legal nature of the transferee or the country in which it is established, as long as the business will be carried on from an establishment in an EEA state. However, direct insurers and pure reinsurers are limited to the legal forms specified in the Consolidated Life Directive, First Non-Life Directive and Reinsurance Directive.

6.1.2.3   UK and EEA states

For this purpose, "UK" means England, Wales, Scotland and Northern Ireland; the Channel Islands, the Isle of Man and Gibraltar do not form part of the UK. Insurers headquartered in Gibraltar are authorised and supervised by the Gibraltarian Financial Services Commission, although the UK has assumed responsibility for ensuring that European standards apply. As a consequence, insurers with a head office in Gibraltar are entitled to passport their insurance activities throughout the EEA and EEA insurers can, similarly, passport into Gibraltar. The Financial Services and Markets Act 2000 (Gibraltar) Order 2001 (SI 2001/3084) provides for this outcome in the UK.

The term "EEA state" is defined by Sch.3 to the FSMA 2000, and as at the date of publication the EEA states (other than the UK) are:

- Austria
- Belgium
- Bulgaria
- Cyprus
- Czech Republic
- Denmark

- Estonia
- Finland
- France
- Germany
- Greece
- Holland
- Hungary
- Iceland
- Italy
- Latvia
- Liechtenstein
- Lithuania
- Luxembourg
- Malta
- Norway
- Poland
- Portugal
- Republic of Ireland
- Romania
- Slovak Republic
- Slovenia
- Spain
- Sweden

On 30 June 2011, it was announced that negotiations for Croatia's accession to the EU had been closed. Croatia is currently expected to become the 28th Member State (and, it follows, an EEA state) on 1 July 2013.

6.1.2.4   *Where is insurance business carried on?*

The test of whether insurance business is "carried on" in the UK or in any other particular location is not exhaustively set out in the FSMA 2000 but should be determined by reference to the tests set out in s.418 of the FSMA 2000 (which sets out certain circumstances in which business not otherwise treated as being carried on in the UK is to be so treated for the purposes of the FSMA 2000). To the extent not in conflict with s.418, reference should also be made to case law under legislation previously providing for the regulation of insurance companies, including s.2 of the Insurance Companies Act 1982 (*see*, for example, *Re Great Western Assurance* [1997] 2 B.C.L.C. 685 (CA)).

In the decision of *Re Sompo Japan Insurance Inc* [2007] EWHC 146 (Ch), Richards J. held that the court's jurisdiction had been established, even though the relevant business was written in Japan and was moved to a UK branch shortly before, and with the sole objective of carrying out, a transfer under the Part VII regime.

6.1.2.5   Excluded cases

There are five categories of excluded transfer, being situations where use of the court procedure is permitted (except in the first case) but not compulsory. The first such case refers to transfers by a friendly society, which must be carried out under separate provisions described at Section 6.1.9 below. Cases two and three concern transfers approved by certain overseas courts or overseas regulators (in these circumstances, it may be desirable to carry out a "case two" or "case three" transfer if there is concern about the legal effect of the overseas procedure on policies or other contracts governed by English law). Case four is where:

(a)   the business to be transferred is the whole of the business of the authorised person concerned;

(b)   all of the policyholders are controllers (as defined in s.422 of the FSMA 2000) of the transferee or of firms within the same group (which is defined in s.421) as the transferee; and

(c)   all of the policyholders who will be affected by the transfer have consented to it.

In practice, case four is likely to apply to relatively few transfers. Case five, on the other hand, may be more helpful as, although restricted to reinsurance, it covers transfers of part of a business and does not depend on establishing a group relationship. It applies where the transfer does not fall within case four and:

(a) the transferor's business consists solely of the effecting and carrying out of contracts of reinsurance;
(b) the business to be transferred is the whole or part of that business;
(c) all of the policyholders who will be affected by the transfer have consented to it; and
(d) a certificate has been obtained under para.2 of Sch.12 in relation to the proposed transfer.

Even where the conditions for either case 4 or 5 are established, there may be good reasons for using the court procedure (such as the fact that, despite the time and costs associated with a court application, it provides much greater certainty of outcome).

It is not clear whether the reference in both cases four and five to "policyholders who will be affected by the transfer" is to the transferring policyholders only or all policyholders of both transferor and transferee, including non-transferring policy-holders. On balance, given the overall thrust of the notification requirements of the legislation (*see* Section 6.1.4.9 below), the groups of policyholders whose position is considered by the independent expert (*see* Section 6.1.4.6 below) and the factors the court takes into account in deciding whether to approve a scheme (*see* Section 6.1.5 below), the better view is probably that the reference is to all policyholders of both transferor and transferee.

6.1.2.6   What is a transfer?

The expression "transfer" denotes an arrangement under which primary liability for the insurance policies forming part of the business transferred is moved from the transferor to the transferee. For practical purposes, the policyholders are treated from the date of transfer as if their contracts had always been with the transferee. A transfer is therefore different from reinsurance; even though reinsurance can, as between trans-feror and transferee, pass economic responsibility in relation to the underlying contracts, it has no effect on legal responsibility to the policyholder.

What the legislation deals with is transfers of insurance business, not merely transfers of insurance policies. Thus, it is possible to have a transfer of an insurance business even where there is only one policy. In *Re Friends' Provident Life Office* [1999] 2 All E.R. (Comm) 437, Chadwick L.J. said:

> "The transfer of long-term business from one company to another may (and usually will) involve the transfer of the legal rights and obligations which have arisen, or which will arise, under existing contracts of insurance; but it will also involve the transfer of the functions which have to be performed by the insurer in 'carrying out' those contracts and, usually, a transfer of the business of 'effecting' future contracts of the same class."

The result was that even though there was in that case only a single contract of reinsurance being transferred, and it was being "transferred" from the reinsurer to the ceding company, there was nevertheless a transfer capable of sanction by the court because a number of other facets of the transferor's "insurance business" were also being transferred.

6.1.2.7   Other matters

Although the term "scheme" is used in s.105 (in the expression "insurance business transfer scheme"), it is not felt to have any particular meaning in this context or to denote any particular form of transfer instrument. For example, the FSA states in the Guidance at para.18.1.5 that a novation or a number of novations could constitute an IBT regulated by the legislation if their number or value were such that the novation was to be regarded as a transfer of part of the business. Likewise, it is clear (*see*Section 6.1.8.5 below) that a transaction documented as a cross-border merger, and taking effect under the legislation relating to such mergers, will also qualify as a "scheme" requiring sanction by the court under Part VII if the other elements of the "insurance business transfer scheme" definition are met.

It is not clear what the scope of the expression "whole or part of the business", as it appears in s.105, is intended to be. The Guidance does not help in this regard and none of the reported cases in this area has explained the expression further. It is therefore sensible to assume that the expression has a very wide meaning and any portion of the business identifiable by reference to any particular criteria is likely to be caught by the legislation.

6.1.3 Uses of IBTs

Most IBTs fall into one of the following three categories:

(a) Where one authorised person wishes to transfer the assets and liabilities of its insurance business to another, for example on an intra-group rationalisation, a "domestication" of a branch business, or as part of the sale of the business, an IBT is the only means of doing this unless one of the excluded cases outlined above applies. Subject to the excluded cases, use of the court procedure is mandatory. It is often possible to achieve a similar commercial result through reinsurance, but this does not have the effect of physically merging funds, nor of actually transferring liabilities so that the transferee becomes liable to the policyholders and the transferor is released from liability.

(b) Where a mutual insurance company established in the UK wishes to demutualise, the accepted means of doing so is by transferring its insurance business to a successor company, either a third-party acquiring company or a company which (or the holding company of which) issues shares to the former members of the mutual. The transfer procedure has therefore been applied to achieve what in a number of other countries is achieved by a specific demutualisation statute.

(c) An IBT can be a useful tool to obtain the sanction of the court, and so make enforceable, (although also involving a transfer of business) what is essentially a fund restructuring such as a reattribution of the inherited estate of a life insurance company.

An IBT is also the means envisaged in s.376(2) of the FSMA 2000 by which an insurance business which is in the process of being wound up could be transferred as a going concern to a solvent insurance company. There are no examples of this happening in recent years.

6.1.4   Procedure

6.1.4.1   Introduction

The procedure for transfers of long-term business and general business is essentially the same, although the issues raised by any transfer will, of course, vary.

6.1.4.2   Timetable

Table 6.1 shows an indicative timetable for a straightforward transfer of insurance business. This contemplates that the nature of the business or the policies to be transferred gives rise to a requirement to consult regulatory authorities in EEA states (as described below) and assumes that the transaction is not a demutualisation and so no vote is required. It also assumes that the procedure is being carried out through the High Court in England rather than the Court of Session in Scotland (as to which *see*Section 6.1.4.15 below).

Table 6.1 Timetable for transfer of insurance business

April	Initial meeting with FSA. Independent expert and all advisers to have been instructed
April–July	Develop proposals and key documents, in discussion with FSA

Early to mid-August	Finalise key documents: scheme document, reports, statement to policyholders, claim form, witness statements
Mid-August	File claim form, scheme document, witness statements (including independent expert's report and draft statement to policyholders) FSA files first Part VII Report (*see* Section 6.1.4.3 below) Submit tax clearance applications
Early September	First court (directions) hearing Three-month EEA state notification by FSA
Mid-September	Documents given to FSA. Notice advertised in gazettes and newspapers Despatch of documents (notice and statement to policyholders) to policyholders, reinsurers, affected commercial counterparties and other persons requesting them

Early to mid-December	Expiry of three-month EEA state consultation period Tax clearances to have been received FSA files second Part VII Report (*see* 6.1.4.3 below) All other evidence and certificates filed in court Unless already held, authorisation of transferee to have been received Court hearing to sanction IBT
31 December	Effective date of transfer

6.1.4.3   *Involvement of the FSA*

The first formal step in planning an IBT is to notify the FSA of the proposal, including a broad outline of the proposed transfer and its purpose (para.18.2.13 of the Guidance). Paragraph 18.2.12 of the Guidance states that the promoters should discuss a proposed transfer with the FSA as soon as reasonably practical, to enable the FSA to consider what issues are likely to arise, such as issues relating to policyholder rights or security, and to agree a practical timetable for the transfer. FSA-authorised firms must do so in order to comply with Principle 11 of the FSA's Principles for Businesses (the "FSA Principles"), which requires them to deal with the FSA in an open and cooperative way.

Although the FSA is not required to approve the transfer formally, it will expect to be kept fully informed as the proposal develops and to review a number of drafts of the formal scheme document, the statement to policyholders and the independent expert's report. The FSA will indicate to the promoters how closely it wishes to monitor the progress of the transfer, including the extent to which it wishes to see draft documentation (para.18.2.13 of the Guidance). The length of time that this initial phase will take depends on the complexities inherent in the proposal and the issues which it raises for policyholder rights and security. It will rarely be less than two to three months.

Since June 2007, the FSA has prepared a written report ("Part VII Report") on all proposed IBTs, which aims to highlight (for the benefit of the court) issues raised by a transfer and the reasons why the FSA objects or does not object to it taking place.

In practice, the FSA prepares a first report (which it expects to file at court shortly before the first court (directions) hearing) and a second report (which it expects to file at court shortly before the final court hearing). Neither report is made public. The first report sets out the FSA's current view on the proposed transfer, whether the FSA intends to be represented by Counsel at the final hearing and its views on waivers being sought from the court. The second report sets out the FSA's considered view on the proposed transfer, whether policyholders or other affected persons have indicated that they intend to appear at the final hearing, the FSA's views on any objections raised by policyholders or others, details of notifications given to policyholders and affected persons and details of the certificates required under the FSMA 2000.

Although the Guidance has not been amended to reflect the FSA's practice of preparing Part VII Reports, para.18.2.51 lists some of the factors that are likely to be relevant to the FSA's opinion on an IBT. These include:

(a) the purpose of the transfer;
(b) how the security of policyholders' contractual rights appears to be affected;
(c) how the transfer compares with possible alternatives, particularly those that do not require FSA or court approval;
(d) how policyholders' rights and reasonable expectations appear to be affected;

(e) the opportunity given to policyholders and others affected by the transfer to consider it, and the adequacy of the information provided;
(f) the opinion of the independent expert;
(g) any views expressed by policyholders.

The FSA's review of transfer proposals, including the application of the Guidance, also reflects the following key themes:

(a) Outcomes–focused regulation—the FSA's stated approach to regulation means that it relies less on the precise wording of its rules and guidance and more on the outcomes that they are intended to secure. In the context of IBTs, it will be important, therefore, for the applicant to show that its proposals are consistent with broader objectives underlying the Guidance.
(b) Treating customers fairly ("TCF")—Based on FSA Principle 6, applicants will need to be able to demonstrate to the FSA that transfer proposals are consistent with TCF, as reflected in rules and guidance and in other FSA statements.

The FSA will need to consider what skills are required to make a proper report on the transfer and what criteria should be applied to the choice of independent expert appointed under s.109 of the FSMA 2000. The independent expert's report may only be made by a person who appears to the FSA to have the skills necessary to enable him to make a proper report and who has been nominated or approved for that purpose by the FSA.

The Guidance sets out at paras 18.2.14–18.2.22 the criteria which the FSA expects to apply to nomination or approval of an independent expert. It indicates that the expert should be an actuary for transfers of long-term business but need not be for a transfer of general business, where the main test will be competence in assessing technical provisions and the uncertainties of the liabilities they represent. The suitability of a particular individual will depend on the nature of the transfer and the firms concerned. The FSA will indicate the criteria it expects the promoters of the transfer to apply in choosing an independent expert and, unless the FSA wishes to make its own nomination (which in practice it rarely, if ever, does), the companies will then select an individual to be notified to and formally approved by the FSA.

An application fee is payable to the FSA for its involvement in an IBT, including its preparation of Part VII Reports. Reflecting the need for greater actuarial input on long-term business transfers, the fee payable for IBTs involving long-term insurance business is £18,500 and for other IBTs is £10,000. The fee is payable by the transferor and it becomes payable when (or before) a firm applies to the FSA for approval of the appointment of the independent expert.

The FSA can also impose a special project fee, which it uses to recover part of the costs it incurs in dealing with certain large-scale and one-off transactions undertaken at the request of firms. In particular, such a fee may be charged on a significant restructuring, including one that involves an IBT.

In October 2011, the FSA issued proposals to revise its approach to charging fees on IBTs. The changes are intended to mitigate the unfairness inherent in seeking to charge both the IBT fee and the special project fee for what is essentially the same transaction.

6.1.4.4 Consultation of regulatory authorities in EEA states

One of the major determinants of the likely timetable is whether any consultation with regulatory authorities in other EEA states is required in order that one or more of the appropriate certificates under Sch.12 to the FSMA 2000 can be given. If the transferee is (or will be) an EEA firm authorised in an EEA state, its home state regulator will need to provide the certificate of solvency specified in para.2 of Sch.12. Otherwise, consultation with EEA regulators might be required because:

(a) the business to be transferred includes business carried on from a branch located in another EEA state;

(b)   the contracts proposed to be transferred include one or more insurance (but not reinsurance) policies for which another EEA state is the "State of the commitment" (in the case of long-term business) or the state "in which the risk is situated" (in the case of general business); or

(c)   the proposed transfer is from a UK branch or agency of a non-EEA insurer authorised by the FSA under art.23 of the First Non-Life Directive or art.51 of the Consolidated Life Directive ("non-EEA insurer") and the proposed transfer is to the branch or agency of another non-EEA insurer in an EEA state other than the UK.

In these three cases, the regulatory authority in that EEA state must be consulted about the transfer and has three months to indicate whether or not it consents to the proposed transfer. If no response is received during that time, the transfer can proceed as consent is presumed.

The expression "State of the commitment" is defined by para.6(1) of Sch.12 to mean:

(a)   if the policyholder is an individual, the EEA state in which he had his habitual residence at the date that he took out the policy; and

(b)   if the policyholder is not an individual, the EEA state in which the establishment of the policyholder to which the policy relates was situated at the date on which the policy was taken out.

Paragraph 6(3) of Sch.12 establishes that references to the EEA state in which a general insurance risk is situated are:

(a)   if the insurance relates to a building or to a building and its contents (as far as the contents are covered by the same policy), to the EEA state in which the building is situated;

(b)   if the insurance relates to a vehicle of any type, to the EEA state of registration;

(c) in the case of policies of a duration of four months or less covering travel or holiday risk (whatever the class concerned), to the EEA state in which the policyholder took out the policy;

(d) in a case not covered by paras (a)–(c):
　(i) if the policyholder is an individual, to the EEA state in which he has his habitual residence at the date when the policy is entered into; and
　(ii) otherwise, to the EEA state in which the establishment of the policyholder to which the policy relates is situated at that date.

The part of these two tests which depends on the "habitual residence" of the policyholder when the policy was taken out gives rise to particular difficulties. This is because the phrase "habitual residence" is a European law concept and there is no single reliable test or set of rules which can be applied to define the meaning of the expression. However, there are certain indicators and factors which can be taken into account when deciding whether a person has habitual residence in a certain state, including:

(a) external appearances such as making a home, location of one's "centre of interest", the development of "normal social relations" and the obtaining of stable employment;
(b) length and continuity of residence; and
(c) intention to reside in the relevant state in the future.

It will be obvious from the nature of these criteria that an insurance company is very unlikely to have gathered information as to habitual residence when a policy was taken out. Indeed, prior to the introduction of these requirements in the Third Insurance Directives on 1 July 1994, there would have been no reason for it to do so.

Practice has shown that the court and the FSA are prepared to be pragmatic in the application of these requirements. Companies typically consult their computer records to identify the number of policyholders with a current residential or registered address in a particular EEA state and, depending on that number, conduct an examination of original files to investigate whether the policyholder was resident in that EEA state when the policy was taken out. In order to invoke the requirement for consultation in relation to a particular EEA state, it is necessary to find only one policy to which the requirements apply, so it is customary to err on the side of caution and consult unless it is very clear that the requirement cannot apply to the relevant EEA state.

Once a certificate has been given by the FSA in relation to a particular EEA state under paras 4 or 5 of Sch.12, it does not matter that there may in fact have been many more policies subject to the requirement in that EEA state than were identified to the overseas regulatory authority. It is usual to include wording in the scheme document which excludes from the transfer any policy to which these requirements apply and in respect of which the relevant certificate has not been given by the FSA. The interests of holders of these "excluded policies" are protected by means of a reinsurance contract entered into between the transferor and transferee.

Difficulties can arise where EEA regulators respond to the FSA's notification in terms which do not allow the FSA to determine clearly whether the regulator has consented, or not refused its consent, to a transfer. Historically, the FSA has been reluctant to interpret such responses as evidence that the relevant EEA regulator has consented or not refused its consent during the three month consultation period, with the conse-quence that the relevant policies risk being excluded from the transfer.

The court has shown, however, that it is willing to take a pragmatic view of ambiguous responses from EEA regulators. In one case, the Italian regulator responded to the FSA's notification by stating that, since the transferor had never applied for the necessary "passport" permission to conduct insurance business in Italy, it had "no elements to support [its] opinion". The court was persuaded that this did not amount to a refusal of consent and so ordered the FSA to produce the necessary certificate. In *Re Commercial Union Life Assurance Co*

Ltd and others [2009] EWHC 2521 (Ch) (the "Aviva Reattribution"), the court concluded that a certificate should be issued in relation to Portugal, notwithstanding that the Portuguese regulator had decided to launch a 60-day consultation with Portuguese policyholders that extended beyond the three month period within which it had to decide whether or not to object to the transfer.

The Guidance sets out (at para.18.2.29) only very brief details of the FSA's requirements before it will agree to start the three-month notification period. In practice, the consultation is generally started at or around the time of the first court (directions) hearing and, if it is necessary for timetable reasons for the period to start earlier, it will be necessary to confirm with the FSA at the outset what exactly it will require.

6.1.4.5 Application to court

Once the documents are finalised, the process is started by a claim form issued in the relevant court as determined under s.107 of the FSMA 2000. In England this is the Companies Court of the Chancery Division of the High Court and the procedure is governed by Parts 8 and 49 of the Civil Procedure Rules 1998 and the related Practice Directions. The application may be made by the transferor or the transferee, or both.

At this stage, the scheme document will be in final form (subject only to any amendment provision specified in the document itself), as will be the independent expert's report. The form of the statement to policyholders will be substantially final, as will the form of notice to be placed in gazettes and newspapers following its approval by the FSA.

6.1.4.6 Independent expert's report

Section 109(3) of the FSMA 2000 provides that the independent expert's report must be made in a form approved by the FSA. The FSA's requirements are set out in the Guidance. An actuary acting as an independent expert will also need to comply with any relevant professional guidance.

The main areas to be covered in the independent expert's report include a description of the purpose of the transfer, a summary of the terms of the transfer (as far as relevant to the report), the expert's opinion of the likely effects of the transfer on all relevant classes of policyholders (both as to the security of their contractual rights and, for long-term business, their reasonable expectations) and an outline of the reasons for that opinion.

Following *Re Sompo Japan Insurance Inc.*[2011] EWHC 260 (Ch), it is also clear that, pending implementation of the Solvency II Directive (2009/138/EC) ("Solvency II"), the independent expert's report will need to address whether preparations being made by the transferee for the introduction of the new regime are sufficient. Furthermore, as the precise timing for Solvency II to come into effect remains undecided, (although as of now it seems likely that it will apply to firms from 1 January 2014) those preparations will need to take proper account of the uncertainty that this creates for firms.

The amount of detail that it will be appropriate to include in the independent expert's report will depend on the complexity of the transfer, the materiality of the details themselves and the circumstances. The principal objective behind the independent expert's report is to inform the court on those matters on which it will require specialist advice (notably, in the case of a transfer of long-term business, actuarial matters) and the Guidance indicates that the report must comply with the rules on expert evidence (which are set out in Part 35 of the Civil Procedure Rules 1998). Reliance will also be placed on it by policyholders, other persons affected by the transfer and by the FSA, which acknowledges in the Guidance that the independent expert's report will be an important factor in enabling it to form its views on the transfer.

In developing his report, the independent expert will have discussions with the FSA and will endeavour to agree its terms (even though it is his own report rather than the FSA's and the FSA is only required to approve its form, not its precise contents, and certainly not its conclusions). In considering any possible area of disagreement, the independent expert and the promoters of the transfer should have regard to the statement by Evans-Lombe J. in *Re AXA Equity & Law Life Assurance Society Plc* [2001] 1 All E.R. 1010, that where the view of the expert differs from that of the FSA on a particular point, the court will tend to prefer the view of the FSA (*see* further discussion at Section 6.1.5 below).

In *Royal & Sun Alliance and British Engine* [2006] EWHC 2947 (Ch), Richards J. commented briefly on disclosure. He said that it was not acceptable that material on which the independent expert had relied, particularly when it was of some significance to an important aspect of the expert's consideration of the transfer, should not be put before the court and be readily available to interested parties. In the 2011 *Sompo*decision referred to above, Briggs J. also dismissed criticism of reliance by the independent expert on other research and review carried out on behalf of the transferor and transferee. In the context of large scale and complex insurance business, the judge thought it both "inevitable and acceptable" that the independent expert should place appropriate reliance, after sufficient review, on the analytical work of other qualified professionals.

6.1.4.7 Report by the holder of the actuarial function/with-profits actuary

It is not a requirement of the FSMA 2000 or the Regulations for a report on the terms of a transfer of long-term business to be prepared by the actuarial function-holder or (where the business transferred includes with-profits business, or the transferor or transferee has other in force with-profits business) the with-profits actuary of either the transferor or the transferee. This has, however, become customary. The Guidance indicates in para.18.2.58 that the FSA would expect to receive reports on the transfer by the actuarial function-holder and, where relevant, the with-profits actuary of both firms at an early stage (note that, in practice, these reports are developed and then finalised alongside the other documents, rather than in advance of them as the Guidance implies). It is also likely that the independent expert will wish to rely on statements in the actuaries' reports on matters such as the future interpretation of policyholders' reasonable expectations, the approach taken to advising the board of directors on actuarial matters arising under the transfer and the with-profits actuary's view on the effect of the transfer on with-profits policyholders. Pending Solvency II taking effect, such additional reports should, like that of the independent expert, aim to address the impact of the new regime on the transferee's post-transfer capital position.

6.1.4.8   Supplementary actuarial reports

Recent turmoil in the financial markets has had an impact on transfers as the court has shown particular interest in how up-to-date the financial information used by the internal actuaries and the independent expert was and whether market fluctuations over the intervening period may impact on the conclusions. This is obviously important because market changes on the scale experienced during the financial crisis could lead to a significant change in the likely effect of a transfer. This could in turn give rise to a need to reconsider whether the transfer should proceed on the basis proposed or at all and, possibly, necessitate the issue of further communications to policyholders.

On one transfer, the parties sought to deal with this issue by obtaining comfort from the independent expert in the form of a letter that the conclusions stated in his report were not affected by market events since the date of the independent expert's report. However, the court questioned the adequacy of this approach and adjourned the final hearing to allow for preparation of a supplemental, reasoned, report.

In practice, parties to transfers should now generally plan to take steps to ensure that the financial information that forms the basis of the internal actuarial and independent expert reports is brought up-to-date shortly before the final hearing, in case the views of those reporting have changed. The FSA will need to be shown any supplementary information since this may affect its views and the content of its report.

Experience has indicated that supplementary actuarial reports should be made available on the websites of the parties to the transfer in sufficient time ahead of the final hearing. On one transfer, a period of three days has been regarded as giving policyholders insufficient time to consider the supplementary actuarial reports and to make representations, with the result that the orders approving the transfers were held on the court file for four days after the final hearing to give policyholders more time to do so. On another transfer, supplementary actuarial reports were made available eight days before the final hearing. This was regarded as sufficient time for policyholders to consider them and make representations. Any interested party who has requested a copy of an actuarial report should be sent any supplementary report.

6.1.4.9   *Statement to policyholders*

Obligations to publicise a proposed transfer are contained in the Regulations. Regulation 3(2), which may be disapplied by the court, establishes that policyholders of the parties to the transfer should be sent notice of the transfer in a form approved by the FSA and as published in newspapers. This information must also be sent to reinsurers whose contracts of reinsurance (in whole or part) are to be transferred or, in specified circumstances, to a third person (such as a broker) authorised to act on behalf of such reinsurers (reg.3(2)(c)). Companies must also give a copy of the independent expert's report, together with a statement setting out the terms of the transfer and containing a summary of the independent expert's report, to any person who requests them (reg.3(4)). They must also provide the FSA with a copy of the application (i.e. claim form and scheme document), independent expert's report and statement (reg.3(5)). Neither reg.3(4) nor the requirement under reg.3(5) may be disapplied by the court.

It is usual for an application to be made to the court for a waiver of the requirement to send all policyholders notification of the proposed transfer on the basis that meeting the requirement in full is almost always a practical impossibility. Instead, the parties put forward proposals for bringing the transfer to policyholders' attention, which will still involve individual notification of at least some policyholders, but may mean not notifying other groups of policyholders in return for more widespread advertising of the scheme than is required by the legislation (*see*further discussion below).

The FSA is likely to be sympathetic to a waiver application where there are constraints on the applicants' ability to meet their statutory obligations in full, perhaps because of incomplete records or reliance on third parties for relevant information, or where it agrees with the parties that notification would be disproportionate. Until very recently, the court has generally been happy to grant waivers in circumstances where the FSA has no objection. Equally, objection from the FSA to any particular waiver application has generally been fatal to that application. A recent line of judgments suggests, however, that the court may be willing to take a more critical approach to applications, notwithstanding that this may lead it to disagree with the FSA.

- In *Ecclesiastical Life Limited v FSA* [2010] EWHC 3871 (Ch), Floyd J. noted at the final hearing that it would be relatively rare for the court to grant a waiver in respect of notification of an entire class of policyholders. Further, whilst in this instance he did not regard a failure to notify a class of policyholders remaining with the transferor as fatal to his approving the scheme, "the importance of the notification provisions cannot be underestimated". These comments were made despite the fact that the FSA had not objected to the waiver that was granted.
- In *Direct Line Insurance PLC v FSA*[2011] EWHC 1482 (Ch), the same judge refused to give a number of waivers at a pre-directions hearing in relation to the notification of transferring policyholders under policies that had been issued through a third party. Reasons for refusing to grant the waivers, at least one of which was objected to by the FSA, included that it would be premature to do so ahead

of discussions with the relevant third party about policy-holder notification. Although Floyd J. acknowledged that policyholders may not be particularly concerned about the identity of the insuring party, this did not necessarily mean that a waiver should be granted.

- At the same pre-directions hearing, Floyd J. was asked to waive the requirement to notify policyholders of the transferee company on the basis that it would be disproportionate to do so in circumstances where their relationship with the transferee would not change and over half of the policies were packaged policies, making it very unlikely that policyholders were in any case aware of or concerned about the identity of the underwriter of their policy. The FSA objected to this application on the basis that the transferee would triple in size and its nature would therefore be changed by the transfer. Again, Floyd J. did not feel ready to grant the waiver requested in the absence of further information, in particular, about how the transfer would be advertised. Subsequently at the directions hearing, however, the waiver was granted once the judge was satisfied with arrangements for wider advertising of the transfer, including quarter page adver-tisements appearing on pages of relevant publications other than the legal announcement pages in them (*see Direct Line Insurance PLC and Churchill Insurance Company Ltd* [2011] EWHC 1667 (Ch)).

More helpfully, perhaps, Norris J. in *Re Aviva International Insurance Ltd* [2011] EWHC 1901 (Ch) confirmed the court's understanding of the practical impossibility firms face in meeting the strict notification requirements of the legislation. Drawing on Floyd J.'s second *Direct Line* decision, Norris J. also indicated that the following factors would be relevant to a waiver application:

- the impossibility of contacting policyholders;
- the practicality of contacting policyholders;
- the utility of contacting policyholders;
- the availability of other information channels through which notice of the application can be made available;

- the proportionality of strict compliance;
- the impact of collateral commercial concerns; and
- the object of the transfer itself and its likely impact on policyholders.

Finally, Norris J. confirmed that, in general, the wider the degree of advertisement that can be given to a scheme, the less important it is to see that individual policyholders are notified in strict compliance with the relevant legislation.

The significance of these decisions is not yet clear. They do, however, highlight the need for clarification in this area. In particular:

- The suggestion in *Ecclesiastical* that it is likely to be rare for a waiver to be granted in respect of an entire class of policyholders is inconsistent with the approach that has often been taken on transfers to date and is worrying.
- Floyd J.'s failure to distinguish between transferring and non-transferring policyholders in his judgment is significant, as the importance of notification requirements is likely to be different for each. Based on the factors set out by Norris J. in the latest *Aviva* decision, it should be considerably more difficult to persuade the court to dispense with the need to notify transferring policyholders of a proposed transfer absent circumstances that make notification impossible. The position is likely to be very different, though, where the same factors are applied to non-transferring policyholders, in which case sensible proposals for wider advertising of the scheme are more likely to be regarded as sufficient.
- In particular for policyholders of the transferee company, if the independent expert concludes that the transfer will not materially affect their interests and the FSA has no objection to a waiver, it is difficult to see what purpose the court exercising its own judgement will serve other than to have a destabilising effect on the scheme.

Although there is no statutory obligation to circulate a more detailed summary of the proposed transfer to policyholders or reinsurers, the Guidance, which has not been updated to reflect the introduction of an obligation to notify reinsurers, states (at para.18.2.48) that it would normally be appropriate to send to policyholders a statement setting out the terms of the transfer and containing a summary of the independent expert's report. The Regulations state that this summary of the report must be sufficient to indicate the opinion of the expert on the likely effects of the transfer on the policyholders of both the transferor and the transferee, and the Guidance contains the FSA's views on this requirement. Case law indicates that particular care should be taken over the content of the policyholder statement where the terms of the proposed transfer provide for a variation of policyholders' rights. In *Re Pearl Assurance (Unit Linked Pensions) Ltd* [2006] EWHC 2291 (Ch), Briggs J. stated that the fact that a proposed transfer is intended to vary contractual rights on a significant scale beyond what is essential to the transfer must "be brought home to all concerned, including in particular the policyholders and the FSA".

The policyholder statement will often contain other related information and disclosures. If it is being published in advance of a vote or other choice to be made by policyholders or members, it will be necessary under the general law to provide sufficient information to enable that decision to be made (*see* for example *Baillie* v *Oriental Telephone and Electronic Company Ltd*[1915] 1 Ch. 503 and *Pacific Coast Coal Mines Ltd* v *Arbuthnot* [1917] A.C. 607 (PC)). In these circumstances, a more detailed policyholder statement will be appropriate. Firms are also required to meet their obligations under FSA Principle 7, namely, to give due regard to the information needs of their policyholders and to communicate information to them in a way which is clear, fair and not misleading. Further, they must have regard to the need to treat their customers fairly under FSA Principle 6.

There is no requirement for either the full text of the scheme document to be on display or made available on request. Any objector who needs to know the complete terms of a proposed transfer to be able to frame his objection properly will, unless the parties are prepared to provide these documents voluntarily (and it is now common practice to place at least the full terms of the scheme on the participant companies' website), need to apply to the court for it to provide a copy under its general jurisdiction.

6.1.4.10 Initial witness statements

The witness statements filed in court at the time proceedings are begun will include information about the transferor and the transferee and their insurance business, the purposes of the transfer, and the companies' proposals as to notification to policyholders of the proposals. This will include details of any categories of policyholder to whom it is not proposed to send documents (*see* Section 6.1.4.9) and persons with whom the companies have lost touch (gone aways). It will also include details of any policies or business to which the requirement to consult with regulatory authorities in EEA states applies. The documents to be exhibited to the witness statements will include the claim form itself with the proposed scheme document annexed, the independent expert's report, reports by the actuarial function-holder (for long-term business transfers) and, where relevant, the with-profits actuary, the form of notice and the policyholder statement to be sent or made available to policyholders.

6.1.4.11 Directions hearing

About seven days after the papers are filed in court, a hearing will be held (generally before a Registrar in chambers, although see the next paragraph). At this hearing, directions will be sought as to publication of notices to policyholders, advertisements in UK newspapers and, if applicable, newspapers in EEA states and as to the date for the final hearing to sanction the IBT.

Waiver applications made in respect of notification requirements are commonly heard at this hearing and in more difficult cases (e.g. those that involve a point of law or that are opposed by the FSA) may be decided by a judge, instead of a Registrar.

The court also confirmed in *Re Names at Lloyd's for the 1992 and prior years of account* [2008] EWHC 2960 (Ch) that it has jurisdiction to decide applications earlier, including before the report of the independent expert has been put before the court, although its willingness to decide them at this earlier stage is likely to depend on whether the independent expert's evidence can be expected to have a bearing on its decision. The recent judgment of Floyd J. in the first *Direct Line* hearing demonstrated the willingness of the court to defer making a decision of waiver applications pending further evidence from the parties.

6.1.4.12   *Notification to policyholders and others*

Following the directions hearing, the companies will arrange for the dispatch of notices and statements to policyholders and reinsurers. The Guidance also indicates that it may be appropriate to notify other persons affected, including anyone with an interest in the policies being transferred that has notified the transferor of their interest. In *Re AIOI Insurance of Europe Ltd* (2005) (unreported), the court took the same view. Richards J. commented that:

> "if there are contracts [, such as outward reinsurance contracts, that are intended to transfer under the IBT] which would trigger rights, or include an express covenant against a transfer, ... [the counterparty] should be notified of the proposed transfer and the [final court] hearing so that they are in a position to attend and make their objections."

These comments are no longer relevant in relation to reinsurance contracts which are governed by reg.3(2)(c) of the Regulations. However, it is thought that other changes to Part VII of the FSMA 2000 that took effect from 30 June 2008 have, in the absence of further guidance of the court, operated to extend the notification obligation expressed by Richards J. to all commercial counterparties of either the transferor or the transferee who have any contractual entitlements that may be caught by s.112A of the FSMA 2000.

It will also be necessary to comply with any further notification requirements as a result of any order made under s.414 of the FSMA 2000, although to date no relevant order has been made.

The Guidance states that the FSA would normally expect notices to be sent to policyholders at least six weeks before the date set for the final court hearing (para.18.2.46 of the Guidance). However, in practice eight weeks should now be allowed for policyholder and reinsurer notifications following the introduction of the FSA's practice of preparing Part VII Reports. In addition, if the transfer proposals provide for the amendment of any principles in the Principles and Practices of Financial Management ("PPFM") of an insurer carrying on with-profits business, at least three months will be needed between notice being given to affected with-profits policyholders and the effective date of the scheme (i.e. not the final court hearing).

The only formal requirement under the Regulations is that a copy of the independent expert's report and a statement setting out the terms of the transfer containing a summary of the independent expert's report should be given to the FSA at least 21 days prior to the final court hearing (reg.4(1)(b)). In *Re Sun Life of Canada Assurance Company*(1999) (unreported), Neuberger J. (following guidance given by the Court of Appeal in *R. v Immigration Appeal Tribunal, Ex p. Jeyeanthan*[1999] 3 All E.R. 231) held that the equivalent provision in legislation previously controlling IBTs was not a mandatory requirement but was instead for the benefit of the FSA, who could waive non-compliance. Even if the FSA were to take the point that insufficient notice had been given, it would still be open to the court to consider whether the FSA had suffered any real prejudice as a result of the non-compliance. If not, the court could hold that there had been substantive compliance with the requirement. It is unlikely that a different conclusion would be reached on the wording of the Regulations.

6.1.4.13 Final court hearing

Assuming that matters have proceeded satisfactorily, the companies will prepare and file a final set of witness statements approximately seven days in advance of the final court hearing. These witness statements will typically:

(a) Prove the various matters set out in the order made on the directions hearing, such as due posting of notices to policyholders and publication of the notice in the gazettes and newspapers.

(b) Exhibit supplementary actuarial reports as referred to in Section 6.1.4.8.

(c) Produce the appropriate certificates as required under s.111(2)(a) of the FSMA 2000.

(d) Confirm the position regarding the authorisation required by the transferee for the purpose of s.111(2)(b) of the FSMA 2000.

(e) Prove that any conditions to which the transfer was made subject, such as the receipt of tax clearances or confirmations, have been satisfied or waived. Although the court generally expects all conditions to have been satisfied or waived before the hearing, a transfer may sometimes be subject to conditions which by their nature cannot be satisfied until a later date, such as a listing condition. Section 111(2)(b) of the FSMA 2000 makes it clear that authorisation of the transferee to carry on the business need only be in place by the time the transfer is to become effective.

(f) Deal with the content of any material objections to the transfer which have been intimated to the companies.

(g) Contain such further argument as may be necessary as to why it is appropriate for the court to sanction the transfer.

At around the same time, the FSA will produce and file its second Part VII Report, confirming its final views on the proposal and addressing any communications which have been received from policyholders. It will also confirm whether the FSA intends to appear by Counsel at the final hearing, which it will now generally do except in very straightforward cases.

The final hearing will be before a judge in open court (*see* Section 6.1.5). It is usual for evidence to be given exclusively by witness statement rather than in person. Any person who alleges that he would be adversely affected by the carrying out of the transfer may appear and argue his case in person or by Counsel. Whether the court should order that the promoters meet the objectors' costs appears to be open for discussion following the decision in *Royal & Sun Alliance and British Engine* [2006] EWHC 2947 (Ch). Counsel for the applicant argued that the practice the court had developed over the past 30 years was not to make an order for costs in favour of an objector who raises reasonable points but does not succeed in defeating the transfer or securing an amendment. Special factors, such as the objector's impecuniosity, would be needed in order to justify an order for costs in his favour. Confusingly, although Richards J. acknowledged that this summary was probably accurate and carried with it a degree of certainty, he did not apply this approach to the question of costs in this case.

Following the hearing, assuming an order has been made sanctioning the IBT, the companies must deposit two office copies of the order with the FSA within 10 days of the making of the order (s.112(10) of the FSMA 2000) and comply with any directions made by the court in relation to publication of notice of the making of the order in EEA states as required under s.114 of the FSMA 2000 or as may be required under s.114A of the FSMA 2000. In many cases the regulatory authorities in the EEA states will indicate how such publication should be made; in other cases, it will be necessary to ask the court for a direction as to how publication should be effected.

6.1.4.14   *Transfers to a non-UK EEA transferee*

As stated above (*see* Section 6.1.1), the Part VII FSMA regime is intended to reflect requirements under the Directives to provide a method for transferring insurance business based on the principle that the transferring insurer's home state regime will apply to all EEA policies being transferred. The same principle will apply under Solvency II, once it takes effect, as the current Directive provisions are essentially replicated in the new regime.

In recent years, there have been a number of transfers of business from a UK company regulated by the FSA to a transferee company headquartered in another EEA state. Most of these have been of reinsurance and have been uneventful; some have involved direct insurance and have raised more difficult issues. A particular issue can be the extent to which the FSA and/or the court can object to the transfer on the basis of concerns about how insurers are regulated in the transferee's home state. For example, capital requirements imposed in the transferee's home state may, pending full implementation of Solvency II, be less stringent than those applying under the current FSA regime, whilst meeting minimum standards under current EU legislation.

We are not aware that the court has been invited to consider transfers in the context of applicable EU law provisions. However, in these circumstances, the position appears to be as follows:

(a) Under the provisions of the Directives, financial supervision of an insurer covered by the Directive is the sole responsibility of the regulatory authorities of the undertaking's home state;

(b) To the extent that such an insurer carries on business in other EEA states through the exercise of the freedom of establishment or the freedom to provide services, the regulatory authorities of the host state may regulate such activities only so far as is consistent with the principle of the "general good";[4]

---

[4] See the European Commission's Interpretative Communication, "Freedom to provide services and the general good in the insurance sector" (2000/C43/03) for application of the "general good" concept in the context of insurance (*see* Chapter 5 for further detail).

(c)   Host state rules will be compatible with the principle of the general good only to the extent that they are directed at a matter which has not been harmonised by EU law; they pursue an objective of the general good; they are non-discriminatory; they are objectively necessary; they are proportionate to the objective pursued; and the objective which they pursue is not already safeguarded by rules of the insurer's home state (or any host state in which it has a branch from which such activities are conducted);

(d)   The provisions in the Directives for the transfer by an insurer of a portfolio of policies to an insurer headquartered in another EEA state have the effect that, at the point of transfer, the home state of the transferee insurer becomes solely responsible for the financial supervision of the business which is the subject of the transfer, to the exclusion of the regulatory authorities of the transferor's home state, and the regulatory authorities of the transferor's home state may not object to the transfer on grounds relating to the financial supervision of the business which is the subject of the transfer;

(e)   Accordingly, it is not open to the FSA to object to the transfer on the basis that the transferee will not be subject to equivalent financial requirements under the relevant EEA state's law to those which the FSA presently applies under UK law. This is a matter exclusively for the home state regulator. Nor may the FSA legitimately demand (or ask the court to demand) any undertaking from the transferee as a condition of its approval of the transfer. The court itself is, likewise, not permitted to refuse to sanction the transfer on any ground related to the financial requirements under the law of the transferee's home state. The court's sole responsibility in this respect is to satisfy itself that the solvency certificate envisaged by the Directives and implementing UK legislation has been provided;

(f)   The first paragraph of the Commission's Interpretative Communication 2000/C43/03 reiterates that this is the correct legal position by stating: "Under the system set up by the Directives, the financial supervision of the business carried on by the insurance undertaking, including business carried on under the rules on establishment or on the freedom to provide services, is always a matter only for that insurance undertaking's home Member State";

(g) To the extent that the transferring business comprises policies written out of the transferor's home state, the regulatory authorities of that state may, after the transfer takes effect, impose on the transferee in respect of such policies any rules which are justified by reference to the principle of the general good, on the basis that such regulatory authorities are, post-transfer, to be regarded as regulatory authorities of a host state in respect of the transferee's management of such policies;

(h) So far as relates to the management, post-transfer, of any with-profits policies which are the subject of the transfer, a key issue is whether all or part of the FSA's current with-profits regime (specifically, rules and guidance contained in Chapter 20 of the Conduct of Business Sourcebook ("COBS 20")) should properly be categorised as prudential or conduct of business requirements. To the extent they are the former, it seems that the principles in (d) above apply i.e. the matter is reserved to the transferee's home state regulator and the FSA cannot seek to apply its rules to any UK business that may have been transferred, leaving UK policyholders in such circumstances unprotected by COBS 20.

Concerns about financial requirements imposed by different regulators should, of course, diminish once Solvency II comes fully into force and prudential regimes are more closely aligned throughout the EEA.

6.1.4.15   Insurance business transfers in Scotland

Section 107 of the FSMA 2000 provides that if a transferor and a transferee are registered or have their head offices in the same jurisdiction, the application for an order sanctioning an IBT must be made to the court in that jurisdiction. If a transferor and a transferee are registered or have their head offices in different jurisdictions, such an application may be made to the court in either jurisdiction. Section 107 of the FSMA 2000 defines "court" as the High Court or the Court of Session in Scotland. The term "High Court" is not defined in the FSMA 2000, but it is defined in Sch.1 to the Interpretation Act 1978 as Her Majesty's High Court of Justice in England and Wales, in relation to England and Wales, and Her Majesty's High Court of Justice in Northern Ireland, in relation to Northern Ireland.

Whilst there is no material difference in the substantive law, there are a number of important differences in procedure in the Court of Session as compared with the High Court. Two in particular should be mentioned:

(a) Any person wishing to object to an application for an order sanctioning the proposed transfer is required to submit a formal objection in the appropriate form (known as "Answers") to the Court of Session. If Answers are lodged, the court will allow a short period for the adjustment of the terms of the applicant's petition and the Answers to focus any issues and a hearing may be fixed to determine those issues. In practice, the court will expect Counsel for the transferee to address any less formal objections (such as letters to the court) at the final hearing and it will also expect the Reporter (*see* below) to refer to these in his report and (where appropriate) to comment.

(b) The Court of Session appoints a Reporter (usually an experienced solicitor in private practice who is independent of the transferor and the transferee) to review compliance by the transferor and transferee with the legislation governing the transfer of insurance business and to investigate whether any conditions to the transfer have been satisfied and/or waived. Prior to the final court hearing, the Reporter produces a report addressed to the court which considers whether each of the requirements of the legislation has been met and draws any defects in compliance to the attention of the Court of Session. The Reporter's remit does not extend to considering the terms or the merits of the transfer.

6.1.5 The decision of the court

Section 110 of the FSMA 2000 provides that both the FSA and any person (including an employee of the transferor or the transferee) who alleges that he would be adversely affected by the carrying out of the transfer are entitled to be heard at the court hearing to sanction the IBT. Section 111(3) of the FSMA 2000 provides that the court (having satisfied itself that the procedural and jurisdictional requirements described above have been satisfied) must consider that, in all of the circumstances of the case, it is appropriate to sanction the transfer.

The FSA is entitled to attend the court hearing and now generally does instruct counsel to appear on its behalf other than in very straightforward cases.

The FSA is not required under its regulatory objectives set out in s.2(2) of the FSMA 2000 to object to an IBT merely because some other transfer might have been in the better interests of policyholders if the transfer itself is not adverse to their interests. However, the Guidance indicates that there may be circumstances where the obligation to treat customers fairly (*see* Section 6.1.4.3) would require the parties to consider or to implement an alternative transfer.

In principle, the parties can proceed with an IBT without FSA approval, although they are unlikely to do so other than in exceptional circumstances and without careful review of the terms of the transfer against the principles applied by the court to the exercise of its discretion.

The leading case on the court's powers before the FSMA 2000 came into force was the decision of Hoffmann J. in *Re London Life Association Ltd* (1989). Curiously, this decision has never been reported, although it has been followed by judges ever since. In *Re AXA Equity & Law Life Assurance Society Plc*[2001] 1 All E.R. 1010, Evans-Lombe J. summarised the *London Life*decision in eight "London Life Principles" which (with minor updates to reflect the language in the FSMA 2000) were as follows:

(a) The FSMA 2000 confers an absolute discretion on the court whether or not to sanction the transfer, but this is a discretion which must be exercised by giving due recognition to the commercial judgment entrusted by the company's constitution to its directors. In the *Pearl Assurance* decision, Briggs J. observed that the "discretion remains nonetheless one of real importance, not to be exercised in any sense by way of rubber stamp".

(b) The court is concerned with whether a policyholder, employee or other interested person, or any group of them, will be adversely affected by the transfer.

(c) This is primarily a matter of actuarial judgment, involving a comparison of the security and reasonable expectations of policyholders without the transfer, with what would be the result if the transfer were implemented. For the purpose of this comparison, the FSMA 2000 assigns an important role to the independent expert, to whose report the court will give close attention.

(d) The FSA, by reason of its regulatory powers, can also be expected to have the necessary material and expertise to express an informed opinion on whether policyholders are likely to be adversely affected. Again, the court will pay close attention to any views expressed by the FSA.

(e) The fact that individual policyholders, or groups of policyholders, may be adversely affected does not mean that the transfer has to be rejected by the court. The fundamental question is whether the transfer as a whole is fair as between the interests of the different classes of persons affected.

(f) It is not the function of the court to produce what, in its view, is the best possible transfer. As between different transfers, all of which the court may deem fair, it is the company directors' choice which to pursue.

(g) Under the same principle, the details of the transfer are not a matter for the court provided that the transfer as a whole is found to be fair. Thus, the court will not amend the transfer because it thinks that individual provisions could be improved upon.

(h) The court, in arriving at its conclusion, should first determine what the contractual rights and reasonable expectations of policyholders were before the transfer was promulgated and then compare those with the likely effect on the rights and expectations of the policyholders if the transfer is implemented.

Whilst this provides a very convenient summary of the principles established by the *London Life* decision, it was prepared in the context of the particular question before Evans-Lombe J. and is therefore not comprehensive as to the criteria which might be applied by the court in other cases. The following further principles can be deduced from the cases:

(a) It appears to be acceptable, in determining the question set out at point (e) above, to take into account the advantages which would be secured by implementation of the transfer for a particular class of persons as a counterweight to potential disadvantages which other groups of persons may suffer. What is required is a balancing exercise, as is clear from the decision in Lindsay J. in *Re Norwich Union Linked Life Assurance Ltd* [2005] BCC 586.

(b) In relation to point (g) above, Hoffmann J had suggested in *London Life* that if the court was of the view that the transfer was unfair, it could indicate that it thought the vice lay in some particular term and that a fresh transfer without that term was likely to be acceptable.

(c) Although Evans-Lombe J. in *AXA* referred only to policyholders, the court will apply the same tests to objections raised by any other category of objector claiming to be adversely affected. It is important to note here that whether or not a third-party objector is adversely affected by a transfer goes to whether the court should exercise its discretion to approve a transfer. This is a different issue to whether the court has jurisdiction to approve an IBT that means that third-party rights are overridden (*see* Section 6.1.6.2).

(d) Evans-Lombe J. stated that in any actuarial matter the court's approach should be to accept the views of the independent expert and the FSA in preference to those of the companies and any objectors where they are in conflict, except where there is a compelling reason, based on proven fact, or demonstrable mistake in calculation or forecast, which points to a contrary view. Where the views of the FSA conflict with those of the independent expert, the court is likely to prefer those of the FSA.

More recently, in the *Aviva reattribution*, Norris J. noted that the court was highly dependent on the independent expert's judgement on issues of a highly confidential nature. Rejection of that judgement would need to be supported by specialist evidence of equal weight that there was a significant technical error. In relation to expressions of judgement contained in an independent expert's report (that something was "fair", "reasonable" or "appropriate"), Norris J. thought that the court may be more confident in making its own assessment. However, it should remain reluctant to overturn the independent expert's opinion, which is "informed by a depth and breadth of specialist knowledge".

It will be apparent that the *London Life* principles and the additional statements set out above are not all necessarily applicable to transfers of general business. However, the reported cases since 1 December 2001 have not suggested that any different test will be applied.

The principles described above should also be used as a guide in deciding how to deal with policyholder or other objections to the transfer. Matters extraneous to the transfer such as complaints about past service, mis-selling, unpaid claims or lack of membership on a demutualisation should, in principle, all be treated by the court as not amounting to a reason why the transfer should not be sanctioned. In contrast, complaints alleging that the transfer would have a material adverse effect on security or policyholders' reasonable expectations as to benefits would potentially lead the court to decline to sanction the IBT. Given the views of the FSA set out in the Guidance, however, it is unlikely that a transfer that gave rise to serious concerns on these points would reach the court. Conversely, experience to date suggests that the court is very unlikely to refuse to approve a transfer that is not objected to by the FSA.

6.1.6 The effect of the court's order

6.1.6.1 Effect generally

The powers of the court when sanctioning an IBT are dealt with in s.112 of the FSMA 2000. A typical transfer will take advantage of many of these powers and accordingly a typical court order will have the following effects:

(a) Policy rights and liabilities transfer without any require-ment for consent by the relevant policyholder so that the transferee becomes directly liable to the policyholder and the transferor ceases to be so liable—indeed, this is the principal objective of the order.

(b) All other assets, rights, contracts and liabilities within the scope of the order also transfer, subject in certain cases to consents as described at Section 6.1.6.2.

(c) The court order is the only instrument needed to effect the transfer (albeit that in any case where registration is needed to perfect a transfer, e.g. real property and shares, the registration requirement is not dispensed with).

(d) The transaction is a transfer by operation of law, as a result of the court's order, of the assets and liabilities within the scope of the order. It is not a transaction of assignment or of novation (novation would, in law, give rise to a new contract, whereas the transfer does not).

(e) As the authority is given by virtue of statute, it does not extend to foreign assets or liabilities which an order of a UK court cannot transfer for want of jurisdiction; such assets or liabilities will need to be transferred by separate documents in accordance with local laws (and may give rise to foreign stamp duties or other consent require-ments). This is recognised by s.112(4) of the FSMA 2000, which provides that a court order sanctioning an IBT may require the transferor to take all necessary steps for securing the transfer of any property or liability included in the order which is governed by the law of another country or territory outside the UK. In the 2007 *Sompo* decision (*see* Section 6.1.2.4), Richards J. applied the "substantial purpose" test to the question of whether non-recognition of a transfer of policies (rather than other property or liabilities) in another jurisdiction should preclude the court from granting its approval. On the basis that more than 27 per cent. of the policies to be transferred under the proposed transfer were governed by English or other UK law, and it was reasonable to suppose that the transfer would be effective in any relevant jurisdiction as regards those policies, the transfer would achieve a substantial purpose. The fact that it also extended to a larger class of business not governed by English law, and in relation to which it might not be effective, was not a good ground for the court to withhold its approval.

This aspect of Richards J.'s judgment was approved and applied by Briggs J. in *Re Sompo Japan Insurance Inc* [2011] EWHC 260 (Ch) where it was probable that a majority in value of the transferring policies were governed by laws other than of part of the UK. Briggs J. qualified his approval, however, by stating that a risk as to the partial ineffectiveness of a given transfer should not undermine the independent expert's analysis in relation to issues such as policyholder security, so as to introduce some distinct element of unfairness or unacceptable level of uncertainty.

6.1.6.2 *Third-party consents*

To meet concerns about the ability of the court to make an order that transfers assets and contracts which by their terms or nature require the counterparty's consent to their transfer (a particular concern in the past was whether the benefit of outwards reinsurance contracts could be transferred without the consent of the reinsurers), the legislation now provides that the court:

(a) has power to order the transfer of outwards reinsurance contracts and other contracts that are ancillary to the main business being transferred under an IBT; and
(b) can override terms of such ancillary contracts that purport to modify or annul a contract upon it being transferred, or

even upon a step being taken towards a transfer, for example making an application to the court for approval of the IBT.

Giving the court power to order the transfer of an ancillary contract does not mean that it must do so; it remains open to the court to decide that, in the circumstances, a contract should be excluded from the transfer. It is not clear whether this point has yet been argued by a third-party wishing to object to a transfer or what approach the court might take in the face of such an argument. In the absence of specific guidance in the legislation, it seems likely that the court would apply the tests of "adverse effect" in s.110 of the FSMA (in similar vein to Hoffmann J. in the 1989 *London Life* decision) and "appropriate in all of the circumstances" in s.111(3) of the FSMA 2000. Application of these tests is likely to be made more complicated, however, by the fact that s.110 is directed at the position of individuals and s.111(3) at the transfer as a whole.

In practice, it may be easier to persuade the court to approve the transfer of ancillary contracts in the context of an intra-group transfer, which is likely to change little in terms of concerns that may be raised by reinsurers e.g. there is no change to underwriting and claims handling systems or personnel and the impact on the reinsurer's capital position is likely to be minimised. Transfers of "expired" reinsurance policies may also face less resistance as they do not involve changes in underwriting policy.

For those contracts not governed by English law, and those third-party consents that the court cannot dispense with and which, despite the best endeavours of the parties, are not forthcoming prior to the transfer date, the language of the scheme document will typically contain a category of "residual assets" (and the associated category of "residual liabilities") designed to cater for these cases. The transfer will normally provide for these assets to remain behind in the transferor and to be held for the benefit of the transferee until the necessary consent, waiver or other event has occurred, whereupon the order of the court will automatically transfer the assets.

6.1.6.3   *Supplemental provisions*

Under s.112(1)(d) of the FSMA 2000, the court order may make such provision (if any) as the court thinks fit with respect to such incidental, consequential and supplementary matters as are, in its opinion, necessary to secure that the IBT is fully and effectively carried out. This provision and its equivalent under previous legislation (but without the words "in its opinion") have been considered in a number of judgments on whether the court's jurisdiction extends to provisions of a transfer that are unrelated to the transferring policies or to provisions that vary the terms of those policies.

In the *Norwich Union* decision ([2005] BCC 586), Lindsay J. decided that, provided that the predominant purpose of an IBT was to transfer insurance policies, there is no statutory requirement that it should do nothing but effect a transfer. Further, approving the approach of Knox J. in *Re Hill Samuel Life Assurance Ltd* [1998] 3 All E.R. 176, a liberal view should be taken of the meaning of the word "necessary" in s.112(2)(d), based on the fact that it formed part of the phrase "necessary to secure that the scheme shall be fully and effectively carried out". The court's jurisdiction would therefore extend to consequential and supplementary matters beyond those that are absolutely vital to an IBT (*see* also Park J. in *Re Reassure United Kingdom Life Assurance Company Ltd* [2006] EWHC 98). It is also clear from case law that the court's jurisdiction to vary the terms of transferring insurance policies extends beyond substituting the transferee for the transferor as insuring party, although it will look to see whether adequate notification of the proposed changes has been given to interested parties, including policyholders and the FSA (*see* Section 6.1.4.9 for comments by Briggs J. in the *Pearl Assurance* decision).

In the light of this line of cases, it will always be necessary to consider critically any provision of the IBT which does not relate to the transferring policies or their future management within the transferee or, even if it does, which interferes with the contractual rights of policyholders.

In *UIA (Insurance) Ltd* [2005] EWHC 2028, the court looked at the application of s.112 in the context of a transfer of long-term business from an industrial and provident society to a company incorporated under the Companies Act 1985 ("CA 1985"). Evans-Lombe J. decided that members' approval of the proposed transfer was not required under s.52 of the Industrial and Provident Societies Act 1965. The transfer was taking place under Part VII of the FSMA 2000 and s.112 should be construed very widely.

6.1.6.4 *Companies in financial difficulty*

Sections 112(8)(c) and 113 of the FSMA 2000 contain provisions dealing with the potential reduction of benefits payable under policies transferred by the IBT. These provisions are intended to apply to companies experiencing financial difficulty and will not be relevant in other contexts.

6.1.7 *Taxation*

6.1.7.1 *Introduction*

In general terms, an IBT is treated in the same way as any other transfer of trade for tax purposes. However, it has been recognised that the application of the general tax rules would result in certain unacceptable tax consequences, especially in relation to life insurance business, which is subject to a special tax regime. As a result, there are specific tax provisions applicable to IBTs (and, in particular, to transfers of life insurance business) which need to be read in addition to the general tax rules. At the time of writing there is an ongoing consultation on the UK tax rules applicable to companies writing long-term business. As a result, the tax provisions described in this section as applying to transfers of life insurance business are likely to be rewritten with effect from 1 January 2013. The scope of any changes, as known at the time of writing, is described below.

6.1.7.2 *Corporation tax—general tax rules applicable to an insurance business transfer*

An IBT is likely to involve, for the transferor, a discontinuance of all or part of its business, and a disposal of assets. The assets disposed of would include "circulating" assets which support the insurance business (usually a portfolio of equities, debt, property and derivative instruments) and permanent assets such as goodwill and shares in subsidiaries.

The application of general UK tax principles would give rise to the following principal consequences:

(a) the transferor would be regarded as making a disposal of its assets subject to corporation tax on chargeable gains ("CGT");
(b) the transferor would be regarded as disposing of its "trading stock" for the purposes of the computation of trading profits;
(c) any tax reliefs (e.g. excess expense relief or loss relief) available to the transferor would not be available for offset against income of the transferee for periods after the transfer.

These consequences are mitigated by the UK legislation in situations where the transferor and transferee are in a group for tax purposes or are under common control. In particular:

(a) Where the transferor and transferee are in a "capital gains tax group" ("CGT group"), s.171 of the Taxation of Chargeable Gains Act 1992 ("TCGA 1992") provides that assets subject to CGT may be transferred between them on a tax-neutral basis.
(b) Where the transferor and transferee are connected parties, and the arm's-length value of the trading stock transferred is greater than the acquisition cost or the actual consideration paid for the stock, it is possible to elect that the value of the trading stock transferred should be deemed to be

the greater of the acquisition cost or the actual consideration paid for the stock (s.167 of the Corporation Tax Act
2009 ("CTA 2009")).

(c) Part 22, Chapter 1 of the Corporation Tax Act 2010 ("CTA
2010") provides that where the parties are under common
ownership (broadly, by the holding, directly or indirectly,
of 75 per cent. or more of the ordinary share capital of both
the transferor and transferee), trading losses of the
transferor are available to the transferee (subject to
streaming provisions which prevent the use of the
transferor's losses against the transferee's existing business). The legislation also ensures that the capital allowances position is transferred from the transferor to the
transferee on a tax-neutral basis.

6.1.7.3 Corporation tax—specific tax regime applicable for life insurance companies

Historically, most life insurance companies ("life companies")
have been taxed on the "I minus E basis". The I minus E basis
recognises that the tax system for a life company achieves two
distinct objectives: to tax investment return "on behalf of"
policyholders with life policies, and to tax life companies on
the profits which they make from insurance business.

Put another way, the life company pays tax as a "proxy" for the
holders of policies which constitute basic life and general
annuity business ("BLAGAB"). The tax is payable at the
income tax basic rate (currently 20 per cent.) and is applied to
income and gains less expenses in relation to BLAGAB policies.

Profits which the life company makes on writing life assurance
business are taxed at the full shareholder corporation tax rate
which, with effect from 1 April 2011, is set at 26 per cent. (and is
set to be reduced to 23 per cent. by 2014). The mechanism for
achieving this is that taxable profits from pension business,
overseas life assurance business, life reinsurance business,
child trust fund business and ISA business (defined in the
legislation, for periods of account from 1 January 2007 for
corporation tax purposes, as together constituting gross roll-up

business ("GRB")) are computed on a "quasi-trading" basis, before the assessable profits are brought into the I minus E computation. In addition, a Life Assurance Trade Profits ("LATP") computation is made to calculate the element of the company's total profits (as determined by the result of the I minus E computation) which should be charged to tax at the full corporation tax rate.

As a result of changes to the life tax regime introduced in ss.431G and 431H of the ICTA 1988 by Finance Act 2007 ("FA 2007"), all life companies are now taxed on the I minus E basis, with the exception of "pure reinsurer" life companies or those whose business consists entirely or mainly of GRB. Such companies are taxed on profits arising from their trade under s.35 of the CTA 2009.

In conjunction with the move to mandatory I minus E basis taxation of most life companies, FA 2007 introduced an automatic measure to ensure that the taxable profits of a life company assessed on the I minus E basis can never be less than its trade profits. The excess of a life company's trade profits is taxed under s.979 of the CTA 2009.

Mutual life companies pay tax at the policyholder rate (20 per cent) on both BLAGAB profits and GRB profits.

In addition, the ordinary tax rules are modified for life companies in a number of respects to ensure "ring-fencing" in respect of different classes of business and in respect of assets or profits referable to policyholders or the company (i.e. in the case of a proprietary company, the shareholders). For example, a CGT charge may arise on the transfer of an asset from one class of business to another.

Finally, life insurance business transfers do not always take place between parties which are under common control. An acquirer may wish to have the business transferred to it in return for a cash payment to the old shareholders or members rather than to acquire the company in which the business is written. It may not be possible to acquire the company in which the business is written (for example if only part of that company's business is being acquired or if the company was incorporated under its own Act of Parliament). Therefore, special provisions are required if it is desirable to achieve tax neutrality on such transfers.

6.1.7.4 Long-term insurance business transfers—2006 and 2011 consultations

During 2006 and 2007 an extensive consultation process (the "2006 Consultation") took place between the life insurance industry and HM Revenue and Customs ("HMRC") on a number of issues identified as being in need of reform. This included the tax treatment of long-term IBTs. The 2006 Consultation's stated aim was to simplify the increasingly complex and cumbersome tax regime governing such transfers, so as to provide greater certainty for industry whilst maintaining revenue protection.

What follows is a summary of the current tax rules at the time of writing applicable to a transfer of long-term business, amended following the conclusion of the 2006 Consultation. Where relevant, reference is made to HMRC's updated guidance on transfers of long-term insurance business (contained in the "Life Assurance Manual"), published in May 2008 and still described on HMRC's website as an "interim publication".

However, it is important to note that as part of the Budget 2011 the UK Government published a technical note ("Solvency II and the Taxation of Insurance Companies") which set out key ministerial decisions on the taxation of life companies from 2013 in response to Solvency II

Then, on 5 April 2011, HMRC published a consultation document "Life Insurance Companies: A New Corporate Tax Regime", which had the effect of commencing a new phase of consultation on the detailed manner by which the ministerial decisions should be implemented. Amongst other things these decisions seek to simplify the tax rules applicable to transfers of long-term business. This new consultation (the "2011 Consultation") should be viewed in the context of the advent of Solvency II, one of the effects of which will be that, from 1 January 2014, FSA regulatory returns will no longer exist in a form which will support the current UK tax legislation.

The key ministerial decisions announced in the technical note and consultation document also:

(a) confirmed that from 2013 the trading profits for tax purposes of a life company will be based on the statutory accounts;

(b) confirmed that there will be no fundamental reform of the I minus E basis for life companies; and

(c) proposed, in the absence of a long-term insurance fund (which under Solvency II will not be required for regulatory purposes), that a 'function-based' tax treatment should apply to life companies, whereby it will be necessary to exclude from the computation of trade profits and BLAGAB profits income and gains from assets identified as being capital in nature.

Key principles to have emerged from the 2011 Consultation to date are addressed below under the heading "Long-term business transfers: 2011 Consultation".

6.1.7.5 Long-term insurance business transfers—corporation tax on chargeable gains

When considering the CGT relief which is available in respect of a transfer of long-term insurance business, it must be borne in mind that the tax charge which would otherwise arise on the transfer would, *prima facie*, be a policyholder tax charge. The legislation reflects the fact that it would be unacceptable for a policyholder tax charge to arise where the company in which the business is situated changes (a shareholder matter).

Relief is provided for by s.211 of the TCGA 1992. This relief is only available if certain conditions are satisfied, as described below. Where the relief is available, the transfer of assets subject to CGT (with the exception of "structural assets", e.g. investments in subsidiaries held in the long-term insurance fund ("LTIF")) is treated as being for a sum which gives rise to neither a gain nor a loss to the transferor (i.e. mirroring the tax neutral treatment for intra-group transfers under s.171 of the TCGA 1992).

The conditions that must be satisfied for relief under s.211 of the TCGA 1992 to be available are as follows:

(a) the transfer is of a business which consists of the effecting or carrying out of contracts of long-term insurance;
(b) the transfer is to another person whether resident in the UK or not;
(c) the transfer is in accordance with a scheme falling within s.105 of the FSMA 2000 (including an excluded scheme falling within Cases 2–5 of s.105(3)) or which would be such a scheme but for the requirement that the transferee carries on the business transferred from a location within the EEA (an IBT) (*see* Sections 6.1.7.18 and 6.1.7.19);
(d) the assets transferred are assets of the transferor's LTIF immediately before the transfer; and
(e) the assets transferred become assets of the transferee's LTIF immediately after the transfer.

Prior to amendments introduced in FA 2007, the relief from CGT on a transfer of long-term business was provided for by s.139 of the TCGA 1992 (as modified by s.211). Section 211 of the TCGA 1992 now stands alone. As a result (and in contrast to the previous relief):

(a) it is no longer a requirement for CGT relief on a transfer of long-term business that no consideration is received by the transferor, other than the assumption of liabilities by the transferee; and
(b) it is no longer necessary to apply to HMRC for clearance, in advance of the transfer, that the transfer is for *bona fide* commercial reasons and does not form part of a scheme or arrangement of which the main purpose, or one of the main purposes, is the avoidance of liability to corporation

tax. In other words, subject to the satisfaction of the conditions outlined above, the nil-gain/nil-loss treatment is automatic. This is one of a number of statutory clearances available on a transfer of long-term business prior to the conclusion of the 2006 Consultation but which have since been replaced by the "targeted anti-avoidance rule" (for more on which, *see* Section 6.1.7.13).

However, s.211 of the TCGA 1992 as amended has restricted the relief previously available as the relief now only applies where the assets are transferred from the transferor's LTIF to the transferee's LTIF. It does not therefore apply to assets held outside the transferor's LTIF. Such assets can only pass to the transferee on a tax-neutral basis if the group transfer relief under s.171 of the TCGA 1992 applies (this will not apply to assets transferred to the transferee's LTIF, as explained below).

6.1.7.6 Long-term insurance business transfers—"box transfers"

Section 440 of the ICTA 1988 deems a disposal to occur (both for CGT purposes and in relation to loan relationships assets, e.g. gilts) where the asset was in one "CGT box" prior to the transfer and in another "CGT box" afterwards.

Following the amalgamation of business referred to at Section 6.1.7.3, s.440(4) provides separate CGT boxes for:

(a) assets linked solely to GRB or foreign business assets;
(b) assets linked solely to BLAGAB;
(c) assets within the LTIF but not linked to any particular category; and
(d) assets outside the LTIF.

Therefore, a deemed charge would arise, for example, if an asset was held within the LTIF prior to the long-term insurance business transfer, but is transferred to the shareholder fund of the transferee (i.e. to outside the LTIF).

Where s.440 applies, the transferor is treated as having disposed of and immediately reacquired the asset for a consideration equal to the fair value of the asset immediately before the transfer. CGT group relief which might otherwise be available is expressly excluded from transfers between LTIF "boxes". However, in practice, this provision is only applied where the change of category is part of an arrangement to which both the transferor and the transferee are party. If this is not the case, the asset is treated as having been transferred between categories by the transferee immediately after the transfer, with the result that any gain or loss accrues to the transferee and not the transferor.

6.1.7.7   *Long-term insurance business transfers—expenses of management*

Again, expenses of management are a component of the "policyholder" I minus E computation and therefore the relief described below prevents the loss of a policyholder-owned relief.

Specific legislation (s.444A of the ICTA 1988) provides that expenses of management which would have been deductible by the transferor under general principles for the accounting period following that in which the transfer takes place will be treated as expenses of management of the transferee and deductible in accordance with general principles, provided that there is a transfer of long-term business from one person to another which constitutes an IBT.

The relief for carrying forward of management expenses was previously only available if the transfer was effected for bona fide commercial reasons and did not form part of a scheme or arrangement of which the main purpose, or one of the main purposes, was the avoidance of liability to corporation tax. This condition, and the accompanying clearance procedure, have now been removed, so that the treatment is automatic (though *see* Section 6.1.7.13 in relation to the "targeted anti-avoidance rule").

The relief also applies to certain other policyholder reliefs such as "excess needs" (a with-profits tax relief) and unused acquisition expenses.

In addition to this relief BLAGAB capital losses may be transferred to the transferee under a long-term insurance business transfer (s.211ZA of the TCGA 1992).

6.1.7.8   *Long-term insurance business transfers—other tax reliefs*

Losses arising to the company from its GRB may also be transferred under s.444A of the ICTA 1988, but only if the transferor and transferee are under at least 75 per cent. common ownership. This change, first introduced in FA 2003, emphasises the "shareholder" nature of the GRB losses. GRB losses are available for offset only against profits of the GRB (the categories of business included within this being taxable as quasi-trades). The tax thereon represents the tax on the profits made by the company in writing the business.

Trading losses arising from the LATP computation (*see* Section 6.1.7.3) or from the writing of non-life business (e.g. permanent health insurance ("PHI")) will be available to the transferee under ordinary principles only where the transferor and transferee are under at least 75 per cent common ownership.

There are provisions in s.444AZA of the ICTA 1988 to allow for the carry-over of GRB losses where the transferor is subject to the I minus E basis of taxation but the transferee is charged to tax under s.35 of the CTA 2009 on all of its long-term business (or vice versa), provided there is 75 per cent common ownership.

6.1.7.9   *Long-term insurance business transfers—other neutrality provisions*

The CGT neutrality provisions apply to assets which are subject to corporation tax on chargeable gains. There are also neutrality provisions to achieve the continuity of taxation between the transferor and transferee in respect of loan relationships (Part 5, Chapter 4 of the CTA 2009), derivatives (Part 7, Chapter 5 of the CTA 2009) and intangibles (s.904 of the CTA 2009), in each case subject to the "box transfer" rules considered in Section 6.1.7.6.

Section 560 of the Capital Allowances Act 2001 provides that where assets are transferred as part of, or in connection with, a transfer of the whole or part of the long-term business of an insurance company to another company and the transfer constitutes an IBT, the transferee shall be entitled to any allowances and charges as would have fallen to be made to or on the transferor.

The amount of the allowances or charges is computed as if everything done to or by the transferor had been done to or by the transferee. In other words there is a complete continuity of the capital allowances position of the transferor and the transfer itself will occasion no balancing charge.

6.1.7.10 Long-term insurance business transfers—anti-avoidance

As explained above, life companies are taxed on a quasi-trading basis in respect of GRB. In addition, an LATP computation is made to calculate the element of the company's total profits (as determined by the result of the I minus E computation) which should be charged to tax at the full corporation tax rate (except in the case of a mutual).

In most cases it should be possible for the transfer of business to be made on a tax neutral basis (i.e. without giving rise to a "trading" profit or loss).

However, the current tax rules incorporate many anti-avoidance provisions in relation to long-term IBTs, mainly in the area of "shareholder" or "company" tax. They are principally targeted at the creation of tax-effective deficits in the transferee (i.e. where liabilities will exceed assets in the transferee) and the extraction of assets from the LTIF on a tax-free basis. The anti-avoidance provisions were significantly amended by the FA 2007 as a result of the 2006 Consultation and are widely drafted, requiring careful consideration.

Taxing the transferor

When assets held within the LTIF of the transferor are not transferred to the LTIF of the transferee (whether left behind in the transferor's LTIF or transferred to the transferee's shareholders' fund), the previously untaxed element of fair value of those assets is brought into account.

As a result of FA 2007, and with effect from 1 July 2008, the amended s.444AB of the ICTA 1988 brings into account for the transferor the previously untaxed element of fair value of the transferor's LTIF assets which do not pass to the transferee's LTIF. Specifically, it will apply if:

(a) any assets of the transferor's LTIF are not transferred to the transferee's LTIF ("non-LTIF assets"); or

(b) immediately after the transfer, the transferor no longer carries on long-term business, but still holds assets which were previously in its LTIF ("retained assets").

Under s.444AB, the excess of the fair value of the non-LTIF assets or retained assets, over the amount already recognised as surplus in the transferor, is taken into account as a taxable receipt in the transferor for its period of account ending immediately before the date of the transfer.

Section 444ABBA of the ICTA 1988 provides that the transferor and the transferee can jointly elect that any additional corporation tax liability arising to the transferor as a result of the transfer of any non-LTIF assets is in fact payable by the transferee.

Excess of assets over liabilities transferred

Prior to 1 July 2008, there was effectively a tax "nothing" position for both the transferor and transferee in the event that there was an excess of assets over liabilities transferred. Section

444AC of the ICTA 1988 (which has now been repealed) exempted the profits arising in the transferee (and disallowed a loss, if the reverse was true).

A new s.444AC of the ICTA 1988 was introduced by the FA 2007 following the 2006 Consultation to limit the exempt profit in the transferee to the amount of the recognised surplus in the transferor (provided that the assets representing that surplus do not constitute non-LTIF assets in the transferee). This section again took effect for transfers of business taking place on or after 1 July 2008. This represented a change in the basis of taxation where the assets transferred exceed the transferred liabilities, resulting in a loss in the transferor, and a profit in the transferee.

6.1.7.11   Long-term insurance business transfers—distributions

It may be the case that, either deliberately or fortuitously, the transferee may around the time of the long-term insurance business transfer be or become a member of the transferor or that the parties have such an existing relationship. In such cases, HMRC may argue that the excess of the value of the transferor's assets over the liabilities assumed by the transferee constitutes a "distribution" for tax purposes (whether an income distribution or a capital distribution). It is considered that treatment of that excess as a distribution (of either kind), even where the transferee is a member of the transferor, is not inevitable (nor in most cases likely), but it is clearly a matter to be borne in mind by those devising the scheme. It may well be advisable, depending on the circumstances, for appropriate confirmation to be obtained from HMRC. If shares are offered on a demutualisation to former members of the mutual, their value might (depending on the exact terms of the scheme) constitute a distribution.

If a surplus transfer is an income distribution for corporation tax purposes, it will fall within the charging provisions of Part 9A of the CTA 2009 (although it is probable that one of the exempt classes of distribution in Part 9A would apply to exempt a charge to tax). In practice, treatment as an income distribution is only likely to be a concern if the surplus transfer constitutes a distribution out of assets of the transferor company in respect of shares in the company (other than a distribution representing a repayment of share capital or a distribution equal to new consideration received by the transferor company). Provided that both the transferor and transferee companies are UK resident and either the transferee owns more than 50 per cent of the transferor's ordinary share capital (or both transferor and transferee are at least 51 per cent subsidiaries of another UK company), then to the extent that the transferred assets are non-cash assets which give rise to a benefit for the transferee a transfer of surplus assets should not in any event give rise to an income distribution for corporation tax purposes.

If a surplus transfer does not fall to be treated as an income distribution, it is still necessary to exclude the possibility that the transfer of surplus assets could instead be treated as a capital distribution under UK chargeable gains legislation. HMRC practice (albeit in the context of a dividend in specie) appears to be that any distribution of non-cash assets excluded from the scope of the income distribution tax charge would not be regarded as a capital distribution.

6.1.7.12 Long-term insurance business transfers—deemed periodical return

It is necessary to consider a life company's obligation to make regulatory returns upon the transfer of its business. HMRC believes a mismatch between regulatory returns and "periods of account" for tax purposes can be manipulated to extract accumulated profits free of tax.

FA 2007 inserted a new s.444AA of the ICTA 1988 (subsequently amended), with effect for periods of account beginning on or after 1 January 2007, providing for there to be deemed periodical returns of the transferor (and therefore deemed periods of account for corporation tax purposes) where the whole of the transferor's long-term business is transferred by way of one IBT (or by two or more IBTs which take effect on the same date).

The first deemed periodical return covers the period to the date immediately before the transfer takes place. As a result, this period becomes a deemed period of account for corporation tax purposes for the transferor. In addition, s.444AA of the ICTA 1988 provides that the date of the IBT itself becomes a deemed period of account for corporation tax purposes for the transferor (so that a second deemed periodical return is created).

Section 444AA(6) of the ICTA 1988 makes it clear that the date of transfer itself is deemed to be a period of account of the transferor only for the purposes of s.444ABD (profits of transferor where value of liabilities exceed value of assets transferred), so that the entries required in this deemed return will be restricted to details of the business transfer out and any reduction in mathematical reserves.

In the event that a transfer takes place on the day following an actual period of account, to avoid the need for a deemed period of account arising, any profit arising to the transferor under s.444ABD of the ICTA 1988 is treated as arising on the last day of the period of account ending immediately before the transfer (this is particularly helpful where the transfer takes place on 1 January).

6.1.7.13   Long-term insurance business transfers—"targeted anti-avoidance rule"

Sections 444AEA–444AED of the ICTA 1988, introduced by FA 2007, contain two targeted anti-avoidance rules ("TAAR") and an accompanying clearance procedure.

The first (s.444AEA of the ICTA 1988) applies if, as a result of the *whole* of the "transfer scheme arrangements", a life assurance trade profits advantage is obtained by either party (or both parties) to the transfer and the obtaining of that advantage was the sole or main purpose, or one of the main purposes, of the *whole* of the transfer scheme arrangements.

The second TAAR (s.444AECA of the ICTA 1988) applies if, as a result of any *part* of the "transfer scheme arrangements", a life assurance trade profits advantage is obtained by either party (or both parties) to the transfer and the obtaining of that advantage was the sole or main purpose, or one of the main purposes, of that *part* of the transfer scheme arrangements.

Transfer scheme arrangements include the transfer itself and any other transfers, contracts of reinsurance, reconstructions or amalgamations or transfers of assets to the transferee not brought into account but which increase the transferee's surplus, in each case which is effected in connection with the transfer.

The transferor or transferee will obtain a life assurance trade profits advantage if its trade profits (i.e. computed under s.35 of the CTA 2009) in the relevant period of account are less than they would have been, or its trading losses are greater than they would have been, but for the whole of the transfer scheme arrangements (for the purposes of the first TAAR) or but for any part of the transfer scheme arrangements (for the purposes of the second TAAR).

The clearance procedure under the TAAR(s) is provided for by s.444AED of the ICTA 1988. An application to HMRC can be made (by either party) on the grounds that either the obtaining of a life assurance trade profits advantage by the applicant was not the sole or main purpose of the whole or any part (as applicable) of the transfer scheme arrangements, or, in the case where the transferor and the transferee are members of the same group of companies, that any aggregate reduction in corporation tax liability across the group arising from a life assurance trade profits advantage is not greater than any aggregate increase in corporation tax liability across the group as a result of the transfer scheme arrangement.

It should be noted that both of the TAARs can apply either to whole or to part transfers. It is the wider "transfer scheme arrangements" which will need to be considered in order to determine whether the life assurance trade profits advantage arises from the "whole" or "part" of those arrangements.

6.1.7.14   Long-term insurance business transfers—VAT

Provided that what is being transferred is the whole of a business or, where part of a business is being transferred, that the part business is capable of separate operation, VAT should not pose any particular problems for IBTs between UK life companies since the transfer will be of a business or part of a business as a going concern ("TOGC") and the transfer will be treated as neither a supply of goods nor a supply of services for VAT purposes (under para.5 of the VAT (Special Provisions) Order 1995 (SI 1995/1268)).

HMRC states, in the Life Assurance Manual, that it "would be expected" that any transfer of long-term business would constitute a TOGC given that a Part VII FSMA transfer must be one where the whole or part of a business is transferred, and the transferred business continues to be carried on by the transferee. It should be noted that HMRC consider that a preliminary reinsurance of the business to a potential trans-feree is not a TOGC, but that such a reinsurance will not prevent the reinsurance and the Part VII FSMA transfer from constituting a TOGC.

Further to qualify as a TOGC, where the assets being transferred include land and buildings in relation to which the transferor has made an election to waive its exemption from VAT, the transferee must also make an election in relation to those properties with effect from the transfer date. An additional requirement was added in 2004, for a buyer to notify the seller that certain anti-avoidance provisions will not apply. This notification is necessary to enable the transfer to qualify as a TOGC. The anti-avoidance provisions are aimed at particular strategies which have been used to improve VAT recovery on "opted" commercial property occupied by partially exempt persons.

In any event, IBTs made between members of a VAT group should not be subject to VAT as the effect is that there is no "supply" for UK VAT purposes.

However, for cross-border IBTs the VAT analysis may require a more detailed analysis due to:

(a) the change in the VAT place of supply rules, with effect from 1 January 2010; and
(b) the decision of the European Court of Justice ("ECJ") in the case of *Swiss Re Germany Holding GmbH* v *Finanzamt München für Körperschaften* (Case C-242/08).

Although in the case referred to above the ECJ held that a cross-border transfer of reinsurance contracts was subject to VAT, it is important to note that it had already been determined by the referring German court that the requisite conditions for treatment as a transfer of a going concern had not on the facts been met.

What this case does highlight is that in all cases it will be important to analyse the proposed IBT at an early stage to determine (i) which jurisdiction's VAT rules will apply, and (ii) whether the applicable conditions for either VAT group treatment or transfer of a going concern treatment will be met. The ECJ decision confirms that any VAT properly charged will be likely to be irrecoverable and would effectively increase the cost of an IBT for the transferee.

6.1.7.15 Long-term insurance business transfers—stamp duty

With the abolition of stamp duty from 1 December 2003 except in relation to shares and certain securities, the significance of stamp duty in the context of transfers of long-term business is much diminished. However, stamp duty or stamp duty reserve tax ("SDRT") may still be charged on the transfer of certain assets such as shares and certain securities. Stamp duty land tax ("SDLT") is chargeable on land transactions. It is therefore important to consider the relevance of stamp taxes where such assets are transferred as part of an IBT.

Where the transferor and transferee are within a group for the purposes of stamp duty (based on beneficial ownership of 75 per cent. of the shares and economic entitlement), stamp duty group relief may be sought (under s.42 of the FA 1930). A similar relief exists in respect of SDLT (under Sch.7 of the FA 2003). The availability of the relief is subject to the meeting of a number of conditions. It is not, as with CGT, denied where transactions are carried out with policyholder assets. The SDRT legislation does not contain any equivalent group relief provisions. Accordingly, any securities within the scope of SDRT should be transferred to the transferee by an instrument of transfer (which can include the court order or a declaration of trust). If this is done, stamp duty group relief may be available and, if it is, this will frank any SDRT liability.

FA 1997 introduced a specific relief intended for "pure" demutualisations, although it is possible to structure a demutualisation which is in substance an acquisition so as to benefit from the relief. The relief is contained in s.96 of the FA 1997. In very brief terms, the relief is available where at least 90 per cent of the members of the transferor (the mutual) are offered shares in the transferee company (or the parent of the transferee) and where any other shares issued by the transferee (or its parent) go to employees or pensioners of the transferor or are issued as a result of an offer to the public. The relief is mirrored for SDLT (s.63 of the FA 2003).

In many cases a transfer of long-term business would not benefit from any of the reliefs set out above. In that case, and where the assets transferred include shares and/or certain other securities, it is necessary to consider the potential heads of stamp duty charge.

The potentially relevant heads of charge are:

(a) Schedule 13, para.1, FA 1999—"transfer on sale". The amount of the duty is calculated as a percentage (0.5 per cent.) of the "amount or value of the consideration for the sale", and such duty is called *ad valorem* duty. In relation to instruments executed on or after 13 March 2008, no *ad valorem*duty is payable where the chargeable consideration in relation to the property transferred is certified at £1,000 or less; or

(b) Schedule 13, para.16 FA 1999—"transfer of property otherwise than on sale". Any instruments effecting a transfer otherwise than on sale executed on or after 13 March 2008 are exempt from stamp duty.

In the straightforward case of a transfer of long-term business where the transferee assumes the transferor's liabilities to the policyholders but no price (either cash or stocks and shares) is payable or to be issued as consideration for the transferred business, whether to the transferor or, on a demutualisation, its members, HMRC's practice as set out in the Life Assurance Manual is that an IBT is liable to stamp duty as a "transfer on sale". However, the guidance goes on to say that in such a straightforward case the assumption of liabilities is not deemed to be chargeable consideration under s.57 of the Stamp Act 1891. This is the same reasoning that had, in the author's experience, previously led HMRC to conclude that the court order would be subject to the (as was) £5 fixed duty (as a "transfer otherwise than on sale"). However, it now seems that, as a "transfer on sale" with no chargeable consideration, there should (upon certification that the £1,000 *de minimis* threshold has not been reached) be no *ad valorem* stamp duty to pay in this straightforward case. Similar reasoning should also ensure that no SDLT arises in a straightforward case where land is transferred to the transferee pursuant to a Part VII FSMA transfer. This is because the assumption of the transferor's liabilities to the policyholders will not be treated as money or money's worth for SDLT purposes.

Certain types of demutualisation or long-term insurance business transfer involve the making of payments (whether in cash or shares) to members (policyholders) of the transferor or to the transferor itself under the scheme. It is a question of construction of the scheme whether the payments are consideration for anything and, if so, what (in particular, whether and to what extent the consideration can be allocated to the assets which attract stamp duty, principally shares, or SDLT (land) as opposed to assets which are now free of stamp duty, such as goodwill). In the Life Assurance Manual, HMRC state that where money or monies worth is paid to the transferor, or to the members or policyholders of the transferor, this will constitute chargeable consideration for the property transferred, and hence be subject to *ad valorem* duty. It is arguable that this is not the case (and no *ad valorem* duty should be chargeable) if the correct construction of the scheme is that, for example, the payments are being made to members to cancel their membership rights and not for the purchase of the business transferred.

Experience suggests that the Stamp Office have in the past also sought to argue that the value of any special bonuses declared in favour of the transferor's policyholders should count as chargeable consideration. However, there is a strong technical argument against this view, particularly as such bonuses are neither provided by the transferee nor received by the transferor. Again, it will be necessary to consider the precise mechanics of any special bonuses and the true construction of the scheme.

In addition, the question of SDRT needs to be considered. Where the order is appropriately stamped, no question of SDRT should arise.

In view of the fact that any consideration, no matter how small, paid to the transferor under the scheme may mean that the order will be a transfer on sale and hence trigger *ad valorem* stamp duty, it is prudent to obtain prior confirmation from HMRC as to the stamp duty treatment (though *see* Section 6.1.7.21).

It is also necessary to consider potential overseas stamp duties which might arise on the transfer of foreign assets.

6.1.7.16 Long-term insurance business transfers—policyholder tax issues

It is necessary to ensure that policyholders' personal tax positions are not adversely affected by the IBT.

Life policyholders may still benefit from a certain relief, life assurance premium relief ("LAPR"), which was phased out in 1984 in respect of qualifying policies and 1968 in respect of non-qualifying policies. However, it was retained for policies written prior to the change.

Such relief can, in certain circumstances, be lost if a new policy is issued in substitution of the existing one or the terms of the existing policy are varied. A possible analysis of the effect of an order under s.111 of the FSMA 2000 might be that policies issued by the transferor are "novated", that is to say cancelled and substituted by new policies in appropriate terms issued by the transferee, and if this analysis were appropriate, LAPR could in certain circumstances be lost. It is therefore important to ensure that the scheme is drafted in such a way as not to constitute a novation (i.e. release and recreation) of liabilities, but a transfer of liabilities by operation of law.

In the Life Assurance Manual, HMRC state that any change in the recipient of premiums under a life policy, due to a transfer taking place, should not affect the availability of LAPR.

HMRC are normally prepared to confirm that other reliefs available to policyholders and annuitants (such as retirement benefit scheme relief, retirement annuity relief and personal pension scheme relief) would be unaffected by the transfer, as would the approved (or, since the wholesale reform of the UK pensions regime in 2006, "registered") status of pensions policies.

The rules providing for whether a life policy is a "qualifying policy" under Sch.15 of the ICTA 1988 were amended by the FA 2006. The principle benefit of qualifying policy status is that the scope of the chargeable event regime, which imposes an income tax charge on policyholders, is restricted for such policies. The rules provide that, in certain circumstances, qualifying policy status will be lost if the terms of the policy are varied. As a result of the FA 2006 change, variations which alter the method used for calculating the benefits secured by the policy will be ignored for the purposes of qualifying status. This amendment is deemed always to have had effect for variations effected as part of an IBT. Again, HMRC have confirmed in the Life Assurance Manual that the "qualifying" status of a policy should not be affected solely by any change to the identity of the insurance company that is party to the policy, nor should a transfer of business result in the substitution of a new policy for an old one. The HMRC guidance also confirms that, for example, a change from a with-profits policy to a linked policy with no surplus entitlement would be covered by the amendment introduced by the FA 2006.

Specific tax issues may arise upon an IBT which has effect to transfer pension policies, In such cases it will be important to ensure that any tax reliefs attaching to the policies are not lost as a result of the IBT. It is also important to consider whether the IBT would have any effect on any transitional rules which might otherwise preserve beneficial tax treatment for policyholders. In all cases, potential tax issues surrounding transfers of pension policies should be considered at an early stage so that, if necessary, the court is made aware of any requirements imposed by HMRC in order for tax reliefs to be retained, or beneficial tax treatment preserved.

6.1.7.17 Long-term insurance business transfers—members' tax issues

It is sometimes questioned whether there is any liability to CGT in relation to members of a mutual company which is the transferor under a long-term IBT where, as is not unusual, the scheme provides for them to become members of the transferee. It is normally very difficult to ascribe any monetary value to the membership rights. Furthermore, s.136 of the TCGA 1992 provides that in the case of a reconstruction (which a demutualisation is likely to be) the issue by the transferee of "shares"—which is expressly declared in this context to include the interest of a member in a company such as the interest of a policyholder in a mutual company—against the cancellation of "shares" in the transferor does not of itself give rise to a disposal by members of the transferor of their interest.

6.1.7.18 Long-term insurance business transfers—cross-border issues and overseas life insurance companies

The tax regime for transfers of long-term business is amended for life companies resident outside the UK but which are engaged in the effecting or carrying out of contracts of long-term insurance in the UK through a permanent establishment (overseas life insurance companies, or "OLICs"). The Overseas Life Insurance Companies Regulations 2006 (as amended) (the "OLICs Regs") amend the definition of LTIF (found at s.431 of the ICTA 1988) as it applies to an OLIC, to include the technical account for long-term business (if accounts prepared in accordance with the Insurance Accounts Directive (91/674/EEC) are used), or such part of the income statement of long-term business included in accounts prepared in accordance with IAS (International Accounting Standards). The result is that it should still be possible for tax-neutral transfers to take place involving OLICs. However, the anti-avoidance provisions described above are still capable of applying to transfers with an OLIC as a party. The amendments reflect the fact that OLICs are charged UK corporation tax in the same way as UK-resident life companies, but only in respect of their UK profits. In relation to OLICs, the definition of an IBT in s.431 of the ICTA 1988 is extended to encompass any "qualifying overseas transfers".

A "qualifying overseas transfer" is defined in the OLICs Regs as so much of the transfer of the whole or part of the business of an OLIC carried on through a permanent establishment in the UK as takes place in accordance with any authorisation granted outside the UK for the purposes of art.14 of the Consolidated Life Directive.

Article 14 of the Consolidated Life Directive permits the relevant authorities in the country in which the head office of an insurer is situated to authorise the transfer of the portfolio of policies to another life office in the Community.

On any cross-border transfer of long-term business, it is particularly necessary to give careful consideration to the VAT treatment of the transfer, for the reasons given in Section 6.1.7.14.

6.1.7.19   Long-term insurance business transfers—the Reinsurance Directive

In consequence of the implementation of the Reinsurance Directive, the definition (in s.431 of the ICTA 1988) for tax purposes of a long-term transfer of business has been amended to mirror the amendment made to s.105(3) of the FSMA 2000.

6.1.7.20   Friendly society insurance business transfers

The reliefs available for transferors of long-term business, as described above, apply equally to transfers of long-term business by a friendly society or to a friendly society notwithstanding that (in the former case) the transfer is an excluded scheme within Case 1 of s.105(3) of the FSMA 2000 (s.463 of the ICTA 1988 and the Friendly Societies (Modification of the Corporation Tax Acts) Regulations 2005 (SI 2005/2014).

FA 2007 has amended s.460 of the ICTA 1988 so that tax exempt life or endowment business ("TELEB") continues (subject to certain conditions) to be exempt from corporation tax if transferred from a friendly society to an insurance company. The transferred TELEB is treated as a separate category of business in the transferee insurance business. However, s.460(13) disapplies the exemption if the contracts are varied so as to increase the premium payable under them.

6.1.7.21   Long-term insurance business transfers—conditionality of scheme on tax clearances

The transfer agreement has traditionally included wording to provide that implementation of the scheme be made conditional on the receipt of satisfactory tax clearances from HMRC. Such clearances would typically have covered the following:

(a)   that s.139 of the TCGA 1992 applies to the transfer to prevent chargeable gains which would otherwise arise in the transferor;

(b)   that s.444A of the ICTA 1988 applies to the transfer with the effect that the relevant reliefs are available to the transferee;

(c)   that policyholders' personal tax positions will not be adversely affected by the transfer (*see* Section 6.1.7.16);

(d)   that the transfer will not constitute a taxable supply for the purposes of VAT (*see* Section 6.1.7.14) (not necessary if an intra-group transfer); and

(e)   that the transfer will not attract *ad valorem* stamp duty (*see* Section 6.1.7.15).

As has already been described in this Chapter, the treatment afforded by s.211 of the TCGA 1992 (which previously applied s.139 of the TCGA 1992 to a transfer of long-term business, but which now stands alone) and s.444A of the ICTA 1988 has, for accounting periods beginning on or after 1 January 2007, been made automatic. These "statutory clearances" have been replaced by the "targeted anti-avoidance rule" (discussed above).

The position with regard to the "non-statutory clearances" referred to above (which is not an exhaustive list) is less clear cut. HMRC have previously said that, in their view, such clearance requests are not necessary in the majority of cases. It had been hoped that the updated HMRC guidance concerning transfers of long-term business would clarify the application of the particular rules, so that parties to such transfers would feel sufficiently comfortable in not continuing to make these clearance applications. The Life Assurance Manual does provide some further guidance on each of these issues (*see* the relevant paragraphs above), but notwithstanding this it remains to be seen whether interested parties will wish to continue to apply for advance clearance in respect of these important matters.

6.1.7.22   *Long-term business transfers: 2011 Consultation*

As referred to above, HMRC launched a consultation on the tax rules applicable to companies writing long-term business on 5 April 2011. The proposals for change have been driven by the advent of Solvency II, which is currently expected to take effect from 1 January 2014. However, it has become clear that the Government, encouraged by the life insurance industry, is looking to use the new regulatory framework to be introduced by Solvency II as a catalyst to simplify and rationalise the UK life tax rules, not least in the area of IBTs.

As part of the 2011 Budget, it was announced that certain key decisions had been taken by the Government as to how the tax rules for long-term business transfers would look from 2013. The role of the 2011 Consultation is to help shape the detailed rules so that these decisions can be reflected in legislation. Draft legislation to introduce changes to the rules is expected in the final quarter of 2011, to be included in Finance Bill 2012.

The key decisions announced as part of the 2011 Budget are that:

(a)   for transfers of long-term business between unconnected parties, the normal accounting rules will be followed for the purposes of calculating trade profits (or losses) of the transferee and transferor;

(b)   for transfers between connected parties, the IBT will be treated as taking place on a tax neutral basis. This has been referred to in the consultation as the "stand in the shoes" approach; and

(c)   the TAAR, in some form or another, is likely to be retained.

Although the details of any new regime remain to be seen, it appears that HMRC and HM Treasury are committed to simplifying the existing UK tax rules as they apply to transfers of long-term business.

6.1.7.23   *General insurance business transfers—introduction*

Although the procedure for transfers of long-term business and general business has been unified, the special tax provisions which achieve CGT deferral and the transfer of certain reliefs apply only to transfers of long-term business. Unlike life insurance companies, general insurance companies are not taxed on "policyholder profits". All general insurance business carried on by a company is a trade, and a transfer of general insurance business will be governed by general tax principles. The discussion at Section 6.1.7.11 will apply equally to general IBTs.

6.1.7.24   *General insurance business transfers—disposal of assets*

Unlike in the case of life insurers, assets representing "circulating capital" of the general insurance business will be taxed as trading profits under s.35 of the CTA 2009. Therefore CGT will not be applicable to the majority of the general insurer's assets. The exception to this would be a mutual general insurer which may be subject to CGT on its assets (because a mutual is not capable of being charged to tax under s.35 of the CTA 2009).

The disposal of assets which are circulating capital will give rise to a trading profit or loss for the transferor. The value at which the assets are deemed to have been sold is generally the arm's-length price, subject to the right to elect to substitute the higher of the acquisition cost and the price actually paid.

Given that general insurance companies are required to mark to market in their accounts, and that trading profits are computed by reference to the accounts, a transfer of assets at market value should not give rise to a significant tax charge. Historically, the view was taken that the realisations basis was the correct taxation basis, and some assets may still be taxed on that basis (with the gain held over until realisation). There are specific tax provisions which permit assets on the realisations basis to be transferred on a tax-neutral basis (s.187 of the CTA 2009).

The main items to which CGT may apply are goodwill and shares in subsidiaries (other than portfolio holdings). If the transferor and the transferee are in the same chargeable gains group, s.171 of the TCGA 1992 will apply so that the transfer will be for no gain/no loss to the extent that the assets transferred are chargeable assets.

6.1.7.25   General insurance business transfers—tax reliefs

There are no special tax provisions applicable to general insurance business. Therefore, unless the transferor and transferee are under common control, trading losses of the transferor will not be available to the transferee, and balancing allowances and charges will arise on the disposal of assets qualifying for capital allowances (subject to a possible election in relation to fixtures).

6.1.7.26   General insurance business transfers—other taxes

As for a life insurance business transfer, a general insurance business transfer should qualify as a TOGC.

In relation to stamp duty, the analysis above relating to long-term insurance business transfers applies equally to the transfer of general insurance business. It should be noted, in particular, that if the transferor is a mutual company, the relief under s.96 of the FA 1997 will also cover a demutualisation in connection with a transfer of general insurance business under a scheme which is an IBT for the purposes of the FSMA 2000 (provided the conditions of s.96 in respect of the transfer are satisfied).

6.1.8 Miscellaneous points on insurance business transfers

6.1.8.1 Amendment of IBTs

Once a transfer has been sanctioned it cannot be amended except in accordance with its terms. It is customary for the scheme document to provide for minor and/or technical amendments to be made without court consent, provided that the FSA has been notified of, and does not object to, the proposed amendments. Otherwise, amendment will usually be provided for with the further sanction of the court.

It is difficult to be categoric about the requirement to obtain court approval for an amendment, as the circumstances of each case may dictate a different approach. The particular procedural and consent requirements (if any) of the scheme in question must be adhered to. Otherwise, it is advisable to agree at an early stage with the FSA what other information it requires and what notification it expects to be given to policyholders (generally this will only be advertising or notification on a website but individual notification may be required).

6.1.8.2 Appeal against the court's order

There is no specific provision in the FSMA 2000, the Regulations or the Guidance dealing with the possibility of appeal against an order of the court sanctioning an IBT. Objectors, therefore, have the same ability to appeal against an order as exists under the general law in relation to any other court order. If this is a real possibility, the parties to the transfer may prefer to delay the effective date of the transfer until it has become clear whether such an appeal will be made.

The court is able to set aside a judgment obtained by fraud even if the transfer has already become effective and even if the result of setting aside the order would be to require the transfer to be unravelled and the transfer of policies, assets and liabilities to be deemed never to have occurred. However, it will not do so if on investigation the court is satisfied that the result would have been the same even if the fraud had not been perpetrated. These two propositions follow from the judgment of Neuberger J in *Fletcherv Royal Automobile Club Ltd*[2000] 1 B.C.L.C. 331, a decision on a scheme of arrangement under s.425 of the CA 1985.

6.1.8.3 Enforcement provisions of scheme document

After the transfer, if the IBT encompasses the whole of its business, the transferor will be left as a shell company, usually with no incentive to take steps to enforce provisions of the scheme document. Failure to observe the terms of the transfer is, in principle, a contempt of court and may be treated accordingly. However, in practice it is necessary for the actuarial function-holder or directors in the transferee, or the FSA, to seek to bring such breaches to the attention of the court.

The scheme document will generally disapply the provisions of the Contracts (Rights of Third Parties) Act 1999, which, if the IBT is a contract for the purposes of that Act (which it may well not be, given that it takes effect by court order rather than agreement of the parties), probably has the effect that an individual policyholder cannot take enforcement action. It is likely, in practice, for it to be simpler for a policyholder to complain to the FSA, who would then consider exercising its general supervisory powers.

6.1.8.4 Part 27 of the Companies Act 2006

If an IBT involves a compromise or an arrangement falling within Part 27 of the Companies Act 2006 ("CA 2006"), Part 26 of the CA 2006 has effect, as modified by Part 27, in relation to that compromise or arrangement. Part 27 applies, for example, to a transfer by a public company to another public company which already has a business of its own where the consideration for the transfer includes shares in the transferee receivable by members of the transferor. In such a case, the meetings required by Part 26 and the other procedural requirements of Part 27 will apply. However, there does not appear to have been a transfer under these provisions since they were first introduced in 1987 in order to comply with EC directives on mergers and divisions of public companies (78/855/EEC and 82/891/EEC).

6.1.8.5   *Application of company law principles*

Nothing in the FSMA 2000 or the Regulations disapplies provisions of the general law or companies legislation relating to maintenance of capital, financial assistance, dividends or transactions having the effect of dividends. Therefore, it is important to consider at an early stage the way in which these rules apply to any given proposal. As regards the rules on financial assistance, it is probable that the correct analysis, which will often need to be considered in circumstances where a transfer is made following an earlier acquisition of the insurance company or its holding company, is that the transfer occurs by order of the court rather than by action of the company itself, and that on this basis the rules do not apply. However, there are mixed views on this point. CA 2006 provisions governing financial assistance removed the prohibition on giving financial assistance if the acquisition is of shares in a private company and the assistance is given by that company or any of its private company subsidiaries. Where the prohibition continues to apply, the analysis will need to be carried out, although if there is a real problem it may be simpler to re-register the transferor as a private company.

In the context of the Cross-Border Mergers Directive (2005/56/EC) (which was implemented in the UK in December 2007), there has been some debate about whether that directive's objectives would be undermined if transfers falling within its scope (which most IBTs will not because they do not result in immediate dissolution of the transferor without winding up) remained subject to Part VII of the FSMA 2000. It is, however, clear on the face of the FSMA 2000 that the court process must be followed if a transfer is caught by Part VII. Further, whilst the wording of the Cross-Border Mergers Directive is not entirely clear on the point, this outcome is at least consistent with the language and purpose of that directive (*see*, in particular, Recital (10) and art.4(1)(b)).

An IBT will generally amount to a transfer of an undertaking within the meaning of the Transfer of Undertakings (Protection of Employment) Regulations 2006 (SI 2006/246) with the result that contracts of employment with any employees of the transferor will pass to the transferee as a result of the court's order.

6.1.8.6 Certificates in relation to transfers outside the UK

Sections 115 and 116 of the FSMA 2000, Part III of Sch.12 to the FSMA 2000 and para.18.3 of the Guidance implement obligations of the UK under EU directives in relation to transfers of insurance business occurring outside the UK. These provisions have the following broad effects:

(a) The FSA may give a certificate confirming that a UK authorised person possesses the required minimum margin of solvency to facilitate an insurance business transfer to the firm under relevant legislation in another EEA state (or from a Swiss general insurance company). The Guidance indicates how that power will be exercised.
(b) Section 116 enables the FSA to publish notice of a transfer authorised in another EEA state and therefore make that transfer effective in law to transfer obligations under the UK policies, and any legal proceedings, within the scope of that transfer.

6.1.8.7 Insurance business transfers in the Channel Islands and the Isle of Man

The Channel Islands and the Isle of Man do not form part of the UK and are not EEA states. Accordingly, transfers of insurance business carried on by an authorised person in those jurisdictions will be subject to the applicable local legal regime for the transfer of insurance business. The tests as to whether a local scheme is required in relation to the local elements of a UK scheme differ in the three jurisdictions and local advice on the need for a scheme in any given case should be sought at an early stage. In Jersey, Guernsey and the Isle of Man a separate scheme document will be required for the transfer of long-term insurance business and, in the case of Jersey only, for the transfer of general business, although this will in most cases be similar to, and conditional upon court sanction of, any associated UK transfer in respect of which application has been made to the court under the FSMA 2000. It is also likely that the reports produced by the independent expert and, if applicable, actuarial function-holder and with-profits actuary and any notices or circulars sent to policyholders by the authorised person or transferee concerned will suffice for the purposes of the relevant local courts in these jurisdictions, provided the position of policyholders with insurance policies written from the relevant branch is specifically addressed. There is no specific legislation governing transfers of general insurance business in Guernsey or the Isle of Man.

6.1.8.8   UK regulatory reform

Under proposals for reform of the UK financial services regulatory architecture, which are expected to take effect from end 2012/early 2013, two organisations will assume responsibility for regulating insurers, in place of the FSA. The Prudential Regulation Authority ("PRA") will be responsible for prudential regulation and conduct of business regulation will fall within the remit of the Financial Conduct Authority ("FCA").

The government has recognised that both the PRA and the FCA will have an interest in IBTs, while arguing that it is "primarily a prudential process" concerned with ensuring that the transferee will be financially sound once the transfer has taken place. It currently proposes, therefore, that the PRA should take the lead on all IBTs, although this will be carried out in consultation with the FCA.

6.1.9 Friendly society amalgamations, transfers and conversions

6.1.9.1 Introduction

Although the continued existence of two Acts of Parliament on the subject (the Friendly Societies Act 1974 and the Friendly Societies Act 1992 ("1974 Act" and "1992 Act" respectively)) gives rise to a number of complexities in other areas, the position in relation to transfers of insurance business by friendly societies is relatively straightforward.

The relevant provision in the 1974 Act (s.82) does not apply to the amalgamation of, or transfer of engagements by, a "registered friendly society", which is defined by s.7(1)(a) of that Act and s.116 of the 1992 Act to mean a friendly society registered under the 1974 Act.

Part VIII of, and Sch.15 to, the 1992 Act contain provisions applying to "friendly societies" as defined for the purposes of that Act, namely societies incorporated under the 1992 Act and registered friendly societies (as referred to above). The consequence is that only the 1992 Act applies to any transfer of insurance business by a friendly society, however it may be registered.

6.1.9.2 Part VIII of the 1992 Act

Part VIII of the 1992 Act deals with three different transactions:

(a) an amalgamation of two or more friendly societies by means of establishment of an incorporated friendly society as their successor, to which all the property, rights and liabilities of each amalgamating society are transferred;

(b) a transfer by a friendly society of all or part of its engagements to another friendly society, an industrial and provident society, a company or any other insurance company; and

(c) the conversion of a friendly society into a company registered under the CA 2006.

Part VIII and Sch.15 also include requirements to be fulfilled by a friendly society which proposes to accept a transfer of business from another friendly society, an industrial and provident society or any other insurance company, notably a requirement that the transfer should be approved by a special resolution of the members of the transferee (with one limited exception where the transfer is between friendly societies and the FSA consents to the approval being given by the committee of management of the transferee).

The Guidance (at SUP 18.4) gives further information as to the way in which the FSA (as successor to the Friendly Societies Commission) will exercise its powers in relation to these three types of transactions. The court is not involved in approving any such transaction.

6.1.9.3 Differences between the amalgamation and transfer provisions

Part VIII of, and Sch.15 to, the 1992 Act, together with the Guidance, set out in detail the requirements for each of the three transactions mentioned above, and it is not necessary to repeat them here. It will sometimes be clear which of the three transactions is the most appropriate, but sometimes more than one would be suitable. The notable differences are as follows:

(a) an amalgamation can only involve two or more friendly societies, whereas a transfer can involve a friendly society and a number of other types of entity, as described above;

(b) an amalgamation leads to the dissolution of the previous societies, and is therefore not suitable where only part of the business is to be transferred, whereas a transfer may relate to all or any part of a friendly society's business;

(c) an amalgamation requires the parties to establish a new incorporated friendly society as the successor to the amalgamating societies;

(d) an amalgamation takes effect simply by virtue of the special resolution and does not require the further instrument of transfer required for a transfer. In both cases, the terms on which the amalgamation or the transfer of engagements is to be made would normally be expected to be set out in the statement sent to members;

(e) it is only on a transfer of engagements, not an amalgamation, that an actuarial report is required under s.87 of the 1992 Act as to the margin of solvency (or, in the case of long-term business, the extent of any excess of assets over liabilities) of the transferee;

(f) further, it is only upon a transfer of long-term business, not an amalgamation of two friendly societies each carrying on long-term business, that the FSA may require under s.88 of the 1992 Act the production of a report by an independent actuary on the terms of the proposed transfer and the likely effects of the transfer on the members of the society who are long-term policyholders; and

(g) the jurisdictional requirements before the FSA can confirm an amalgamation are substantially more straightforward than the requirements for a transfer. In particular, it is necessary on a transfer to notify regulatory authorities in EEA states in similar circumstances to those applicable to insurance companies (*see*Section 6.1.4.4) and in the case of general business, the FSA only has power to transfer the contracts entered into before the date of the application, not all contracts entered into up to the transfer date.

The requirements as to statements to members and as to the right to make representations at the hearing are substantially similar, whether the transaction is proposed to take effect as an amalgamation or as a transfer. See Chapter 11 for further information about mergers and transfers by friendly societies.

The procedural requirements in relation to a conversion of a friendly society into a company, which might be appropriate in the event of the proposed demutualisation of a friendly society, are similar to the simpler requirements applicable to amalgamations.

As an alternative to using the transfer procedure under the 1992 Act, a friendly society may convert itself into a company prior to transferring its business under Part VII of the FSMA. However, given the additional processes involved, this would be unlikely to be desirable unless there were a specific reason to use the Part VII mechanism (for example, because of the court's wider jurisdiction under Part VII than the FSA's powers under the 1992 Act).

The Building Societies (Funding) and Mutual Societies (Transfers) Act 2007 gives HM Treasury power to modify legislation relevant to transfers of business by a building society, friendly society or an industrial and provident society. It is intended to increase the extent to which transfers of business can take place between different types of mutual. To date, this power has only been exercised to facilitate transfers by building societies; transactions that have taken advantage of the legislation include the merger in 2009 of Britannia Building Society with Co-operative Financial Services. There have been no changes to date to legislation relating to friendly society transfers.

6.2 Solvent schemes of arrangement

6.2.1 Introduction

A scheme of arrangement ("Scheme") is a compromise or arrangement between a company and its members or creditors (or any one or more classes of them) under Part 26 of the CA 2006. Schemes involving compromises or arrangements with members are commonly used as a mechanism for effecting takeovers or other corporate reorganisations, but such Schemes do not have any special application to insurance and reinsurance companies and therefore they are not considered further here. References below to "insurers" and "insurance" include "reinsurers" and "reinsurance".

This section focuses on creditors' solvent Schemes ("Solvent Schemes") as used between an insurance company and its policyholders. It also covers (*see* Section 6.2.7) how a Scheme can be used to effect a solvent restructure of the business of a life assurance company. Solvent Schemes—sometimes also known as "cut off" or "estimation" Schemes—have their origin in Schemes traditionally used by insolvent insurance companies in provisional liquidation, under which dividends are paid as claims become agreed in the ongoing insolvent run-off of the insurer. Such Schemes were often seen as a more flexible and cost-effective alternative to formal liquidation. Solvent Schemes take a different approach in that they seek to terminate the run-off process by "cutting off" present and future liabilities under policies in return for a once and for all payment. Claims must be made before a specified date ("bar date") or become unenforceable.

Over the last few years, an increasing number of Solvent Schemes have been implemented. They can (sometimes following an IBT under Part VII of the FSMA 2000) be a useful tool for solvent insurance companies to bring an early end to all or part of their business and in that way release capital which would otherwise be tied up in run-off for many years.

However, some policyholders have criticised the overall fairness of Solvent Schemes. Common complaints include that Schemes involve a re-transfer of risk and a forced commutation of potentially valuable and irreplaceable insurance cover in return for a payout calculated by an actuarial "estimation methodology" which may undervalue contingent "incurred but not reported claims" ("IBNR claims"), thus undervaluing the policy. An estimation process is by its nature prone to uncertainty and the financial outcome for policyholders will not be the same as if the policy were left to run its course.

Policyholder dissatisfaction has led to two high-profile court challenges to Solvent Schemes since 2005 (*Re British Aviation Insurance Company Ltd* [2006] B.C.C. 14 ("BAIC") and *Re Sovereign Marine & General Insurance Co Ltd*[2006] B.C.C. 774 ("Sovereign Marine"). At least two Solvent Schemes have been abandoned following concerted policyholder objections to their implementation. In other cases, objecting policyholders have been able to use legal uncertainty over aspects of Solvent Schemes and the threat of objection to negotiate favourable cash commutations that have allowed those Schemes to proceed unchallenged. However, the Scheme process is evolving to address a number of policyholder complaints, albeit that the fundamental uncertainty of the estimation process and concerns over fairness still remain.

6.2.2   Scope of Scheme provisions

6.2.2.1   "Arrangement" or "compromise"

Part 26 of the CA 2006 came into force on 6 April 2008, replacing most of the provisions previously appearing in Part XIII of the CA 1985, including s.425. Although the format of the legislation has changed, the requirements are substantially the same.

The term "arrangement" is defined by s.895(2) of the CA 2006 to include a reorganisation of the company's share capital by consolidation or subdivision. Otherwise, neither "compromise" nor "arrangement" is defined, although the court decided in *Re NFU Development Trust Ltd* [1973] 1 All E.R. 135 (and recently followed in *Re Uniq Plc* [2011] EWHC 749 (Ch)), that there must be an element of accommodation or compromise on both sides. A Scheme can therefore be used to give effect to almost any form of internal reorganisation or arrangement with creditors, or classes of them, provided the necessary creditor approvals and court sanction are obtained. An attempt by opposing policyholders to argue that a Solvent Scheme could only be put forward if the insurance company had a "problem requiring a solution" rather than a desire to return capital to shareholders was ultimately rejected by the Inner House of the Court of Session in Scotland (*Scottish Lion Insurance Company Ltd*[2009] C.S.I.H. 6).

In *Re Lehman Brothers International (Europe) (in administration) (No.2)* [2009] EWCA Civ 1161 ("Lehman"), the Court of Appeal had to consider whether Lehman Brothers International (Europe) ("LBIE") could propose a scheme of arrangement to compromise the claims of its clients who had proprietary rights to securities they had delivered to LBIE under custody agreements, margin lending and derivatives transactions. The

Court of Appeal dismissed an appeal against the first instance decision of the High Court that it did not have jurisdiction to sanction such a scheme. The Court of Appeal held that a Scheme must be an arrangement between a company and its creditors, i.e. an arrangement which dealt with their rights inter se as debtor and creditor. A proprietary claim to trust property was not a claim in respect of a debt or liability of the company. A beneficiary who had a beneficial interest in property held on trust by LBIE was not a "creditor" and therefore the court's jurisdiction to sanction a Scheme did not extend to the release of rights over property held by LBIE on trust. This was different from the release of rights over the Scheme company's own property by way of security, which could be subject to a Scheme.

6.2.2.2 Meaning of "company"

For the purposes of establishing the court's jurisdiction over a Solvent Scheme, a "company" is defined as being any company liable to be wound up under the Insolvency Act 1986 ("IA 1986") or the Insolvency (Northern Ireland) Order 1989 (SI 1989/2405 (NI 19)) (*see* s.895(2) of the CA 2006). This covers all UK companies, although the Scottish court has sole jurisdiction to deal with Schemes proposed by Scottish companies, and the practice, though similar, does vary.

The court also has jurisdiction over Schemes proposed by overseas companies pursuant to the court's jurisdiction to wind up an unregistered company under s.221 of the IA 1986. However, the court will only exercise this jurisdiction if a sufficient connection with England is shown (*see In the Matter of Drax Holdings Ltd* [2004] 1 All E.R. 903; *Sovereign Marine, Re La Seda de Barcelona Sa* [2010] EWHC 1364 (Ch); and *Re Rodenstock GmbH* [2011] EWHC 1104 (Ch), the latter of which is discussed in more detail below) or, in the case of an EEA insurer (but not a pure reinsurer), under the Insurers (Reorganisation and Winding Up) Regulations 2004 ("IRWUR").

In *Re DAP Holding NV* [2005] EWHC 2092 (Ch), a Scheme was proposed by 17 insurance companies and one pure reinsurer, all incorporated in the Netherlands. Whilst the court would not have had jurisdiction to wind up the reinsurer under the EC Regulation on Insolvency Proceedings 2000 ("EC Insolvency Regulation") (because its "centre of main interests" or "COMI" was not England and it did not have an establishment in England), it was still "liable to be wound up" under the IA 1986. COMI and establishment were held to be transient matters and nothing in the EC Insolvency Regulation precluded an English court from concluding that a foreign company was liable to be wound up in England; of course, a sufficient connection with England was needed for the court to be able to sanction the Scheme but that went to the discretion of the court rather than the existence of the jurisdiction. The 17 insurance companies were also "liable to be wound up" under the IA 1986 by virtue of reg.5 of the IRWUR—reg.4 of the IRWUR prohibited a court from winding up an EEA insurer but reg.5 expressly provided that, for the purposes of s.425 of the CA 1985 (the predecessor to s.895 of the CA 2006), an EEA insurer was to be treated as a company "liable to be wound up" under the IA 1986.

In *Re Rodenstock GmbH* , a German company whose COMI was in Germany proposed an English law Scheme to its senior lenders (the senior facilities agreement was governed by English law). Whilst the court acknowledged that the EC Insolvency Regulation and the Brussels Regulation on Jurisdiction and Enforcement of Judgments in Civil and Commercial Matters both curtailed the English court's jurisdiction to wind up foreign companies (and the English court would not have had winding up jurisdiction over the Scheme company in that case), it was held that these two regulations did not narrow the meaning of "liable to be wound up" for the purposes of the jurisdictional test in s.895 of the CA 2006; nor did they narrow the English court's international jurisdiction in relation to Schemes. The court did consider, though, that the case raised serious questions over the extent of the court's jurisdiction and discretion to sanction a Scheme, given the Scheme company's apparent limited connections with England and the fact that Germany has no equivalent process to a Solvent Scheme.

The English governing law and exclusive jurisdiction clause in the senior facilities agreement (to which all senior lenders were parties) persuaded the court in this instance that the German company had sufficient connection with the English jurisdiction for the court to sanction the Scheme. The court made it clear, however, that this was a fact-specific decision. The judgment left open the question of how the court might exercise its discretion to sanction if all the Scheme creditors of the company proposing the Scheme were domiciled outside England and they entered into separate agreements with the Scheme company (even though those agreements were each governed by English law).

6.2.3 Procedure

6.2.3.1 Introduction

Scheme procedure is essentially the same for long-term and general business. Part 26 of the CA 2006 provides for the following three stages:

(a) Initial application to court for an order that the requisite policyholders' meeting or meetings be summoned and for directions for the conduct of, and voting at, those meetings (the "convening hearing"). Policyholders are required to be given notice of the convening hearing and may attend the hearing to raise certain issues before the court (*see* below).
(b) The relevant meetings of policyholders are called and held.
(c) If the requisite majorities of policyholders vote in favour of the Scheme (*see*Section 6.2.3.6), a second court hearing to seek the court's sanction of the Scheme (the "sanction hearing"), following which the Scheme becomes effective (and so legally binding on the company and its policyholders) on delivery of the court's order to the registrar of companies.

Once the Solvent Scheme becomes effective, claims must be submitted along with supporting information by the policy-holders to the Scheme company by a specified bar date (usually between four and six months after the Scheme has become effective, depending upon its terms). The Claims are then either agreed by the Scheme company or, if disputed, referred to adjudication.

Although the FSA does not have a formal role to play on Schemes, it will wish to review any Scheme proposals put forward by an insurance company to see whether they are consistent with that firm's ongoing obligation to satisfy the FSA's Principles. In July 2007, the FSA published a process guide (the "Guide") describing its approach to Schemes and inviting comments (*see* Section 6.2.6). However, the Guide has not been updated to reflect such comments.

6.2.3.2 Application to court

The company will not want to incur significant transactional costs in preparation of a Scheme without having first gauged the likely level of policyholder support for the Scheme. The largest and key policyholders whose support will be needed will, therefore, in practice be identified and canvassed for their "in principle" views on the Scheme. This process can be used as a tool to refine the design of the Scheme to address policyholders' concerns.

Lawyers will prepare the detailed terms of the Scheme, the Explanatory Statement and other related documents. The Scheme is the formal legal document containing the terms of the Scheme proposal. The Explanatory Statement is an accom-panying document which sets out in clear terms the key features, benefits and disadvantages of the Scheme.

The FSA must be consulted on the terms of the Scheme and may provide comments. It will ultimately be asked to provide a letter confirming that it has no objections to the terms of the Scheme.

Once the terms of the Scheme are finalised and the FSA has confirmed it has no objections, the formal process of putting the Scheme before policyholders for their consideration and approval can be started. Before an application is made to the Companies Court asking it to convene the necessary meeting(s) of policyholders, a "Practice Statement" letter must be sent to policyholders and widely advertised in specialist insurance press (*see Practice Statement: Schemes of Arrangements with Creditors* [2002] 1 W.L.R. 1345). The letter notifies the relevant policyholders of the proposed application to court, the terms of the Scheme in outline and the purpose that it is intended to achieve and the meetings of policyholders that the Company believes are required for the purposes of voting on the Scheme. The purpose of the letter is to encourage policyholders to raise any class objections (*see* Section 6.2.5 for more information on the question of classes) so that such issues (which go to the court's jurisdiction to sanction a Scheme) can be dealt with up-front at the convening hearing. The letter also allows policyholders to raise any concerns they may have on the proposed conduct of those meetings.

The next step following the sending of the Practice Statement letter is to issue an application for permission to call the meetings of policyholders (in their respective classes, if relevant). Section 896 of the CA 2006 formally introduces for the first time a power to apply to the court for permission to convene class meetings, reflecting previous practice under the CA 1985. The application form must be accompanied by a supporting witness statement, which includes statutory information about the company and describes the terms of the proposed Scheme. The witness statement must also describe the number of policyholder meetings to be held and the manner in which the meetings are to be advertised. The application form will exhibit the Scheme document.

6.2.3.3 Hearing of application to convene meetings

The convening hearing will be before a registrar or a judge, who decides whether to grant an order convening a meeting or meetings of policyholders. Meetings need only be called of classes of policyholders involved in the Scheme (*see Re RAC Motoring Services Ltd* [2000] 1 B.C.L.C. 307). The Scheme company will seek directions from the court as to the appointment of a chairman to:

(a) oversee the conduct of the meeting(s);
(b) ascribe a value to policyholders' claims for voting purposes; and
(c) report back to the court on the outcome of the vote(s).

The Scheme company is also likely to seek approval from the court to the proposed voting procedures for the policyholders' meeting(s), which must include, as required by s.899 of the CA 2006, the ability for policyholders to vote by proxy. The company will also typically need to show the court that the process by which policyholders' votes will be valued for the purposes of voting at the Scheme meetings is fair and appropriate.

The court will instruct the company to send to each of the policyholders a notice of the relevant meeting(s) together with a copy of the Scheme document, the Explanatory Statement and a court-approved form of proxy. The court will review the steps taken by the company to identify and notify policyholders of the Scheme and to obtain current addresses for policyholders. Ordinarily, details of the Scheme meeting(s) will be circulated to insurance brokers who have placed business with the company in the past. Finally, in terms of notification, the court will direct how the policyholders' meeting(s) should be advertised including, where appropriate, overseas.

The court will determine the period of notice which must be given for the meeting(s). The timeframe for returning proxy and voting forms can vary significantly, although in some cases three or four months is usually given. Longer periods may be required if overseas policyholders are involved or the Scheme is particularly complicated.

A report or letter will need to be produced from the FSA confirming that the FSA does not object to the Scheme proceeding to the vote stage.

One of the key issues for applicants is the need to identify whether different legal rights of policyholders are affected by the Scheme proposals such that they may need to vote in different classes (i.e. in separate meetings). Under s.899(1) of the CA 2006, the court has no jurisdiction to sanction the Scheme if the class meetings have not been properly convened. For the meetings to be properly convened, the classes must be properly constituted and the votes properly allocated. The identification of classes of policyholders and how their voting rights are determined are discussed at Section 6.2.5.

Prior to the introduction of the Practice Statement procedure, it was a matter entirely for the Scheme company to determine the extent to which separate class meetings should be held, which determination would then be scrutinised at the sanction hearing. The Court of Appeal criticised this approach in *Re Hawk Insurance Co Ltd* [2001] 2 B.C.L.C. 480 ("Hawk"), saying that it led to unnecessary delay and expense and that such matters should be considered earlier in the Scheme process. The Practice Statement was introduced as a result.

In *Re Scottish Lion Insurance Company Ltd* [2006] S.L.T. 606, the Scottish court decided that the company must, as part of its preparations for a Scheme, provide creditors with names and contact details for all other creditors who would or may have a claim under the Scheme so that they might in effect be able to "consult together" as the Scheme requires them to do. Scheme applicants have resisted this concept in England and the Scottish practice has not been adopted, although in one case the English court ordered that the Scheme company's website should contain a forum to facilitate policyholder contact and discussion.

6.2.3.4 Explanatory Statement

The Explanatory Statement, which must accompany the notice to policyholders of the relevant meeting(s), is required by s.897 of the CA 2006 to:

(a) explain the effect of the Scheme; and
(b) state:
(i) any material interests of the directors of the company (whether as directors, or as members, or as creditors of the company, or otherwise); and
(ii) the effect on those interests of the Scheme, to the extent that it is different from the effect on the equivalent interests of other persons.

Each director is under an obligation to inform the company of any matters relating to himself necessary to allow the company to comply with its obligations under s.897 (*see* s.898 of the CA 2006).

Where notice is given by advertisement, the advertisement must either include the Explanatory Statement or state where one can be obtained (*see* s.897(1)(b)). If a request is then made for the Explanatory Statement, it must be provided free of charge (*see* s.897(4)). Breach of any of the requirements in s.897 is a criminal offence by the company and any defaulting officer (*see* s.897(5)–(8)). In practice, companies usually post a copy of the Explanatory Statement on their website together with other Scheme documents.

When deciding whether to sanction the Scheme, the court will consider whether the Explanatory Statement is fair and, as far as is possible, enables policyholders (or the relevant class or classes of policyholders) to make an informed decision about whether to vote in favour of the Scheme.

6.2.3.5 Changes relevant to the policyholder vote

If, before the relevant meetings are held, there is a change in any of the information supplied to policyholders that might affect how policyholders decide to vote on the Scheme, the court may refuse to sanction the Scheme unless either the policyholders are informed of the change prior to the meeting, or the change is such that no reasonable policyholder would alter his decision as to how to act on the Scheme if the changes had been disclosed (*see Re Jessel Trust Ltd* [1985] B.C.L.C. 119 and *Re Minster Assets Plc* [1985] 1 B.C.C. 99299).

6.2.3.6   *Policyholder meeting(s)*

The resolution to approve the Scheme must be passed by the relevant majority of each class of policyholders. The relevant majority is a majority in number representing at least 75 per cent. in value of the policyholders or class of policyholders, if relevant, voting, whether in person or by proxy. This is a dual test:

(a)   those who vote in favour of the Scheme must be a majority in number of those members of the class who are present and voting; and
(b)   those in favour must represent at least three-quarters in value of the interest of those present and voting.

It is the chairman's job to attribute a value to each policyholder's vote, which can be a difficult and potentially arbitrary process where the policyholder and the Scheme company hold different views on the value of IBNR claims that might arise under the policy. The court has decided (e.g. *see* the *BAIC* decision) that the chairman's decision could be challenged if he:

(a)   failed to act honestly;
(b)   acted perversely, that is, he reached a decision that no reasonable chairman could have reached; or
(c)   failed to conduct the meeting substantially in accordance with the procedure laid down by the court at the convening hearing.

Following the policyholders' meeting(s), a detailed witness statement by the chairman reporting on the results of the meeting(s) must be filed with the court in support of the company's application for sanction of the Scheme. A witness statement must also confirm that the court's requirements for the service of notice of the meeting(s) have been met.

Recent Schemes have recognised the potential conflict of interest inherent in the chairman of the Scheme meetings being connected with the company, whether as a director or professional adviser. They have, therefore, adopted the concept of an "Independent Vote Assessor" to assess and report to the court on the treatment of claims for voting purposes. In practice, however, such Independent Vote Assessor (whilst independent) will often—but not always—have been nominated by the company.

In another decision concerning the Scottish Lion Scheme, the Scottish court ruled that the submission of voting forms and supporting documentation for the purposes of the Scheme meetings was part of a court process and the creditor thereby waived any legal professional privilege which existed over those documents (*Scottish Lion Insurance Company Ltd* [2011] C.S.I.H. 18). Creditors were deemed to have disclosed the documents in the knowledge that disclosure to the court or to other Scheme creditors might be necessary at some point to sanction the Scheme or deal with opposition to the outcome of the voting process.

6.2.3.7   Court sanction

After the meeting(s), an application may be made to the court to sanction the Scheme (*see* s.899(2) of the CA 2006). The request for sanction is heard by a Companies Court judge in open court. The legislation does not contain any guidance on when and how the court should exercise its discretion to approve a Scheme. The approach taken by the courts (*see*, for example, Plowman J. in *Re National Bank Ltd* [1966] 1 All E.R. 1006) suggests that the following key tests are applied:

(a) Compliance with statutory requirements—the court will need to be satisfied that all legislative requirements have been met before it sanctions a Scheme.

(b) Fair representation of the class and statutory majority acting *bona fide*—even if the statutory majority of policy-holders votes in favour of a Scheme, the court must be satisfied that those who attended the meeting are representative of the class and that the majority who voted at the meeting acted in good faith, or it may take the view that the result does not represent a true decision of the class.

(c) The Scheme is one which a reasonable person would approve—in the *Dorman Long* case [1934] Ch. 635, Maugham J. described the test as "whether the proposal is such that an intelligent and honest man, a member of the class concerned and acting in respect of his interest might reasonably approve".

6.2.3.8   Scheme objectors

Ideally, objections to the Scheme based on class issues should be dealt with at the convening hearing in accordance with the Practice Statement. Failure to do so does not prohibit the making of such objections at the sanction hearing, albeit that to do so runs the risk of an adverse costs order being made against the policyholder. The costs in challenging a Scheme can be substantial.

6.2.3.9   Filing of the court's order

The Scheme becomes effective once a copy has been delivered to the registrar of companies (*see* s.899(4) of the CA 2006) and is legally binding on:

(a) all policyholders or all policyholders within the relevant class(es) eligible to vote on the Scheme, regardless of whether they voted in favour of the Scheme, apart from any policyholders who opted out of the Scheme; and

(b) the company.

Once the Scheme has been sanctioned by the court, it becomes a statutory Scheme and cannot be amended by agreement. Nor is it possible to insert a provision in the Scheme for it to be amended. The only way to amend an existing Scheme is by way of a new Scheme.

6.2.4 Key features of Solvent Schemes

6.2.4.1 Business covered by Scheme

The business to be schemed will ordinarily have been in run-off for a number of years so that a reasonably reliable view can be taken on the likely level of claims, which helps make valuation of claims as amenable as possible to estimation and reduces uncertainty. However, some business will be inherently unsuitable for inclusion in a Scheme (e.g. the claims position may be very uncertain or there may be substantial ongoing complex coverage disputes). Some practical points are as follows:

(a) Policyholders with particularly significant claims should be consulted at an early stage and their views obtained on the Scheme and the proposed estimation methodology.
(b) Solvent Schemes only cover insurance/reinsurance liabilities. Any other general claims will be paid in the ordinary course of business.
(c) It is crucial that the applicant has a thorough understanding of its business so that it can identify accurately those parts that are intended to be covered by the Scheme and, in turn, so that it can provide an accurate description of the proposed Scheme for policyholders.
(d) Consideration will have to be given to the treatment of any remaining reinsurance assets which cover the Scheme business. Reinsurers are not (as debtors) ordinarily bound by the terms of the Scheme, so a strategy is needed to allow the Scheme company to collect its remaining reinsurances or to take a view that the potential loss of reinsurance cover is outweighed by the overall benefits of the Scheme.

(e)   Some types of insurance business are unsuitable for a Scheme. For example, compulsory insurance policies (e.g. employer's liability; motor insurance) cannot be schemed – public policy and law dictate that cover should remain in place.

(f)   The estimation methodology will need to be fair and should not disproportionately devalue those claims that are by their nature very difficult to estimate, including long-tail IBNR claims.

6.2.4.2   Moratorium on claims

A Solvent Scheme will provide for a moratorium on all proceedings being started or continued against the company in respect of claims under policies that are included in the Scheme.

6.2.4.3   Security and letters of credit

If a policyholder has security over the assets of a Scheme company or the benefit of a letter of credit, the Scheme will provide that the policyholder can only enforce its security or draw on the letter of credit in accordance with the terms of that security or letter of credit and up to the amount of the claim that the policyholder has against the Scheme company, including claims to be established pursuant to the terms of the Scheme. The amount recovered under the security or letter of credit will be set off against the admitted Scheme claim of the policyholder.

6.2.4.4   Set-off

The Scheme will provide that sums owed by any policyholder to the company will be set off against amounts owed to the policyholder in respect of its admitted Scheme claims. Usually, set-off is only applied where the amount owed by the policyholder to the company has been established or agreed. However (and perhaps controversially), some recent Schemes proposed by reinsurance companies now seek to apply the estimation methodology not just to claims of policyholders but also to the claims which the company has against those of its policyholders which are also its reinsurers, for the purposes of calculating a net sum owing either way after the application of set-off. Whether this attempt to value the company's reinsurance claim in this way is supportable in the light of the *Lehman* decision (*see* Section 6.2.2.1) is open to question.

6.2.4.5   Bar date

Policyholders must file their claims (and supporting evidence) before the bar date specified in the Scheme. Claims received after that date will not be accepted for payment and will be deemed to have been paid and satisfied in full. In the *BAIC* decision, the court criticised a bar date that gave policyholders only 120 days from when the Scheme took effect to submit their claims, and indicated that a year should have been allowed instead. However, subsequent Schemes have been sanctioned with bar dates of less than a year, and six months is now more usual.

6.2.4.6   Estimation methodology

Typically, the estimation methodology should contain sufficient detail to allow for the independent valuation of a policyholder's claim and it is likely to address, in particular, IBNR claims, which raise the most difficult valuation issues. However, it will usually also contain the flexibility needed to apply the policyholder's own methodology for estimating claims if it seems more appropriate than the approaches proposed in the estimation methodology.

Otherwise, the estimation methodology will contain a summary of the actuarial methods expected to be applied, by business (e.g. aviation, marine) or loss type (e.g. asbestos, pollution, health), to estimating claims. Such methods might include a "best estimate" basis of valuation, or the mean average of the distribution of possible outcomes. "One size fits all" does not apply.

6.2.4.7 Claims adjudication and dispute resolution

If discussions between the policyholder and Scheme adminis-
trator do not end in agreement, an adjudication process will
usually be triggered whereby the amount of the claim in
dispute is determined by an appointed adjudicator without
recourse to the courts.

6.2.4.8 Reversion to run-off

Many recent Solvent Schemes contain a "reversion to run-off"
clause as a safeguard for the company against an unexpectedly
high level of claims or other difficulties related to implementation of the terms of the Scheme (e.g. problems in obtaining
reinsurance recoveries with which to fund payments to
creditors based on claims estimated under the Scheme). In such
event, the company can decide to terminate the Scheme on
notice to policyholders and revert to running off the business
in the ordinary course.

6.2.4.9 Opt-out

A Scheme can be designed to allow policyholders to opt out of
the Scheme process. Where a policyholder opted out, he would
not be entitled to vote on the Scheme and his legal rights
against the Scheme company should remain unaffected.

An "opt-out" was provided as part of the Scheme of Phoenix &
London Assurance Ltd ("Phoenix") (*see* Section 6.2.7).

6.2.5 Determination of "classes" for Schemes

6.2.5.1 Consulting with a view to the common interest

The starting point for the test for whether policyholders form
part of the same class for the purposes of a Scheme is the
judgment of the Court of Appeal in *Sovereign Life Assurance Co
(in liquidation)* v *Dodd* [1892] 2 Q.B. 573. The appropriate
class(es) for the purposes of considering and voting on a
Scheme will be those made up of "persons whose rights are not

so dissimilar as to make it impossible for them to consult together with a view to their common interest". This test is not always easy to apply and its application and outcome will depend on the facts of each Scheme.

The Court of Appeal considered the question of classes in some detail in relation to an insolvent Scheme proposed by Hawk Insurance Company (which was in provisional liquidation) as an alternative means of valuing and paying claims under an insolvent liquidation, which applies inflexible rules to the potential disadvantage of policyholders (e.g. all claims must be converted and paid in sterling, not dollars); *see Hawk.*

The Hawk Scheme was a "rough and ready" cut-off Scheme, with many similarities to a Solvent Scheme. All insurance claims (including unsettled paid claims, outstandings and IBNR claims) had to be submitted for valuation before a bar date. Claims which could not be agreed would be referred to a Scheme adjudicator under the dispute resolution process. Once insurance claims had been admitted either by agreement or by adjudication, the Scheme would pay a dividend on admitted claims at three rates:

(a) 100 per cent of unsettled paid claims;
(b) 75 per cent of claims in respect of outstandings; and
(c) 50 per cent in respect of IBNR claims.

Applying the *Sovereign Life* test, the Court of Appeal decided that neither the rights of policyholders that were released or varied, nor the new rights given under the Scheme, were so dissimilar as to make it impossible for policyholders (being the persons entitled to those rights) to consult together with a view to their common interest. The "common interest" of the Hawk policyholders was in achieving a simple, inexpensive and expeditious winding up of the company's affairs outside of a formal liquidation.

The court ruled that, in the circumstances of the insolvency of Hawk, all policyholders had the same existing rights prior to the Scheme against the company. Namely, in a winding up of

Hawk, "they will all be entitled to submit claims in the winding up and to have those claims admitted or rejected". By way of example, there was no difference in this regard between the rights of policyholders with contingent IBNR claims and the rights of ordinary trade creditors. It was just that, in order to give effect to the rights of the former, it would be necessary to estimate the value of their claims.

Further, the different distribution percentages for different categories of claims under the Scheme were simply aimed at achieving a "just estimate" valuation (as would be required in a liquidation) in relation to what those claims might be. The purpose was to provide a "rough and ready" basis for the admission of claims by the insurer in order to achieve the parties' common interest of "achieving a relatively simple, inexpensive and expeditious winding up of the company's affairs outside a formal liquidation".

6.2.5.2 The BAIC case

Following the decision in *Hawk*, a number of "one class" Solvent Schemes were proposed and sanctioned by the court without any judicial consideration of how the test in *Hawk* could or should be applied to a solvent insurance company.

BAIC was a solvent aviation underwriter that had been in run off since 2002. It had underwritten insurance and reinsurance cover in the aviation market since the 1940s and had (amongst others) insured a number of US aviation products manufacturers under product and general liability insurance policies. These policyholders alleged that they were facing a future wave of asbestos claims arising out of their manufacturing processes, for which they held insurance cover issued by BAIC and which claims (it was argued) would be IBNR claims which would be subject to the estimation methodology in the Scheme. A number of these US policyholders regarded Solvent Schemes as unfair in principle. They were dissatisfied with the outcome of previous Schemes and challenged the BAIC Scheme. Claims under BAIC policies were at various stages of development and uncertainty, from unsettled paid claims through to contingent claims in respect of outstandings and IBNR.

No objection to BAIC's proposed intention to convene a single "one class" Scheme meeting of policyholders was raised at the convening hearing. However, various challenges were made at the sanction hearing, including that IBNR claimants should have been placed in a separate class for voting purposes. The objectors argued that the court had no jurisdiction to sanction the Scheme.

Lewison J. gave extensive consideration to the decision in *Hawk* and its application to a Solvent Scheme. In particular, he noted that it is important to identify what policyholders' rights would be "in a no scheme world". The key to answering this question was to identify the appropriate "comparator" (which, in the case of *Hawk*, had been an insolvent liquidation). In analysing policyholders' rights as required by *Hawk*, the question was: what is the realistic alternative to the Scheme and, under that alternative, do policyholders form a single class?

BAIC argued that the appropriate comparator for a Solvent Scheme was a solvent liquidation (where contingent claims would need to be valued before being paid by the company (being the same process in effect as proposed under the Scheme)). US policyholders opposing the Scheme argued that, on the facts, BAIC was not insolvent and had no intention of going into a voluntary solvent liquidation (it may also have been relevant that the Scheme did not comprise all of BAIC's business, in which case solvent liquidation was not a realistic alternative). Therefore, the only realistic alternative to the Scheme was the continued solvent run-off of BAIC's business under which contingent IBNR claims of the type claimed by the US policyholders would be paid as and when they arose over the duration of the run-off. Lewison J. agreed.

Because the appropriate comparator in *BAIC* was a solvent run-off of the company's business, the court held that the rights of policyholders with contingent claims such as IBNR (the existence of which was uncertain and which would require estimation under the Scheme) and the rights of policyholders with unsettled paid claims (whose claims had been established and did not require estimation) were "sufficiently different" that it was not possible for them to consult together sensibly "in their common interest". In truth, they had no common interest at all. Accordingly, the court had no jurisdiction to sanction the Scheme because the single Scheme meeting was not properly constituted.

In addition to his judgment on classes, the judge considered various other objections to the BAIC Scheme in relation to fairness. He found that, even if he had decided that he had jurisdiction to sanction the Scheme (i.e. the classes were properly constituted), he would have exercised his discretion to refuse to sanction the Scheme on the grounds of fairness because he was persuaded that it was unfair for BAIC to compulsorily re-transfer risk to policyholders for the benefit of the shareholders of BAIC, particularly in respect of valuable occurrence policies that could not be replaced at any price.

6.2.5.3   *The Sovereign Marine case*

A year after the *BAIC* judgment, the question of class constitution was back before the court in the *Sovereign Marine* case. Sixteen insurance companies were proposing separate cut-off Schemes in respect of their liabilities arising out of the WFUM Pools business (apart from UK compulsory liability insurance) and were seeking the court's permission to convene (in each case) a single meeting of policyholders to vote on each Scheme.

The principal objection of the opposing policyholders (which included a number of US policyholders who had succeeded in their objections to the BAIC Scheme) was that the Solvent Schemes, as proposed, failed to constitute a separate class of Scheme policyholders in respect of IBNR and that, if each Solvent Scheme was to proceed, a separate meeting of IBNR policyholders to vote on each Scheme must be convened.

Based on the ruling in *BAIC*, the objecting US creditors argued (this time at the convening hearing) that the comparator for *all* Solvent Schemes was a solvent run-off. As such, it was a general principle that all Solvent Schemes required a separate meeting of policyholders with IBNR claims. The court disagreed and held that *BAIC* did not establish such a general rule but that the principles set out in *Hawk* should be applied to the facts of each case.

After consideration of a substantial amount of evidence from both sides, Warren J. considered that there was a huge range of uncertainty in the estimation and valuation of claims. For example, some notified outstanding claims could be very uncertain where the claim is still (for instance) subject to litigation. On the other hand, some IBNR claims could be more certain than some outstanding claims where the IBNR relates to a very developed category of claim or to a specific event the occurrence of which the insurer is aware (though the claim had not yet been notified). Most uncertain of all are IBNR claims in relation to unknown latent damage with little or no claims history. In those cases, both the existence and quantum of the claim may be unknown.

The judge concluded that the rights of a policyholder with an outstanding claim or unsettled paid claim at the certain end of the range of uncertainty were so different from those of a policyholder with an IBNR claim at the uncertain end of the range that:

> "it is impossible for them to consult together (in respect of those divergent rights) for the purposes of voting on the Scheme (just as it was impossible for the different classes of claimant to consult together in BAIC)."

It followed that, for 13 of the *Sovereign* companies where the appropriate comparator was a solvent run-off, there should be two separate class meetings: one in relation to IBNR claims and one in relation to all other claims. The judge found that a single class of creditors was appropriate for each of the remaining three *Sovereign* companies—Sovereign Marine, which was insolvent, and its two solvent subsidiaries (which were scheming their entire business and so voluntary liquidation was an appropriate comparator).

6.2.5.4 *Summary of class issues*

To summarise:

- The application of the class test to each proposed Scheme will always depend on the particular facts of the case.
- The application of the test depends on consideration of policyholders' rights (but not interests) before and after the Scheme.
- Applying the appropriate comparator is important; that is, where are the parties likely to be in the absence of a Scheme?
- Policyholders with IBNR claims may need to form a separate class for the purposes of a Solvent Scheme where the alternative is an ongoing solvent run-off.

It is important not to fragment the classes so as to produce a large number of small classes. The creation of a large number of classes could give undue power to the members of those classes who could veto the Scheme.

6.2.6 *The FSA process guide to decision making on Schemes of Arrangement for insurance firms (the "Guide")*

The FSA published the Guide in July 2007 to indicate how it expects to input in the Scheme process when Schemes are proposed by insurance companies (solvent or insolvent).

Schemes are not governed by the FSMA 2000 but, applying FSA Principle 11 (*see* Section 6.1.4.3), if an insurance company is proposing to implement a Scheme, it must inform the FSA. FSA Principles 6 and 7 (*see* Section 6.1.4.9) are also relevant to the FSA's evaluation of Schemes, in the context of its broader objectives of maintaining public confidence in the financial system and protecting consumers.

Whilst the role of the FSA is not to give formal approval to a Scheme, it has stated that it will object to those Schemes which pose a risk to its objectives. It is unlikely to object to a Scheme if it is satisfied that the firm's proposed course of action falls within the range of possible reasonable actions, depending on what is fair in the circumstances.

The FSA will, if appropriate, issue a letter of non-objection at both the convening hearing and sanction hearing stage.

Some factors that the FSA will take into account in reviewing Schemes include:

(a) whether the proposed Scheme would pose a threat to the achievement of the FSA's objectives;
(b) whether the insurance company has acted properly in relation to the FSA Principles;
(c) the degree of experience and expertise that different consumers may have in relation to different kinds of regulated activity;
(d) types of policyholders subject to the Scheme;
(e) the degree of solvency of the insurance company. The FSA would not normally object to a Scheme proposed by an insolvent company or marginally solvent company provided that, having regard to the company's resources, the Scheme treats policyholders fairly. In the case of substantially solvent firms, the FSA would need to be satisfied that the policyholders are in no worse position than a solvent run-off;
(f) types of business subject to the Scheme—for example, it is more difficult to assess whether policyholders are being treated fairly in the case of long tail business where policies are occurrence-based and the claims have not occurred yet;
(g) the age of liability exposures: the longer an insurance company has been in run-off, the more likely its largest and more volatile exposures will already have been commuted;
(h) whether the Scheme is being implemented in relation to an insurance pool, in which case the FSA is likely to base its

decision on consideration of the pool as a whole rather than considering the solvency of each insurance company within the pool;

(i) whether the Scheme offers suitable additional benefits for policyholders and/or safeguards for dissenting policyholders, as indications of treating policyholders fairly;

(j) whether a "Policyholder Advocate" should be appointed to protect policyholders, for example, in relation to Schemes which affect the interests of private retail policyholders or small commercial policyholders, or where the Scheme is likely to be complex or controversial.

6.2.7 Schemes of arrangement and their application to life assurers

Schemes can also be used to restructure the business of a life assurance company, both in a solvent and insolvent context. The Scheme can compromise the rights of policyholders of a life assurance company by amending policyholders' contractual rights under their policies.

A Scheme can be used to effect a solvent restructure of the company's business by offering clear benefits to its policyholders, for example, a less constrained investment strategy and/or uplifts to policy values in return for the removal of guarantee terms under their policies. This was the approach adopted in the *Phoenix* Scheme, which was approved overwhelmingly by its policyholders.

The *Phoenix* Scheme gave policyholders an opportunity to opt out of the Scheme and so retain their guaranteed pension rate under their policy. The opt-out was a novel feature for a Solvent Scheme and was particularly welcomed by the court and the FSA.

Chapter 7

Sale and Administration of Non-Investment Insurance

Duncan Barber,
Partner: Linklaters LLP

7.1 The requirements for insurance intermediaries

Anyone who carries on certain activities relating to insurance in the UK must be authorised by the Financial Services Authority ("FSA"), be exempt from authorisation or become the appointed representative of someone who is authorised. This will be so even if the insurance activities are secondary to the person's main business. These activities are known as "insurance mediation activities" and are governed by a series of rules that are set out in the FSA Handbook ("FSA rules").

The current regime has been in place since 2005, when the UK government implemented the EU Insurance Mediation Directive[1] ("IMD" or "Directive"). The Directive applies to persons who provide insurance mediation services to third parties for remuneration and requires registration with a local regulator and the implementation of certain prudential rules and conduct of business rules. The Directive sets out a system of passporting so that insurance intermediaries which meet the requirements to be registered in their home state and are so registered may provide services into, or set up and establish in, another EU Member State (which by virtue of the EEA Agreement[2] extends to any other EEA state[3]).

---

[1] Directive 2002/92/EC.
[2] "EEA Agreement" means the agreement on the European Economic Area signed

The FSA rules implementing the Directive in the UK are designed to comply with the Distance Marketing Directive[4] which seeks to improve consumer protection in respect of the distance marketing of financial services contracts (i.e. those concluded by means of distance communication which do not involve the simultaneous physical presence of the parties).

As well as governing the requirement to be authorised, the FSA rules cover matters such as capital resources, client money, professional indemnity insurance, requirements for individuals working in the business and persons controlling the business to be approved by the FSA, and detailed conduct of business rules which govern matters such as information to be provided to customers, cancellation rights and claims handling.

This Chapter focuses on the application of these rules to insurance intermediaries in relation to non-investment insurance contracts (*see* Section 7.8.1 for an explanation of non-investment insurance contracts). Chapter 10 focuses on the rules which apply to insurance intermediaries in relation to investment insurance contracts. Most insurers will be carrying on insurance mediation activities in conjunction with their underwriting activities, and to the extent of those insurance mediation activities insurers will also be "insurance intermediaries" for the application of the conduct of business rules. As will be seen from the wide scope of the activities and limited exemptions, it is by no means just insurance companies and insurance brokers that are caught by the FSA's regulation of insurance intermediaries.

7.1.1 *Insurance Mediation Directive 2 ("IMD2")*

The European Commission is looking to enhance the insurance intermediary framework through the introduction of IMD2. Aspects of the current regime are set to change as the European

---

at Oporto on 2 May 1992, together with the Protocol adjusting that Agreement signed at Brussels on 17 March 1993, as modified or supplemented from time to time.

3   EEA states are the EU Member States plus Iceland, Liechtenstein and Norway.
4   Directive 2002/65/EC.

Commission is expected to publish a formal legislative proposal for the revision of the Directive in early 2012. The European Commission's consultation exercise focused on the following potential areas for amendments:

(a) A high and consistent level of policyholder protection embodied in EU law: the Commission consulted on extending existing information requirements to direct sales, whether the existing exemption from information requirements for large risk insurance products should be retained and the introduction of a definition of "advice";

(b) Effective management of conflicts of interest and transparency: the Commission consulted on applying high level principles concerning conflicts of interest and transparency to insurance intermediaries and insurance undertakings possibly based on the MiFID conflicts regime and how transparency around remuneration could be improved, taking into account the need for a "level playing field";

(c) Introducing clearer provisions on the scope of the IMD: the Directive provides that activities akin to insurance mediation activities which are carried on by an insurance undertaking or an employee of an insurance undertaking who is acting under the responsibility of the insurance undertaking employer will not be considered to be insurance mediation. The Commission consulted on the extension of the scope of the IMD to cover all market participants (e.g. banking and insurance companies) which have insurance mediation as part of their activities;

(d) Increased efficiency in cross-border business: proposals consulted on included the integration of definitions of "freedom of establishment" and "freedom to provide services" and a more transparent use of general good rules in the context of passporting;

(e) Achievement of a higher level of professional requirements: the Commission consulted on minimum basic common principles for professional requirements, with Member States having the freedom to adopt specific standards for both intermediaries and direct sale; and

(f)   Distribution of insurance Packaged Retail Investment Products ("PRIPs"): the Commission consulted on the addition of a chapter on the selling practices for insurance PRIPs to take account of the specificities of the insurance business and providing that selling practice rules for insurance PRIPs should be aligned with MiFID rules to ensure appropriate consumer protection.

The extent to which the Commission's proposals will be carried over to the final text of IMD2 will not be known until 2012. However, current UK insurance mediation rules are already in line with many of the proposals consulted on by the Commission. For example, insurance mediation activities are already regulated in relation to all UK market participants, including insurance undertakings. The FSA Handbook also includes training and competence ("TC") rules relating to professional requirements. Proposals to introduce definitions of various terms such as "freedom of establishment" or "freedom to provide services", while adding clarity, should not have a significant effect on existing rules. The Commission's proposals around improving remuneration transparency, if introduced, would result in remuneration type disclosures for insurance undertakings. The joint response of HM Treasury and the FSA to the consultation process did not support the introduction of a requirement on insurance undertakings to disclose some type of "commission equivalent" based on the cost of acquiring the business. It also did not support any restriction at a national level on the ability to make specific provisions on intermediary remuneration where it was felt that action was required for consumer protection.

7.2   Insurance mediation activities

The Financial Services and Markets Act 2000 (Regulated Activities) Order 2001[5] (the "RAO") provides that contracts of insurance are "relevant investments" for the purposes of several of the regulated activities:

---

[5]   SI 2001/544.

(a) dealing in relevant investments as agent (art.21);
(b) arranging (bringing about) deals in relevant investments (art.25(1));
(c) making arrangements with a view to deals in relevant investments (art.25(2));
(d) assisting in the administration and performance of a contract of insurance (art.39A);
(e) advising on relevant investments (art.53); and
(f) agreeing to carry on any of the activities set out above (art.64).

7.3   Requirement for authorisation

Authorisation is required if a firm is or will be carrying on a regulated activity that involves any one or more of the activities listed at Section 7.2:

(a) in relation to contracts of insurance;
(b) by way of business in the UK; and
(c) where the activities are not otherwise excluded or exempt.

The FSA's guidance in relation to the requirement to obtain authorisation for insurance mediation activities is set out in Chapter 5 of The Perimeter Guidance Manual ("PERG") in the FSA Handbook. The FSA guidance will not bind the courts, but, if a person acts in line with the guidance in the circumstances contemplated by it, the FSA will proceed on the basis that the person has complied with aspects of the requirement to which the guidance relates.

Anyone carrying on one or more regulated activities in the UK without being authorised or becoming an appointed representative will be committing a criminal offence unless he is exempt from the requirements. It may also render agreements he enters into himself or that he arranges on behalf of third parties unenforceable. A person is authorised if he either:

(a) holds a permission given by the FSA under Part IV of the Financial Services and Markets Act 2000 ("FSMA 2000"); or

(b) otherwise qualifies for authorisation—for example, as an EEA firm using passporting rights.

7.3.1 Contracts of insurance

The first question to be asked when considering whether authorisation is required for a particular activity is whether that activity relates to contracts of insurance. The definition of contracts of insurance in the RAO is not exhaustive, but it does make some specific extensions and limitations of the general common-law meaning of a contract of insurance. For example, art.3(1) of the RAO states that certain fidelity bonds and similar contracts of guarantee, which are usually not contracts of insurance at common law, are to be treated as contracts of insurance, whereas funeral plan contracts, which are likely to be thought of as contracts of insurance at common law, are not contracts of insurance for the purposes of the RAO. No distinction is drawn between a contract of direct insurance and a contract of reinsurance for the purposes of the RAO. Subject to the above modifications, the FSA has indicated that it will follow the common law definition of a contract of insurance and has provided some guidance as to its understanding of the common law in this regard in Chapter 6 of PERG.

7.3.2 Are the activities insurance mediation activities?

The next question to ask is whether the activities are insurance mediation activities as referred to at Section 7.2.

7.3.2.1 Dealing in contracts of insurance as agent

The activity is defined in art.21 of the RAO in terms of buying, selling, subscribing for or underwriting contracts as agent. An intermediary would be carrying on this activity whether he acted on behalf of the insurer or on behalf of the policyholder if he has the power to bind his principal.

7.3.2.2   *Arranging deals in, and making arrangements with a view to transactions in, contracts of insurance*

Article 25 of the RAO describes two types of regulated activities concerned with arranging deals in respect of contracts of insurance. These are:

(a)   making arrangements for another person (whether as principal or agent) to buy a contract of insurance (art.25(1)); and

(b)   making arrangements with a view to a person who participates in the arrangements buying a contract of insurance (whether as principal or agent) (art.25(2)).

Examples of activities which the FSA believes fall within art.25(1) for insurance mediation are negotiating with the insurance undertaking the terms of a contract of insurance on behalf of the customer and vice versa, or assisting in the completion of a proposal form and sending it to the insurance undertaking (the latter may also amount to dealing as agent—*see* Section 7.3.2.1 above). Article 25(2), unlike art.25(1), does not require that the arrangement would bring about the transaction to which it relates but merely that it was the intention at the time that the relevant activities were undertaken. The FSA's guidance in PERG 5.6.4G indicates that this regulated activity would include activities of persons who help potential policyholders to fill in or check application forms in the context of ongoing arrangements between these persons and insurance undertakings. In contrast, the FSA considers that a mere passive display of literature advertising insurance (e.g. leaving leaflets advertising insurance in a dentist's or vet's waiting room and doing no more) would not amount to the art.25(2) activity.

Article 72C of the RAO excludes from the ambit of art.25(1) and (2) activities that consist of the provision of information to the policyholder or potential policyholder, provided that:

(a) they are carried on by a person carrying on any profession or business which does not otherwise consist of regulated activities; and
(b) the provision of information may reasonably be regarded as being incidental to that profession or business.

The FSA regards being "incidental" as requiring "an inherent link between the activity and the firm's main business" (PERG 5.6.7G). For example, introducing dental insurance may be incidental to a dentist's activities; introducing pet insurance would not. However, the exclusion only extends to information given to the policyholder or potential policyholder and not to the insurance undertaking. An intermediary which forwards a proposal form to an insurance undertaking would not be able to take advantage of the exclusion. Similarly, an intermediary which does more than provide information (e.g. by helping a potential policyholder to fill in an application form) cannot take advantage of this exclusion.

Article 27 of the RAO contains an exclusion that applies to arrangements which might otherwise fall within art.25(2) which simply amount to the provision of the means by which one party to a transaction (or potential transaction) is able to communicate with other such parties. This would apply to persons such as internet service providers or telecommunications networks.

Article 28 of the RAO excludes a policyholder himself from the requirement to become authorised as a result of arranging a contract of insurance for himself, provided that he is the only policyholder. However, it does not exempt insurers. This means that a policyholder arranging (or assisting in the administration or performance of) a joint or composite insurance policy risks carrying on a regulated activity in relation to the other policyholders. Those who will be carrying on a regulated activity in this respect unless an exemption applies or they are not carrying on the activities "by way of business" (*see* Section 7.3.3) include project companies that arrange insurance to cover all parties interested in a particular development, corporate risk departments that arrange insurance to cover every entity within the larger corporate group, and anyone who routinely extends the benefit of their insurance cover to employees and/or subcontractors. Insurers will be carrying on the regulated activity of arranging contracts of insurance in addition to effecting and carrying out contracts of insurance.

Premium finance companies may be able to rely on the exclusion in art.32 of the RAO which applies to arrangements for the provision of finance, provided that the arrangements they put in place, taken as a whole, have as their sole purpose the provision of finance to fund premiums. That is, this is not ancillary to any arranging activity.

Article 33 of the RAO creates an exclusion for introducing, but it does not apply to arrangements relating to contracts of insurance. However, the FSA's guidance states that it will apply where the introduction is for independent advice on investments generally and the introducer is indifferent as to whether or not a contract of insurance rather than any other type of investment may ultimately be bought. The FSA's rationale is that in that case the arrangement does not relate specifically to a contract of insurance but to investments generally.

7.3.2.3 Assisting in the administration and performance of a contract of insurance

Broadly, this relates to activities carried out by a firm after the insurance contract has been entered into for and on behalf of policyholders, in particular in the event of making a claim. In order to be carrying on this activity, both the administration *and* the performance of a contract of insurance must be being carried out (art.39A of the RAO)—one or the other on its own is insufficient. This makes it difficult to judge whether some activities are regulated under this provision. Although the FSA's guidance on this regulated activity in PERG 5.7 draws some distinctions between "administration" and "performance", much of its guidance overlaps, which means it is not easily analysed or applied and therefore does not prove very helpful.

However, the exclusion in art.39B of the RAO is much more helpful in making it certain that claims management on behalf of an insurer which amounts to:

(a) expert appraisal;
(b) loss adjusting on behalf of an authorised insurer or a reinsurer; and
(c) managing claims for an authorised insurer or a reinsurer,

is excluded from the regulated activity.

The exclusion in art.72C of the RAO for provision of information also applies to this regulated activity.

7.3.2.4   *Advising on contracts of insurance*

Article 53 of the RAO makes advising on contracts of insurance a regulated activity. This covers advice which is:

(a) given to a person in his capacity as an insured or potential insured, or as agent for an insured or potential insured; and
(b) on the merits of the insured or his agent:
    (i)   buying, selling, subscribing for or underwriting a particular contract of insurance; or
    (ii) exercising any right conferred by a contract of insurance to buy, sell, subscribe for or underwrite a contract of insurance.

For advice to fall within art.53, it must:

(a) relate to a particular contract of insurance;
(b) be given to a person in his capacity as an investor or a potential investor;
(c) be advice (as contrasted with information); and

(d) relate to the merits of the person buying, selling, subscribing for or underwriting (or exercising any right to do so) a contract of insurance or rights to or interests in life policies.

As a result of (a) above, generic or general advice will not fall under art.53. Indeed, the FSA's guidance states that advice that a person should take out insurance of a particular class without identifying any particular insurance undertaking that provides such insurance would not be a regulated activity under art.53.

Article 54 of the RAO excludes advice given in periodical publications, regularly updated news and information services and broadcasts from the regulated activity of advising on contracts of insurance. The exclusion applies provided that the principal purpose of the publication or service taken as a whole (including its advertising content) is not to advise on investments or to lead or enable persons to buy, sell, subscribe for or underwrite relevant investments.

7.3.3 *By way of business*

To require authorisation, insurance mediation activities need to be carried on "by way of business". The Treasury has been granted power pursuant to the FSMA 2000 to specify the circumstances in which a person is or is not to be regarded as carrying on regulated activities by way of business. This has been set out in the Financial Services and Markets Act 2000 (Carrying on Regulated Activities By Way of Business) Order 2001.[6], Under reg.3(4), a person is not to be regarded as carrying on by way of business any insurance mediation activity unless he takes up or pursues that activity for remuneration. In the FSA's opinion, there are two principal elements to the business test in the case of insurance mediation activities:

(a) Does the person receive remuneration for these activities?

---

[6] SI 2001/1177.

(b) If so, does he take up or pursue these activities by way of business?

Both elements must be satisfied in order for the FSA to consider that the activities are carried on *by way of business*. In considering the individual elements, a clear overall indication against either element should mean that the test is failed.

The FSA seems to interpret "remuneration" very similarly to the way in which "consideration" is interpreted in general contract law. In other words, it need not be full remuneration and can even take the form of an indirect economic benefit which the person expects to receive as a result of carrying on insurance mediation activities. The remuneration does not have to be provided or identified separately from remuneration for other goods or services provided and there is no minimum amount. Therefore, if a person carries out any of the regulated activities together with other activities, his fees for his services as a whole will be taken to include remuneration for the insurance mediation activities for the purpose of this test. Finally, there is no need for the remuneration to be provided by any particular party (such as a proposed insured or insurer).

Even if there is remuneration, the FSA notes that the activities would usually also need to be carried on by way of business. The FSA's guidance on this point takes account of several factors (none of which individually can be conclusive). These include the degree of regularity and continuity of the activity, the existence of a commercial element to the activity, the scale of the activity and the proportion which the activity bears to other activities carried on by the same person, but which are not regulated. While these are identified as separate points for consideration, the FSA's guidance on these points is to a greater extent circular, in all cases returning to whether the *mediation* activities are essential to the success of the firm's other business activities, both financially and in any other material respect. The FSA summarises this component of the test by saying that the activities need to be carried on with a degree of regularity *and* must be carried on for a commercial purpose; that is, the firm must be expecting a direct financial benefit of some kind. However, the FSA also notes that an isolated activity may be by way of business if it provides a sufficiently large reward or is otherwise particularly relevant to the person's other business activities. The FSA cites a typical example where the business test would be satisfied as being someone whose main business is not insurance mediation activities, but who recommends or arranges specific insurance policies in the course of carrying on that other business and receives a fee, commission or other indirect financial benefit for doing so, or his main business activities are enhanced as a consequence of providing the mediation service.

The FSA has compiled a table included in PERG 5.4.8G in which it sets out the types of activities that it considers will and will not constitute "remuneration" and "by way of business". For example, recovery of actual costs will not be remuneration, but in practice unless only out-of-pocket costs are recovered it may be difficult to prove that a payment only reimburses actual costs. Particularly relevant is the analysis of whether the activities play a material part in the success and profitability of the other business activities of the person in question: if there is no link, then the activity is unlikely to result in an indirect benefit.

The overall effect is that there is little clarity around the "by way of business" test and a case-by-case analysis is required.

In the case of certain specific activities, in particular the arranging of group insurances and the arranging of project insurances by a project-specific company, the FSA has provided additional guidance. The FSA is expected to continue doing so in respect of activities the regulation of which was not the primary target of the Directive and which have been caught by the FSA rules not directly following the Directive wording.

7.3.4   *In the UK*

Section 19 of the FSMA 2000 provides that the requirement to be authorised only applies in relation to regulated activities which are carried on "in the UK". Persons carrying on insurance mediation activities from a registered office, head office or branch in the UK will clearly be carrying on regulated activities in the UK. Certain other activities are deemed to be carried on in the UK by virtue of s.418 of the FSMA 2000. In practice, the FSA will also take into account where each of the steps involved in carrying on the relevant activity is carried out.

For firms which are authorised to carry on insurance mediation activities in other EEA states, there will be no need to seek a permission under Part IV of the FSMA 2000. Instead, they can utilise the passport procedure such that they can obtain authorisation to carry on insurance mediation activities in the UK through an application made to their home state regulator.

See also the overseas persons exemption at Section 7.3.5.4.

7.3.5   *General exclusions*

There are various exclusions which apply to insurance mediation activities (specifically, those caught by arts 21, 25(1) and (2), 39A and 53 of the RAO). These are broadly as follows.

7.3.5.1   *Connected contracts of insurance*

Article 72B of the RAO excludes from FSA regulation certain insurance mediation activities carried on by providers of non-motor goods or providers of services related to travel. For the exclusion to apply, the contracts of insurance must satisfy a number of conditions, principally that:

(a)   the annual premium for the contract does not exceed €500;
(b)   the contract has a total duration (including through renewals) of five years or less;

(c)   in relation to travel risks, the travel booked with the travel provider relates to attendance at an event organised or managed by that provider and the party seeking insurance is not an individual or a business with a group annual turnover of less than £1 million or the travel booked is only the hire of an aircraft, vehicle or vessel which does not provide sleeping accommodation; and

(d)   the contract does not cover liability risks (except that liability risks may be included in the cover for a travel policy where that cover is ancillary to the main cover provided by the contract) and is complementary either to non-motor goods being supplied, or travel services being provided, by the provider.

7.3.5.2   *Large risks situated outside the EEA*

Article 72D of the RAO provides an exclusion for large risks contracts of insurance to the extent that the risk or commitment covered by the contract is situated outside the EEA. Broadly, these are risks relating to:

(a)   railway rolling stock, aircraft, ships, goods in transit, aircraft liability and shipping liability;

(b)   credit and suretyship relating to the policyholder's commercial or professional liability; and

(c)   land vehicles, fire and natural forces, property damage and motor vehicle liability where the policyholder is a business of a certain size.

7.3.5.3   *Activities carried on in the course of a profession or non-investment business*

Article 67 of the RAO excludes from regulation any activity which:

(a)   is carried on in the course of carrying on any profession or business which does not otherwise consist of the carrying on of regulated activities in the UK; and

(b) may reasonably be regarded as a necessary part of other services provided in the course of that profession or business.

However, the art.67 exclusion is disapplied by art.4(4A) of the RAO in relation to insurance mediation and reinsurance mediation activities (which are respectively defined for the purposes of the RAO by arts 2.3 and 2.4 of the Directive) where the relevant risk or commitment is located in an EEA state. Article 2.3 of the Directive includes a widely drafted definition of "insurance mediation" being:

> "the activities of introducing, proposing or carrying out other work preparatory to the conclusion of contracts of insurance, or of concluding such contracts, or of assisting in the administration and performance of such contracts, in particular in the event of a claim."

A similar definition of "reinsurance mediation" is set out in art.2.4 of the Directive.

By virtue of Part XX of the FSMA 2000, professional firms (broadly firms of solicitors, accountants, actuaries, conveyancers and surveyors) may carry on insurance mediation activities in the course of their professional activities without authorisation. For this to be the case, and in line with the Directive, the provision of any regulated activities must be incidental to the provision by the firm of its professional activities (s.327(4) of the FSMA 2000). Registration with the FSA is required; but this is the responsibility of the professional body that supervises the relevant profession once informed by the firm carrying on the insurance mediation activities (*see* art.94 of the RAO and PROF 7.1 of the FSA Handbook). The firm must comply with its professional body's rules instead of the FSA rules.

7.3.5.4   Overseas persons

Article 72 of the RAO provides a potential exclusion for persons with no permanent place of business in the UK. This allows persons located outside the EEA to deal with authorised persons in the UK, for example authorised insurance brokers and insurance undertakings operating in the Lloyd's market, and to receive and pursue unsolicited approaches from persons in the UK, provided such approach complies with the financial promotions regime under s.21 of the FSMA 2000.

7.3.5.5 *Appointed representatives*

Persons who carry on insurance mediation activities in the UK as appointed representatives of insurers will not require authorisation (s.39 of the FSMA 2000). An appointed representative is a person who is a party to a contract with an authorised person which permits or requires him to carry on certain regulated activities. The appointed representative's principal must accept responsibility for the appointed representative's actions when acting for it. SUP 12 of the FSA Handbook contains rules and guidance relating to appointed representatives. The insurance mediation activities that can be carried on by an appointed representative differ depending on the type of contracts of insurance in relation to which the activities are carried on.

Assessment of the requirement for authorisation can be carried out using Figure 7.1 (a flowchart provided by the FSA in PERG 5.15.2G).

7.4 Financial safeguards

Article 4.4 of the Directive requires Member States (which by virtue of the EEA Agreement extends to any other EEA state) to put in place measures to protect customers against the risk that an insurance intermediary will be unable to transfer premiums to an insurer or will be unable to transfer the amount of a claim or premium refund to the customer. The four measures proposed by art.4.4, some or all of which must be adopted by EEA states, comprise:

NO | Are you, or will you be, carrying on a *regulated activity* that involves insurance mediation? | YES | Consult Articles 21, 25, 39 A and 53 of the *RAO* and *PERG* 5.5 to 5.11

NO | Will you be carrying on these *regulated activities* by way of business? | YES | Consult Section 22 of the *Act* and *PERG* 5.4

NO | Are you, or will you be, carrying on a *regulated activity* in the *UK*? | YES | Consult Section 418 of the *Act* and *PERG* 5.12

YES | Are your activities excluded in full under the *RAO*? | NO | Consult Part II of the *RAO* and *PERG* 5.3.7G to 5.3.8G, 5.6.5G to 5.6.23G, 5.7.7G, 5.8.24G to 5.8.26G, 5.11 and 5.12.9G to 5.12.10G

YES | Are your activities exempt under Part XX of the *Act* because you are a member of the professions? | NO | Consult Part XX of the *Act*, the *Non-Exempt Activities Order* and *PERG* 5.14.1G to 5.14.2G

YES | Are you *an exempt person* under Sections 38 or 39 of the *Act*? | NO | Consult the *Exemption Order*, the *Appointed Representatives Regulations* and *PERG* 5.13

Authorisation not required

YES | Are you a *firm* established in another *EEA state* which has obtained registration in that state in relation to the *regulated activity*? | Authorisation required

NO

Contact the *Home State regulator*, who will then contact the *FSA*, with a view to your *authorisation* under Schedule 3 to the *Act* (*see PERG 5*).

Apply for *Part IV permission* from the *FSA* under Part IV of the *Act*

Where relevant, obtain exemption under the *Act* as an *appointed representative* (Section 39)

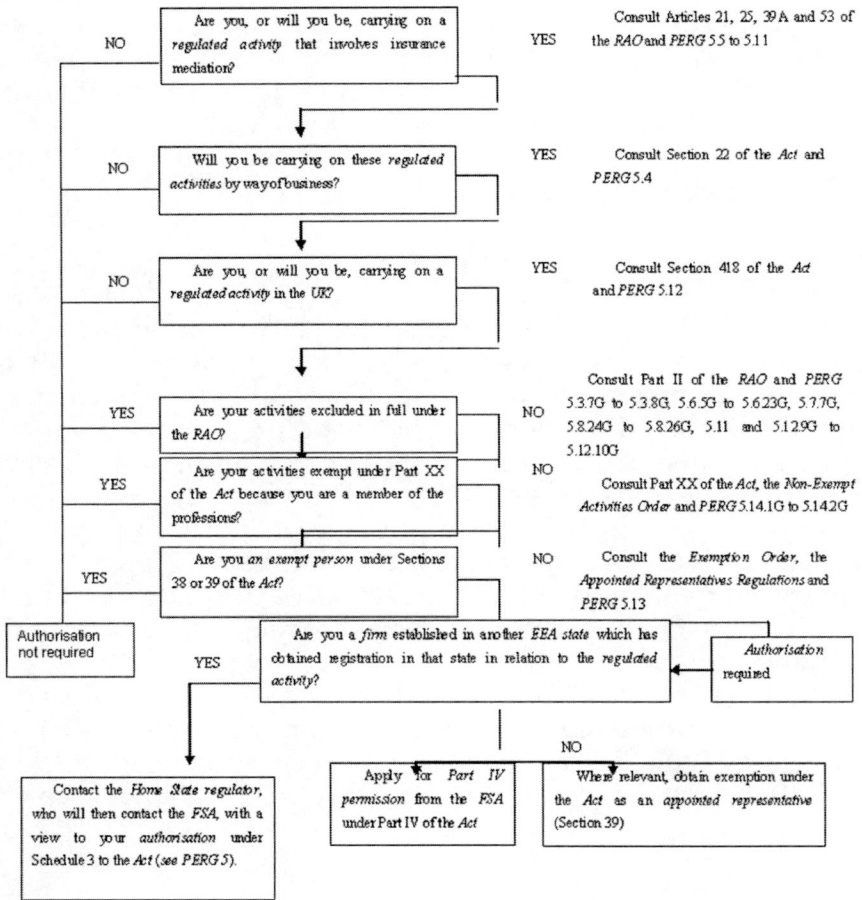

Figure 7.1 The requirement for authorisation

(a) provisions whereby the insurer accepts any risk to the customer arising from the intermediary holding client money;
(b) a requirement for the intermediary to have financial capacity of four per cent of annual premiums received;
(c) a requirement for the intermediary to maintain strictly segregated client accounts; and
(d) a requirement for a guarantee fund.

In addition, art.4.3 of the Directive requires intermediaries to hold professional indemnity insurance or a comparable guarantee against liability arising from professional negligence.

The FSA has implemented arts 4.3 and 4.4 of the Directive in the Prudential Sourcebook for Mortgage and Home Finance Firms, and Insurance Intermediaries ("MIPRU") as set out below.

7.4.1 *Professional indemnity insurance*

Insurance intermediaries which are not themselves insurers or Lloyd's managing agents are required to hold professional indemnity cover. Minimum limits of professional indemnity insurance cover for an intermediary are:

(a) for a single claim, €1,120,200 (MIPRU 3.2.7(1)R); and
(b) in aggregate, €1,680,300 or, if higher, 10 per cent of annual income (broadly calculated as brokerage, fees, commissions and other related income due to the firm in relation to its insurance mediation activities) up to £30 million (MIPRU 3.2.7(2)R).

Under Principles for Businesses 3 and 4, it is the responsibility of the firm's senior management to satisfy itself on a reasonable basis that the minimum level of cover of professional indemnity insurance is adequate to meet foreseeable contingencies.

The insurance must not be subject to an excess which exceeds:

(a) in the case of a company which does not hold client money or other client assets, the higher of £2,500 and 1.5 per cent of annual income (MIPRU 3.2.11R); and

(b) for a firm which does hold client money, the higher of £5,000 and 3 per cent of annual income (MIPRU 3.2.12R).

Additional capital must be used to complement a higher excess (MIPRU 3.2.14R). The insurance must include appropriate cover in respect of legal defence costs (MIPRU 3.2.4R(4)) and cover in respect of awards of the Financial Ombudsman Service against the firm (MIPRU 3.2.4R(6)). The insurance must be from an insurer authorised in one of the jurisdictions set out in MIPRU 3.2.1R.

Instead of obtaining insurance, it is possible to obtain a "comparable guarantee" from another authorised person which has net tangible assets of more than £10 million (MIPRU 3.1.1R). A "comparable guarantee" is a written agreement on terms equivalent to the terms required for professional indemnity insurance to finance the claims that might arise as a result of a breach by the firm of its duties under the regulatory system or civil law. If the intermediary's group includes an authorised person with such net tangible assets, the comparable guarantee must be from that person.

The personal indemnity insurance rules for insurance intermediaries in MIPRU 3 do not apply to insurers (or reinsurers) or managing agents.

7.4.2   Client money

A regulated insurance intermediary can adopt one or both (in respect of discrete parts of its business) of two different approaches to handling client money under the FSA's Client Assets sourcebook ("CASS") which in turn reflect the options given in art.4.4 of the Directive. The first is to provide by law or contract for a transfer of risk from the insurance intermediary to the insurance undertaking (CASS 5.2). The second is that client money is strictly segregated by being transferred to client accounts which cannot be used to reimburse other creditors in the event of the firm's insolvency (CASS 5.3 and 5.4 provide different means of achieving such segregation).

The client money rules for insurance intermediaries in CASS 5 do not apply to insurers (or reinsurers) or managing agents.

7.4.2.1 Holding money as agent of the insurance undertaking ("risk transfer") (CASS 5.2)

The insurance intermediary can agree with the insurance undertaking that it will hold cash such as premiums received from policyholders or payments received from the insurance undertaking in respect of claims as agent for the insurance undertaking such that the insurance undertaking remains responsible for those monies until they have been appropriately applied. By virtue of CASS 5.2.3R, a firm must not agree to:

(a) deal in investments as agent for an insurance undertaking in connection with insurance mediation activities;

(b) act as agent for an insurance undertaking for the purpose of settling claims or handling premium refunds; or

(c) otherwise receive money as agent of an insurance undertaking,

unless:

(d) it has entered into a written agreement with the insurance undertaking to that effect;

(e) it is satisfied on reasonable grounds that the terms of the policies issued by the insurance undertaking to the firm's clients are likely to be compatible with such an agreement;

(f) (in the case of (a)) the agreement expressly provides for the firm to act as agent of the insurance undertaking for the purpose of receiving premiums from the firm's clients; and

(g) (in the case of (b)) the agreement expressly provides for the firm to act as agent of the insurance undertaking for the purpose of receiving and holding claims money or premium refunds prior to transmission to the client making the claim or entitled to the premium refund in question.

7.4.2.2 Statutory trust (CASS 5.3)

Section 139(1) of the FSMA 2000 provides that rules may make provisions which result in client money being held by a firm on trust (England and Wales and Northern Ireland) or as agent (Scotland). In the event of failure of the firm, costs relating to the distribution of client money would have to be borne by the trust. The money is held on trust for the clients according to their respective interests in it except that, on a failure of the firm, payment of the costs properly attributable to the distribution of the client money would take priority (CASS 5.3.2R). The terms of CASS 5.3, 5.5 and 5.6 (the latter to be known as the "client money (insurance) distribution rules") must be incorporated by reference into the terms of the trust.

7.4.2.3 Non-statutory client money trust (CASS 5.4)

CASS 5.4 permits a firm to declare a trust on terms which expressly authorise it, in its capacity as trustee, to make advances of credit to the firm's clients. An example of such credit would be where a premium is forwarded to an insurer on behalf of a client before the money has been received from the client. Intermediaries are not entitled to lend money from non-statutory client money trusts to themselves. A firm may comply with the non-statutory client money trust rules for one part of its business while complying with the statutory trust rules for the other parts (CASS 5.4.2R).

As well as systems and controls requirements, including written confirmation from its auditor that the firm has in place systems and controls which are adequate to manage client money transactions and any credit risk arising from the trust arrangement, the firm must have and at all times maintain capital resources of not less than £50,000 if it wishes to use the non-statutory client money trust (CASS 5.4.4R). This amount of £50,000 is not incremental to the capital requirements of the firm discussed at Section 7.4.3. In addition, the firm's terms of business or other client agreements must adequately explain the non-statutory trust and the client's informed consent must be obtained to its use.

Similarly to the statutory trust, the non-statutory client money trust requires assets to be held for the clients for whom that money is held by the firm according to their respective interests in it subject to the payment of costs properly attributable to the distribution of the client money on the failure of the firm. CASS 5.4, 5.5 and 5.6 must be incorporated by reference into the terms of the trust. The debt arising from advances out of the trust assets and any security therefore must be held for the benefit of the trust (CASS 5.4.8R).

7.4.2.4   *Other client money requirements*

Client accounts/segregation

A firm must hold client money separate from the firm's money (CASS 5.5.3R).

A firm must segregate client money by either paying it as soon as practicable into a client bank account or otherwise paying it out (e.g. to the client or the firm itself when it is due and payable to the firm, for example by way of drawdown of commission) (CASS 5.5.5R).

Client accounts must generally be with an "approved bank" (which includes any UK authorised bank or building society) (CASS 5.5.38R) and can be a general client bank account (i.e. a common pool (CASS 5.5.13R)) or a designated client bank account (for those clients who request not to be part of a pool, such clients may request that money be deposited with a bank which is not an approved bank (CASS 5.5.39R)). The firm must notify the bank and obtain acknowledgment that the money in the account is held on trust (CASS 5.5.49R–5.5.51R). If the firm becomes insolvent and there is a shortfall of money, the client money (insurance) distribution rules in CASS 5.6 will govern the distribution of available assets.

CASS 5.5 contains other, very detailed, requirements in relation to matters such as investment of non-statutory trust assets, interest and investment returns on client assets, transfer of client money to third parties (e.g. other brokers), the firm's selection of a bank, in relation to holding or passing money outside the UK and client money calculation (to check that money segregated at banks is sufficient to meet the firm's obligations to clients) and reconciliation.

Appointed representatives

In relation to its appointed representatives, the principal firm must either:

(a) establish and maintain procedures to ensure that client money received by its appointed representatives or other agents of the firm is:
  (i) paid into a client bank account of the firm as soon as is practicable or is otherwise paid out; or
  (ii) forwarded to the principal firm so as to ensure that the money arrives at the specified business address by the close of the third business day after receipt.
(b) The firm must also ensure that its appointed representatives or other agents keep client money separately identifiable from other money until the client money is paid into a client bank account or sent to the firm (CASS 5.5.19R–5.5.21R) or ensure on a regular basis that it holds, in its client bank account, an amount equal to its reasonable estimate of the amounts from time to time held by its appointed representatives or other agents. In order to verify this, the principal is required to carry out no less frequently than every 10 business days reconciliations of the amount it has paid into its client bank account with the amount actually received and held by the appointed representative (CASS 5.5.23R). The firm must then make a corresponding payment into, or withdrawal from, the account.

In addition, the principal firm will be liable to account to the appointed representative's customers for any client monies owed by the appointed representative to its customers (CASS 5.5.18(3)R).

Client money distribution (CASS 5.6)

CASS 5.6 sets out the client money (insurance) distribution rules which seek to facilitate the timely return of client money to a client in the event of the failure of a firm or a third party at which a firm holds client money.

Safekeeping of clients' documents and other assets (CASS 5.8)

If, in the course of its insurance mediation activities, the firm takes into its possession for safekeeping any client title documents (such as documents evidencing title to a contract of insurance) or other tangible assets, it must take reasonable steps to ensure that any such documents/items of property are kept safe and are not delivered to any other person except in accordance with instructions given by the client and a record must be kept as to the identity of such documents/items of property and the dates on which they were received by the firms and delivered to the client (CASS 5.8.3R). Such a record must be kept for at least three years after the document/property is delivered to the client.

7.4.3 Capital resources requirements

A firm with permission to carry on insurance mediation activities is required to fulfil certain capital resources require-ments. The capital resources requirements do not apply to a firm which is an insurer, authorised bank, building society, friendly society or Lloyd's managing agent (MIPRU 4.1.4R and 4.1.11R). A firm of this nature has its own capital resources requirements. Equally, a firm which carries on only designated investment business does not have to apply the capital resources requirements (MIPRU 4.1.6R). Special rules apply for credit unions and social housing firms (MIPRU 4.1.11G and 4.1.13G). The insurance mediation capital resources rules distinguish between a firm holding client assets and one that does not on the basis that the FSA believes that there would be a greater risk to consumers, and there would be a greater adverse impact on market confidence, if a firm holding client money or other client assets were to fail.

A firm is required at all times to ensure that it is able to meet its liabilities as they fall due (MIPRU 4.2.1R). In addition, a firm must at all times maintain capital resources equal to or in excess of its relevant capital resources requirement (MIPRU 4.2.2R).

The capital resources requirement for a firm carrying on insurance mediation activity (and no other regulated activity) which does not hold client money or other client assets in relation to its insurance mediation activity is the higher of:

(a) £5,000; and
(b) 2.5 per cent of the annual income from its insurance mediation activity and any mortgage mediation activity it carries on (MIPRU 4.2.11R(1)).

If a firm holds client money or other client assets in relation to its insurance mediation activity (and carries no other regulated activity), its capital resources requirement is the higher of:

(a) £10,000; and
(b) 5 per cent of the annual income from its insurance mediation activities and any mortgage mediation activity (MIPRU 4.2.11(R)(2)).

The annual income is the brokerage fees, commissions and other related income due to the firm in respect of or in relation to its mediation activities earned by the intermediary that is its own income (MIPRU 4.3.3R). In other words, it is the commission it receives net of amounts due to the product provider, but before any payments are made to the firm's appointed representatives, if any.

The minimum capital requirement is increased to £50,000 for intermediaries wishing to segregate retail client money into a non-statutory trust (as explained further at Section 7.4.2.3).

For firms which also carry on designated investment business, the capital resources requirement is the higher of the requirement in accordance with the capital resources rules for intermediaries disregarding its designated investment business and the financial resource requirement which is applied by the Interim Prudential sourcebook for investment business ("IPRU(INV)") or the Prudential Sourcebook for Banks, Building Societies and Investment Firms ("BIPRU") (MIPRU 4.2.5R).

A firm must calculate its capital resources from the items in MIPRU 4.4.2R (share and other capital; audited reserves; interim net profits; revaluation reserves; general provisions against liabilities; and subordinated loans meeting the requirements of MIPRU 4.4.7R and MIPRU 4.4.8R) from which it must deduct the items in MIPRU 4.4.4R (investments in own shares; intangible assets (including the full balance sheet value of goodwill); interim net losses and excess of drawing over net profits). Further details of these items are provided in MIPRU.

7.5 Financial Services Compensation Scheme

The activity of insurance mediation constitutes a separate sub-scheme within the Financial Services Compensation Scheme ("FSCS"). The FSCS only covers insurance mediation business conducted on or after 14 January 2005. The compensation limit is 100 per cent of the first £2,000 and 90 per cent of the remainder for business conducted before 1 January 2010, and 90 per cent of the claim for business conducted on or after 1 January 2010 (100 per cent of the claim for compulsory classes of insurance).

7.6   Supervision Manual ("SUP")

7.6.1   Applicable chapters of SUP

All chapters of SUP other than 4, 17 and 18 (unless the insurance intermediary is also an insurer) will apply to a firm carrying on insurance mediation activities in relation to a related insurance contract or when communicating or approving a non-investment financial promotion. Certain aspects of SUP as it applies to insurance intermediaries are summarised below.

7.6.2   Approved persons (SUP 10 and MIPRU 2)

SUP 10.4.5R sets out a table of "controlled functions". Individuals carrying out any of those functions in relation to a firm's regulated activities must be approved by the FSA (s.59 of the FSMA 2000).

Responsibility for a firm's insurance mediation activity must be allocated to a director or senior manager (MIPRU 2.2.1R). That person may be an approved person performing a "governing function" (a director), other than a non-executive director, or the "apportionment and oversight function" (the person who must be appointed under the Senior Management Arrangements, Systems and Controls module of the FSA Handbook to deal with the apportionment of responsibilities and oversee the establishment and maintenance of systems and controls) (MIPRU 2.2.2R).

A firm must establish that a reasonable proportion of those within its management structure who are responsible for, and all other persons directly involved in, its insurance mediation activity demonstrate the knowledge and ability necessary for the performance of their duties (e.g. through experience and training). All of these individuals must be of good repute (e.g. have not been convicted of relevant serious criminal offences or been adjudged bankrupt) (MIPRU 2.3).

7.6.3   Controllers and close links (SUP 11)

By virtue of para.4 of the Financial Services and Markets Act 2000 (Controllers) (Exemption) Order 2009,[7] a simplified regime applies on the change of control of a UK firm that is not a bank, investment firm, management company or direct insurer authorised under European directives. FSA approval will be required by persons wishing to acquire holdings of shares or voting power (as defined in s.422 of the FSMA extending to third parties holding shares on that person's behalf or with whom agreement has been reached giving such person control of the third parties' voting power) in relation to such a firm (or a parent undertaking) where this amounts to 20 per cent or more of the firm. This contrasts with the requirements for persons wishing to become controllers of other regulated firms who must obtain approval before obtaining 10 per cent and then through additional thresholds for 20 per cent, 30 per cent and 50 per cent.

In addition to this, UK firms that are not banks, investment firms, management companies or direct insurers authorised under European directives are required to notify the FSA of any persons that become or cease to be 20 per cent controllers (whether directly or through holdings in a parent undertaking of the intermediary) (SUP 11.4.2AR and 11.6.4R), so that the FSA can ensure that it has the information it requires to monitor the firm (SUP 11.2.2G).

7.6.4   Passporting (SUP 13)

The detailed procedures and notification requirements for UK firms wishing to establish branches in, or provide services into, other EEA states are set out in Chapter 13 of the Supervision Manual.

---

[7]   SI 2009/774.

7.7 Other FSA Handbook modules

The general FSA Handbook modules which apply to all firms with Part IV permissions apply in the same way to insurance intermediaries, including the Principles for Businesses ("PRIN"), Statements of Principle and Code of Practice for Approved Persons ("APER"), the Fit and Proper test for Approved Persons ("FIT"), Senior Management Arrangements, Systems and Controls ("SYSC"), Training and Competence sourcebook ("TC"), Enforcement Manual ("ENF"), Dispute Resolution: Complaints ("DISP") and Compensation source-book ("COMP").

As can be seen at Section 7.8 below, the FSA is placing an increasing emphasis on the Principles for Businesses in relation to its regulation of the activities of insurance intermediaries. Key principles in this regard include:

(a) Principle 6—customers' interests: a firm must pay due regard to the interests of its customers and treat them fairly.
(b) Principle 7—communications with clients: a firm must pay due regard to the information needs of its clients and communicate information to them in a way which is clear, fair and not misleading.
(c) Principle 8—conflicts of interest: a firm must manage conflicts of interest fairly, both between itself and its customers and between a customer and another client.

The FSA has focused particularly on treating customers fairly or "TCF" (Principle 6). All firms are now expected to have appropriate management information in place to test whether they are treating their customers fairly. All firms are expected to be able to demonstrate to themselves and to the FSA that they are consistently treating their customers fairly. The FSA views the ICOBS rules (*see* Section 7.8) as an important element of what treating customers fairly means for firms selling insurance policies to retail customers.

The more detailed "common platform" systems and controls requirements (being SYSC 4–10 which relate to MiFID[8] and CRD[9] firms) apply to insurance intermediaries as "non-scope firms" but exclude insurers, which will be covered as part of the FSA's Solvency II work.

Finally, ICOBS (*see* Section 7.8) sets out the conduct of business rules for sales of non-investment insurance. Chapter 10 covers the conduct of business rules for sales of investment insurance contracts.

7.8   Insurance: Conduct of Business Sourcebook ("ICOBS")

Conduct of business requirements were introduced in 2005 in the Insurance Conduct of Business Handbook ("ICOB") at the time of implementation of the Insurance Mediation Directive. The FSA subsequently reviewed ICOB to create a more principles-based approach for sales of non-investment insurance replacing it with the "Insurance: New Conduct of Business Sourcebook" or "ICOBS" which came into force on 8 January 2008.

The FSA's general approach to ICOBS entails:

(a)   reliance on the Principles for Businesses and a small number of high-level standards expressed as rules;

(b)   being supplemented by a small number of specific rules in areas where repeated failings show rules are needed to make the FSA's expectations clear and to constrain behaviour that works against the interests of consumers;

(c)   a general presumption against retaining or creating detailed rules except where necessary to implement directives or where a detailed rule is the only practical way of achieving a particular regulatory outcome; and

(d)   focusing on outcomes not detailed compliance.

---

[8]   Markets in Financial Instruments Directive, 2004/39/EC.
[9]   Capital Requirements Directive, 2006/49/EC.

In ICOBS, the FSA differentiates between two groups of products:

(a) protection products—term, critical illness, income protection and payment protection insurance ("PPI"—defined as "payment protection contracts" for the purposes of the FSA Handbook—*see* Section 7.8.5.2)—where the FSA perceives that there is a greater risk of consumer detriment; and

(b) "other" products—all general insurance except PPI.

The FSA's July 2007 consultation paper (CP 07/11) and the resulting policy statement (PS 07/24) on Insurance Selling and Administration provide useful background in interpreting the detailed rules in ICOBS. The FSA published a post-implementation review of ICOBS in June 2010 but the level of non-compliance identified meant it was unable to draw conclusions as to the effectiveness of its principles-based approach. The Competition Commission published an order detailing measures to introduce competition into the market for payment protection insurance ("PPI") on 24 March 2011 (*see* Section 7.8.5.2).

7.8.1 Application and purpose (ICOBS 1)

7.8.1.1 Products

ICOBS applies to non-investment insurance contracts. "Non-investment insurance contracts" are general insurance contracts (i.e. non-life) and pure protection contracts (i.e. life insurance contracts where the benefit is payable only in the case of death or incapacity due to injury, sickness or infirmity and which have no surrender value in excess of the premium paid), but not long-term care insurance contracts. The reason for the exclusion of long-term care insurance is that it is regulated as an investment product under the COBS rules. The COBS rules in relation to investment insurance contracts are covered in Chapter 10 below.

7.8.1.2   Activities

In broad terms, ICOBS applies to the selling and administration of non-investment insurance contracts by both insurers (including Lloyd's managing agents) and intermediaries. This includes the provision of advice, the effecting and the carrying out of non-investment insurance contracts which insurers conduct as product providers (e.g. activities such as producing the contracts and paying claims) and the communication and approval of financial promotions and activities connected with them (ICOBS 1.1.1R—the "general application rule").

Note that INSPRU 1.5.13(1)R prevents an insurer from carrying on an insurance mediation activity in respect of a third-party's products unless a natural fit or necessary connection can be shown between the insurer's insurance business and the third party's products.

The general application rule is modified in ICOBS 1 Annex 1 according to the type of firm (Part 1), its activities (Part 2) and its location (Part 3). Limitations and exclusions to the application of ICOBS include the following.

Large risks (ICOBS 1 Annex 1, Part 2, paragraph 2.1R)

ICOBS does not apply to insurance intermediaries carrying on insurance mediation activities in relation to contracts of large risks (as defined by art.5(d) of the First Non-Life Directive[10] and including, for example, aircraft and ships and credit and suretyship for professional policyholders (*see* Section 7.3.5.2)):

(a)   where the risk is located outside the EEA; or
(b)   for commercial customers where the risk is situated within the EEA.

---

[10]   Directive 73/239/EC.

Reinsurance contracts (ICOBS 1 Annex 1, Part 2, paragraph 1.1R)

ICOBS does not apply to activities relating to reinsurance contracts.

Pure protection contracts: election to apply COBS rules (ICOBS 1 Annex 1, Part 2, paragraph 3)

ICOBS does not apply to pure protection contracts to the extent that a firm has elected to comply with COBS in respect of that business, treating the pure protection contract as a "life policy" and a "designated investment" and not as a "non-investment insurance contract". The COBS rules are covered in Chapter 10 below.

However, notwithstanding these exclusions, the Principles for Businesses continue to apply so, for example, guidance advises firms to provide evidence of cover promptly to customers and that for group policies information should be provided to be passed on to each other policyholder in line with Principle 7 and the FSA has introduced a new section into ICOBS as a result of the Retail Distribution Review which must be complied with even by firms which elect to comply with COBS for their pure protection business.

The provision imposes additional disclosure obligations to ensure that, where a Firm agrees an adviser charge with a consumer, the consumer understands how the firm is remunerated for the pure protection sale and, if applicable, that the firm will receive a commission in addition to its adviser charge (ICOBS 4.6). Additional disclosure obligations contained in COBS are imposed on such sales. The new provision will become effective on 31 December 2012.

7.8.1.3 Firms

ICOBS 1 Annex 1, Part 1 includes modifications of the application of the rules for third-party processors (outsourced service providers), Lloyd's managing agents, authorised professional firms, appointed representatives, service companies and the Society of Lloyd's itself.

While ICOBS does not apply directly to a principal firm's appointed representative, in determining compliance with ICOBS anything done or omitted by the appointed representative will be treated as having been done or omitted by the firm (ICOBS 1.1.1R and ICOBS 1 Annex 1, Part 1, para.4).

Where a chain of intermediaries exists between the insurer and the customer, ICOBS applies only to the intermediary in contact with the customer and not to any intermediaries in the middle of the chain. However, intermediaries in the middle of the chain are likely to be carrying out regulated activities which will require authorisation (ICOBS 1 Annex 1, Part 2, para.4.1R).

7.8.1.4 *Jurisdiction*

ICOBS will generally only apply to activities carried out from an establishment in the UK (ICOBS 1.1.1R). Paragraphs 3–8 of ICOBS 1 Annex 1 Part 4 set out some very detailed guidance in relation to modifications to this general rule on territorial scope. The need for this arises particularly because of the number of different directives which are implemented in ICOBS, being the Directive, the Non-Life Directives,[11] the Consolidated Life Directive,[12] the Motor Insurance Directives,[13] the Distance Marketing Directive and the Electronic Commerce Directive.[14]

The EEA territorial scope rules are unlikely to apply if a UK firm is doing business from a UK establishment for a client located in the UK in relation to a UK product. However, if there is a non-UK element, the firm should consider whether:

---

[11] The First Non-Life Directive, the Second Non-Life Directive (Directive 88/357/EEC) and the Third Non-Life Directive (Directive 72/49/EEC).

[12] Directive 2002/83/EC.

[13] Directive 72/166/EEC, Directive 84/5/EEC, Directive 90/232/EEC and Directive 2000/26/EC.

[14] Directive 2000/31/EC.

(a) it is subject to a directive;
(b) the business it is conducting is subject to a directive; and
(c) the particular rule is within the scope of a directive.

If the answer to all three questions is yes, the modification in Paragraphs 3–8 of ICOBS 1 Annex 1 Part 4 may change the effect of the general application rule (ICOBS 1 Annex 1, Part 4, para.2.2G).

7.8.2   General rules (ICOBS 2)

7.8.2.1   Customers

ICOBS distinguishes between firms dealing with consumers and firms dealing with commercial customers. Whereas a policyholder includes anyone who is entitled to make a claim on a policy, only a policyholder or prospective policyholder who makes the arrangements preparatory to his concluding a non-investment insurance contract (directly or through an agent) is a "customer". A "consumer" is a customer acting for a purpose outside his or its trade, business or profession, while a "commercial customer" is a customer who is or which is not a consumer (ICOBS 2.1.1G). When in doubt as to whether a customer is a consumer or a commercial customer, a firm must treat the customer as a consumer (ICOBS 2.1.2R). If a customer is acting in the capacity of both a consumer and a commercial customer in relation to a particular non-investment insurance contract, a customer is a commercial customer (ICOBS 2.1.3G). ICOBS 2.1.4G provides a table of certain customer classification examples.

7.8.2.2   Communications to clients and financial promotions (ICOBS 2.2)

Under s.21 of the FSMA 2000, a restriction is imposed on the communication of financial promotions (defined as an invitation or inducement to engage in investment activity (such as buying a contract of insurance) that is communicated in the course of business) unless the communication is made by an authorised person or the content of the financial promotion has been approved by an authorised person. However, the Financial Services and Markets Act 2000 (Financial Promotion) Order 2005[15] (the "Financial Promotion Order") provides exemptions for certain types of financial promotion.

ICOBS 2.2 deals with a communication or approval of a financial promotion of a non-investment insurance contract to be communicated in the UK unless it can be communicated by an authorised person without approval.

When a firm communicates information (including a financial promotion) to a customer or other policyholder, it must take reasonable steps to communicate it in a way which is clear, fair and not misleading (ICOBS 2.2.2R).

Before approving a financial promotion, a firm must take reasonable steps to ensure that the financial promotion is clear, fair and not misleading. If, subsequently, a firm becomes aware that a financial promotion is not clear, fair and not misleading, it must withdraw its approval and notify any person that it knows to be relying on its approval as soon as reasonably practicable (ICOBS 2.2.3R).

ICOBS 2.2.4G provides guidance on the application of the clear, fair and not misleading rule in relation to pricing claims, including financial promotions that indicate or imply that a firm can reduce the premium, provide the cheapest premium or reduce a customer's costs. The guidance includes that the financial promotion should be consistent with the result reasonably expected to be achieved by the majority of the customers who respond, unless the proportion of those customers who are likely to achieve the pricing claims is stated prominently (ICOBS 2.2.4G).

7.8.2.3 *Inducements (ICOBS 2.3)*

ICOBS 2.3 reminds a firm of its duty to manage conflicts of interest fairly under Principle 8 and that this principle extends

---

[15] The Financial Services and Markets Act 2000 (Financial Promotions) Order 2005 (SI 2005/1529).

to soliciting or accepting inducements where this would conflict with the firm's duties to customers. Firms are reminded that, when offering such inducements, they should consider whether doing so conflicts with their obligations under Principles 1 and 6 to act with integrity and treat customers fairly. The unfairness or otherwise of an inducement is therefore a judgment which is left to individual firms. Guidance adds that inducements include, but are not limited to, cash, cash equivalents, commission (to include all remuneration), goods and hospitality.

7.8.2.4   Record-keeping requirements (ICOBS 2.4)

ICOBS 2.4 refers firms to SYSC 3.2.20R which requires firms to take reasonable care to make and retain adequate records of matters and dealings which are the subject of requirements and standards under the regulatory system, which include ICOBS. The guidance reminds firms of the need to deal with requests for information from the FSA as well as queries and complaints from customers which may require evidence matter such as:

(a)   the reasons for personal recommendations;
(b)   what documentation has been provided to the customer; and
(c)   how claims have been settled and why (ICOBS 2.4.1G).

7.8.2.5   Exclusion of liability (ICOBS 2.5)

In addition to provisions of the general law such as the Unfair Terms in Consumer Contracts Regulations 1999,[16] a firm must not seek to exclude or restrict, or to rely on any exclusion or restriction of, any duty or liability it may have to a customer or other policyholder unless it is reasonable for it to do so and the duty or liability arises other than under rules in or made under FSMA 2000 (ICOBS 2.5.1R) or any directly applicable provisions of a Directive or Regulation.

---

[16]   SI 1999/2083 (as amended).

7.8.3 Information about the firm, its services and remuneration (ICOBS 4)

7.8.3.1 Purpose and application

ICOBS 4 applies to insurance intermediaries (but not insurers) (ICOBS 4.1.1R).

7.8.3.2 General requirements for pre-contract status and fees disclosure

Status disclosure (ICOBS 4.1.2–4.1.8)

Certain information as to the status of the intermediary, contained in ICOBS 4.1.2R, 4.1.6R and (for consumers only) 4.1.7R, must be provided to the customer before conclusion of an initial non-investment insurance contract and, if necessary, on its amendment or renewal. This information includes:

(a)   the insurance intermediary's name and address;
(b)   the fact that it is included in the FSA Register and means for verifying this;
(c)   details on ownership above a 10 per cent threshold of or by an insurance undertaking;
(d)   details of how to complain and that complaints may subsequently be referred to the Financial Ombudsman Service or any other applicable named complaints scheme.

It also includes a requirement to inform the customer whether:

(a)   it gives advice on the basis of a fair analysis of the market;
(b)   it is under a contractual obligation to conduct insurance mediation business exclusively with one or more insurance undertakings; or
(c)   it is not under a contractual obligation to conduct insurance mediation business exclusively with one or more insurance undertakings and does not give advice on the basis of a fair analysis of the market.

If a firm does not advise on the basis of a fair analysis of the market, it must inform the customer that he has a right to request the name of each insurance undertaking with which the firm may and does conduct business and must comply with such a request. A firm must also confirm whether it is giving a personal recommendation (that is, a recommendation that is "advice on investments" falling within art.53 of the RAO) or merely information.

Information on fees (ICOBS 4.3) and commissions (ICOBS 4.4)

A customer must be provided with details of the amount (failing which the method of calculation) of any fees, other than premium monies, payable through the life of a policy for an insurance mediation activity before liability is incurred to pay the fee or before conclusion of the contract, whichever is earlier. On a request by a commercial customer, an insurance intermediary must promptly disclose, in cash terms (estimated, if necessary), any commission (to include all forms of remuneration) received by it and any associate in connection with a policy. The requirement to disclose commission does not apply in the case of a consumer. However, the information may be provided by the firm on a voluntary basis.

Means of communication (ICOBS 4.1.9R)

Information provided in compliance with ICOBS 4 must be provided in a clear, accurate and comprehensible manner and in a durable medium. A "durable medium" is defined as paper or any instrument which allows the storage of information in a way which is accessible for future reference for a period of time which is adequate for the purposes of the information and which allows the unchanged reproduction of the information stored. This includes computer disks, CD-ROMs and e-mails, but excludes websites unless the information remains accessible for future reference in the way described.

The information may be disclosed orally on the request of a customer or when immediate cover is required. For telephone sales, the information may be given in accordance with the distance marketing rules in ICOBS 3.1.14R (*see* Section 7.8.6.2). The customer must be provided with the required information in a durable medium immediately after the conclusion of the contract.

ICOBS 4 Annex 1G sets out a sample initial disclosure document which can be used to meet the status disclosure, scope of service and fee disclosure requirements (ICOBS 4.5).

7.8.3.3 *Additional requirements for protection policies for insurance intermediaries and insurers (ICOBS 4.2)*

ICOBS 4.2 applies only to pure protection contracts and payment protection contracts (*see* Section 7.8.5.2 for definition of payment protection contract) for consumers.

The main additional requirement is that, in a sale that does not involve a personal recommendation (a "non-advised sale"), a firm must take reasonable steps to ensure a customer understands that he is responsible for deciding whether a policy meets his demands and needs (ICOBS 4.2.4R(1)). If a firm anticipates providing, or provides, information on any main characteristic of a policy orally during a non-advised sale, taking reasonable steps includes explaining the customer's responsibility orally (ICOBS 4.2.4(3)R). A policy's main characteristics include its significant benefits, its significant exclusions and limitations, its duration and price information (ICOBS 4.2.4(4)R). Guidance on significant exclusions and limitations is provided in ICOBS 6 Annex 2, para.3.1G (*see* Section 7.8.5.6).

7.8.4 *Identifying client needs and advising (ICOBS 5)*

7.8.4.1 *General*

A firm arranging a payment protection contract must take reasonable steps to ensure that the customer only buys a policy under which he is eligible to claim benefits. If, at any time while arranging the policy, it finds that parts of the cover do not apply, the firm must inform the customer so he or she can take an informed decision on whether to buy the policy (ICOBS 5.1.2R).

Guidance is provided in very similar terms in relation to any other policies covered by ICOBS, citing in particular the need for firms to comply with Principle 6. Firms are reminded in guidance of the need to explain to customers the duty to disclose all circumstances material to a policy and the consequences of any failure to do so and to ensure that the customer is asked clear questions about any matter material to the insurance undertaking (ICOBS 5.1.4G).

Additional guidance applicable only to payment protection contracts is that reasonable steps required in relation to eligibility are likely to include checking that the customer meets any qualifying requirements for different parts of the policy (ICOBS 5.1.3G).

7.8.4.2 Statement of demands and needs (ICOBS 5.2)

ICOBS 5.2 applies to:

(a) an insurance intermediary in relation to any policies (other than a connected travel insurance contract); and
(b) an insurer where it has given a personal recommendation to a consumer on a payment protection contract or a pure protection contract.

A firm must, before the conclusion of a contract, specify, in particular on the basis of information provided by the customer, the demands and needs of that customer as well as the underlying reasons for any advice given to the customer on that policy (ICOBS 5.2.2R). The level of detail to be provided will depend on the complexity of the policy proposed. The means of communication is as set out at Section 7.8.3.2.

Guidance is provided on statements of demands and needs for non-advised sales which allows for generic statements in literature such as application forms and product documents which explains demands and needs by reference to responses given by the customer or merely explains the demands and needs which the policy meets (ICOBS 5.2.4G).

7.8.4.3   Advised sales (ICOBS 5.3)

A firm must take reasonable care to ensure the suitability of its advice for any customer who is entitled to rely on its judgment (ICOBS 5.3.1R). Guidance in ICOBS 5.3.2G explains that, for payment protection contracts or pure protection contracts, a firm should:

(a)   establish the customer's demands and needs including by obtaining further relevant information from the customer, for example details of existing insurance cover;

(b)   take reasonable care to ensure that the policy is suitable for the customer's demands and needs, taking into account its level of cover and cost, and relevant exclusions, excesses, limitations and conditions; and

(c)   inform the customer of any demands and needs that are not met.

If an insurance intermediary informs a customer that it gives advice based on a fair analysis of the market, it must base that advice on analysis of a sufficiently large number of contracts of insurance available on the market to enable it to make a recommendation in accordance with professional criteria, regarding which non-investment insurance contract would be adequate to meet the customer's needs (ICOBS 5.3.3R).

7.8.5   Product information (ICOBS 6)

7.8.5.1   General

ICOBS 6 is designed to ensure that a customer has the necessary information in good time and in a comprehensible form so that he can make an informed decision about the arrangements proposed. ICOBS 6.1.5R requires firms to take reasonable steps to ensure that this is the case.

If both the insurer and the insurance intermediary in question operate from an establishment maintained in the UK, the insurer is responsible for producing, and the insurance intermediary for providing to the customer, the information required by ICOBS 6 and the distance communication rules (ICOBS 6.1.1R). Where there is no insurance intermediary, the insurer is responsible for producing and providing the information (ICOBS 6.1.2R). The insurer is responsible for providing information required on mid-term changes and the insurance intermediary is responsible for producing price information if it agrees this with the insurer. The insurer must provide information in good time to enable the insurance intermediary to comply with the rules in ICOBS 6, or promptly on an insurance intermediary's request (ICOBS 6.1.3R). The general responsibilities of insurers and insurance intermediaries are modified by ICOBS 6 Annex 1R if one of the firms is not based in the UK and in certain other situations (ICOBS 6.1.4R).

If a policy is bought by a customer in connection with other goods or services, a firm must, before conclusion of the contract, disclose its premium separately from other prices and also disclose whether buying the policy is compulsory (ICOBS 6.1.13(1)R). In the case of a distance contract, disclosure of whether buying the policy is compulsory may be made in accordance with the timing requirements under the distance communication rules (ICOBS 6.1.13(2)R).

Where ICOBS 6 requires information to be provided before conclusion of a contract, this must typically be in writing or another durable medium. In the case of distance contracts, this information may instead be provided by a firm in accordance with the distance communication timing requirements in ICOBS 3 (ICOBS 6.1.13R(2) and ICOBS 6.1.14R). ICOBS 6.1.10G notes that a firm may wish to provide information in a policy summary (*see* Section 7.8.5.6) or key features document. Policy summaries are only mandatory for payment protection contracts and pure protection contracts (*see* Section 7.8.5.5).

A "distance contract" is a contract concluded using distance communication only, involving no simultaneous physical presence between the firm and the consumer, for example telephone, internet, e-mail or post. A contract is not a distance contract if:

(a) making or performing it does not constitute or form part of a regulated activity;
(b) it is entered into on a strictly occasional basis outside a commercial structure dedicated to the concluding of distance contracts; or
(c) a consumer, and an intermediary acting for a product provider, are simultaneously physically present at some stage before the conclusion of the contract.

See Section 7.8.6 for an explanation of the distance communication requirements.

Although the specific guidance on white-labelling which was included in ICOB has not been retained in ICOBS, the effect is unchanged as in all cases the identity of the insurance undertaking providing the cover must be communicated to the customer.

7.8.5.2 *Payment protection contracts*

Many of the rules in ICOBS are focused particularly on payment protection contracts. A "payment protection contract" is defined as a non-investment insurance contract which has elements of a general insurance contract and the benefits of which are described as enabling a policyholder to protect his ability to continue to make payments due to third parties, or can reasonably be expected to be used in this way. The FSA confirmed in PS 07/21 that the definition is intended to cover income protection policies. The use of the words "which has elements of a general insurance contract" is intended by the FSA to clarify the position for mixed contracts which have elements of both general insurance and a pure protection contract. This is perhaps best clarified by setting out the FSA's explanation from PS 07/21 of the position that will apply to payment protection contracts with elements of both pure protection contract and general insurance contract (for example a payment protection contract with a life insurance element). The FSA states that the position for such policies is as follows:

(a) rules that apply to all products (for example, the high-level suitability and product disclosure rules) apply to the whole policy;

(b) rules applying only to pure protection contracts (for example, the Consolidated Life Directive disclosures in ICOBS 6.3.1R and 6.3.3R—*see* Section 7.8.5.4) apply to the life insurance element;

(c) rules applying only to general insurance contracts (the Third Non-Life Directive disclosures in ICOBS 6.2.2R–6.2.4R—*see* Section 7.8.5.3) apply to the general insurance parts of the policy;

(d) the information required by the Consolidated Life Directive and Third Non-Life Directive can be given in accordance with the Distance Marketing Directive timing requirements (ICOBS 6.1.14R); and

(e) where there are specific rules for payment protection contracts (for example, the eligibility rule in ICOBS 5.1.2R and the price disclosure requirements in ICOBS 6), these apply to the whole policy. So a policy that meets the definition of payment protection contract would be subject to the payment protection rules for the whole policy.

On 24 March 2011, the Competition Commission published a legally-binding Order[17] following its investigation of competition in the PPI market in the UK. The Order includes a package of measures which seek to address the lack of competition in the market which the Competition Commission had identified following a lengthy investigation. These measures include a point of sale prohibition on PPI during the sale of a credit product; a prohibition on single premium policies; a standard, consistent form for personal PPI quotes; and annual statements so that policyholders know the value of protection they are receiving for their money and can readily check what that would cost from other providers. Most of these measures relate to personal loan PPI ("PLPPI"), first-charge mortgage PPI ("MPPI"), credit card PPI ("CCPPI") and second-charge

---

[17] The Payment Protection Insurance Market Investigation Order 2011.

mortgage PPI ("SMPPI"). The point of sale prohibition does not apply to retail PPI. The Order will be regulated by the Office of Fair Trading which will also receive first six-monthly (for two years) then annual "compliance reports" including both commercial and regulatory information. The Competition Commission Order falls outside the scope of this book but summary details are provided given the overlap with the FSA's ICOBS rules.

The point of sale prohibition addresses the "point of sale" advantage enjoyed by sellers of credit by prohibiting the sale of PPI at the same time as the related credit product for PLPPI, MPPI, CCPPI and SMPPI. This prohibition operates to prevent a firm from concluding a PPI transaction until at least seven days after conclusion of the credit sale, or if later, the provision of a personal quote. The prohibition does not prevent firms from undertaking the full PPI sales discussion at the credit point-of-sale and firms can contact customers from seven days after conclusion of the credit sale to conclude the PPI sale. The firm can also conclude a PPI transaction from 24 hours after conclusion of the credit sale where the customer initiates contact with the firm.

Barclays Bank PLC (supported by Lloyds Banking Group and Shop Direct Group Financial Services Ltd) had challenged the lawfulness of the decision to impose the package of measures outlined by the Competition Commission in the Competition Appeal Tribunal, principally in relation to the point of sale prohibition. This challenge was upheld in part, with the Tribunal holding that, in assessing whether it was a proportionate measure to increase competition in the PPI market, the Competition Commission had failed to take account of the loss of convenience to consumers in banning the sale of PPI at the same time as a related credit product. The Tribunal remitted the matter to the Competition Commission and directed it to address certain additional matters in the remittal. The Commission found that the loss of convenience to consumers did not alter its initial conclusions and that the point of sale prohibition was a proportionate measure as part of the overall package of measures to increase competition.

The Order took effect from 6 April 2011. Certain information requirements will come into force on 1 October 2011 and the point of sale prohibition and other measures on 6 April 2012.

Following publication of the Commission's report leading to the Order, the FSA released a clarification confirming that the ICOBS requirements and standards for PPI sales, as described elsewhere in this Chapter, remain in place in relation to the sale of PPI (*see* e.g. Section 7.8.5.5). The FSA clarification also confirms that:

(a) oral information on PPI given at the credit point-of-sale cannot be relied upon as meeting the oral disclosure requirements and informed decision standard for PPI sales following the end of the prohibition period (including an earlier customer-initiated discussion);

(b) when a firm contacts a customer by telephone or other means involving oral discussion following the end of the prohibition period (including an earlier customer-initiated discussion), it must ensure that the information provided is sufficient for the customer to make an informed decision and that all the required ICOBS PPI disclosures are made at this point (ICOBS 4.2.4R, 6.4.2R and 6.4.5R);

(c) where the firm contacts customers by letter or other written communication following the end of the prohibition period (including an earlier customer-initiated discussion), the communication must be clear, fair and not misleading and the firm must take steps to ensure that the customer's decision to buy PPI is an active opt-in decision taken after it has provided appropriate information on which the customer can base an informed decision (ICOBS 4.2, 5.2 and 5.3); and

(d) prior to conclusion of a PPI contract, any advice or personal recommendations made at the credit point-of-sale or the PPI point-of-sale must be communicated as set out in ICOBS 5.2.2R and 5.2.3R.

In more recent open correspondence with the Competition Commission, the FSA has pointed out that, although the Order intends to capture insurance products which are a direct replacement for PPI, it does not in their view capture "debt waiver" and "debt freeze" arrangements because they do not amount to insurance. Under these arrangements, the debt or payment obligations would be suspended for a period, resulting in a similar effect to PPI but, importantly, no payment to or on behalf of the debtor. The FSA does note that the Principles for Businesses should apply to the banks selling these products and that any mortgage sale featuring this type of arrangement would have to comply with the detailed mortgage conduct of business rules in MCOB.

7.8.5.3 Pre-contract information: general insurance contracts (ICOBS 6.2)

ICOBS 6.2 derives from the Third Non-Life Directive and as such it only applies to general insurance contracts.

Before a general insurance contract is concluded, a firm must inform a customer who is a natural person of the law applicable to the contract, the arrangements for handling policyholders' complaints (including the existence of a complaints body—in the case of the UK, usually the Financial Ombudsman Service) and the EEA state in which the head office or branch with which the contract is to be concluded is situated (ICOBS 6.2.2R and 6.2.3R).

The contract or other document granting cover, together with the insurance proposal where it is binding on the customer, must state the address of the head office or, where appropriate, the branch of the insurance undertaking which grants the cover (ICOBS 6.2.4R).

A firm must provide a consumer with the information on cancellation rights set out in ICOBS 6.2.5R in good time before conclusion of the contract.

7.8.5.4 *Pre- and post-contract information: pure protection contracts (ICOBS 6.3)*

ICOBS 6.3 derives from the Consolidated Life Directive and as such it only applies to pure protection contracts.

ICOBS 6.3.1R lists the information which must be provided to a customer before a pure protection contract is concluded. The list is considerably more detailed than that set out in ICOBS 6.2 in relation to general insurance contracts. ICOBS 6.3.3R requires that the customer be updated on changes to certain of the initial information throughout the term of the pure protection contract.

7.8.5.5 *Additional requirements for protection policies (ICOBS 6.4)*

The distinction in ICOBS between protection policies and other contracts to which ICOBS applies is starkly apparent in ICOBS 6. Only the high-level rules in ICOBS 6.1 (and ICOBS 3 for distance contracts) apply to contracts which are not protection policies. ICOBS 6.4 sets out super-equivalent rules (being rules additional to directive requirements) which apply to payment protection contracts and pure protection contracts:

(a) If a firm provides information orally during a sales dialogue with a customer on a main characteristic of a policy, it must do so for all of the policy's main characteristics (guidance in ICOBS 6.4.3G adds that this will include its significant benefits, significant exclusions and limitations (*see* Section 7.8.5.6 which summarises identical guidance on significant exclusions and limitations), its duration and price information) (ICOBS 6.4.2(1)R).

(b) A firm must take reasonable steps to ensure that the information provided orally is sufficient to enable the customer to make an informed decision based on that information, without overloading the customer or obscuring other parts of the information (ICOBS 6.4.2(2)R).

(c) A firm must provide a consumer with a policy summary in good time before the conclusion of the contract (ICOBS 6.4.4R).

(d) For payment protection contracts, a firm must draw a consumer's attention to the importance of reading the payment protection contract before the end of the cancellation period to check that the policy is suitable for the consumer (which must be done orally if the firm provides information on any main characteristic of the policy orally) (ICOBS 6.4.5R).

(e) A firm must provide price information in a way calculated to enable the customer to relate it to a regular budget (ICOBS 6.4.6R). (Guidance in ICOBS 6.4.7G adds that price information is likely to include at least: the total premium; for policies over one year with reviewable premium, the period for which the pre-quoted premium is valid and the timing of reviews; other fees, administrative charges and taxes payable by the customer through the firm; and a statement identifying separately the possibility of any taxes not payable through the firm.)

Where a premium will be paid using a credit agreement other than a revolving credit agreement, a firm must provide price information in a way calculated to enable the customer to understand the additional repayments that relate to the purchase of the policy and the total cost of the policy. A firm must explain to a customer, if applicable, that the premium will be added to the amount provided under the credit agreement and that interest will be payable on it (ICOBS 6.4.9R).

Guidance is provided in relation to policies bought as secondary products to revolving credit agreements (such as store cards or credit cards). Price information should be given in a way calculated to enable a typical customer to understand the typical cumulative cost of taking out the policy. The rationale for this guidance is that with revolving credit arrangements such as credit cards, there is no defined price which can be specified at the beginning, so the firm cannot provide specific price information in a way calculated to enable the customer to understand the additional repayments and the total cost of the policy. The guidance adds that a firm should ensure that this element of price information is not undermined by any information given orally (ICOBS 6.4.10G).

In relation to mid-term changes, a firm must provide a customer with information about any change to the premium (unless the change conforms to a previously disclosed formula) and any term of the policy, together with an explanation of any implications of the change where necessary (ICOBS 6.4.11R). Firms are reminded of the need to consider whether these changes are compatible with the original policy as a matter of contract law and also to consider whether any reserved right to make variations is itself unfair under the Unfair Terms in Consumer Contracts Regulations 1999 (SI 1999/2083, as amended).

7.8.5.6 Policy summary for consumers (ICOBS 6 Annex 2)

This Annex sets out the contents and other requirements for policy summaries as referred to in ICOBS 6.1.10 and 6.4.4. Paragraph 2.1 sets out the information which the policy summary must contain and requires that the policy summary contain no other information. The contents requirements include significant features and benefits and significant or unusual exclusions or limitations (and cross-references to the relevant policy document provisions for the exclusions or limitations).

Paragraph 3 of ICOBS 6 Annex 2 includes guidance on significant or unusual exclusions or limitations. It states that a significant exclusion or limitation is one that would tend to affect the decision of consumers generally to buy. An unusual exclusion or limitation is one that is not normally found in comparable contracts. In determining what exclusions or limitations are significant, a firm should, in particular, consider the exclusions or limitations that relate to the significant features and benefits of a policy and factors which may have an adverse effect on benefits payable under it. Examples of significant or unusual exclusions or limitations given in the guidance are as follows:

(a) the contract only operates through certain means of communication, for example telephone or internet;
(b) deferred payment periods;
(c) moratorium periods;
(d) exclusion of certain conditions, diseases or pre-existing medical conditions;
(e) limits on the amount of cover;
(f) limits on the period for which benefits will be paid;
(g) restrictions on eligibility to claim such as age, residence or employment status; and
(h) excesses.

A firm may provide a document that has the contents of a key features document instead of a policy summary (ICOBS 6 Annex 2, para.4.1R). Key features documents are used in relation to the sale of investment insurance contracts and are governed by COBS 13 (*see* Section 10.10 of Chapter 10).

7.8.5.7   *Complaints-handling procedures for payment protection contracts (DISP Appendix 3)*

The assessment and redress of PPI complaints has been a high-profile topic, including the unsuccessful case brought by the British Bankers' Association which sought to overturn the FSA's approach and its proposed rules and guidance (see "Challenge to DISP complaints-handling rules in PPI mis-selling case", below).

Appendix 3 to the Dispute Resolution: Complaints sourcebook ("DISP") now sets out the approach which firms should use when handling and assessing complaints in relation to the sale of PPI and in determining appropriate redress where complaints are upheld. The guidance relates to the sale of any PPI contract whenever the sale took place and irrespective of whether it was on an advised or non-advised basis; conducted through any sales channel; in connection with any type of loan or credit product, or none; and for a regular premium or single premium payment (DISP, Appendix 3, 3.1.1G). It also applies whether the policy is currently in force, was cancelled during the policy term or ran its full term (DISP, Appendix 3, 3.1.1G).

Assessing a complaint (DISP, Appendix 3, Section 3.2)

When assessing a complaint, the firm should consider, in light of all the information provided by the complainant and otherwise already held by or available to the firm, whether there was a breach or failing by the firm (DISP, Appendix 3, 3.2.1G). When undertaking this assessment the firm should seek to establish the true substance of the complaint, rather than taking a narrow interpretation of the issues raised (DISP, Appendix 3, 3.2.2G). This might involve contacting the complainant directly (DISP, Appendix 3, 3.2.3G); considering other evidence of breach or failing not raised in the complaint (DISP, Appendix 3, 3.2.5G); and taking into account other information it already holds about the sale (DISP, Appendix 3, 3.2.6G).

Where a complaint is made, the firm should assess the complaint fairly, giving appropriate weight and balanced consideration to all available evidence, including what the complainant says and other information about the sale that the firm identifies (DISP, Appendix 3, 3.3.1G). The firm is not expected automatically to assume there has been a breach or failing (DISP, Appendix 3, 3.3.1G).

Approach to considering evidence (DISP, Appendix 3, Section 3.3)

Section 3.3 of DISP Appendix 3 sets out in some detail the approach firms should take when considering evidence of a complaint. This guidance drives at firms getting to the bottom of what happened during sales and asks firms not to rely on technical matters or the drawing of inferences to reject complaints. For example, firms should assess the reliability of the complainant's account fairly and in good faith and should make all reasonable efforts to clarify ambiguous issues or conflicts of evidence before making any finding against the complainant (DISP, Appendix 3, 3.3.7G).

Determining the effect of a breach or failing (DISP, Appendix 3, Section 3.6)

Where the firm determines that there was a breach or failing, the firm should consider whether the complainant would have bought the PPI contract in the absence of that breach or failing (DISP, Appendix 3, 3.6.1E). In the absence of evidence to the contrary, the firm should presume that the complainant would not have bought the PPI contract he bought if the sale was "substantially flawed". A full list of examples of "substantially flawed" sales is set out in DISP, Appendix 3, 3.6.2G and includes, *inter alia*, pressuring the complainant into purchasing, failing to disclose certain information, providing misleading or inaccurate information and, where relevant, not ensuring suitability or eligibility.

Approach to redress (DISP, Appendix 3, Section 3.7)

Where the firm concludes in accordance with DISP App 3.6 that the complainant would still have bought the PPI contract he bought, no redress will be due (DISP, Appendix 3, 3.7.1E). Where the firm concludes that the complainant would not have bought the PPI contract he bought (and is not using the alternative redress approach for single premium policies or other appropriate redress), the firm should, as far as practicable, put the complainant in the position he would have been if he had not bought any PPI contract (DISP, Appendix 3, 3.7.2G).

Where the firm determines that it is to pay redress, the firm should pay to the complainant a sum equal to the total amount paid by the complainant in respect of the PPI contract including historic interest where relevant. If the customer received any rebate (for example, through cancelling the policy before it ran full term and received a refund), the firm may deduct the value of the rebate from the amount otherwise payable (DISP, Appendix 3, 3.7.3E). There are separate rules for the situation where a single premium policy was added to a loan, which involve restructuring the loan for live single premium policies and, for cancelled policies, paying the difference between the actual loan balance at the point of cancellation and what the loan balance would have been if no premium had been added (DISP, Appendix 3, 3.7.4E). An alternative approach to redress for single premium policies is also laid out in DISP, Appendix 3, 3.7.7E–3.7.15E. This alternative approach allows the bank to assume that, where certain breaches or failings have occurred, the customer would have purchased a regular premium PPI contract as opposed to a single premium PPI contract (DISP, Appendix 3, 3.7.7E). Redress is then calculated accordingly.

DISP makes it clear that the remedies in DISP App 3.7 are not exhaustive and that when applying a remedy other than those listed in DISP, the firm should satisfy itself that the remedy is appropriate to the matter complained of and is appropriate and fair in the individual circumstances (DISP, Appendix 3, 3.8.1E and 3.8.2E).

Root cause analysis (DISP, Appendix 3, Section 3.4)

Where a firm receives complaints about its sales of PPI contracts, it should analyse the root causes of those complaints including, but not limited to:

(a) the concerns raised by the complainants (both at the time of sale and subsequently);
(b) the reasons for both rejected claims and complaints;
(c) the firm's stated sales practices at the relevant times;
(d) evidence of the actual sales practices at the relevant times, where this is available;
(e) relevant regulatory findings; and
(f) relevant decisions by the Financial Ombudsman Service ("FOS").

Where consideration of the root causes of complaints suggests recurring or systemic problems in the firm's sales practices, the firm should, in assessing an individual complaint, consider whether the problems were likely to have contributed to a breach or failing in the individual case, even if those problems were not referred to specifically by the complainant (DISP, Appendix 3, 3.4.2G).

Further, where a firm identifies recurring or systemic problems in its sales practices, either for its sales in general or for those from a particular location or sales channel, it should (in accordance with Principle 6 (Customers' interests) and to the extent that it applies) consider whether it ought to act with regard to the position of complainants who may have suffered detriment from, or been potentially disadvantaged by, such problems but who have not complained ("non-complainants"). The firm should take appropriate and proportionate measures to ensure that non-complainants are given appropriate redress or a proper opportunity to obtain it (DISP, Appendix 3, 3.4.3G), which might include undertaking proactively a redress or remediation exercise to contact non-complainants (DISP, Appendix 3, 3.4.3G(2)).

Challenge to DISP complaints-handling rules in PPI mis-selling case

In *R. (on the application of British Bankers Association) v The Financial Services Authority* [2011] EWHC 999 (Admin) (20 April 2011), the British Bankers' Association (BBA) sought to challenge the legality of the FSA policy statement which introduced these new rules—most notably in relation to the role that the FSA's Principles for Businesses (the "Principles") are to play in the complaints-handling procedure. In rejecting the three arguments presented by the BBA and upholding the new rules and guidance as lawful, the High Court made the following points:

- Section 150 of the Financial Services and Markets Act 2000 ("FSMA") does not prevent obligations under the Principles arising between a firm and its customers. "Actionable" as it is used in s.150 prevents individuals from bringing an action against a firm for breach of the Principles in a court of law—it does not prevent the firm from owing obligations to the customer or being required to pay compensation to a customer for breach of the Principles. As such, the Financial Ombudsman Service ("FOS") is entitled (and in fact has a duty) to take the

           Principles into account in deciding what is "fair and reasonable in all the circumstances" when reviewing a complaint.

- It was lawful for the FSA or FOS to rely on the Principles (specifically Principle 6 as it is applied in DISP, Appendix 3, 3.4.3G) in relation to PPI complaints where there has been no breach of the specific technical rules in the Handbook. The Principles are the "ever present substrata" in the regulatory framework to which the specific rules are then added. The FSA and FOS do not apply specific rules as an exhaustive statement of firms' obligations.

- Finally, the FSA is not prevented from utilising its other powers where the conditions for a "consumer redress scheme" are satisfied under s.404 of the FSMA. In other words, the FSA was entitled to introduce more detailed guidance on the steps a firm should take in conducting "root cause analysis" (including identifying Principle 6 as the source of the obligation to pay compensation to non-complainants), as opposed to tackling the issue of widespread PPI mis-selling through a consumer redress scheme under s.404 of the FSMA.

The FSA press release (20 April 2011) which followed the High Court's judgment makes it clear that the FSA now expects firms to deal swiftly with outstanding complaints on PPI mis-selling in accordance with Appendix 3 of DISP. The decision confirms that, where the rules are silent, the Principles provide considerable scope for a retrospective change in the FSA's expectations in this area.

7.8.6   *Distance communications (ICOBS 3)*

7.8.6.1   *Application*

ICOBS 3 deals with implementation of the relevant provisions of the Distance Marketing Directive and the E-Commerce Directive.

ICOBS 3.1 applies to a firm that carries on any distance marketing activity from an establishment in the UK, with or for a consumer in the UK or another EEA state.

ICOBS 3.2 applies to a firm carrying on an electronic commerce activity from an establishment in the UK with or for a person in the UK or another EEA state. An "electronic commerce activity" is defined as an "information society service" (in summary, any service normally provided for remuneration, at a distance, by means of electronic equipment for the processing (including digital compression) and storage of data at the individual request of a service recipient) which is or but for art.72A (Information society services) of the RAO (and irrespective of the effect of art.72 (Overseas Persons) of that Order) would be a regulated activity.

7.8.6.2 Provision of information for distance contracts (ICOBS 3.1)

The "distance marketing information" set out in ICOBS 3 Annex 2R must be provided in good time before the conclusion of a distance contract (*see* Section 7.8.5.1 in relation to the definition of distance contract) (ICOBS 3.1.3R).

All contractual terms and conditions and information referred to in the distance marketing disclosure rules must be communicated to the consumer in writing or another durable medium in good time before the conclusion of any distance contract (ICOBS 3.1.8R).

In the case of a telephone communication, only the "abbreviated distance marketing information" (set out in ICOBS 3 Annex 3R) needs to be provided during that communication, provided that the consumer has explicitly consented (ICOBS 3.1.14R). However, the full distance marketing information must still be provided in writing or another durable medium in good time before the conclusion of any distance contract unless another exemption (such as the exemption for "means of distance communication not enabling disclosure" explained in the paragraph below) applies (ICOBS 3.1.14R).

The "means of distance communication not enabling disclosure" exception allows a firm to provide the distance marketing information and the contractual terms and conditions in writing or another durable medium immediately after the conclusion of a distance contract, if the contract has been completed at a consumer's request using a means of distance communication that does not enable the provision of that information in that form in good time before the conclusion of any distance contract (ICOBS 3.1.15R).

The rules prohibit a firm from accepting a waiver by a consumer of any of the rights created or implied by the distance marketing rules in ICOBS 3.1 (ICOBS 3.1.18R).

7.8.6.3   Electronic communications (ICOBS 3.2)

ICOBS 3.2 applies to firms undertaking insurance selling and administration activities by electronic means (e-mail and websites) and places requirements on them that apply in addition to any other relevant ICOBS requirements. ICOBS 3.2 applies to a firm carrying out these activities from an establishment in the UK, with or for a person in the UK or another EEA state.

7.8.7   Cancellation (ICOBS 7)

ICOBS 7 details the cancellation rights of consumers on the inception and the renewal of non-investment insurance contracts and distance contracts. A limited number of exclusions apply (e.g. in the case of travel and baggage insurance policies or policies where the events being insured are of less than one month's duration) (ICOBS 7.1.3R).

A retail customer has a right to cancel, without penalty and without giving any reason, within:

(a) 30 days for a non-investment insurance contract which is, or has elements of, a pure protection contract or payment protection contract; or

(b) 14 days for any other contract of insurance or distance contract (ICOBS 7.1.1R).

Where a contract contains elements of both a general insurance contract and a pure protection insurance contract, a 30-day cancellation period applies.

The right of cancellation commences from the later of:

(a) the conclusion of the contract, and
(b) the receipt of the contractual terms and conditions and other pre-contractual information required by ICOBS.

In the case of pure protection contracts, the time limit in (a) begins when the customer is informed that the contract has been concluded (ICOBS 7.1.5R).

The effect of a consumer exercising his right to cancel is that he withdraws from the contract and the contract is terminated (ICOBS 7.2.1R). Where a consumer exercises the right to cancel, he may only be required to pay for the service actually provided by the firm in accordance with the contract (ICOBS 7.2.2(1)R). A firm must, without undue delay and no later than within 30 days of receipt of the notice of cancellation, return to the consumer any sums which it has received from him in accordance with the contract (ICOBS 7.2.6R). Consumers are under a similar obligation to return sums or property received from the firm (ICOBS 7.2.7R). Proportionate deductions may be made by the firm in respect of services provided which may include reasonably incurred costs and, in relation to the insurance cover, would usually be expected to be proportionate to the time on risk, though "a more accurate method" may be used if there is "a material unevenness of the incidence of risk" (ICOBS 7.2.3G and 7.2.4G).

A firm must not require a consumer to pay any amount following cancellation:

(a) unless it can prove that the consumer was duly informed of the amount payable;

(b) if it commenced the contract before the expiry of the cancellation period without the consumer's prior request;
(c) in the case of cancellation of a pure protection contract; or
(d) in the case of cancellation of a payment protection contract unless a claim is made during the cancellation period and settlement terms are subsequently agreed (ICOBS 7.2.2(3), (4) and (5)R).

7.8.8 Claims handling (ICOBS 8)

7.8.8.1 General rules

The purpose of ICOBS 8 is to ensure that claims are handled fairly and settled promptly and that customers are provided with information on the claims-handling process and, where relevant, an explanation of why a claim is rejected or not settled in full.

Insurers must:

(a) handle claims fairly and promptly;
(b) provide reasonable guidance to help a policyholder make a claim and appropriate information on its progress;
(c) not unreasonably reject a claim; and
(d) settle claims promptly once settlement terms are agreed (ICOBS 8.1.1R).

ICOBS 8.1.2R provides that, except where there is evidence of fraud, a rejection of a consumer policyholder's claim is unreasonable if it is for:

(a) non-disclosure of a fact material to the risk which the policyholder could not reasonably be expected to have disclosed;
(b) misrepresentation of a fact material to the risk, unless the misrepresentation is negligent; or
(c) a breach of warranty or condition, unless the circumstances of the claim are connected with the breach and unless (for a pure protection contract):

(i) under a "life of another" contract, the warranty relates to a statement of fact concerning the life to be assured and, if the statement had been made by a life to be assured under an "own life" contract, the insurer could have rejected the claim under ICOBS 8.1.2R; or

(ii) the warranty is material to the risk and was drawn to the customer's attention before the conclusion of the contract.

7.8.8.2 *Motor vehicle liability insurers*

ICOBS 8.2 implements rules from the Motor Insurance Directives requiring appointment by UK motor vehicle liability insurers (persons carrying on class 10 general insurance business) of claims representatives in each EEA state other than the UK in relation to claims following injury to a person outside the injured person's EEA state of residence caused by vehicles insured through an establishment in, and normally based in, an EEA state other than the injured person's state. The rules deal with claims in respect of injuries caused by UK-based vehicles. ICOBS 8.2 also sets out rules for the handling of these claims including time limits for the responses to claims and a requirement to pay interest if those limits are breached.

7.8.8.3 *Duties of insurance intermediaries*

ICOBS 8.2 sets out guidance for insurance intermediaries. It does not purport to summarise the full extent of the general law on the duties of an insurance intermediary.

The key guidance relates to conflicts of interest. Under ICOBS 8.3.3G, insurance intermediaries are reminded of Principle 8 and SYSC 10. SYSC 10 requires insurance intermediaries to take all reasonable steps to identify conflicts of interest and maintain and operate effective organisational and administrative arrangements to prevent conflicts from constituting or giving rise to a material risk of damage to its clients. Firms should also consider whether declining to act would be the most reasonable step where it is not possible to manage a conflict.

7.8.9 *Price comparison websites*

Following the release of proposed guidance in June 2011,the FSA has published finalised guidance on the selling of general insurance policies through price comparison websites in October 2011.[18] The guidance is relevant to price comparison websites, aggregator business models and firms developing online price comparison business models in order to sell regulated products. The main business model operated by firms involves the use of a proprietary price comparison tool to give customers an opportunity to enter their requirements and receive a series of quotes. The customer is then re-directed to an insurer or insurance intermediary to purchase the policy in question.

The guidance follows on from guidance released by the FSA in May 2008 and further thematic work conducted by the FSA in 2010 which uncovered a lack of understanding in the industry on the regulated activity being conducted by these firms, leading to a failure to abide by the relevant rules. The guidance is being introduced to address three areas of particular concern to the FSA: (i) failure to observe the general prohibition and restrictions on financial promotions in ss.19 and 21 of the FSMA; (ii) non-compliance with ICOBS requirements; and (iii) non-compliance with the Senior Management Arrangements, Systems and Controls sourcebook ("SYSC").

In relation to ICOBS, the FSA found in its thematic work that because the firms sampled took the view that they were "introducing" customers to an authorised firm they fell short of the requirements in a number of key areas, including:

---

[18] FSA Guidance—"Guidance on the: Selling of General Insurance Policies through Price Comparison Websites", June 2011.

(a) placing an unfair burden on consumers to ensure they purchase a policy under which they are eligible to claim or that they make their own disclosure of material facts to the insurer;

(b) not making it clear to consumers which firm is responsible for the comparison being provided or which firm is acting as introducer and which firm is arranging the sale of the policy, making it difficult for consumers to know who to complain to if they wish to do so;

(c) not making it clear whether the firm is providing advice or only information;

(d) failing to take responsibility for producing the demands and needs statement; and

(e) failing to take sufficient responsibility for checking that the eligibility and material risk data collected through their online questionnaire mapped accurately to the eligibility and risk criteria of the policies sold.

The proposed guidance asks firms to review their disclosure documentation, sales procedures and their terms and conditions to ensure that these are compliant with all relevant regulatory requirements including the Principles for Businesses ("PRIN"), ICOBS and the Unfair Terms in Consumer Contracts Regulations 1999. The guidance directs the relevant firms to pay particular attention to addressing issues (a)–(e) outlined above and to ensure that the firm does not seek in its terms and conditions to exclude liability for the regulated activities it is undertaking.

Chapter 8

Special Rules Relating to Certain Categories of Insurance Business and Special Features of the Reinsurance Directive

Ambereen Salamat,

Head of Financial Services Regulation: Holman Fenwick Willan LLP

8.1 Special rules relating to certain categories of insurance business: Introduction

Whether as a result of membership of the European Union ("EU"), or due to domestic reasons, certain categories of insurance business in the UK are subject to special rules. Also, some classes of insurance are compulsory in the UK. These include:

(a) Motor third-party liability.
(b) Employers' liability.
(c) Third-party liability in respect of:
    (i) nuclear installations;
    (ii) ship owners in respect of oil pollution;
    (iii) air carriers;
    (iv) riding establishments;
    (v) dangerous wild animals.
(d) Professional indemnity in respect of:
    (i) solicitors;

(ii) insurance brokers;

(iii) licensed conveyancers.

Of the compulsory classes, this Chapter reviews only motor and employers' liability insurance. It also deals with the special rules that apply to long-term care, legal expenses, export credit insurance, as well as to co-insurance and travel insurance.

8.2   Motor insurance

8.2.1   *Compulsory cover*

The insurance of motor vehicles against the risk of liability for injury to, or the death of, third parties caused by the driver's negligence has been compulsory since 1930. The scope of compulsory cover has expanded since that time as a result not only of case law, but also European law.

Prior to 27 October 2009, there were five separate Motor Insurance Directives[1] dealing with compulsory motor insurance. Following the European Commission's adoption of a proposal for a codified version of these Directives on 27 February 2008, a Sixth Motor Insurance Directive[2] has been approved and implemented with effect from 27 October 2009. The Sixth Motor Insurance Directive was intended to remove obsolete provisions and modernise the structure and terminology of the existing Motor Insurance Directives[3] in order to provide better clarity and easier interpretation of the rules relating to motor insurance. The existing Motor Insurance Directives have been repealed and their provisions codified, without any change to their substance, in the Sixth Motor

---

[1] Council Directives 72/166/EEC, 84/5/EEC, 90/232/EEC, 2000/26/EC and 2005/14/EC.

[2] Council Directive 2009/103/EC, the Sixth Motor Insurance Directive, codifying and repealing Council Directives 72/166/EEC, 84/5/EEC, 90/232/EEC, 2000/26/EC and 2005/14/EC.

[3] Council Directives 72/166/EEC, 84/5/EEC, 90/232/EEC, 2000/26/EC and 2005/14/EC.

Insurance Directive. As UK national law had already implemented the provisions of the existing Motor Insurance Directives, no further national legislation has been required to implement the provisions of the Sixth Motor Insurance Directive and, for ease, any references in this Chapter to the existing Motor Insurance Directives are to be construed as references to the appropriate Articles in the Sixth Motor Insurance Directive.[4]

8.2.2 First, Second and Third Motor Insurance Directives and their implementation

The First, Second and Third Motor Insurance Directives (as repealed and codified under the Sixth Motor Insurance Directive) all influenced motor insurance. The chief aim of Council Directive 72/166/EEC[5] was to ensure that all insurers in individual Member States provided the minimum compulsory indemnity against third-party liability required by the national law of the relevant State. However, under the Directive, it was not necessary for the same levels of compulsory third-party cover to be set by the individual Member States. By the Second Council Directive 84/5/EEC,[6] each Member State was obliged to put in place a similar form of compulsory third-party cover, giving protection not only against personal injury but also against material damage to third-party property. This Directive also set minimum indemnity limits and required every Member State to establish a body tasked with providing compensation for injuries caused by uninsured or unidentified drivers. Finally, the Third Council

---

[4] A correlation table at Annex II of Council Directive 2009/103/EC details how the repealed Articles in Council Directives 72/166/EEC, 84/5/EEC, 90/232/EEC, 2000/26/EC correspond to the Articles of Council Directive 2009/103/EC.

[5] Council Directive 72/166/EEC, as amended by Council Directive 72/430/EEC, was implemented in the UK by the Motor Vehicles (Compulsory Insurance) Regulations 1973 (SI 1973/1820), as subsequently replaced by the Motor Vehicles (Compulsory Insurance) (No.2) Regulations 1973 (SI 1973/2143). This Directive has now been repealed and its provisions codified under arts 1 to 8 and 31 of Council Directive 2009/103/EC.

[6] Second Council Directive 84/5/EEC was implemented in the UK by the Motor Vehicles (Compulsory Insurance) Regulations 1987 (SI 1987/2171). This Directive has now been repealed and its provisions codified under arts 3, 9, 10, 12, 13 and 31 of Council Directive 2009/103/EC.

Directive 90/232/EEC[7] required insurers to give third-party cover anywhere within the EU on the basis of a single premium.

The relevant provisions relating to compulsory insurance in the UK are set out in Part VI of the Road Traffic Act 1988 ss.143–161 ("the Act"). Section 143 is the key operative provision. It makes insurance compulsory against liability in respect of death or bodily injury to third parties, including passengers, and in respect of liability for damage to a third party's property. The section makes it an offence for any person to use, or to cause or permit any other person to use, a motor vehicle on a road unless there is in force, in relation to such use, a policy of insurance or such security in respect of third-party risks as complies with the requirements of the Act.

To comply with the Act, policies must be issued by an authorised insurer (i.e. a person who has permission under Part IV of the Financial Services and Markets Act 2000 ("the FSMA 2000") (or an EEA firm of the kind mentioned in para.5(d) of Sch.3 to the FSMA 2000, which has permission under para.15 of that Schedule) to effect or carry out relevant contracts of insurance and is a member of the Motor Insurers' Bureau[8]). The policy must insure the person specified in it:

(a)   against liability in respect of death or bodily injury to any person or damage to property caused by, or arising out of, the use of the vehicle on a road or other public place in Great Britain.[9] The term "person" includes any passenger

---

[7]   Third Council Directive 90/232/EEC was implemented in the UK by the Motor Vehicles (Compulsory Insurance) Regulations 1992 (SI 1992/3036) by way of amendments to s.145 of the Road Traffic Act 1988. This Directive has now been repealed and its provisions codified under arts 11–19, 23 and 31 of Council Directive 2009/103/EC.

[8]   Sections 95, 145(2) and (5) of the Road Traffic Act 1988.

[9]   Section 145(3)(a) of the Road Traffic Act 1988 as amended by reg.2(3) of the Motor Vehicles (Compulsory Insurance) Regulations 2000 (SI 2000/726).

but not the driver[10] and the policy must provide cover even where damage is caused by a deliberate act of the insured;[11] and

(b) in the case of a vehicle normally based in the territory of another Member State, against any civil liability occurring as a result of an event related to the use of the vehicle in Great Britain if:

    (i) the law of that Member State would require such insurance in respect of an event occurring in that country, and

    (ii) the cover required by that law would be higher than that required by (a) above;[12] and

(c) in the case of a vehicle normally based in Great Britain, against any liability in respect of the use of the vehicle in the territory (other than Great Britain) of each of the Member States according to:

    (i) the law on compulsory motor insurance of the State where the event occurred; or

    (ii) if it would give greater cover, the law which would apply if the place where the event occurred was Great Britain;[13] and

(d) against the statutory liabilities for payment for emergency treatment (s.145(3)(c) of the Act).

8.2.3 Fourth Motor Insurance Directive and its implementation

The Fourth Motor Insurance Directive (as repealed and codified under the Sixth Motor Insurance Directive)[14] was required to be implemented by Member States on or before 19

---

[10] *R. v Secretary of State for Transport Ex p. National Insurance Guarantee Corporation Plc* [1996] C.O.D. 425.

[11] *Bristol Alliance Lts Partnership v Williams* [2011] EWHC 1657 (QB).

[12] Section 145(3)(aa) of the Road Traffic Act 1988, inserted by reg.2(1) of the Motor Vehicles (Compulsory Insurance) Regulations 1992 (SI 1992/3036).

[13] Section 145(3)(b) of the Road Traffic Act 1988, as amended by reg.2(2) of the Motor Vehicles (Compulsory Insurance) Regulations 1992 (SI 1992/3036).

[14] Council Directive 2000/26/EC, Fourth Motor Insurance Directive amending 73/239/EEC and 88/357/EEC. This Directive has now been repealed and its provisions codified under arts 1 and 20–31 of Council Directive 2009/103/EC.

January 2003. This Directive provided for improved information, easier procedures and quicker settlement of claims. It has been implemented by various legislative measures in the UK.

New rights to issue proceedings directly against the insurer of the person responsible for an accident were provided.[15] Parties suffering loss or injury are entitled to claim in their Member State of residence against a claims representative appointed there by the insurer of the responsible party, with the result that the damage suffered by such injured parties is dealt in accordance with procedures familiar to them. Appointing such claims representatives is now a threshold condition for authorisation to carry on motor insurance business[16] and insurers are required to confer various powers and duties on their claims representatives.[17] In particular, claims representatives are required to collect all necessary information and to take appropriate action to settle such claims on behalf of the relevant insurer.

Injured parties should receive a reasoned offer of compensation or reasoned reply to the points raised in their claim form from the insurer or its claims representative within three months of presenting their claim. Where this is not complied with, interest will be payable on the amount of compensation offered or awarded.[18]

In compliance with the Directive, the Motor Insurers' Information Centre ("MIIC") has been established as the UK's Information Centre to help people seek compensation in respect of motor vehicle accidents occurring in a Member State other than their state of residence.[19] The MIIC provides access to information (such as the name and address of the insurer of

---

[15] The European Communities (Rights Against Insurers) Regulations 2002 (SI 2002/3061).

[16] The Financial Services and Markets Act 2000 (Variation of Threshold Conditions) Order 2002 (SI 2002/2707) amending para.2 of Sch.6 to the Financial Services and Markets Act 2000; FSA Rules and Guidance COND 2.2A.

[17] FSA Handbook ICOBS 8.2.3R.

[18] FSA Handbook ICOBS 8.2.6R–8.2.11G; the Financial Services and Markets Act 2000 (Fourth Motor Insurance Directive) Regulations 2002 (SI 2002/2706).

[19] The Motor Vehicles (Compulsory Insurance) (Insurance Centre and Compensation Body) Regulations 2003 (SI 2003/37).

motor vehicles normally based in the UK, the number of the insurance policy in respect of any identified vehicle) so as to allow its dissemination to injured parties in certain circumstances. In appropriate cases, the MIIC is obliged to seek similar information from organisations with like functions established in other Member States. Each motor insurer is required to retain relevant information about each motor policy that it has written for at least seven years after the expiry date of the policy. Further, the MIIC is empowered to require insurers to supply it with this information in respect of UK-based vehicles, together with details of their claims representatives.

Again, and pursuant to this Directive, the Motor Insurers' Bureau ("MIB") has been approved as the compensation body for the UK. If the injured party resident in the UK proves to the MIB that the insured person is liable to him, then to the extent that he can prove loss and damage, the MIB must compensate him. That said, certain conditions need to be satisfied:

(a) the injured party's right to claim must arise in respect of loss or injury resulting from an accident caused by the use of a motor vehicle in a public place;
(b) the accident must have occurred in a Member State (other than the UK), or in a country subscribing to the Green Card Scheme;[20] and
(c) the vehicle causing the accident must normally be based in, and insured in, a Member State other than the UK.

The claimant must have sought compensation from the liable insurer or its claims representative but must not have commenced legal proceedings. The insurer must have failed to make a reasoned reply within three months.

---

[20] By virtue of agreements between the various Motor Insurers' Bureau, the Green Card provides that compulsory motor insurance in one participating country will be effective in another. The victim of an accident is to be compensated by the Motor Insurers' Bureau in the country in which he is injured following which that Motor Insurers' Bureau is able to seek an indemnity from either the foreign insurer or the Bureau which provided the Green Card. The Green Card operates simply as an international insurance certificate valid for the dates mentioned in it and the countries referred to in it.

Further, in certain circumstances, a person who resides in the UK may be able to claim compensation from the MIB where either the vehicle which caused the damage, or the requisite insurer, cannot be identified.

8.2.4 *The Fifth Motor Insurance Directive and its implementation*

The Fifth Motor Insurance Directive (as repealed and codified under the Sixth Motor Insurance Directive),[21] aimed at improving the legal protection of accident victims, was required to be implemented by 11 June 2007 and was implemented in the UK by the Motor Vehicles (Compulsory Insurance) Regulations 2007 (the "2007 Regulations"). Its main provisions include:

(a) Requiring amounts of compulsory cover to be increased to:
  (i)   €1 million per victim in the case of personal injury (or €5 million per claim where Member States so opt);
  (ii) €1 million per claim (irrespective of the number of victims) in the case of damage to property,
  with future increases in line with inflation.
  The 2007 Regulations go beyond the requirements of the Directive, as s.145(4)(b) of the Act requires unlimited insurance cover in respect of personal injury, and the sum of £1 million per claim in the case of damage to property.
(b) Personal injuries and damage to property suffered by pedestrians, cyclists and other non-motorised users of the road are to be covered by the compulsory insurance of the vehicle involved in the accident where they are entitled to compensation according to national civil law.
  This requirement is provided for in s.145(3)(a) and (4)(b) of the Act.

---

[21] Council Directive 2005/14/EC, Fifth Motor Insurance Directive amending Council Directives 72/166/EEC, 84/5/EEC, 88/357/EEC and 90/232/EEC and Directive 2000/26/EC was implemented in the UK by the Motor Vehicles (Compulsory Insurance) Regulations 2007 (SI 2007/1426). This Directive has now been repealed and its provisions codified under Council Directive 2009/103/EC.

(c)   There should be an option to limit or exclude compensation in the event of damage to property on the basis that the vehicle is not identified. However, this should not apply where compensation has been paid for significant personal injuries to any victim of the same accident in which damage to property was caused. Member States may provide for an excess of no more than €500 for which the victim of the damage to property may be responsible. Whether the personal injuries are considered significant should be determined in accordance with the national legislation and administrative provisions of the Member States where the accident takes place. In establishing this, the Member States may take into account whether the injury required hospital care.

This requirement is provided for by the terms of the Untraced Drivers Agreement, the Uninsured Drivers Agreement and the relevant Supplementary Agreements to these.[22] (These are formal agreements between the Secretary of State for Transport and the MIB that provide for the MIB to pay defined compensation in specific circumstances for personal injury to victims in respect of road accidents where the liable party cannot be identified or is uninsured and there is, therefore, no insurance cover.)

(d)   The insurance cover should remain valid during the whole term of the contract, irrespective of whether the vehicle remains in another Member State for a particular period, without prejudice to the obligations under the Member State's national legislation with respect to the registration of vehicles. This is to combat the practice of some insurers cancelling the policy in the event that the vehicle remains outside the Member State of registration for longer than a specified period.

This requirement is provided for in s.145(3)(b) of the Act.

(e)   That it is made easier to obtain insurance cover for vehicles imported from one Member State into another, even though the vehicle is not yet registered in the

---

[22] The definition of significant personal injury and the limitations on compensation in the event of damage to property adopted in the UK are provided in the Supplementary Agreement between the Secretary of State for Transport and the MIB dated 15 April 2011 which amended the Untraced Drivers Agreement 2003.

Member State of destination, by introducing a temporary derogation from the general rule determining situation of risk. For a period of 30 days from the date when the vehicle is delivered, made available or despatched to the purchaser, the Member State of destination will be construed as the Member State where the risk is situated. This requirement was implemented by the Financial Services and Markets Act 2000 (Motor Insurance) Regulations 2007.[23]

(f)   That it is made easier for a policyholder to change insurer by giving the policyholder the right to request at any time a statement concerning the claims, or the absence of claims, involving the vehicle(s) covered by the policy at least during the preceding five years of the contractual relationship. The insurer should provide this statement within 15 days of the policyholder's request. The "no claims discount statement" in Great Britain conforms to this requirement.

8.3   Long-term care insurance

8.3.1   *What is long-term care insurance?*

Long-term care insurance ("LTCI") products are designed to help consumers provide for all or part of long-term care if they need to move to a residential home or need nursing care in their own home. LTCI products can take various forms but generally fall into two distinct types:

(a)   Pre-funded policies:
      (i)   pure protection insurance contracts ("LTCI pure protection contracts") which are insurance only products with no investment element; or

---

[23] Financial Services and Markets Act 2000 (Motor Insurance) Regulations 2007 (SI 2007/2403). The FSA has amended the glossary definition of "state of the risk" to allow a UK resident purchaser who imports a vehicle into the UK from another European Economic Area state to take out insurance as if it were a UK risk.

(ii) investment bonds that are specifically tied to an LTCI pure protection contract ("LTCI investment bonds"), which can be funded by either single or regular premiums.

(b) Immediate care plans: these are investment-based products which help to fund the costs of long-term care at the point when it is required ("LTCI immediate care plans"). They provide a regular income stream in exchange for a lump-sum payment.

8.3.2 Regulation of LTCI

LTCI investment bonds and LTCI immediate care plans are regulated as "designated investments" and are subject to the provisions of the Conduct of Business Sourcebook ("COBS") for investment business. They are regulated as part of the "packaged products"[24] regime in COBS.

LTCI pure protection contracts are regulated as "non-investment insurance contracts" and are subject to the provisions of the Insurance: Conduct of Business Sourcebook ("ICOBS"), except where a firm has elected to comply with COBS, in which case the firm must then treat the LTCI pure protection contract as an investment. A firm must make a record of its election to comply with COBS.[25]

8.3.3 Application of COBS rules

COBS came into force from 1 November 2007. It takes into account the FSA's objective of moving towards a "more principles-based approach" to regulation. This resulted in a shorter sourcebook which places greater emphasis on principles and higher-level rules. Under this regime, firms have more discretion to achieve outcomes that are appropriate for their particular business.

This section only deals with the provisions of COBS.

---

[24] "Packaged Products" include life policies, pensions, collective investment schemes and investment trust savings schemes.
[25] ICOBS 1 Annex 1 Part 2 (3.1R).

8.3.4   Raising the standards for all LTCI business

The FSA introduced additional requirements for advised sales of types of LTCI products as well as certain specific product types.

8.3.4.1   Advice and suitability

COBS sets out guidance on the obligations to assess suitability of investment products including LTCI products.

Where a firm is making a personal recommendation in relation to a designated investment, it should obtain all relevant information (such as information regarding the customer's knowledge, experience and financial situation) to determine a customer's demands and needs and take into account existing cover, the level of cover provided by the policy, cost, relevant exclusions and conditions. It should inform the customer of any demands and needs not met.[26]

8.3.4.2   Information and product disclosure

Requirements relating to the provision of information for all LTCI products need to be complied with so that the customer can make an informed decision about the arrangements proposed. The information will vary depending on a number of factors including the knowledge, experience and ability of a typical customer and the policy's overall complexity.

A Key Features document must be provided to the customer and must include enough information about the nature and complexity of the product, how it works, any limitations or minimum standards that apply and the material risks and benefits of buying or investing, so that the customer can make an informed decision about whether to proceed.[27] Communicating with clients (COBS 4), Preparing product information (COBS 13), Providing product information to clients (COBS 14)

---

[26]   COBS 9 Suitability.
[27]   COBS 13.3 Contents of a Key Features Document.

and Reporting information to clients (COBS 16) set out the rules on information disclosure.

8.3.4.3 *LTCI investment bonds*

The FSA has given careful consideration to the appropriateness of these products for funding the costs of long-term care and requires insurers to include additional risk warnings and disclose product information in their Key Features documents, drawing attention to:

(a) the risk that the income produced by the bond may be insufficient to continue to meet the premiums of the underlying pure protection contracts; and

(b) the potential consequences of this, including, where this is the case, the fact that capital may be partially or completely eroded or cover reduced.

In addition, insurers are required to:

(a) provide customers with an annual statement on the performance of the investment plan, including the current fund value and the latest projected value of the bond; and

(b) alert the customer to any potential shortfall and advise him to seek advice on his investment.

8.3.4.4 *Claims handling*

COBS 17 specifically addresses claims handling for LTCI products. It sets out rules on providing information to claimants dealing with claims, responding to and rejecting claims. In particular, COBS 17 provides:

(a) when a claim is made, the policyholder must promptly receive a claim form, information on claims handling and applicable medical criteria;

(b) as soon as reasonably practicable after making a claim, the policyholder must be informed how the claim will be settled or why it has been rejected; and

413

(c)   a claim must not be unreasonably rejected or rejected for non-disclosure of a material fact that the policyholder could not reasonably have been expected to disclose, non-negligent misrepresentation or breach of warranty (unless the circumstances of the claim are connected to the breach, the warranty was material to the risk and the policyholder was aware of this).

The purpose of these rules is to ensure that claims are handled fairly and processed and settled promptly.

8.4   Legal expenses insurance

The Insurance Companies (Legal Expenses Insurance) Regulations 1990[28] impose specific requirements on insurers carrying on legal expenses insurance business[29] in the UK. Prior to the adoption of these Regulations, insurers writing policies that contained provision for the payment of the insured's or a third-party's legal costs incurred in connection with a claim were regarded as writing an ancillary risk. Since the adoption of the Regulations, insurers are no longer entitled to treat such risks as ancillary to other classes.

The Regulations do not apply to:[30]

(a)   legal expenses insurance contracts concerning disputes or risks relating to the use of seagoing vessels;
(b)   anything done by a person providing civil liability cover for the purpose of representing the insured in an enquiry or proceedings which is at the same time done in the insurer's own interest under such cover; or

---

[28]   SI 1990/1159 implementing Council Directive 87/344/EEC of 22 June 1987 on the coordination of laws, regulations and administrative provisions relating to legal expenses insurance.
[29]   Falling within contracts of general insurance Class 17 in Part I of Sch.1 to the Financial Services and Markets Act 2000 (Regulated Activities) Order 2001 (i.e. "contracts of insurance against risks of loss to the persons insured attributable to their incurring legal expenses (including costs of litigation)").
[30]   Regulation 3 of the Insurance Companies (Legal Expenses Insurance) Regulations 1990 (SI 1990/1159).

(c) legal expenses cover provided by an assistance insurer where that cover is provided under a contract the principal object of which is the provision of assistance for persons who fall into difficulties while travelling, while away from home or their permanent residence and where the costs are incurred outside the state in which the insured normally resides. In this event, the contract must clearly state that the cover in question is limited to the circumstances referred to and is ancillary to that assistance.

The Regulations provide that legal expenses cover must be the subject of a separate policy, or dealt with in a separate section of a single policy in which the nature of the cover is specified.[31] Further, an insurer carrying on legal expenses business must adopt at least one of the following arrangements to avoid conflicts of interest:[32]

(a) Ensure that no member of staff engaged in the management of claims under legal expenses insurance contracts, or with legal advice in respect of such claims, carries on at the same time any similar activity:
   (i) in relation to another class of general insurance business carried on by that insurer; or
   (ii) in another insurer having financial, commercial or administrative links with the first insurer, which carries on one or more classes of general insurance business.
(b) Entrust the management of claims in respect of legal expenses insurance to an undertaking having separate legal personality. This undertaking will need to be mentioned in the separate policy or section of the policy, as the case may be.

---

[31] Regulation 4 of the Insurance Companies (Legal Expenses Insurance) Regulations 1990 (SI 1990/1159).
[32] Regulation 5 of the Insurance Companies (Legal Expenses Insurance) Regulations 1990 (SI 1990/1159).

(c) Afford the insured, in the policy, the right to entrust the defence of his interests, from the moment that he has the right to claim from the insurer under the policy, to a lawyer of his choice.

The legal expenses insurance policy must expressly recognise[33] that, where under the policy recourse is had to a lawyer to represent the interests of the insured in any enquiry or proceedings, the insured shall be free to choose that lawyer. Further, the policy must also expressly recognise that the insured shall be free to choose a lawyer to serve his interests whenever a conflict of interest arises.[34] Any provisions of a policy that depart, or in any way qualify the freedom to choose a lawyer, will breach the Regulations.[35]

The Regulations require that any dispute between the insurer and the insured may be referred to arbitration and the policy must expressly mention the right of the insured to have recourse to such a procedure.[36]

8.5   Employers' liability insurance

The two main pieces of legislation governing employers' liability insurance are the:

(a) Employers' Liability (Compulsory Insurance) Act 1969 (the "1969 Act"); and
(b) Employers' Liability (Compulsory Insurance) Regulations 1998 (the "1998 Regulations").[37]

---

[33] Regulation 6 of the Insurance Companies (Legal Expenses Insurance) Regulations 1990 (SI 1990/1159).

[34] Exemptions set out in reg.7 of the Insurance Companies (Legal Expenses Insurance) Regulations 1990 (SI 1990/1159).

[35] See decision of European Court of Justice in *Eschig v UNIQA Sachversichcherung AG* (C-199/08) in (10 September 2009). The FSA issued a guidance letter on 12 August 2010, which highlighted the decision and reminded firms of the requirement to comply with the Council Directive 87/344/EEC and the Insurance Companies (Legal Expenses Insurance) Regulations 1990.

[36] Regulation 8 of the Insurance Companies (Legal Expenses Insurance) Regulations 1990 (SI 1990/1159).

[37] Employers' Liability (Compulsory Insurance) Regulations 1998 (SI 1998/2573), as

8.5.1 Compulsory insurance

Section 1(1) of the 1969 Act is the key operative provision. It makes it compulsory for every employer carrying on any business in the UK to insure, and maintain insurance, against liability for bodily injury or disease sustained by their employees, and arising out of and in the course of their employment in Great Britain in that business. Therefore, all employers with places of business in Great Britain, except for local authorities, nationalised industries and those expressly exempted by the 1998 Regulations, must take out the required insurance. Section 5 makes an employer not so insured in accordance with the 1969 Act when required guilty of an offence and liable on summary conviction to a fine. Further, where an offence committed by a corporation has been committed with the consent or connivance of, or facilitated by any neglect on the part of, any director or other officer, that person as well as the corporation shall be deemed to be guilty of that offence and shall be liable to be proceeded against and punished accordingly.

The 1969 Act requires insurance only in respect of employees which are defined in s.2(1) as:

> "an individual who has entered into or works under a contract of service or apprenticeship with an employer whether by way of manual labour, clerical work or otherwise, whether such contract is expressed or implied, oral or in writing."

To comply with the 1969 Act, policies must be approved and must be issued by an authorised insurer. An authorised insurer is defined by the 1969 Act as a person who has permission under Part IV of the FSMA 2000 (or an EEA firm of the kind mentioned in para.5(d) of Sch.3 to the FSMA 2000, which has permission under para.15 of that Schedule) to effect or carry out relevant contracts of insurance.

---

amended several times but most recently by the Employers' Liability (Compulsory Insurance) (Amendment) Regulations 2011 (SI 2011/686).

The 1998 Regulations provide that cover under one or more policies of insurance shall be, or shall in aggregate be, not less than £5 million in respect of claims relating to any one or more employees arising out of any one occurrence. It should be noted that where an employer is a company with one or more subsidiaries, the requirement as to the minimum amount of cover is taken to apply to that company, together with any subsidiaries, as if they were a single employer.

An approved policy means a policy of insurance not subject to any conditions or exceptions prohibited under the 1998 Regulations. In particular, the policy must not contain any conditions which provide that no liability shall arise under the policy, or any such liability so arising shall cease, if:

(a)   some specified thing is done or omitted to be done after the happening of the event giving rise to a claim under the policy;
(b)   the policyholder does not take reasonable care to protect his employees against the risk of bodily injury or disease in the course of their employment;
(c)   the policyholder fails to comply with the requirements of any enactment for the protection of employees against the risk of bodily injury or disease in the course of their employment; or
(d)   the policyholder does not keep specified records or fails to provide the insurer with or make available information from such records.

Further, there is prohibited any condition which requires:

(a)   a relevant employee to pay; or
(b)   an insured employer to pay the relevant employee, the first amount of any claim or any aggregation of claims.

8.5.2   Certificates of insurance

The 1998 Regulations provide that every employer entering into a contract of insurance in accordance with the requirements of the 1969 Act shall be issued by the insurer with whom he contracts (no later than 30 days from the date on which the insurance commences or is renewed) a certificate of insurance in the form and containing the particulars specified in Sch.1 to the 1998 Regulations.

Copies of the certificate must be displayed for the information of the employees at each place of business at which the employer employs relevant employees. This requirement can be satisfied through making an electronic form of the certificate available in a place where each employee has reasonable access to it. Further obligations are set out in the 1998 Regulations in relation to production of certificates by the employer and inspection of policies of insurance by the inspector authorised by the 1969 Act.

8.5.3 Recent developments

As a result of concerns that some employees suffering from industrial diseases could not trace their employers' liability policy, an online tracing service was established in 1999 by the insurance industry. Although this improved access to compensation, the success rate of finding relevant insurers was relatively low, which led to proposals from the Department for Work and Pensions ("DWP") for the creation of a new Employers' Liability Tracing Office ("ELTO"), in its consultation paper of 10 February 2010.[38] The ELTO has now replaced the previous tracing service established in 1999. The ELTO provides a central database of all new and renewed employers' liability policies from April 2011, any policies prior to April 2011 which have had new claims against them and any policies identified through the previous tracing service.

The FSA also introduced new rules in the Insurance: Conduct of Business Sourcebook ("ICOBS") requiring all employers' liability insurers to publish relevant policy information to assist past and present UK employees in tracing details of their

---

[38] *Accessing Compensation – Supporting people who need to trace Employers' Liability Insurance – public consultation,* Department for Work and Pensions, 10 February 2010,

employers' liability insurance. From 6 March 2011, firms are obliged to produce an employers' liability register ("ELR") and supporting documents.

ICOBS 8.4.4 R requires all general insurers and Lloyd's managing agents whose insurance business includes UK employers' liability insurance to:

- produce an ELR complying with the relevant requirements in ICOBS 8.4.4R (2) and ICOBS 8 Annex 1;
- obtain a written statement, from a director of the firm responsible for the production of the ELR, that to the best of the director's knowledge the register has been properly prepared in accordance with the requirements of ICOBS 8.4; and
- obtain an independent assurance report addressing the accuracy and completeness of the ELR, prepared by an auditor satisfying FSA requirements and addressed to the directors of the firm.

The content of the ELR is elaborated in ICOBS 8.4.4R (2) and includes the establishment of a database which allows for requests for information and searches from individuals with potential claims, as well as potentially liable employers and insurers. ICOBS 8 Annex 1 provides a template form for the information to be included in the ELR and states that all information detailed in the form must be included for each policy entered into or renewed on or after 1 April 2011. Further, all information in the form, which the firm holds, must be included for each policy in relation to which a claim is made on or after 1 April 2011. Such information must be made available no later than three months from the date of entry, renewal or making of the claim.

Firms must notify the FSA within one month of ICOBS 8.4 becoming applicable to them, stating whether they are carrying on UK employers' liability insurance, and if so, details of where their ELR is made available, contact details of a person at the firm, the period over which it provided cover, or, if still continuing, the date that cover commenced as well as their FSA Firm Reference number.[39]

The information on the ELR can be made available by firms either through their own website or by arranging for a qualifying tracing office to make it available on its website.[40] There are certain conditions, set out at ICOBS 8.4.9R, which must be satisfied by a tracing office to qualify and its directors have to publish a statement confirming this is the case. Although the FSA cannot compel firms to use the ELTO, its website provides details of specialist tracing offices which have satisfied the aforementioned conditions, but which, as at 30 June 2011, consisted only of the ELTO.

The ELR must be updated with any new or more accurate information arising out of the entry into or renewal of, or a claim made in relation to, a policy, three months from the date of entry, renewal or the date on which the claim was made; and in all other cases, three months from the date upon which the firm received the new or more accurate information.[41] Firms must otherwise update the ELR no less frequently than once every three months.

Although the new provisions of ICOBS came into force on 6 March 2011, there are various transitional provisions allowing for the smooth transitioning of the requirements. Firms were required to initially notify the FSA of any actual or potential liability for UK employers' liability claims by 6 April 2011 and where applicable, ELRs established by 1 April 2011.

---

[39] ICOBS 8.4.6R.
[40] ICOBS 8.4.7R.
[41] ICOBS 8.4.11R (2).

8.6   Export credit insurance

8.6.1   What is an export credit?

An "export credit" is an agreement which allows a buyer of exported goods and/or services to defer payment over a period of time. That said, there appears to be no comprehensive definition of "export credit" under either European or English law.

8.6.2   What is export credit insurance?

Witherby's Dictionary of Insurance defines export credit insurance as "insurance for exporters against the risk of non-payment for political and/or commercial reasons". Export credit insurance is conventionally divided into:

(a)   short term, providing insurance for up to two years; and
(b)   medium and long term, providing insurance for two years or more.

Whereas short-term export credit insurance can generally be obtained from the private insurance market,[42] medium- and long-term export credit insurance is generally provided by various forms of government support.

Such government involvement highlights the crucial role that medium- and long-term export credit insurance plays in international trade and therefore constitutes an important commercial policy instrument. It is because government involvement raises potential concerns regarding distortions of free and fair competition, that medium- and long-term export credit insurance has been the focus of the Organisation for Economic Co-operation and Development ("OECD").

---

[42]   Admittedly, some privately owned and controlled export credit insurers that only provide short-term insurance may be supported by their governments through guarantees or equivalent reinsurance arrangements for some segments of their business.

When drafting its export credit insurance legislation, the EU has been influenced by both the OECD and concerns of government involvement. The UK has either implemented European law, or deemed presently enacted legislation as sufficient. A brief review of short-, medium- and long-term export credit insurance legislation is set out below.

8.6.3 Influence of the OECD's arrangement on EU export credit insurance

The basis of much of European law on export credit insurance has been drawn from the OECD, specifically the OECD's Export Credit Division. The OECD's Export Credit Division facilitates work relating to the policies and practices of OECD member governments who provide officially supported export credits.

Through Council Decision 2001/76/EC, the OECD Arrangement on Officially Supported Export Credits[43] (the "Arrangement") has been implemented into European law.

The main purpose of the Arrangement is to provide a framework for the orderly use of officially supported credits.[44] The Arrangement seeks to encourage competition among exporters from the OECD-exporting countries based on quality and price of goods and services exported rather than on the most favourable officially supported terms. It applies to officially supported credits with repayment terms of two years or more, relating to exports of goods and/or services or to financial leases.

Official support is not prohibited, but certain limitations on the terms and conditions of export credits that benefit from it are laid down. These include minimum premium benchmarks, the minimum cash payments to be made at or before the starting

---

[43] The Arrangement came into being in April 1978 and is a "gentlemen's agreement" amongst its participants.

[44] Official support can take the form of direct credits/financing, re-financing, interest rate support, aid financing (credits and grants), export credit insurance and guarantees.

point of credit, maximum repayment terms and minimum interest rates which benefit from official financial support.

The Arrangement has been reviewed and amended several times. On 3 March 2011, the OECD published the latest version of the Arrangement.[45] That said, the EU has not formally adopted by Council Decision any of the versions of the Arrangement subsequent to the original version in 1978.

8.6.4   EU export credit insurance legislation: the First Council Directive

It is through the First Council Directive 73/239/EEC[46] that the EU has power to legislate in the area of export credit insurance. The Annex which forms part of the Directive, classifies risk according to classes of insurance. Export credit is included in insurance business classified under general business class 14 by the Directive as follows:

"14. Credit

- insolvency (general)
- export credit
- instalment credit
- mortgages
- agricultural credit."

8.6.5   Implementation of the First Council Directive

The UK has implemented the First Council Directive and defined the same class of general business as:

"Contracts of insurance against risks of loss to the persons insured arising from the insolvency of debtors of theirs or

---

[45] Arrangement on Officially Supported Export Credits (March 2011) TAD/PG(2011)4.

[46] First Council Directive 73/239/EEC of 24 July 1973 on the coordination of laws, regulations and administrative provisions relating to the taking-up and pursuit of the business of direct insurance other than life assurance.

from the failure (otherwise than through insolvency) of debtors of theirs to pay their debts when due."[47]

There is clearly a divergence between the wording of the First Council Directive and that of the legislation in the UK. It can be argued that the manner in which class 14 has been defined in the UK is capable of a different, and narrower, meaning than in the First Council Directive. It should be noted that where the wording of a Directive is sufficiently precise and unambiguous, it will have direct effect and be relied upon before the national courts.[48]

8.6.6 Short-term export credit insurance

Six European Commission Communications to Member States deal directly with short-term export credit insurance. They are:

(a)   Communication 97/C281/03;[49]
(b)   Communication 2001/C217/02;[50]
(c)   Communication 2005/C325/11;[51]
(d)   Communication 2009/C16/01;[52]
(e)   Communication 2010/C329/06;[53] and
(f)   Communication 2011/C6/05.[54]

---

[47]   Part I of Schedule 1 of the Financial Services and Markets Act 2000 (Regulated Activities) Order 2001 (SI 2001/544), contracts of general insurance class 14.
[48]   *Association Basco-Béarnaise des Opticiens Indépendants* v *Préfet des Pyrénées-Atlantiques* Case C-109/99.
[49]   Communication of the Commission to Member States pursuant to art.93(1) of the EC Treaty applying arts 92 and 93 of the Treaty to short-term export credit insurance, 17 September 1997.
[50]   Communication of the Commission to Member States amending the Communication pursuant to art.93(1) of the EC Treaty applying arts 92 and 93 of the Treaty to short-term export credit insurance, 2 August 2001.
[51]   Communication of the Commission to Member States amending the communication pursuant to art.93(1) of the EC Treaty applying arts 92 and 93 of the Treaty to short-term export credit insurance, 22 December 2005.
[52]   Communication of the Commission to Member States on Temporary Community framework for State aid measures to support access to finance in the current financial and economic crisis, 1 January 2009.
[53]   Communication of the Commission to Member States amending the communication pursuant to art.93(1) of the EC Treaty applying arts 92 and 93 of the Treaty to short-term export credit insurance, 7 December 2010.
[54]   Communication from the Commission to Member States on Temporary

The aim of the Communications is to remove distortions of competition which arise from the financial advantages of state aid given to public or publicly supported export credit insurers[55] who export within and beyond the EU.

Communication 97/C281/03 took effect from 1 January 1998 for an initial period of five years. However, this period has been extended until 31 December 2012 by the European Commission.[56]

Member States were requested to amend, where necessary, their export credit insurance systems for marketable risks[57] so that the granting of different forms of state aid (including state guarantees for borrowing or losses, relief or exemption from taxes) to public or publicly supported export credit insurers in respect of those risks ended within one year of publication of the Communication. Further, public or publicly supported export credit insurers were to be required, as a minimum, to keep a separate administration and account to show that they did not enjoy state aid in their insurance of marketable risks.

The Commission stated in Communication 2005/C325/11 that it had considered the capacity of the market to adapt to a further extension of the definition of marketable risk to cover a wide range of commercial risks, but decided to leave the definition unchanged. However, where the cover offered by

---

Community framework for State aid measures to support access to finance in the current financial and economic crisis, 11 January 2011.

[55] Defined as those export credit agencies which are supported by the government through guarantees or equivalent reinsurance arrangements for certain parts of their business.

[56] Amendments to the 1997 Communication, 2010/C329/06.

[57] "Marketable" risks are defined for the purposes of the Communication as commercial and political risks on public and non-public debtors established in the countries listed in the Annex. For such risks, the maximum risk period (that is, manufacturing plus credit period with normal Berne Union starting point and usual credit term) is less than two years. All other risks (that is, catastrophe risks (i.e. war, revolution, natural disasters, nuclear accidents etc.), not so-called "commercial, catastrophe risks" (catastrophic accumulations of loss on individual buyers or countries) which may be covered by excess of loss reinsurance and are commercial risks and commercial and political risks on countries not listed in the Annex) are considered to be not yet marketable. The definition is as stated in Communication 97/C281/4 and amended by Communication 2001/ C217/2.

private insurers to small companies with a limited export turnover is unavailable or insufficient, the Commission will consider its export-related risks as temporarily non-marketable in Member States where there is no adequate offer by the private market.

As a consequence of the recent financial crisis, the Commission stated in Communication 2009/C16/01 that although a lack of insurance and reinsurance capacity did not exist in every Member State, it could be anticipated that cover for marketable risks could be temporarily unavailable in certain countries. It therefore provided for a simplified and faster procedure for Member States to demonstrate lack of a market by providing sufficient evidence of the unavailability of cover for the risk in the private insurance market. This temporary measure was due to expire on 31 December 2010, but has been extended until 31 December 2011 by Communication 2011/C6/05.

8.6.7   Medium- and long-term export credit insurance

8.6.7.1   Council Directive 98/29/EC

Council Directive 98/29/EC[58] is the main Directive dealing with medium- and long-term export credit insurance. The aim of the Directive is to ensure that export policy is based on uniform principles and that competition between enterprises in the EU is not distorted. The Directive applies to insurance for transactions related to the export of goods and/or services originating in a Member State insofar as this support is provided directly or indirectly for the account of, or with the support of, one or more Member States involving a total risk period of two years or more.

---

[58] Council Directive 98/29/EC on harmonisation of the main provisions concerning export credit insurance for transactions with medium- and long-term cover. Council Directive 98/29/EC was not required to be implemented by the UK as the Export and Investment Guarantees Act 1991 was considered to make provision for the requirements of the Directive.

8.6.7.2   Common principles for export credit insurance: UK focus

The common principles for export credit insurance are set out in the Annex to Council Directive 98/29/EC. Pursuant to the Annex, the covered risks relate to risks of loss arising from manufacturing or credit risk. The covered causes of loss are as follows:[59]

(a)   insolvency of the private debtor[60] and, if any, its guarantor, either *de jure* or *de facto*;
(b)   default of the debtor and, if any, its guarantor;
(c)   decision of the buyer under a supplier credit[61] to interrupt or cancel the commercial contract, or to refuse to accept the goods and/or services without being entitled to do so;
(d)   any measure or decision of the government of a country other than the country of the insurer, or that of the policyholder, which prevents performance of the loan agreement or the commercial contract respectively;
(e)   general moratorium decreed either by the government of the country of the debtor, or by that of a third country through which payment in respect of the loan agreement or the commercial contract is to be effected;
(f)   political events, economic difficulties, or legislative or administrative measures which occur or are taken outside the country of the insurer, and which prevent or delay the transfer of funds paid in respect of the loan agreement or the commercial contract;
(g)   legal provisions adopted in the country of the debtor declaring payments made by the debtor in local currency to be valid discharge of the debt, notwithstanding that, as a result of fluctuations in exchange rates, such payments, when converted into the currency of the commercial

---

[59] The causes of loss set out are reflected in the Export Credit Guarantee Department's Export Insurance Policy.
[60] A private debtor is any debtor that is not a public debtor. A public debtor is any entity which, in whatever form, represents a public authority and which cannot, either judicially or administratively, be declared insolvent.
[61] The term "supplier credit" is said to apply to a commercial contract providing for an export of goods and/or services originating in a Member State between one or more suppliers and one or more buyers, whereby the buyer undertakes to pay the supplier on cash terms or on credit terms.

contract or the loan agreement, no longer cover the
amount of the debt at the date of transfer of funds;

(h) any measure or decision of the government of the country
of the insurer or of the policyholder, including measures
and decisions of the EU, relating to trade between a
Member State and third countries, such as a ban on
exports, insofar as its effects are not covered otherwise by
the government concerned; and

(i) cases of *force majeure* occurring outside the country of the
insurer, which could include war, including civil war,
revolution, riot, civil disturbance, cyclone, flood, earth-
quake, volcanic eruption, tidal wave and nuclear accident,
insofar as its effects are not insured otherwise.

Member States must ensure that those institutions providing
cover for such transactions directly or indirectly in the form of
export credit insurance for the account of the Member State or
with the support of the Member State, must do so in
accordance with the provisions of the Directive if destined for
countries outside the EU and financed by buyer credit,[62]
supplier credit[63] or paid on cash terms.

8.6.7.3 *Equalisation reserves*

Part 1.1 of the Prudential Sourcebook for Insurers ("INSPRU")
applies to general insurance business.[64] Every firm[65] carrying
on credit insurance business in the UK, unless it is a
non-directive insurer[66] or a pure reinsurer,[67] is required to

---

[62] The term "buyer credit" is said to apply to a loan agreement between one or more
financial institutions and one or more borrowers financing a commercial contract
providing for an export of goods and/or services originating in a Member State,
whereby the lending institution(s) undertake to pay the supplier(s) under the
underlying transaction on cash terms on behalf of the buyer(s)/borrower(s),
while the buyer(s)/borrower(s) will reimburse the lending institution(s) on credit
terms.

[63] *See* fn. 61.

[64] It now sets out the requirements of Council Directive 87/343/EEC.

[65] An authorised person is not a professional firm unless it is an authorised
professional firm.

[66] *See* the definition in the FSA Handbook Glossary.

[67] A pure reinsurer is defined by the FSA Handbook Glossary as an insurer whose
insurance business is restricted to reinsurance.

maintain an equalisation reserve for the purpose of providing against above average fluctuations in claims in respect of general business of that description.

In the case of a UK insurer, the requirement to maintain an equalisation reserve does not apply where the net premiums written in any financial year in respect of its credit insurance business are less than four per cent of the net premiums written by it in that financial year and less than €2.5 million.[68] In the case of a non-EEA insurer, the same thresholds relate to business being carried on through a branch in the UK.

8.6.7.4 IFRS 4 and its impact on the recording of equalisation reserves

Against the backdrop of accounting practices for insurance contracts being diverse and often differing from practices in other sectors, the International Accounting Standards Board[69] ("IASB") released International Financial Reporting Standard 4, *Insurance Contracts*[70] ("IFRS 4"), for financial statements beginning on or after 1 January 2005. IFRS 4 impacts upon the financial recording of equalisation provisions.

The IASB's position, outlined in IFRS 4, prohibits provisions for possible claims under contracts that are not in existence at the reporting date, such as equalisation provisions. The IASB's view is that:

(a) an insurer shall not recognise as a liability, any equalisation provisions relating to possible future claims under future insurance contracts; and

(b) claim reserves are only permissible to the extent that they relate to actual liabilities.

---

[68] INSPRU 1.4.44R.

[69] The IASB is an independent, privately funded accounting standard-setter based in London. The IASB is committed to developing, in the public interest, a single set of high-quality, understandable and enforceable global accounting standards that require transparent and comparable information in general-purpose financial statements.

[70] IASB Discussion Paper, "Preliminary Views on Insurance Contracts".

The IASB's insurance project has now moved into the second stage of development ("Phase II"), but it appears that its position on equalisation reserves remains unchanged. In May 2007, the IASB launched a public consultation on the main components of an accounting model for insurance contracts[71], which was followed by the publication of an exposure draft in July 2009,[72] neither of which covered the subject of equalisation reserves. The IASB, jointly with the Financial Accounting Standards Board, is continuing to review responses to the proposals in the exposure draft, with a further version expected before 2012.

8.7 Co-insurance

The Co-insurance Directive[73] ("the Directive") prohibits restrictive legislation on co-insurance and allows authorised insurers throughout the EU to cover international co-insurance risks. Undertakings which:

(a) have their head office in a Member State; and
(b) are subject to the First Non-Life Directive[74] and satisfy its requirements,

are entitled to participate in co-insurance under the conditions laid down by the Directive and may not be made subject to any other provisions, at least as far as the conduct of co-insurance operations is concerned.

To be covered by the Directive, a co-insurance operation must satisfy the following conditions:

(a) the risk must be covered by a single contract at an overall premium and for the same period by two or more

---

[71] Part of the IASB's Insurance project, Phase I, issued March 2004.
[72] IASB Exposure Draft: Insurance Contracts (ED/2010/8) (July 2010)
[73] Council Directive 78/473/EEC of 30 May 1978 on the coordination of laws, regulations and administrative provisions relating to Community co-insurance.
[74] First Council Directive 73/239/EEC of 24 July 1973 on the coordination of laws, regulations and administrative provisions relating to the taking up and pursuit of the business of direct insurance other than life assurance.

> insurance undertakings (co-insurers), each for its own part, one of which is the leading insurer;
> (b) the risk must be situated in the EEA;
> (c) for the purpose of covering the risk, the leading insurer must be authorised to carry on insurance business in accordance with the First Non-Life Directive;
> (d) at least one of the co-insurers must participate in the contract by means of a head office, agency or branch established in a Member State other than that of the leading insurer;
> (e) the leading insurer must fully assume the leader's role in co-insurance practice and, in particular, must determine the terms and conditions of insurance and rating.[75]

The risk covered must fall within one of the following classes (subject also to the conditions that, by reason of its nature or size, the risk calls for the participation of several insurers for coverage): 4, 5, 6, 7, 8, 9, 11, 12, 13 and 16.[76] The requirements of the Directive are contained in the Regulated Activities Order 2001.[77]

An EEA firm authorised in its home state is excluded from the requirement to be authorised by the FSA where it is conducting insurance business in the UK other than through a branch but pursuant to a Community co-insurance operation in which it is participating (otherwise than as a leading insurer).[78]

The Directive has been recast into the Solvency II Directive. There have been no substantive changes to the Directive except those necessary to improve drafting and readability, or to delete articles which are obsolete.

---

[75] Note that the provisions in the Solvency II Directive which deal with coinsurance, include an additional condition that "the risk is a large risk", which was not previously contained in Council Directive 78/473/EEC.

[76] Article 1(1) of the Directive 78/473/EEC states it does not apply to co-insurance operations covering risks classified under Class 13 which concern damage arising from nuclear sources or from medicinal products.

[77] The Financial Services and Markets Act 2000 (Regulated Activities) Order 2001 (SI 2001/544), art.11 Community Co-insurers.

[78] "Community co-insurance operation" and "leading insurer" have the same meaning as in the Directive 78/473/EEC.

8.8 Travel insurance

Connected travel insurance ("CTI") is travel insurance sold alongside a holiday or other related travel. Travel providers, such as travel agents, tour operators, coach tour operators, airlines, ferry companies, train companies and accommodation providers, often make available travel insurance connected to travel arrangements as a service for their customers. The sale of stand-alone travel insurance became regulated in the UK under the Insurance Mediation Directive ("IMD") in January 2005. However, CTI was exempt under the IMD and the Treasury replicated the IMD exclusion for the sale of CTI in the Regulated Activities Order 2001.[79]

The Regulated Activities (Amendment) (No.2) Order 2007[80] amended the Regulated Activities Order 2001[81] and came into force on 1 January 2009. It limited the scope of the CTI exemption to circumstances where the sale of a contract of insurance is linked to travel organised by the travel provider where the person seeking insurance is not an individual or a business with a group annual turnover of less than £1 million, or the hire of a vehicle. The Treasury decided to continue to make the exemption available to event management firms in respect of commercial customers and car hire firms as no evidence of consumer detriment as a result of such sales was found.

In addition, on 1 January 2009, the FSA introduced new exemptions and exclusions for firms selling regulated CTI products reflecting its aim for a lighter regime than the IMD requires in relation to the sale of stand-alone travel insurance. These include:

(a) an exclusion for CTI intermediaries from the need to establish that a reasonable number of persons in their

---

[79] The Financial Services and Markets Act 2000 (Regulated Activities) Order 2001 (SI 2001/544).

[80] The Financial Services and Markets Act 2000 (Regulated Activities) (Amendment) (No.2) Order 2007 (SI 2007/3510).

[81] The Financial Services and Markets Act 2000 (Regulated Activities) Order 2001 (SI 2001/544) art.72B.

management structure and all persons directly involved in insurance mediation activities demonstrate the knowledge and ability necessary to perform their duties, and all persons in their management structure and any staff directly involved in insurance mediation activities are of good repute;[82]

(b) a status disclosure exemption for CTI products, whereby firms only need to provide the procedures allowing customers and other interested parties to register complaints about the firm with the firm and the Financial Ombudsman Service (where applicable);[83]

(c) an exclusion for CTI intermediaries from the disclosure requirements at ICOBS 4.1.6R, which must be complied with prior to conclusion of an initial contract of insurance and on its amendment or renewal; and

(d) an exclusion for CTI intermediaries from the statement of demands and needs provisions at ICOBS 5.2.[84]

8.9 Special features of the Reinsurance Directive: Introduction

The Reinsurance Directive was implemented into the FSA's Handbook and UK legislation in stages. The first stage, dealing with solvency, insurance special purpose vehicles ("ISPVs") and other minor matters, was implemented by the FSA's amendments to its Handbook on 25 October 2006.[85] The second stage, relating to passporting and portfolio transfer provisions, was implemented by the Treasury on the deadline date, 10 December 2007, by way of three statutory instruments.[86]

---

[82] MIPRU 2.3.1R.

[83] ICOBS 4.1.5R .

[84] ICOBS 5.2.1R(1).

[85] FSA 2006/42—The Prudential Sourcebook for Insurers Instrument 2006, summarised in Handbook Notice 59.

[86] The Reinsurance Directive Regulations (SI 2007/3253), the Financial Services and Markets Act 2000 (Reinsurance Directive) Order 2007 (SI 2007/3254) and the Financial Services and Markets Act 2000 (Reinsurance Directive) Regulations 2007 (SI 2007/3255). An explanatory note covering all three SIs is also available.

The Reinsurance Directive established a supervisory regime for all reinsurers with their headquarters in the EU and allows EU reinsurers to carry on business throughout the EU by way of freedom of establishment (*see* Chapter 5 for more information). It also allows EU reinsurers to transfer portfolios of inwards reinsurance business (*see* Chapter 6 for more information).

However, the Reinsurance Directive introduced a number of special features which have no parallel in the Life and Non-Life Directives. These are:

(a) ISPVs;
(b) risk transfer; and
(c) reciprocal recognition with other regulatory regimes.

This Chapter focuses on the first of these special features, which (in the manner implemented by the FSA) created a new type of reinsurance vehicle in the UK. It also touches briefly on the treatment of risk transfer by the FSA.

For the time being, at least, the question of reciprocal recognition is one for EIOPA rather than individual Member States.

8.10   Insurance Special Purpose Vehicles

8.10.1   What is an ISPV?

The provisions in the Reinsurance Directive permitting the establishment of ISPVs were introduced at a relatively late stage in its development, after lobbying from Ireland, in order to facilitate insurance securitisations within the EU.

The FSA adopted the Reinsurance Directive's definition of an ISPV with only small changes, defining an ISPV as:

"an undertaking, other than an insurance undertaking or reinsurance undertaking which has received an official authorisation in accordance with Article 6 of the First Non-Life Directive, Article 4 of the Consolidated Life

Directive or Article 3 of the Reinsurance Directive:

(a) which assumes risks from such insurance undertakings or reinsurance undertakings; and
(b) which fully funds its exposures to such risks through the proceeds of a debt issuance or some other financing mechanism where the repayment rights of the providers of such debt or other financing mechanism are subordinated to the undertaking's reinsurance obligations."

A number of key points can immediately be identified in relation to a UK ISPV:

(a) The ISPV cannot be an insurance or reinsurance undertaking which is also authorised under the Non-Life, Life or Reinsurance Directives. However, an existing insurance or reinsurance undertaking can apply for variation of permission to become an ISPV, but it must ensure that it meets the definition of an ISPV and that it does not retain any insurance or reinsurance business that does not satisfy that definition.
(b) The ISPV can only assume risks from insurance or reinsurance undertakings authorised under the Non-Life, Life or Reinsurance Directives. This would include a syndicate at Lloyd's, since the Society of Lloyd's is a UK regulated entity authorised in accordance with the Directives.
(c) The ISPV cannot assume risks from a non-EEA headquartered entity.
(d) The ISPV cannot assume risks directly from a non-insurance entity.
(e) The ISPV must fully fund its exposure through the proceeds of a debt issuance or other financing mechanism. The FSA expressly states that, in order to be fully funded, the ISPV must have actually received the proceeds of the debt issuance or other financing mechanism and will not,

therefore, grant Part IV Permission to an ISPV where any part of the financing is on a contingent basis, for example by way of a standby facility or letter of credit.[87]

(f) The repayment rights of the providers of the debt or other financing mechanism must be subordinated to the undertaking's reinsurance obligations.

8.10.2 Establishment and authorisation of a UK ISPV

In the UK, an ISPV must apply for authorisation from the FSA, including the permissions pursuant to Part IV of the FSMA 2000 in relation to effecting and carrying out contracts of insurance as principal (*see* Chapter 2, Section 2.7 for more information on the application procedure in general). The FSA has announced that it will require less information from an ISPV than it requires from a conventional insurer or reinsurer and will place greater emphasis on self-certification and senior management responsibility.

The ISPV must satisfy the threshold conditions set out in Sch.6 to the FSMA 2000 (*see* Chapter 2, Section 2.6 for further details of the threshold conditions). The FSA's website allows an applicant to build its own application pack.[88] In the case of an ISPV, this includes the standard "Core Details" and "Individuals" forms and the "Owners and Influencers Appendix", as well as a "Supplement for Insurance Special Purpose Vehicles" form and a tailored "Checklist and Declaration". The applicant will also need to supply the following supporting documentation:

(a) staff organisational chart;
(b) business plan information;
(c) compliance procedures/monitoring programme;
(d) details of its professional advisers;
(e) a forecast opening balance sheet;
(f) a forecast balance sheet after 12 months of trading; and
(g) form SH01 (Companies House return of allotment of shares).

---

[87] INSPRU 1.6.3G.
[88] *See* www.fsa.gov.uk/pages/Doing/How/insurance/index.shtml.

The "Supplement for Insurance Special Purpose Vehicles" form and the accompanying notes are particularly helpful in guiding an applicant through the key issues that will need to be addressed in the application for authorisation. The notes to this form specify some of the detail that must be included in the regulatory business plan, information relating to the scope of permission that may be required, information that the FSA requires in relation to financial resources, background information in relation to personnel carrying out controlled functions and specific compliance matters that must be addressed.

8.10.2.1   Regulatory business plan

The regulatory business plan must deal with a number of core issues, including the following:

(a)   the name of each ceding company, the identity of its regulator and a name and contact details of an individual at the relevant regulator (where that regulator is not the FSA); this will enable the FSA to check that the ISPV assumes risks only from Directive-authorised entities;

(b)   details of the contractual arrangements of the ISPV (*see* Section 8.10.2.2) and its investment policy;

(c)   details of the main business risks that the ISPV is likely to face (including that it remains fully funded and solvent and continues to meet its obligations to the providers of its finance) and how it intends to manage those risks;

(d)   details of any outsourcing arrangements that are required by the ISPV in order to carry on its business; and

(e)   an assessment of the competence and capability of its personnel.

8.10.2.2   Contractual arrangements

The contractual arrangements to which the ISPV is to be party are to some extent controlled by INSPRU. INSPRU 1.6.9R requires that a UK ISPV must include in each of its contracts of reinsurance terms which secure that its aggregate maximum liability at any time under those contracts does not exceed the amount of its assets at that time. INSPRU 1.6.11R requires a UK

ISPV to ensure that under the terms of any debt issuance or other financing arrangement, the rights of the providers of that debt or other financing are fully subordinated to the claims of creditors under its contracts of reinsurance. INSPRU 1.6.12R prohibits a UK ISPV from entering into any contracts or assuming any obligations which are not necessary for it to give effect to the reinsurance arrangements which represent the special purpose for which it has been established.

The ISPV is required to obtain an independent legal opinion in order to satisfy itself that each contractual obligation that it enters into with a ceding company is legally effective and complies with the requirements of INSPRU 1.6.9R–1.6.12R. Although not clear from the FSA's guidance, it seems likely that the opinion will also need to address the debt or other financing arrangements, confirming that the contractual obligations are legally effective and compliant with the requirements of INSPRU 1.6.11R in particular.

Although the legal opinion does not form part of the application documentation, the FSA reserves the right to request a copy during the application process and/or the waiver process (*see* Section 8.10.3.2). It would be sensible for the legal advisers to consider this when including any limitations on the parties who may rely on the opinion.

8.10.2.3 *Financial resources*

The ISPV is required to explain how it will meet its requirements:

(a) to be fully funded; and
(b) to ensure that at all times its assets are greater than its liabilities.

Further information on these requirements is set out at Section 8.10.3.3. The FSA has structured its authorisation process so that the raising of funds need not commence until it has issued a notice that it is minded to grant the application for Part IV Permission.

The ISPV may then, if it has not already done so, raise its finance as proposed in the application. The FSA expects this process to be concluded soon after the "minded to authorise" notice has been given. The ISPV must then certify that it has received the proceeds of its fund raising, that it now meets the requirement for its reinsurance liabilities to be fully funded and that it fulfils the solvency requirement.

Provided the FSA is satisfied with the ISPV's certificate, and that nothing else in its application has changed, it will grant the Part IV Permission, following which the firm may carry out the regulated activities set out in its scope of permission, including effecting and then carrying out the contract(s) of reinsurance with the ceding company or companies.

In the context of this proposed structure, care needs to be taken to ensure that other regulated activities are not carried out by the ISPV before it has received its authorisation.

8.10.2.4 Compliance

The ISPV must have the appropriate compliance procedures in place to meet its regulatory obligations and, as a minimum, it must have in place procedures to meet the FSA's rules in relation to the following subject areas:

(a) the FSA's Statement of Principles and its Code of Practice ("APER");
(b) fit and proper criteria for approved persons (FIT 2);
(c) notifications to the FSA (SUP 15);
(d) reporting requirements (SUP 16);
(e) systems and controls in relation to financial crime and money laundering (SYSC 3.2.6 and SYSC 3.2.6A-J);
(f) business continuity (SYSC 3.2.19);
(g) record keeping (SYSC 3.2.20); and
(h) operational risk (SYSC 13).

An ongoing compliance monitoring programme should also be included as part of the application.

8.10.2.5 Application fee and process

The application fee payable to the FSA is the same as its standard fee for a moderately complex application (currently £5,000).

As far as timescale is concerned, no distinction is drawn in the FSMA 2000 between the authorisation of an ISPV and the authorisation of any other insurer or reinsurer, so that the same 6-month statutory period from the date the FSA receives a completed application (or 12 months if the application is not fully completed) applies as it would to any new insurer or reinsurer.

8.10.3 Financial supervision

8.10.3.1 Supervision of the ceding company

The FSA's primary focus, in relation to financial supervision, is on the impact that arrangements with a UK ISPV will have on the individual capital assessment ("ICA") of any UK ceding companies (*see* below), rather than the ISPV to which those risks are ceded. This novel approach to the regulation of an FSA-authorised entity allows the FSA to apply only a very light touch to the financial supervision of the ISPV, while ensuring that the cedant is not taking inappropriate credit in its own financial statements.

The effect of this is that, where a UK cedant wishes to take credit for risks ceded to an ISPV in another EEA Member State, the FSA will carry out a form of secondary financial supervision of the ISPV, through the cedant's waiver application (*see* Section 8.10.3.2) and through its monitoring of the cedant's ICA. Conversely, a UK ISPV which assumes risks only from cedants in other EEA Member States will be subject only to the light-touch regulatory regime outlined below.

A UK ceding company may treat amounts recoverable from an ISPV in a number of ways:

(a) as an admissible asset;
(b) as reinsurance for the purposes of calculating its mathematical reserves; or
(c) as reinsurance reducing its minimum capital requirement ("MCR"),[89]

provided it has first obtained a formal waiver from the FSA permitting that treatment.

For more information on the financial supervision of insurers and reinsurers generally, see Chapter 4.

8.10.3.2   *The waiver application*

In order to claim credit for risks transferred to an ISPV, under s.148 of the FSMA 2000 an FSA-regulated firm will be required to apply for a waiver of certain rules contained in INSPRU which provide, *prima facie*, that an FSA-regulated firm cannot claim credit in those circumstances.

The FSA considered that this approach, which may appear slightly artificial, was the simplest manner in which to implement the Reinsurance Directive's specific requirement that credit could only be taken for amounts recoverable from a special purpose vehicle where the ceding company had made an "application, with supporting evidence" and the regulator had agreed. The waiver procedure was the closest to the procedure laid down in the Reinsurance Directive and, rather than introduce a new process, the FSA adapted its rules accordingly.

INSPRU 1.6.14G–1.6.18G sets out the information which the FSA would expect to receive as part of an application for a waiver, and the factors (together with the factors in s.148 of the FSMA 2000) to which the FSA will have regard in deciding whether or not to grant such a waiver together with the amount which it will allow the ceding company to bring into account.

---

[89] INSPRU 1.6.13G.

Where the ISPV is a UK ISPV, the FSA will need to be satisfied that the ISPV complies with the rules applying to a UK ISPV in respect of its assets and liabilities and its contractual arrangements set out in INSPRU 1.6.5R–1.6.12R (for more information on which, *see* Section 8.10.2.2). If the ISPV is not a UK ISPV, the FSA expects to receive:

(a) confirmation that the ISPV has received an official authorisation in accordance with art.46 of the Reinsurance Directive in the EEA state in which it has been established;
(b) details of the debt issuance or other financing mechanism by which the ISPV's reinsurance liabilities are funded;
(c) information about the ISPV's key management and control functions, including details of the ISPV's auditors, arrangements for claims handling and any material outsourcing arrangements; and
(d) information about the structure of any group of which the ISPV is a member.

A cedant may only take credit for reinsurance (including a contract of reinsurance with an ISPV as any analogous non-reinsurance financing arrangements) if and to the extent that there has been an effective transfer of risk from the firm to a third party (*see* Section 8.11). The FSA will require evidence that the contract of reinsurance satisfies the risk transfer principles.

Information must also be provided about the impact that the arrangements with the ISPV will have on the ceding company's ICA, including evidence that all of the residual risks associated with the arrangements (including credit, market, liquidity and operational risks) are reflected in the assessment.

Further, the FSA will require an analysis of the potential for risk to revert to the ceding company or any of its associates under realistic adverse scenarios or for liabilities to arise in respect of the risks transferred for which no provision has been made by the ceding company.

8.10.3.3   Supervision of the ISPV

As noted above, the ISPV must at all times comply with two basic rules:

(a)   it must be fully funded in respect of its reinsurance obligations; and
(b)   it must meet the solvency requirement, which is that, at all times, its assets must be greater than or equal to its liabilities.[90]

As already described, in order to be considered fully funded the ISPV must have actually received the proceeds of its debt issuance or other financing (*see* Section 8.10.1), and its contracts of reinsurance must include terms that ensure that its maximum liability under those contracts is capped at a level that is no greater than its assets (*see* Section 8.10.2.2).

The same contractual cap will assist in satisfying the solvency requirement, although other expenses, for example staff and accommodation costs, claims-handling arrangements, professional fees and outsourcing costs, will also need to be addressed. These other issues can be addressed in a number of ways, for example by a contractual indemnity from the relevant ceding company.

A UK ISPV must ensure that its assets are invested in accordance with the rules that apply to pure reinsurers (*see* Chapter 4). Its assets must be held by it, or on its behalf, or by or on behalf of the relevant ceding company.

A UK ISPV must submit a copy of its annual audited financial statements within three months of its accounting reference date.[91] It may also be required to submit other annual reports under SUP 16, for example in relation to its controllers and close links.

---

[90] INSPRU 1.6.5R.
[91] *See* www.fsa.gov.uk/Pages/Doing/how/help/faqs/ispv/index.shtml

8.11   Risk transfer

The Reinsurance Directive permits each regulator to lay down specific provisions concerning the pursuit of finite reinsurance activities, including adequate internal control mechanisms and accounting, prudential and statistical information requirements.

Although the FSA chose not to introduce any specific rules relating to finite reinsurance, it did take the opportunity to develop rules and guidance relating to risk transfer which it had already been considering. The FSA consulted on the new provisions as part of its consultation on the Reinsurance Directive.[92]

The consultation paper and the replies to comments received in relation to the consultation paper (which are contained in Handbook Notice 59) make it clear that the FSA wished to implement rules on a principles-based approach. As a result, the rules and guidance implemented consist of just six sections, and although there are a number of examples contained in the guidance (*see* Section 8.11.2), it should not be considered as limiting the basic rule in any way.

8.11.1   The basic rule

The basic rule is contained in INSPRU 1.1.19AR and is referred to briefly at Section 8.10.3.2 as it applies equally to transactions with an ISPV as it does other contracts of reinsurance and "analogous non-reinsurance financing arrangements". It provides that a "firm may only take credit for reinsurance if and to the extent that there has been an effective transfer of risk from the firm to a third party".

8.11.2   Guidance

Guidance on the rule is included in INSPRU 1.1.19BR– 1.1.19FG.

---

[92] Consultation Paper 06/12, "Implementing the Reinsurance Directive".

Analogous non-reinsurance financing arrangements would include securitisations and contingent loans as well as "any other arrangements in respect of contracts of insurance that are analogous to contracts of reinsurance in terms of the risks transferred and the finance provided". This latter provision contemplates the treatment of insurance-linked securities and contingent loan arrangements as analogous to reinsurance.

Chapter 4 above deals in more detail with the ways in which a ceding company can take credit for reinsurance under the rules in GENPRU and INSPRU, but the following examples are included in INSPRU 1.1.19CG:

(a)   treating the reinsurer's share of technical provisions as an admissible asset;

(b)   reducing the ceding company's solvency requirements by making a deduction for reinsurance; and

(c)   bringing into account amounts receivable under the reinsurance when valuing cash flows for the purpose of a prospective valuation of mathematical reserves.

The ceding company must take into account any factors which might result in the risk transfer not being effective in all circumstances in which it may wish to rely on the transfer. Some examples of negative factors include:

(a)   whether the documentation associated with the reinsurance reflects the economic substance of the transaction;

(b)   whether the extent of the risk transfer is clearly defined in the documentation and is incontrovertible;

(c)   whether there are any terms or conditions in the risk transfer documentation the fulfilment of which the ceding company does not have full control over, for example:

   (i)   the ability of the third party to cancel the transaction unilaterally, except for the non-payment of monies due from the ceding company to the third party under the risk transfer documentation, particularly where that ability is triggered by an increased likelihood that the third party may experience losses under the transaction;

(ii) any additional costs to the ceding company in circumstances where the third party is likely to experience losses under the transaction;

(iii) any mechanism to alter the transferred risk for the purposes of reducing the likelihood that the third party might experience losses under the transaction;

(iv) any provision that could prevent the third party from being obliged to pay out in a timely manner any monies due under the transaction; or

(iv) any provision that could allow the maturity of the transaction to be reduced; and

(d) whether the transaction is legally effective and enforceable in all relevant jurisdictions.

Ceding companies should also take into consideration, when evaluating risk transfer, any circumstances in which the benefit to the ceding company of the transaction might be reduced, for example in the context of an ISPV where the ceding company has invested in the bonds issued by, or other financing arrangements of, that ISPV.

Chapter 9

The Regulation of Long-Term Insurance

Charles Rix,
Partner: Hogan Lovells International LLP

Steven McEwan,
Of Counsel: Hogan Lovells International LLP

9.1 Introduction

Since the last edition of this book, the regulation of long-term insurance has been in a state of relative calm. The calm has been broken on occasion, most notably by proposals to impose greater restrictions on the management of with-profits funds, which threaten to have significant implications for with-profits insurers, particularly mutuals, and by the greater scrutiny with which FSA now reviews management performance. However, the changes have not been of the intensity of, for example, the introduction of the Pillar 2 capital requirement in 2004 or the reform of the requirements for treating with-profits customers fairly in 2007.

Readers will be well aware that this calm is a calm before a storm—a storm for which insurers have been working extremely hard to prepare. When it is implemented, Solvency II will have a very significant effect on the regulation of long-term insurance. Its effects will primarily relate to the regulation of assets, liabilities and regulatory capital (commonly referred to as "prudential" regulation), though the regulation of conduct of business will inevitably be affected to some extent as well, and there will be major changes to reporting and disclosure requirements. Some idea of the volume of work required to implement Solvency II emerged when insurers reported on their financial position under draft Solvency II rules as part of Quantitative Impact Study 5 (QIS 5) in 2010, with one insurer estimating that it required the equivalent of 80 full time members of staff working over three months.

The regulatory architecture is changing as well. In the EU, the European Insurance and Occupational Pensions Authority ("EIOPA") now has significantly more power than CEIOPS, the committee from which it took over in 2011. And in the UK, the government's proposals to reorganise the FSA will have major implications for insurers who, assuming the proposals are implemented, will in future be subject to prudential regulation by the Prudential Regulation Authority and conduct of business regulation by the Financial Conduct Authority.

The calm referred to above refers only to the insurance regulatory environment. There has of course been significant turmoil in the financial markets throughout the financial crisis in the banking sector which began in 2007. The FSA and its approach to insurance regulation deserve much credit for the fact that UK insurers appear to have come through the financial crisis relatively unscathed.

As this chapter focuses on long-term insurance (commonly referred to as "life" insurance, though this term can conceal certain of its important features such as annuities and pensions), it is worth reflecting briefly on what distinguishes it from general insurance (commonly referred to as "non-life" insurance). In addition to the subject matter of the policies themselves, two main differences can be observed.

First, as the name suggests, the risks assumed and service provided under long-term insurance policies are typically of long duration. General insurance policies typically endure for much shorter periods, often with no obligation on the insurer to renew the policy. However, this distinction does not apply to all policies. There is nothing to prevent a long-term insurance policy covering only a single year, or even a shorter period. Claims under some general insurance policies may be made long after the period of coverage of the policy, as happened as a result of the effects of exposure to asbestos not emerging for many years after the cover period of the relevant insurance policies, and general insurers may in some cases spread claim payments over many years in accordance with structured settlements.

Second, long-term insurance policies are often used as a vehicle for long-term saving, providing an alternative to investment products and other forms of pension provision. General insurance policies do not accumulate a savings value which is returned at the end of the policy. Again this distinction does not apply to all policies. For example, a standalone term assurance policy, a very common type of long term insurance policy which provides for a lump sum payment on death within a fixed period, does not accumulate a savings value.

This chapter covers all aspects of the regulation of long-term insurance with the exception of the marketing of long-term insurance which is covered in Chapter 10. Inevitably, because the basic framework of regulation of long-term insurance and general insurance is essentially the same, some aspects of the regulation of long-term insurance have been covered in other chapters. The description in this chapter of regulation in these areas has therefore been kept brief and cross-references to other chapters are made where appropriate. More in-depth analysis has been provided in those areas which are unique to long-term insurance, particularly unit-linked insurance and with-profits.

Where it has been useful to do so, this chapter comments on the impact which Solvency II is expected to have when it is implemented. However, the main object of this book is to be a practical guide to current regulation, so extensive analysis of Solvency II has been avoided. Its likely impact is summarised generally in Chapter 4. For the same reason, this chapter does not (other than above in this introduction) make reference to the proposed reorganisation of the FSA, though this topic is discussed in Chapter 1.

9.2   The origins of the current regulatory regime

When the Financial Services and Markets Act 2000 ("FSMA 2000") came into force on 1 December 2001, the Financial Services Authority ("FSA") became the sole regulator of almost all of the UK financial services industry (a notable exception is the consumer credit industry which is regulated by the Office of Fair Trading). This represented a fundamental change from the previous system under which there had effectively been different regulators for banking, insurance and investment management. Not surprisingly, one of the FSA's initial objectives was to harmonise the regulation of different financial services sectors. The FSA also adopted a risk-based approach to regulation. Under this approach, the FSA aims to allocate its resources in a way which is proportionate to the risk posed by each regulated firm or sector to the FSA's regulatory objectives. As a general rule, larger firms are likely to receive more intensive supervision than smaller firms under this approach.

Since 1 December 2001, the FSA has undertaken a complete overhaul of the regulation of the life assurance industry. This is partly due to European Commission initiatives and partly due to the FSA's own initiatives.

There have, of course, been other catalysts for reform of the regulation of the life insurance industry—in particular, the mis-selling practices in relation to personal pension policies and freestanding additional voluntary contributions to pension policies that came to light in the 1990s, which resulted in significant amounts of compensation having to be paid by the firms involved, and the near demise of Equitable Life at the beginning of the 2000s, which led to a series of reviews and reports,[1] and ultimately in new rules which have fundamentally changed the regulatory approach to with-profits business.

The FSA has also developed a principles-based approach to regulation. The use of principles in financial services regulation is not a new concept—they have been used in the UK since 1990. What has changed is the shift in focus from prescriptive rules to the use of the Principles, as set out in the FSA's "Principles for Businesses" which forms part of the FSA Handbook, as the primary form of regulation. In April 2007 the FSA published "Principles-based regulation: Focusing on the outcomes that matter", in which it confirmed its intention to move to a *"more* principles-based approach" (emphasis added). This approach encompasses several key concepts.

The first key concept is the use of broad-based standards in preference to detailed rules. The Principles are purposive and drafted in general terms, and can be applied to a wide range of situations, and explained and developed in a wide variety of ways, including informal guidance, industry letters, case studies, discussion papers, speeches by FSA staff and endorsement of guidance issued by industry bodies. They are directly enforceable against insurers, without the need for a breach of any specific FSA rule. The FSA has made it clear that it will increasingly seek to rely on the Principles alone when taking enforcement action. In April 2011, this approach received support from the High Court which held that the Principles were actionable even in the absence of specific rules.[2]

The second key concept is the idea that principles-based regulation is focused on outcomes rather than processes. The third key concept is greater involvement from senior management. The corollary of a focus on broad principles and

---

[1]   Among the reviews and reports were the "With-Profits Review" conducted by the FSA, the Baird Report examining the FSA's role in the regulation of Equitable Life, the Tiner Project, in which the FSA undertook a comprehensive review of insurance regulation, and the Penrose Report, an independent report commissioned by HM Treasury setting lessons to be learnt in relation to the conduct, administration and regulation of life insurance business.

[2]   R. (on the application of British Bankers' Association) v the Financial Services Authority [2011] EWHC 999 (Admin).

outcomes rather than processes is that senior management are required to develop a more sophisticated approach to regulatory practices and take greater responsibility for the evolution of reporting and monitoring structures. Only by doing so can they ensure that their firm is achieving the necessary outcomes.

Principles-based regulation is by no means "light-touch" regulation. It does of course require the regulator to make decisions in relation to its application of its resources and what firms and issues to focus on but that approach has advantages over a more static, "one size fits all" rules-based approach. Although the FSA may be placing less public emphasis on principles-based regulation than it did previously,[3] it is equally noteworthy that almost all of the Final Notices that the FSA has published in respect of enforcement actions during 2011 have included a finding of a breach of a principle. It is also notable that the FSA regulation of long-term insurance has become considerably more intrusive and rigorous than it was in the past.

9.3   The regulatory framework

The framework for the regulation of life insurance businesses in the UK is established by the FSMA 2000 under which the FSA is appointed as the regulator of the financial services sector. The FSA describes itself as an independent non-governmental body accountable to HM Treasury. In performing its role as the regulator of the UK financial services industry, the FSA is required to act in a way which is compatible as far as reasonably possible with its regulatory objectives (*see* Chapter 1).

All FSA authorised firms are required to conduct their affairs in accordance with the FSA's 11 Principles for Businesses (*see* Chapter 1). These principles in particular require a firm to:

---

[3]   An interesting comparison can be made between the 2006–2007 Annual Report, where principles-based regulation is referred to 52 times, and the 2010–2011 Annual Report in which there are no references to principles-based regulation.

(a) conduct its business with integrity and with due skill, care and diligence;
(b) take reasonable care to organise and control its affairs responsibly and effectively, with adequate risk management systems;
(c) maintain adequate financial resources;
(d) pay due regard to the interests of customers and treat them fairly; and
(e) deal with the FSA in an open and cooperative way.

All FSA-regulated firms have a duty pursuant to Principle 11 to cooperate with the FSA and to disclose to the FSA anything of which it would reasonably expect to receive notice. Firms are also subject to requirements to provide information in accordance with the rules and detailed guidance in the Supervision Manual ("SUP").[4] In addition, insurers are required to prepare annual insurance returns for the FSA under the Interim Prudential Sourcebook for Insurers ("IPRU(INS)") (*see* Chapter 4) and are subject to certain specific notification requirements under the Prudential Sourcebook for Insurers ("INSPRU") and the General Prudential Sourcebook ("GENPRU"), for example any breach or expected breach of the capital resources requirement.

Although the FSMA 2000 gives the FSA power to use its own initiative to make rules in relation to the regulation of financial services businesses, in practice many of its rules are made for the purposes of implementing EU Directives. EU regulation of insurance is largely driven by the fundamental rights of freedom of establishment and freedom to provide cross-border services originally provided for by the EC Treaty. Among other things, this has resulted in insurers which are authorised to conduct business in one EEA state being permitted, under the EEA passporting regime, to conduct insurance business in other EEA states without the need for further authorisation and subject to the supervision of their home state regulator (so called "home state regulation") (*see* Chapter 5).

---

[4] Of particular note is SUP 15.3.11, which requires notification to the FSA of significant breaches of FSA rules, including significant breaches which may occur in the foreseeable future.

Many of the UK's rules for the regulation of life insurance derive from the three "generations" of Life Directives (First Life Directive (79/267/EEC), Second Life Directive (90/619/EEC) and Third Life Directive (92/96/EEC)). These directives were briefly supplemented by a fourth directive (2002/12/EC) amending the solvency margin requirement for life assurance business in 2002 (as part of the Solvency I amendments) before all four directives were consolidated in a single Consolidated Life Assurance Directive in 2002 (2002/83/EEC). These directives established a single market for direct life insurance in the European Union which is extended by agreement to the full European Economic Area. There are a number of other European Directives which particularly affect the regulation of long-term insurers in the UK, including the following:

(a)   The Reinsurance Directive (2005/68/EC), which requires EU Member States to exercise prudential supervision of reinsurance businesses. In the UK, firms conducting only reinsurance business (referred to as "pure" reinsurers) were already regulated on broadly the same basis as firms conducting only direct insurance business or conducting both direct and reinsurance business. The implementation of the Reinsurance Directive has therefore not significantly impacted UK rules applicable to reinsurers, although it has resulted in some softening of the rules as they apply to pure reinsurers[5] and the introduction of new rules on insurance special-purpose vehicles ("ISPVs") (*see* Chapter

---

[5]   The key differences in the FSA rules applicable to pure reinsurers are:
(a)   for pure reinsurers, the definition of "admissible assets" refers to a set of principles-based requirements set out in INSPRU 3.1.61A rather than to a specific list of assets set out in GENPRU 2 Annex 7;
(b)   pure reinsurers are exempt from the detailed rules which apply for the purpose of determining the admissibility of derivatives and stock lending transactions under INSPRU 3.2 (although some of the same principles are covered in the requirements in INSPRU 3.1.61A);
(c)   pure reinsurers are exempt from the market risk and counterparty limits which apply under INSPRU 2.1.22;
(d)   pure reinsurers are not required to localise their holdings of assets under INSPRU 1.1.30 or to currency-match their assets under INSPRU 3.1.53;
(e)   pure reinsurers are exempt from the "close-matching rules" which apply to direct insurers who carry on linked business (see Section 9.5.8 below), though in practice a pure reinsurer would probably only take advantage of this exemption in relation to index-linked business and not property-linked business;

8). The FSA has made rules relating to ISPVs in INSPRU 1.6. These rules permit a special-purpose company established in an EEA state to act as a reinsurer without being subject to the regulatory capital requirements to which normal reinsurers would be subject. Instead, the ISPV must fully fund its reinsurance liabilities by issuing debt or through some other financing mechanism. A UK insurer is only permitted to take advantage of reinsurance from an ISPV where it obtains a waiver from the FSA allowing it to do so.

(b) The Insurance Groups Directive (98/73/EC), which requires EU Member States to monitor the capital resources of insurance groups and to exercise general supervision over intra-group transactions within insurance groups. On an annual basis a UK insurer is required to calculate and to report the group capital position at the level of the insurer itself, at the level of its ultimate EEA insurance parent undertaking and at the level of its ultimate (worldwide) insurance parent undertaking (if different from the ultimate EEA insurance parent undertaking). The main objective of this calculation is to identify the financial position of the group after eliminating:

    (i)   double-counting of the same capital where it benefits two or more regulated entities in the same group; and

    (ii) reliance on surplus capital held in certain group entities which is not freely transferable around the group.

(f) under INSPRU 1.1.90, pure reinsurers may take up to 50 per cent (rather than only 15 per cent) credit for reinsurance in the calculation of their capital resources requirement;

(g) in determining what non-insurance business a pure reinsurer may carry on, the requirement under INSPRU 1.5.13A appears to be more liberal than the corresponding requirement for other insurers under INSPRU 1.5.13; and

(h) under IPRU(INS) rule 8.3, a non-UK insurer carrying on direct business through a UK branch must maintain a chief executive in respect of its UK branch business, but a non-UK pure reinsurer is exempt from this requirement.

In addition to these differences, the capital requirement for life protection reinsurance business, where written by a pure reinsurer or a mixed insurer (an insurer which carries on both direct business and a significant amount of reinsurance business), is determined using the calculation normally employed for general insurance business (being the greater of the premiums amount, the claims amount and the brought forward amount).

A "hard" group capital requirement applies at the level of the insurer itself and at the level of the ultimate EEA insurance parent undertaking, but not at the level of the ultimate (worldwide) insurance parent undertaking (if different from the ultimate EEA insurance parent undertaking). A "hard" requirement is a requirement whose breach will constitute a breach of FSA rules, with the effect that it will be necessary for some immediate action to be taken so that the breach does not continue. It is distinguished from a "soft" requirement with which the insurer is expected to comply but where failure to comply could be addressed more gradually or left unremedied if thought appropriate. An insurer is also required to provide details of material connected-party transactions as part of its annual FSA returns (*see* Chapter 4). Under Solvency II, the "soft" worldwide group capital requirement will become a hard requirement. This is one of the areas of Solvency II which are expected to have the most implications for international insurance groups, though the effect may be mitigated by transitional provisions if they can be agreed at EU level.

(c) The Financial Groups Directive (2002/87/EC), which requires Member States to exercise supplementary supervision over financial conglomerates—that is, groups which consist of one or more entities in the insurance sector and one or more entities in the banking and investment sector and which meet certain further criteria. Supplementary supervision includes monitoring of capital adequacy, risk concentration, intra-group transactions, internal control mechanisms and risk management processes. Where a UK insurer is the head of a financial conglomerate or where the insurance sector is the most important financial sector in the financial conglomerate, the capital adequacy position of the financial conglomerate will, subject to certain exceptions, be determined according to the same rules as are used for determining the group capital position of an insurance group for purposes of the rules implementing the Insurance Groups Directive. As in the case of the group capital calculation for insurance groups, the main objective of the capital adequacy calculation for financial conglomerates is to identify the capital position after eliminating double-counting of capital and reliance on non-transferable surplus capital. The capital adequacy requirement is a "hard" requirement at EEA level but will only be applied as a hard requirement at worldwide level if the FSA so requires. The capital adequacy calculation and details of significant risk concentration levels and intra-group transactions are required to be provided to the FSA on an annual basis by the entity responsible for reporting on behalf of the financial conglomerate (*see* Chapter 4).

(d) The Distance Marketing of Financial Services Directive (2002/65/EC), under which protection was given to customers of financial products marketed and sold by telephone or by electronic means, without face-to-face contact. The Directive established a set of EU-wide rules prescribing specified minimum information to be given to customers before entering into such a contract (referred to as a "distance contract") and giving cancellation rights within a minimum period after the conclusion of the contract. The provisions of the Directive were implemented in the UK partly by the Financial Services (Distance Marketing) Regulations 2004 and partly by FSA rules and guidance.[6] Prior to implementation, cancellation rights were already generally available to policyholders in relation to long-term insurance contracts, as had been required by the Consolidated Life Assurance Directive. Implementation of the Distance Marketing of Financial Services Directive has resulted in a complex matrix of rights to cancel which is in some respects counter-intuitive[7] (*see* Chapter 10).

---

[6] For a contract relating to life insurance, a consumer has the right to cancel the contract within 30 calendar days from the date when the consumer is informed that the distance contract is concluded (a period longer than the 14 calendar-day period which applies for other types of distance contracts): *see* reg.10(4) of the Regulations (which applies to distance contracts) and COBS 15.2.1 (which applies to both distance contracts and non-distance contracts). However, firms may voluntarily give consumers wider rights to cancel than are required by the Regulations or the FSA rules. There are numerous further rules in COBS which require information to be provided whether the contract is a distance contract or a non-distance contract.

[7] COBS 15.2.1. It should be noted that the right to cancel does not apply to a linked

(e) The Insurance Mediation Directive (2002/92/EC), under which Member States are required to regulate insurance mediation activities (broadly introducing, advising, selling as agent and assisting in the administration and performance of insurance contracts). Prior to the implementation of this Directive, the UK already had an extensive regulatory regime governing insurance mediation activities in relation to life insurance, so implementation had less of an impact on the life insurance industry than on the general insurance industry where intermediaries were not previously regulated (*see* Chapter 10 below).

9.4 General regulatory requirements for long-term insurance

9.4.1 The requirement for authorisation

Under the so-called general prohibition set out in s.19 of the FSMA 2000, any person wishing to carry on long-term insurance business in the UK must have permission to do so from the FSA unless it is exempt from the need for authorisation or is able to rely on the EEA "passporting" regime under which an insurer which is authorised in another EEA state and which satisfies certain conditions will be treated as authorised to carry on insurance business in the UK even though it does not obtain permission from the FSA to do so. Carrying on long-term insurance business means effecting and/or carrying out contracts of long-term insurance business. Contravention of the general prohibition is a criminal offence and insurance contracts under which insurance is provided by an unauthorised person are unenforceable against the policyholder (although they are not unenforceable against the unauthorised person).

---

policy if it is a distance contract, though it does apply to a linked policy which is not a distance contract: *see* COBS 15 Annex 1 para.1.10, implementing art.6(2) of the Directive and FSA Consultation Paper 196 at para.2.26. This appears to be at odds with art.35 of the Consolidated Life Assurance Directive.

Permission to conduct long-term insurance business must cover each class of long-term insurance business that the insurer intends to carry on. The classes of long-term insurance business are as follows:

(a) Class I (life and annuity);
(b) Class II (marriage and birth);
(c) Class III (linked long-term);
(d) Class IV (permanent health);
(e) Class V (tontines);
(f) Class VI (capital redemption);
(g) Class VII (pension fund management);
(h) Class VIII (collective insurance);
(i) Class IX (social insurance).

In accordance with the prohibition in the Consolidated Life Assurance Directive on the authorisation of new composite insurers, the FSA will not give a new permission for an insurer to carry out both long-term insurance business and general insurance business. This prohibition does not apply where a general insurer's permission to carry on long-term insurance business would be restricted to reinsurance business. By contrast, a long-term insurer would not be permitted to carry on general business restricted to reinsurance business, except on a supplementary basis.

It is recognised that long-term insurers will typically wish to be able to provide supplementary protection against personal injury, accident, disability or sickness and that general insurers who provide protection against personal injury, accident, disability or sickness will also wish to provide protection against death. The Consolidated Life Assurance Directive therefore permits long-term insurers to be authorised to carry on general insurance business falling within class 1 (accident) and class 2 (sickness) and general insurers who carry on only class 1 (accident) and class 2 (sickness) business to be authorised to carry on long-term insurance business. Under the Regulated Activities Order, a contract whose principal object is that of a long-term insurance contract, and which is effected or carried out by a long-term insurer, will be regarded as a long-term insurance contract notwithstanding the fact that it contains "related and subsidiary" provisions such that it might also be regarded as a general insurance contract. In practice the FSA has taken a relatively restrictive approach to the application of this provision in the past.

9.4.2   Governance

A UK insurer is required to satisfy the threshold conditions both as a condition of becoming authorised by the FSA and as a condition of continuing to be authorised (*see* Chapter 2). The FSA may vary or cancel a firm's Part IV permission if it appears to the FSA that the firm is failing or is likely to fail to satisfy the threshold conditions. Threshold Condition 5 requires a long-term insurer to satisfy the FSA that it is a fit and proper person having regard to all the circumstances, including (among other factors) the need to ensure that its affairs are conducted soundly and prudently. Guidance on this Threshold Condition states that the governing body of a firm is to be made up of individuals with an appropriate range of skills and experience to understand, operate and manage the firm's regulated activities. If appropriate, the governing body is to include non-executive representation at a level which is appropriate for the control of the regulated activities. A firm also has a duty to maintain a clear and appropriate apportionment of responsibilities among its directors and senior managers.

9.4.3   Approved persons

Like other regulated firms, a long-term insurer must ensure that no person performs a prescribed "controlled function" on its behalf unless he has been approved by the FSA as being fit and proper to perform that controlled function (*see* Chapter 3). Approved persons are required to comply on an ongoing basis with the part of the FSA Handbook referred to as "APER" (the Statements of Principle and Code of Practice for Approved Persons). For long-term insurers, the controlled functions include the actuarial function and the with-profits actuary function as well as the functions common to other regulated firms such as the director function, the chief executive function, the money laundering reporting function and the apportionment and oversight function.

9.4.4 Actuarial Function Holder and With-Profits Actuary

Under SUP 4.3.1 a long-term insurer is required to appoint a person to carry out the actuarial function (the "Actuarial Function Holder"). A firm carrying out with-profits business must also appoint a person to carry out the with-profits actuary function (the "With-Profits Actuary"). The Actuarial Function Holder is responsible for monitoring the financial condition of the firm and advising on capital needs. The With-Profits Actuary focuses specifically on the With-Profits business of the firm.

Actuarial Function Holders and With-Profits Actuaries are subject to so-called "whistleblowing" duties under which they must give information on certain matters to the FSA relating to the firms by which they are appointed. These matters include material contraventions of enactments under which the FSA has power to prosecute and failure to meet the threshold conditions for FSA authorisation. Actuaries who provide information to the FSA under these provisions will be protected by the Public Interest Disclosure Act 1998. In addition, the FSA's rules require firms to take reasonable steps to ensure that the Actuarial Function Holder and the With-Profits Actuary do not also perform the function of chairman or chief executive of the firm or any other function which could give rise to a conflict of interest.

9.4.5 Internal systems and controls

Long-term insurers (like other firms) are subject to Principle 3, which requires them to take reasonable care to organise their affairs responsibly and effectively, with adequate risk management systems. Systems and controls are required to be established having regard to the different categories of risk identified in the FSA Handbook: liquidity risk, group risk, operational risk, prudential risk, credit risk, market risk and insurance risk. A firm is required to have in place "sound, effective and complete processes, strategies and systems" that enable it to identify and manage these risks and other risks which are relevant to the firm.

Since the introduction of the individual capital adequacy regime in 2005, long-term insurers have been required to prepare and submit to the FSA "individual capital assessments" analysing the adequacy of their capital resources. The assessments are required to be consistent with the insurer's management practice, systems and controls and are required to cover the risks referred to above. Poor systems and controls will mean greater risk and may therefore result in a greater amount of capital being required to be held.[8] For more detail *see* Chapters 2 and 3.

9.4.6 *Mathematical reserves*

The liabilities which insurers are required to recognise in respect of contracts of insurance (*see* Chapter 4) are referred to as "technical provisions". For long-term insurance business, technical provisions include "mathematical reserves", which represent the liabilities in respect of such business which have not yet fallen due for payment. Mathematical reserves are required to be determined in accordance with FSA rules. The remainder of the technical provisions for long-term insurance business represent liabilities which have already fallen due for

---

[8] There is no express obligation to hold the amount of capital which, based on an individual capital assessment, would appear to be required, although it would be difficult for a firm to argue that it was satisfying the requirement to hold "adequate" capital resources if its capital resources were less than the amount which its own individual capital assessment indicated were required. Following a review of the individual capital assessment, and any subsequent analysis carried out by the FSA itself, the FSA may give "individual capital guidance" to the insurer, identifying the amount of capital which the FSA considers the insurer should hold in order to comply with the general requirement under GENPRU 1.2.26 to maintain adequate overall financial resources. The individual capital guidance is not binding on the insurer, but the FSA has power to vary the insurer's Part IV Permission in order to impose an obligation on it to hold the amount of capital which the FSA considers necessary.

payment, and these technical provisions are required to be determined in accordance with various national and international accounting rules.

An important feature that distinguishes mathematical reserves from other technical provisions, including, with certain exceptions, technical provisions for general insurance business, is that they are determined as the net present value of expected future cash flows. The determination is "net" because it is made by netting future cash inflows and future cash outflows relating to the long-term insurance business, including premiums, expenses, benefits payable and amounts to be received or paid under reinsurance contracts. The determination is of the "present value" of future cash flows because it is made by discounting the value of the cash flows to reflect the passage of time before they will be paid or received. This enables the firm to take into account the yield that it expects to achieve from the assets held to cover its liabilities, from reinvesting sums received from those assets and from the investment of future premium receipts (the yield itself not being treated as a cash flow when determining the mathematical reserves).

Mathematical reserves are required to be established on a "prudent" basis. Firms are required to include margins for adverse deviation which are sufficiently prudent to ensure that there is no significant foreseeable risk that liabilities to policyholders in respect of long-term insurance contracts will not be met as they fall due. This can be compared with the approach used in determining the realistic value of liabilities of a with-profits fund, where a "best estimate" approach is used with no margins for adverse deviation.

With certain exceptions, mathematical reserves are required to be calculated separately for each long-term insurance contract, with additional reserves being established on an aggregated basis for risks that are not specific to individual contracts. It is therefore possible for the mathematical reserves in respect of an individual contract to be negative, so that they are offset against positive mathematical reserves for other contracts, though this is not permitted if the contract has a guaranteed surrender value. The total mathematical reserves established by the firm cannot be less than zero. (An example of a contract which may have negative reserves is a term assurance policy where the expenses are borne by the firm mainly in the first year of the policy and recouped gradually from premiums over the term of the policy. In this scenario the expected future cash inflows from premiums will exceed the expected future cash outflows from claims. Cash outflows minus cash inflows will therefore be negative, giving rise to negative mathematical reserves.)

More detailed rules apply to particular aspects of the valuation of cash flows, including the discount rate to be used in determining present values, the value to be attributed to expected future premiums, provisions for expenses, mortality and morbidity assumptions, the exercise of policyholder options, persistency assumptions and the valuation of reinsurance cash flows.

9.4.7 Restriction of business to insurance

Rule 1.5.13 of INSPRU provides that an insurer (other than a pure reinsurer[9]) "must not carry on any commercial business other than insurance business and activities directly arising from that business". This rule is based upon the provisions of the first Life Directive which sought to restrict the ability of an insurance company to carry on non-insurance related activities on a commercial basis. The Directive's provisions were implemented as Section 16 of the Insurance Companies Act 1982 and subsequently incorporated into the FSA Handbook with some slight amendments. Guidance in the FSA Handbook cites the investing of assets and employing insurance staff as examples of permitted non-insurance activities as these arise directly from the insurance business.

In the past it was questioned whether transactions entered into by an insurer under which it carried on non-insurance business

---

[9] Pure reinsurers are subject to what appears to be a more liberal provision requiring them not to carry on any business other than the business of reinsurance "and related operations": INSPRU 1.5.13A.

might be void or unenforceable as being in breach of statutory duty.[10] It is now clear that they would not be: s.151(2) of the FSMA 2000 provides that contravention of FSA rules does not make a transaction void or unenforceable. Nevertheless, an insurer would still be subject to the enforcement powers of the FSA for breach of FSA rules if it enters into such transactions.

It should be noted that r.1.5.13 restricts the carrying on of *commercial* business by an insurer where it is not insurance business or activities directly arising from that business. In this respect it is less restrictive than s.16 of the Insurance Companies Act 1982, which applied to "any activities", whether they comprised commercial business or not. Non-insurance activities of an insurer which do not constitute commercial business will therefore not be prohibited by the rule. The position under s.16 went beyond art.6(2)(b) of the Consolidated Life Assurance Directive. In referring to commercial business, r.1.5.13 follows art.6(2)(b).

It is also interesting to compare the position for pure reinsurers. INSPRU 1.5.13A, which is the corresponding provision limiting the non-reinsurance activities of pure reinsurers, provides that a pure reinsurer must not carry on any "business" other than the business of reinsurance and "related operations". Notably the prohibition on "business" is wider than the prohibition on "commercial business", though the exception for "related operations" is probably also wider than the exception for "activities directly arising from that business" which applies to direct insurers under INSPRU 1.5.13. Solvency II will retain the same respective formulations of the restrictions for insurers and pure reinsurers: see art.18(1)(a) and (b).

---

[10] See *Fuji Finance Inc v Aetna Life Insurance Co Ltd* [1996] 4 All E.R. 608, Court of Appeal.

9.4.8 *Identification and separation of long-term insurance business assets*

Long-term insurance policies may remain in force for many years. Often they are relied upon by policyholders as investment products in which significant value is accumulated. They cover the risks which are of most personal importance to policyholders:

(a) on the policyholder's death, a long-term insurance policy may provide a lump sum or an income for the policyholder's dependants or it may discharge his debts so that his dependants are free of them;

(b) alternatively, it may act like a pension fund by providing the means to purchase an annuity for the policyholder's retirement.

For these reasons, special rules govern the management and application of assets which an insurer holds in respect of its long-term insurance business.

An insurer is required to keep a separate accounting record of the assets which it holds to cover the liabilities arising from its long-term insurance business and of the premiums and other receivables in respect of those assets and that business. These assets and receivables, referred to as its "long-term insurance assets", form the "long-term insurance fund" of the insurer. An insurer may have more than one long-term insurance fund where it identifies separate assets in connection with different parts of its long-term insurance business. For example, where an insurer has a with-profits fund, it may maintain a with-profits fund and a non-profit fund, each of which would be a separate long-term insurance fund. However, internal linked funds maintained in connection with linked policies would not normally be regarded as separate long-term insurance funds.

Restrictions apply on the application of assets of a long-term insurance fund. Such assets must be applied only for the purposes of the insurer's long-term insurance business. Guidance is provided on what will constitute the purposes of the long-term insurance business. The purposes include:

(a) the payment of claims, expenses and liabilities (including repayment of a loan when it was incurred for the purposes of the long-term insurance business) arising from the long-term insurance business;

(b) acquisition of lawful access to fixed assets to be used in the long-term insurance business; and

(c) the purchase or investment of assets, including an exchange at fair market value of assets (including money) between the fund and other assets of the firm.

A firm may also apply assets of a long-term insurance fund by transferring them under a stock-lending transaction (whether as the securities being loaned or, where the firm is the borrower, as collateral) where the transfer is for the benefit of the long-term insurance business. Assets of a long-term insurance fund may not be made the subject of a mortgage or charge other than in respect of a long-term insurance liability. Except in the case of a mutual insurer (whose assets will consist solely of its long-term insurance funds), they may not be used to pay financial penalties imposed by the FSA. A firm is not permitted to transfer assets out of a long-term insurance fund except where they represent an established surplus determined by an actuarial investigation carried out within the past three months.[11] An insurer must not declare a dividend when the value of its long-term insurance assets is less than its liabilities attributable to the long-term insurance business. Further restrictions are imposed on the use of assets in with-profits funds.

---

[11] The expression "transfer assets out", as used in INSPRU 1.5.27, is somewhat vague. Clearly it does not refer to the application of assets for the purposes of the firm's long-term insurance business, as such application is implicitly permitted. It would restrict the making of a gift, the payment of a dividend or the reallocation of assets so that they are no longer treated as part of the long-term insurance funds (a process sometimes referred to as a transfer to the shareholders' fund) and probably also the voluntary prepayment of a contingent loan liability unless in each case the amount transferred formed part of an established surplus.

Although the assets of a long-term insurance fund must be applied only for the purposes of the insurer's long-term business, policyholders have no legal or beneficial interest in them. The assets of the insurer which are held outside of its long-term insurance funds are sometimes described as the "shareholders' fund". However, such a reference is misleading as these assets are not freely available to shareholders. They will be available to cover any liabilities of the insurer which are not allocated to the long-term insurance fund, including any general insurance business liabilities, and also any liabilities which cannot be discharged from the assets of the long-term insurance funds because those assets are insufficient.

9.4.9 Winding-up rules

On a winding-up of an insurer, the debts of the insurer would be paid in the order specified in the Insurers (Reorganisation and Winding Up) Regulations 2004. The order is:

(a) first, preferential debts (employees and pension scheme contributions);
(b) second, insurance debts (debts to which an insurer is or may become liable under a contract of insurance other than a contract of reinsurance); and
(c) third, all other debts.

For an insurer which carries on only long-term insurance business, this will mean that, after payment of preferential debts, all of the remaining assets of the insurer, whether or not allocated to long-term insurance funds, would be available to meet debts under its contracts of direct long-term insurance, with only the residue of its assets being applied to pay other debts (including debts due under reinsurance contracts[12]). For an insurer which carries on both long-term insurance business

---

[12] For this reason it is usual for insurers who obtain reinsurance to seek security from the reinsurer for debts owed under the reinsurance contract. Such security is usually obtained in the form of a *pari passu* floating charge over some or all of the assets of the reinsurer. The effect of such a charge is that, on a winding-up of the reinsurer, the insurer will receive the amount which it would have received if the debts owed to it under the reinsurance contract had been insurance debts. *See* also Section 9.5.9.

and general insurance business, long-term insurance assets would be applied in priority to the payment of preferential debts attributable to the insurer's long-term insurance business and its long-term insurance debts, and only if there were any residue would such assets be available for the payment of preferential debts attributable to its general insurance business or its general insurance debts or other debts.

9.4.10   Transactions with connected persons

Previously IPRU(INS) 3.4 placed restrictions on the use of long-term insurance assets in transactions with connected persons. This rule has now been revoked as it was considered complicated and difficult to construe and was generally waived by the FSA. However, certain rules do continue to apply to transactions with connected persons. Restrictions apply to the use of assets of a with-profits fund to make a loan to, or to give a guarantee to or for the benefit of, a connected person. In selecting assets for its linked policies, a firm must ensure that there is no reasonably foreseeable risk of a conflict of interest with its linked policyholders. An insurer is required to provide details of material connected party transactions as part of its annual FSA returns.

9.5   Linked business

9.5.1   Introduction

The classes of long-term insurance business listed above in s.9.4.1 include class III: linked long-term. Contracts comprising this class of business are described in the Financial Services and Markets Act 2000 Regulated (Activities Order) 2001 (SI 2001/544) (the "Regulated Activities Order" or "RAO") as:

"contracts of insurance on human life or contracts to pay annuities on human life where the benefits are wholly or partly to be determined by reference to the value of, or the income from, property of any description (whether or not specified in the contracts) or by reference to fluctuations

471

in, or in an index of, the value of property of any description (whether or not so specified)".

With-profits policies and linked policies provide the principal means by which policyholders may use insurance policies for long-term investment. Under a linked policy, the benefits are determined directly by reference to the performance of particular assets or indices during the term of the policy, irrespective of either the performance of other aspects of the insurer's business or the past or expected future performance of those assets. This feature distinguishes linked policies from with-profits policies, where benefits depend on the discretionary bonus rates which are declared by the insurer which often (though not always) depend on the performance of the insurer's overall business and, through the practice of smoothing, on performance in previous years and expected future performance.

To the extent that the benefits under the policy are determined by reference to particular assets or indices, and the insurer covers the policy by investing in the same assets or indices, the insurer will be subject to no investment risk in respect of the policy—all of the investment risk will be taken by the policyholder. As a result, insurers are permitted to hold a lower amount of capital resources in respect of such policies than they are required to hold in respect of other types of policy, so linked business is generally less expensive for an insurer to operate than other types of business.

Linked policies may be issued in a pure form, where the benefits depend solely on the performance of particular assets or indices.[13] More commonly, however, they include ancillary

---

[13] The question has arisen whether such a policy is truly a contract of insurance, since it would appear that there is no assumption of risk by the insurer. It has been held that such a policy will constitute a contract of insurance provided that payment would be required to be made on the death of the policyholder or on his survival to a certain date, even if payment might also be required to be made at other times, for example on early surrender of the policy by the policyholder: *Fuji Finance Inc* v *Aetna Life Assurance Co Ltd* [1997] Ch. 173. This is consistent with the Regulated Activities Order which includes, within the list of contracts of insurance, contracts "wholly" determined by reference to the relevant assets or indices.

provisions under which the insurer will guarantee that a certain minimum payment will be made on the death or critical illness of the policyholder during the term of the policy or on maturity of the policy at a certain date. The policy may also provide for waiver of premium benefits during illness or redundancy of the policyholder, so that the policyholder will accrue benefits even though he temporarily ceases to pay the premium. Where a self-invested personal pension scheme ("SIPP") is covered by an insurance policy, the policy will generally take the form of a linked policy.

Linked policies typically allow the policyholder from time to time to change the assets and indices by reference to which the policy benefits are determined. Some policies, commonly referred to as "hybrid" policies, provide both linked benefits and with-profits benefits and allow the policyholder to vary the proportions of the two types of benefits.

It is not only investment policies that may take the form of a linked policy. Annuity policies may also take the form of a linked policy. A linked annuity policy will provide for the level of income to be determined by reference to the performance of particular assets or indices rather than, for example, by reference to a fixed escalation rate or an escalation rate based on interest rates or inflation.

A policy may be a linked policy without either the insurer or the policyholder expressly intending that it should be. For example, a term assurance policy might include a provision whereby the benefits payable, in the event of the death of the policyholder, will be increased each year by reference to an index of property values. This would make the policy a linked policy and the index would need to be an "approved index" (*see* below).

When considered as an investment product, a linked policy operates similarly to an investment in a collective investment scheme, such as a managed fund, a UCITS scheme, a limited partnership, an open-ended investment company or a unit trust. Linked policies and collective investment schemes are therefore typically targeted at the same investors, and details of performance of the two products are commonly listed together in market publications. Linked policies have the advantage that the provider, as an insurer, is able to supplement the policy with insurance benefits, such as a guaranteed payment on death. If a linked policy constitutes pension business, the insurer will not be taxed on the income and gains on the assets covering the policy and this benefit will be passed on to the policyholder by reason of the value of the assets being greater than if deductions had to be made for payment of tax. On the other hand, insurance regulation imposes more restrictive limits on the assets by reference to which the benefits under linked policies can be determined, most notably in respect of derivatives, so managers of collective investment schemes generally have greater flexibility which, in theory, may give them the ability to generate higher returns (or make larger losses).

9.5.2 Sources of rules and guidance

Linked policies are recognised in the Consolidated Life Assurance Directive, in which they are referred to in various provisions as "assurances linked to investment funds".

The FSA Handbook contains rules relating to linked policies in a number of different sourcebooks. Chapter 21 of the *Conduct of Business Sourcebook* ("COBS") sets out principles by which firms must operate their linked business and rules limiting the types of assets and the indices by reference to which policy benefits may be determined.

The rules of the *Prudential Sourcebook for Insurers* ("INSPRU") which deal with the calculation of the capital resources requirement of an insurer include special provisions relating to long-term insurance business class III (i.e. linked policies), requiring a lower amount of capital resources for these policies than for other types of policy. The rules of the *General Prudential Sourcebook* ("GENPRU") and INSPRU which deal with the determination of the amount of a firm's capital resources also provide that certain deductions that apply in respect of other types of business do not apply in respect of assets held to cover linked liabilities.

INSPRU also lays down rules on matching of assets and liabilities for index-linked liabilities and property-linked liabilities which are in some respects less restrictive than the rules which apply in respect of other liabilities.[14]

Linked policies are recognised distinctly in FSA returns and in the accounts of insurers. For example, insurers are required to identify the value of assets held to match linked liabilities and to provide valuation summaries of property-linked contracts and index-linked contracts. In its audited annual company accounts an insurer must state the value of assets held to cover linked liabilities in a separate line in the assets section of its balance sheet and it must state the amount of its technical provisions for linked liabilities in a separate line of the liabilities section of its balance sheet.

The FSA rules are supplemented by industry guidance in the *Guide of Good Practice for Unit Linked Funds* published by the Association of British Insurers. The FSA has indicated that it expects this guide to be applied by the insurance industry as the "foundation of unit-linked fund governance".

Because of the similarity of linked policies to investments in collective investment schemes, insurers operating linked policies have in the past referred to FSA rules and guidance relating to collective investment schemes, which are now contained in the Collective Investment Schemes Sourcebook. Reference to these rules and guidance is still sometimes made

---

[14] INSPRU 1.1.34(4)(b) provides that the ordinary rules requiring matching of assets and liabilities do not apply to index-linked liabilities or property-linked liabilities (except to the extent of any guaranteed benefit) and INSPRU 3.1.54 provides that the rules requiring currency matching of assets and liabilities do not apply to assets held to cover index-linked liabilities or property-linked liabilities. INSPRU 3.1.57 imposes rules for covering property-linked liabilities and INSPRU 3.1.58 imposes rules for covering index-linked liabilities. These rules do not apply to pure reinsurers, which are subject to more general principles set out in INSPRU 3.1.61A.

in practice, though to a lesser extent than before 2007 now that a fuller set of FSA rules for linked policies has been settled.

9.5.3   Unit-linked policies and unit-linked funds

A common form of linked policy is a unit-linked policy. Generally, the insurer will have established one or more internal funds, referred to as unit-linked funds or linked funds, each of which will have a specific investment policy. Each unit-linked fund will be operated on a basis whereby, in the books of the insurer, it is notionally ring-fenced from the rest of the insurer's business, so that all income and gains on the assets are recorded as being paid into it.

Premiums will be allocated to one or more of these funds at the direction of the policyholder. In return for the premium, the policyholder will be allocated units in the funds. The number of units allocated will depend on the current unit price of units in the fund, which will be calculated, broadly, by dividing the net asset value of the fund by the current number of units.

When a payment is to be made to the policyholder under the policy, some or all of the units allocated to the policyholder will be cancelled. The payment to the policyholder will depend on the number of units cancelled and the unit price at the time of cancellation. If the unit price has increased, the policyholder will receive a payment greater than the premiums he has paid. On the other hand, if the unit price has fallen, the policyholder will receive a payment which is less than the premiums he has paid.

The method of calculating the unit price is clearly of key importance in ensuring fairness to policyholders—both in relation to the payment made to an individual policyholder on cancellation of his units and in relation to the effect on the unit-price of the fund by reason of the allocation of units to other policyholders and the cancellation of units of other policyholders. The *Guide to Good Practice for Unit Linked Funds* sets out guidance for the determination of unit prices and states that:

"Unit prices should be calculated in a fair and transparent manner, which means: (1) Cross-subsidy among policyholders or individual funds should be avoided as far as reasonably possible; and (2) the pricing mechanism should not be used as a deliberate means of extracting value from the fund or from policyholders."

9.5.4 *Property-linked liabilities and index-linked liabilities*

The FSA rules distinguish between:

(a) "property-linked liabilities", which are linked to cash and assets. Property-linked liabilities include liabilities linked to unit-linked funds which contain property which fluctuates in value from time to time. However, they also include liabilities linked to specific property, such as residential property held in a self-invested personal pension scheme; and

(b) "index-linked liabilities", which are linked to indexes.[15]

The rules governing the two types of liabilities differ slightly, primarily in terms of how the liabilities may be covered by the insurer. The two types of liabilities are also reported separately on the insurer's FSA returns. In drafting a linked policy, it is necessary to take care to ensure that the policy creates the type of liability which the insurer intends. For example, a policy under which benefits are linked to the FTSE-100 Index will

---

[15] As defined in Annex I of the Consolidated Life Assurance Directive, class III business is "assurance . . . linked to investment funds". Article 25 extends this to include a "share index or some other reference value". The definition of linked business in the Regulated Activities Order (quoted at Section 9.5.1 above) refers to "fluctuations in, or in an index of, the value of property of any description". Read literally, this would require an index used for linked business to be "an index of . . . the value of property" (and this is supported by the definition of "index-linked benefits" in the FSA Glossary), which would appear to be narrower than "some other reference value" in art.25. For example, it might be questioned whether an average earnings index is an index of the value of property, though it is clearly a reference value. In practice, however, the FSA seems to take a wide interpretation of the meaning of an index of the value of property, since it introduced specific rules to permit the use of an average earnings index for linked business in certain circumstances: *see* COBS 21.3.5. *See* also Section 9.5.7.1.

create index-linked liabilities, whereas a policy linked to a unit-linked fund holding FTSE-100 Index swaps will create property-linked liabilities.

9.5.5   The structure of the FSA rules

Following consultation during 2007, the FSA introduced new rules governing linked business which became effective in October 2007. These rules can be divided into three categories:

(a)   general principles with which insurers carrying on linked business are required to abide;
(b)   more detailed rules setting out the indices and the types of assets by reference to whose value benefits under linked policies may be linked: these indices and assets are referred to as "permitted links"; and
(c)   rules requiring insurers to ensure "close matching" between the assets which are held to cover the liabilities under linked policies and the amount of those liabilities: these rules are referred to as the "close matching rules".

A firm will only be able to enter into linked business in respect of which it is able to comply with the rules in all three categories. For example, a firm wishing to link benefits to assets which would be permitted links may be unable to do so if the unavailability of the assets for purchase in the market would mean that it could not comply with the close-matching rules.

9.5.6   Principles for firms engaged in linked long-term insurance business

In what is a good example of principles-based regulation, the FSA has produced a set of general principles with which insurers carrying on linked business must comply. These principles cover the following matters:

(a)   valuation;[16]

---

[16] COBS 21.2.1: "A firm must ensure that the values of its permitted links are

(b) liquidity;[17]
(c) borrowing and other liabilities;[18]
(d) policyholder acceptance of risk profile;[19]
(e) systems and controls;[20]
(f) conflicts of interest;[21]

---

determined fairly and accurately". The reference to "permitted links" should probably be read as referring to linked liabilities and linked assets.

[17] COBS 21.2.2: "A firm must ensure that its linked assets: (1) are capable of being realised in time for it to meet its obligations to linked policyholders; and (2) are matched with its linked liabilities as required by the close matching rules". This principle has replaced the previous requirement that individual assets should be "readily realisable" so that the liquidity requirement now applies to a unit-linked fund as a whole (*see* PS 07/17, para.2.4). This principle will avoid the problems that previously arose where the temporary suspension in trading of shares of a particular company would cause a technical breach of the rules. The principle remains of particular relevance where a unit-linked fund is invested in real property, since the time which it takes to sell property may make it difficult to realise cash quickly.

[18] COBS 21.2.3: "A firm must ensure that there is no reasonably foreseeable risk that the aggregate value of any of its linked funds will become negative". This principle is designed to prevent the scenario where, for the account of a unit-linked fund, a firm borrows money and uses it to purchase assets which subsequently fall in value, with the result that the liabilities of the fund exceed the value of its remaining assets. The effect of such a scenario would be that the policy payouts would be reduced to zero, but since they cannot be reduced below zero (as the firm cannot require policyholders to make further payments to meet the liabilities), the firm would bear the investment risk, which is contrary to the basis on which linked business operates (and the reduced capital requirements that apply). A specific rule applies to "gearing" in relation to investment in "permitted land and property", so that, with certain exceptions, the borrowing must not exceed 10 per cent of the gross asset value of the fund. Rules require that derivatives should be "covered", which should prevent them being used in a way which causes the value of a unit-linked fund to become negative.

[19] COBS 21.2.4: "A firm must notify its linked policyholders of the risk profile and investment strategy for the linked fund: (1) at inception, and (2) before making any material changes". It may be questioned whether this principle requires an insurer to notify policyholders where it makes a material change to the specific risk profile and investment strategy which it has applied in practice where the change is still consistent with the profile and strategy which was previously described to policyholders.

[20] COBS 21.2.5: "A firm must ensure that its systems and controls and other resources are appropriate for the risks associated with its linked assets and linked liabilities". In the consultation process, the FSA indicated that this would include being able to understand and explain (to the FSA) the risks arising from the linked assets. It would follow that firms should ensure that they gain a real understanding of the linked assets and not simply rely on external fund managers to determine what is appropriate.

[21] COBS 21.2.6: "(1) A firm must ensure when selecting linked assets that there is no reasonably foreseeable risk of a conflict of interest with its linked policyholders. (2) If a conflict does arise, the firm must take reasonable steps to ensure that the

(g) substance over form;[22] and
(h) communication with the FSA.[23]

---

interests of the linked policyholders are safeguarded". Read literally, this rule would seem to have the effect that where the firm realises that a conflict of interest will arise from purchasing a particular asset, it should not purchase the asset. In the consultation process, the FSA gave as an example the decision to purchase a commercial property. If a person connected with the firm was a tenant, the purchase of the asset would give rise to a conflict of interest (for example, in a decision whether to evict the tenant for rent arrears), so the firm should not purchase the property. If the firm had already purchased the property then it would have to act so as to safeguard the interests of policyholders. The question arises whether this principle would apply to investment in units in a collective investment scheme managed by a person connected with the firm. Such investment would potentially give rise to a conflict in that the manager would be remunerated according to the value of the assets under management, so a decision by the firm to redeem units would result in lower remuneration for the manager. It seems unlikely that the FSA would have intended this result, as such investments are common. The principle may be compared with the rules in SYSC 10 which apply to banks and investment firms, which accept that conflicts of interest will arise and emphasise the need for the firm to manage them. A question also arises whether the principle applies only to the "selection" of assets (as a literal construction would imply) or whether it applies also to transactions in which the assets are applied, for example, stock-lending transactions with connected persons using the linked assets. On a literal interpretation, the principle would not extend to transactions in which the assets are applied, but in the consultation process the FSA specifically identified stock-lending transactions as another example of where a conflict of interest may arise.

[22] COBS 21.2.7: "In applying the rules in this section, a firm must consider the economic effect of its permitted links and linked assets ahead of their legal form". In the consultation process, the FSA explained that this principle would work in two ways. It would prevent a firm from arranging an asset so that it meets the literal characteristics of a permitted link while its economic effect was of an asset which was not a permitted link—for example, a deposit whose return was based on an index which was not a permitted index. On the other hand, it would allow the FSA to permit (presumably by granting a waiver) the inclusion of assets which do not satisfy the formal requirements of permitted links—for example, because of different forms of ownership of property in other jurisdictions. The FSA stated that it did not intend the principle of economic effect to apply to investments in authorised collective investment schemes, so a firm would not be required to look through to the investments of an authorised collective investment scheme to determine what their true economic effect would be.

[23] COBS 21.2.8: "A firm must notify the FSA in writing as soon as it becomes aware of any failure to meet the requirements of this section". Given the generality of the principles, it might be asked whether notification would be required where the firm thinks that, on one possible interpretation of the principles, there has been a failure to meet the requirements. Taking this principle together with Principle 11, it would be prudent to notify the FSA where the scenario poses any material risk to policyholders.

Drafting these rules as general principles means that there is less risk that firms will find themselves in breach of the rules because of short-term technical infringements, such as occurred when shares in Railtrack were suspended from trading in 2001 and, as a result, they no longer satisfied the previous "readily realisable" requirement. On the other hand, the open texture of general principles means that there may be less certainty about what is consistent with them—for example, on what constitutes a "conflict of interest" or what constitutes a "reasonably foreseeable risk". This creates the difficulty that the firm which adopts the least conservative interpretation may offer the most attractive returns to policyholders, thereby penalising firms who are the most conservative in their approach to compliance.

9.5.7 The indices and assets by reference to which benefits may be determined

FSA rules provide that an insurer may not contract to provide benefits under a linked policy that are determined:

(a) wholly or partly, or directly or indirectly, by reference to fluctuations in any index other than an "approved index";
(b) wholly or partly by reference to the value of, or the income from, or fluctuations in the value of, property other than one or more of 11 specified types of assets.[24]

9.5.7.1 Approved indices

In order to be an approved index, an index must fall into one or more of four categories included in the definition of "approved index" in the FSA Glossary. This definition was not changed by

---

[24] COBS 21.3.1(2): "(a) approved securities; (b) listed securities; (c) permitted unlisted securities; (d) permitted land and property; (e) permitted loans; (f) permitted deposits; (g) permitted scheme interests; (h) [deleted—*see* below]; (i) cash; (j) permitted units; (k) permitted stock lending; and (l) permitted derivatives contracts". Item (h) was originally "income from (a) to (g)", but it was unnecessary because income is already covered by the opening wording of COBS 21.3.1(2) and the inclusion of (h) may have created the implication that income received in a form which was not otherwise a permitted link would have been a permitted link, which was not intended.

the rules which followed the main 2007 consultation process, but it was subsequently extended to include the average earnings index, as explained more fully below.

Two categories of approved index are defined generally, depending on the characteristics of the index, rather than the particular subject matter of the index. In each case the index must be based on constituents that are permitted links (that is, other approved indices or the assets which constitute permitted links), but in one case the index must be calculated independently, published at least once a week and calculated on a publicly available basis according to rules satisfying certain conditions and in the other case there must be a listed derivative contract in respect of the index.

The other two categories of approved index are more specific. First, the index may be an index of retail prices published by the government of a Zone A state (states being members of the EEA, full members of the OECD and certain others). In May 2011, the FSA issued guidance that it considers that, in the UK, this includes both the Consumer Prices Index and the Retail Prices Index. Second, it may be the average earnings index, but only when used for the purposes of orders made under s.148 of the Social Security Administration Act 1992 by the Department for Work and Pensions. These orders apply where the underlying liabilities are to pay a guaranteed minimum pension under a defined benefit occupational pension scheme.

The need for inclusion of the average earnings index is a good example of where the rules which apply to linked business can restrict firms even where they are not deliberately setting out to write linked business. Firms entering into bulk annuity contracts to buy out the liabilities of defined benefit pension schemes were finding that such schemes could include liabilities linked to the average earnings index. If the firm were to assume the liability, it would therefore be providing benefits linked to the average earnings index which, until it was included in April 2008, was not an approved index. The reason for excluding it was the view that it would not be possible for a firm to comply with the close matching rules in relation to business linked to the average earnings index (*see* Section 9.5.8), but the FSA is now satisfied that it may be possible to comply with the close matching rules and has issued guidance on this matter.

9.5.7.2 *Assets which comprise permitted links*

The assets which constitute permitted links consist of:

(a) securities which are approved securities,[25] listed securities[26] or permitted unlisted securities;[27]
(b) land and property which is permitted land and property;[28]
(c) loans and deposits which are permitted loans[29] or permitted deposits;[30]

---

[25] An "approved security" is a security issued or guaranteed by the government of a Zone A state; a loan to or deposit with the central bank of an EEA state or one of a number of international institutions; or a debenture issued before 1995 by the Agricultural Mortgage Corporation Ltd or the Scottish Agricultural Securities Corporation Ltd.

[26] A "listed security" is a security included in an official list, but, because of the principle of substance over form, it may exclude a unit in a scheme or fund where, although the unit is listed, it does not fall within the definition of permitted scheme interest or permitted unit. *See* footnote 33 below. Similarly, it would be likely to exclude a derivative or quasi-derivative that was listed but which was not a permitted derivatives contract. Note that, as at the time of writing, in the UK, a security will only be included in an official list where it is included in the main market of the London Stock Exchange. It will not be included in an official list if, for example, it is listed only on AIM.

[27] A "permitted unlisted security" is any investment which is not a listed security but which is realisable in the short term. Under previous rules, the holding of unlisted securities was limited to 10 per cent by value of the unit-linked fund, but this limit was removed in 2007. There is no definition of "realisable in the short term", but previous rules required that unlisted securities should be capable of being realised within seven working days. The definition, by referring to "any investment", would imply that it would include investments which do not fall within the definition of "security" and, perhaps, units in collective investment schemes which fail to satisfy the definition of "permitted scheme interest". However, it is not clear that the FSA intended this result: *see* fn.33.

[28] To constitute "permitted land and property", an interest in land must be:
(a) considered by the firm to be located in a territory with a properly functioning market indicated by a number of specified criteria;
(b) either owned directly by the firm or held in a structure that does not pose materially greater risk to linked policyholders than direct ownership; and
(c) satisfies the gearing requirement, where applicable (*see* Section 9.5.7.3 (c)).

[29] A "permitted loan" is a loan to:
(a) an approved credit institution (broadly, an EEA bank);

(b)   an approved financial institution (broadly, the central bank of an EEA state or one of a number of international institutions);

(c)   an approved investment firm (this is not defined, but probably includes a UK authorised investment firm and a MiFID investment firm); or

(d)   any person provided that the loan is documented in a written agreement setting out certain terms and is fully secured by a mortgage or charge on permitted land and property that, except where the loan is made to a body corporate, is not used wholly or mainly for domestic purposes.

Note the requirement in (d) for the loan to be "fully secured", which would have the effect that if the value of the security fell below the value of the loan, the loan would cease to be a permitted link.

[30]   A "permitted deposit" is a deposit with:

(a)   an approved credit institution (broadly, an EEA bank);

(b)   an approved financial institution (broadly, the central bank of an EEA state or one of a number of international institutions); or

(c)   an approved investment firm (this is not defined, but probably includes a UK authorised investment firm and a MiFID investment firm).

(d) units in schemes and funds which are permitted scheme interests[31] or permitted units[32] or, possibly, listed securities;[33]

---

[31] Whether a unit (which would include a share or interest under trust or limited partnership interest) in a scheme or fund (including a unit trust or an open-ended investment company or a limited partnership) constitutes a "permitted scheme interest" depends in part on whether the policyholders whose benefits are linked to it are all institutional investors (trustees of defined benefit occupational pension schemes). If they are, then the units can be in:
(a) an authorised fund (that is, an open-ended investment company or a unit-trust scheme authorised by the FSA)
(b) a "recognised scheme" (a scheme authorised in an EEA state under the UCITS Directive and recognised in the UK and certain other broadly equivalent schemes recognised in the UK);
(c) a scheme falling within the UCITS Directive;
(d) a "non-UCITS retail scheme" (a scheme authorised in the UK which may be marketed to retail customers);
(e) a "qualified investor scheme" (a scheme authorised in the UK which may be marketed only to sophisticated investors) or its EEA equivalent; or
(f) an unregulated collective investment scheme that invests only in permitted links and publishes its prices regularly.
If some or all of the policyholders whose benefits are linked to the units in the scheme or fund are not institutional investors, then the scheme must fall into one of points (a) to (f) above, with two additional requirements which apply to (e) and (f). First, in the case of a qualified investor scheme, the scheme must invest only in permitted links and publish its prices regularly. Second, the total value of the units in schemes in (e) and (f) which are held in a linked fund must not exceed 20 per cent of the gross asset value of that linked fund. Note that an "unregulated collective investment scheme" must still be a "collective investment scheme", so it must not be excluded from the definition by the Financial Services and Markets Act 2000 (Collective Investment Schemes) Order 2001 (SI 201/1062). A potential pitfall resulting from this Order is that a scheme in which each of the unit holders is in the same group as the operator will be excluded from the definition of collective investment scheme.
[32] A "permitted unit" is a unit in any real or notional fund that invests only in permitted links and is managed either wholly by the insurer or wholly or partly by (a) an agent on behalf of the insurer or (b) a reinsurer in relation to a reinsurance contract with the insurer; for which agent or reinsurer the insurer retains all responsibility towards its linked policyholders. One example of a permitted unit would arise where a firm invests the assets of a linked fund in units in another of its own linked funds. Reinsurance is considered in more detail below: *see* Section 9.5.9.
[33] It is not clear whether units which do not satisfy the definition of "permitted scheme interest" or "permitted units" but which do satisfy the definition of "listed security" or "permitted unlisted security" will be permitted links. On a literal interpretation, they will be, but it is necessary to consider what the FSA intended by the principle in COBS 21.2.7 whereby a firm must consider the economic effect of its permitted links and linked assets ahead of their legal form. The FSA's reference to GENPRU Annex 7(3) in para.3.19 of CP 07/07 would suggest that it would not accept that such units would be permitted links.

(e)   stock-lending agreements and repos which constitute permitted stock lending;[34] and

(f)   derivatives and quasi-derivatives which are permitted derivatives contracts.[35]

Examples of assets which do not constitute permitted links are commodities (such as gold, oil or paintings) and derivatives which do not satisfy the requirements of being permitted derivatives contracts because they are not effected or issued on

---

[34] "Permitted stock lending" arises where a firm enters into a stock-lending transaction that satisfies INSPRU 3.2.36A–3.2.42. These rules impose conditions on:

(a)   the assets that may be the subject of the transaction (which in the case of linked business must be permitted links);

(b)   the identity of the counterparty; and

(c)   the adequacy and availability of the collateral obtained to secure the obligation of the counterparty.

For the purposes of linked business, three further provisions are made:

(a)   if the linked policyholders bear the whole of the risk, they must receive the whole of the recompense (net of fees and expenses);

(b) the extent of any risk that the policyholders bear must be disclosed to them; and

(c)   where the risk is borne outside the linked fund, the linked fund should receive a fair and reasonable recompense for the use of the assets of the linked fund: INSPRU 3.2.36A.

[35] A "permitted derivatives contract" is a derivative (a contract for differences, an option or a future) or quasi-derivative (an asset which has the effect of a derivative, such as a credit linked note) which satisfies INSPRU 3.2.5 to INSPRU 3.2.35 as applied in relation to assets covering liabilities in respect of linked business. These rules impose conditions on:

(a)   the purpose for which the derivative or quasi-derivative is held (which must be efficient portfolio management or reduction of investment risk);

(b)   the assets held to "cover" the derivative or quasi-derivative (which, where the firm may be required to transfer particular assets or the income from particular assets, must be those assets which must be permitted links, and, where the firm may be required to pay a monetary amount, must be permitted links that are sufficient in value so that the firm reasonably believes that following reasonably foreseeable adverse variations, it could pay the monetary amount in the right currency when it falls due); and

(c)   the manner in which the derivative is effected or issued (which must be on or under the rules of a regulated market or off-market with an approved counterparty on certain terms and such that it will be capable of valuation).

An important change which was introduced following the 2007 consultation process was that, in determining whether a derivative or quasi-derivative is held for the purpose of efficient portfolio management in relation to permitted links, it is no longer necessary to show that it is held for one of the three specific purposes listed in INSPRU 3.2.6 (*see* also PS 07/17, para.2.28). This will remove the previous doubt that existed regarding whether a firm could hold an inflation-linked swap (or other index-linked swap) in a linked fund where it wished to provide property-linked benefits linked to inflation.

or under the rules of a regulated market or with an approved counterparty. It is not clear whether units in a collective investment scheme which do not satisfy the definition of "permitted scheme interest" but do satisfy the definition of "listed security" or "permitted unlisted security" are intended to be permitted links.[36]

9.5.7.3   Limits on certain assets

Certain assets are subject to limits on the amount which may be held in a particular unit-linked fund. Except for unit-linked funds which are made available exclusively to institutional linked policyholders, no more than 20 per cent of the gross assets of a unit-linked fund may consist of interests in unregulated collective investment schemes.

Investment in land and property in a unit-linked fund must be restricted so that the borrowing against it, taken together with borrowing against property held in unregulated collective investment schemes in which units are held by the unit-linked fund, does not exceed 10 per cent of the gross asset value of the unit-linked fund. However, in certain circumstances this limit does not apply when the relevant policyholder requests, directly or indirectly, the firm to hold the land or property.

In the past, a 10 per cent limit applied to investment by unit-linked funds in unlisted securities. This limit was removed by the FSA in 2007.

9.5.8   The close-matching rules

FSA rules require an insurer to maintain close matching between the assets covering linked liabilities and the linked liabilities.

INSPRU 3.1.57 requires that property-linked liabilities are covered as closely as possible with the assets to which those liabilities are linked or a property-linked reinsurance contract

---

[36] *See* fn.33.

or a combination thereof. In practice, covering property-linked liabilities is often achieved by maintaining the unit-linked funds containing the assets to which the liabilities are linked, including, where a reinsurance contract is effected, the units in the reinsurer's unit-linked fund which are held under the reinsurance contract. In this scenario, the assets constituting the permitted links and the assets covering the liabilities will be the same.

This rule is supplemented by guidance in INSPRU 1.5.35, under which a firm should not apply unit-linked assets for any purpose other than to meet the relevant liabilities. INSPRU 1.5.36 requires that the firm must select, allocate and manage its unit-linked assets taking into account its contractual obligations and its regulatory duty to treat customers fairly.

INSPRU 3.1.58 sets out a wider variety of methods of covering the index-linked liabilities. The methods include holding "a portfolio of assets whose value or yield is reasonably expected to correspond closely with the index-linked liabilities". The rule also allows the insurer to cover index-linked liabilities with an index-linked reinsurance contract or with an approved derivative or an approved quasi-derivative (that is, a derivative or quasi-derivative which satisfies the admissibility requirements).

The requirement to maintain close matching does not apply to pure reinsurers, which are required to comply with the principles in INSPRU 3.1.61A. In practice, however, a pure reinsurer would be unlikely to operate its property-linked business differently from an insurer carrying on direct business.

9.5.9 Use of reinsurance

As noted at 9.5.8 above, an insurer may satisfy the close-matching rules, in whole or in part, with a property-linked or an index-linked reinsurance contract. Under such a contract, the reinsurer would agree that, upon the insurer making a claim, it would pay benefits to the insurer linked to the same property or index to which the insurer's liabilities under the primary unit-linked policy are linked.

It is common for a property-linked reinsurance contract to provide that the insurer will acquire units in unit-linked funds of the reinsurer. This type of reinsurance contract serves a dual function. First, it is used to cover the property-linked liabilities of the insurer as described in Section 9.5.8 above. Second, the units which the insurer acquires under it are treated as assets of the unit-linked fund of the insurer, to which the benefits payable by the insurer are linked.[37] In order to serve this second function, it is necessary for the units to be permitted links. Specifically, the units must be "permitted units"—that is, units in a real or notional fund (the unit-linked fund of the reinsurer) that invests only in permitted links and is managed by a reinsurer for whom the insurer retains all responsibility towards its linked policyholders.

The requirement for the insurer to retain towards its linked policyholders all responsibility for the reinsurer is mirrored by the requirement that a firm that has entered into a reinsurance contract in respect of its linked policies "must nevertheless discharge its responsibilities under its linked long-term insurance contracts as if no reinsurance contract had been effected". These two requirements leave some doubt about exactly how far the insurer's responsibilities extend. It would appear that the FSA intends the insurer to be responsible to policyholders for negligence or a breach of contract by the reinsurer to the extent that this impacts adversely on policyholders. However, it does not appear that the FSA intends the insurer to assume the credit risk of the reinsurer provided that it makes adequate disclosure to policyholders of the implications of any credit risk exposure they face in relation to the solvency of the reinsurer. The FSA has stated that there is no requirement for an insurer to hold capital against the possibility that a reinsurer may default, unless the terms of the policy are that the insurer, and not the policyholder, is exposed to that risk.

---

[37] Although the reinsurance is treated as an asset for the purposes of the unit-linked rules, it is nevertheless treated as reducing mathematical reserves for the purposes of reserving rules.

It is therefore important in drafting a linked policy to make clear whether the policyholder or the insurer will bear the credit risk of the reinsurer. In addition to the policy provisions, marketing material should clearly disclose the risk to which the policyholder will be subject. Where the policyholder will bear the credit risk of the reinsurer, it may also be necessary to disclose that if the reinsurer becomes insolvent, the policyholder may not be able to make a claim under the Financial Services Compensation Scheme for any resulting loss which he suffers.

Since 2004, it has become important for an insurer which enters into a property-linked reinsurance contract to seek security over the long-term insurance assets of the reinsurer. This is because the Insurers (Reorganisation and Winding Up) Regulations 2004 have the effect that, on the winding-up of a UK reinsurer, insurance debts owed to the reinsurer's direct policyholders will be paid in priority to other unsecured debts, including debts owed to insurers to whom the reinsurer provides reinsurance. By way of exception, the Regulations provide that secured debts will be paid in priority to direct insurance debts. It has therefore become standard practice in the context of property-linked reinsurance contracts for the reinsurer (where it also writes direct business) to enter into a *pari passu* floating charge in favour of the insurer on terms that, in enforcing the charge, the insurer will recover no more than the amount which it would have recovered if the debt owed to it under the reinsurance contract had ranked *pari passu* with the insurance debts owed to the reinsurer's direct policyholders.

Where an insurer enters into a property-linked reinsurance contract, it should take care to ensure that the terms of the reinsurance match the terms of the linked policy. This is particularly important in relation to rights which the reinsurer may have in certain circumstances under which it may defer payment to the insurer. Difficulties will arise if the insurer does not have an equivalent right to defer payment to the policyholder.

An insurer which effects a significant volume of reinsurance of its unit-linked business should have regard to the requirement to notify the FSA of large reinsurance exposures and to explain how they are being safely managed. Where the credit risk of the reinsurer is borne by policyholders, rather than by the insurer, the insurer will not technically have an exposure to the reinsurer. However, where the credit risk is of such a size that it would be a large reinsurance exposure if the insurer were bearing it, the insurer may nevertheless consider that it should notify the FSA of the reinsurance in accordance with Principle 11 and explain how the credit risk is being safely managed.

9.6   With-profits business

9.6.1   Introduction

The most complex area of long-term insurance regulation is the regulation of with-profits business. The basic objective of a with-profits policy—to provide the policyholder with a smoothed investment return on the premiums paid to the insurer—is deceptively simple and masks a whole range of issues which can arise essentially from the discretion that a firm has under the terms of the policy (for example, in relation to investment and bonus policy, smoothing and new business). It was this discretion, and the conflicts of interest which can arise from this discretion between policyholders and shareholders and different groups and generations of policyholders, which was the focus of the reforms which were introduced in 2004 in relation to the FSA's regulation of with-profits business. These reforms aimed to ensure greater consistency and predictability in the use by firms of the discretion available to them in relation to with-profits business, to improve transparency and communication with policyholders and to improve the governance of with-profits firms. The objectives of the reforms were neatly summarised by John Tiner when initial proposals for the reform of with-profits regulation were announced in January 2003 in the following terms:

"This package of measures will shine a searchlight into life insurers' boardrooms. It will show how discretion is exercised in with-profits funds and ensure that boards and senior management are accountable not only for the decisions they take but also for ensuring that they obtain actuarial advice where appropriate and can demonstrate that they have given proper attention to policyholders' interests".

The rules and guidance on with-profits regulation operate as a focus for the FSA's principles-based approach to regulation. Compliance with the rules and guidance is not sufficient: firms must also comply with the underlying principles. The FSA's Principles for Businesses which are particularly relevant to with-profits business are as follows:

(a) Principle 6: a firm must pay due regard to the interests of its customers and treat them fairly.
(b) Principle 3: a firm must take reasonable care to organise and control its affairs responsibly and effectively, with adequate risk-management systems.
(c) Principle 7: a firm must pay due regard to the information needs of its clients, and communicate information to them in a way which is clear, fair, and not misleading.
(d) Principle 8: a firm must manage conflicts of interest fairly, both between itself and its customers and between a customer and another client.

9.6.2 What is a with-profits policy?

Under a with-profits policy, the policyholder is normally promised a relatively modest guaranteed sum on death or on survivorship to a particular age. This sum is augmented by the declaration of regular (usually annual) bonuses by the firm, broadly reflecting the profits made by the company from the premiums paid by the policyholder, topped up by a final bonus paid on maturity of the policy. Regular bonuses are normally guaranteed (in other words, they increase the guaranteed payout that the policyholder can expect on maturity) and are referred to as "reversionary" bonuses. By contrast, final bonuses, sometimes referred to as "terminal" bonuses, are not normally guaranteed. The firm will deduct charges from the policy for administration and investment management and also for costs such as the cost of guarantees.

Bonuses on the policy are "smoothed" from one year to another in order to shield policyholders from short-term fluctuations in investment markets. This means that the firm has to have sufficient reserves to pay "over the odds" when markets fall but, at the same time, must hold back part of the investment returns that it makes when there are steep rises.

Most firms aim to pay the policyholder "smoothed asset share" on the maturity of the policy (assuming that the guaranteed value of the policy is not higher; if the guaranteed value is higher then the guaranteed value will be paid). The asset share is broadly an accumulation of premiums paid by the policy-holder plus (or minus) investment returns less charges, expenses and tax.

A policyholder who cashes in his policy before maturity is said to have surrendered the policy. In these circumstances, the policyholder will normally have no right to guaranteed amounts under the terms of his policy and will therefore receive an amount based on the value of his policy (i.e. the asset share) with deductions made for the firm's costs in administering the surrender.

Payouts to policyholders in advance of maturity may be subject to the application of a "Market Value Reduction" or "MVR" (this is sometimes known as a "Market Value Adjuster" or "MVA"). An MVR will typically be applied where the payout could otherwise exceed the value of the underlying assets as a result of adverse market movements.

With-profits policies are normally allocated to with-profits funds that are either 90:10 or 100:0. In a 90:10 fund, at least 90 per cent of the profits of the fund which the directors of the firm decide to distribute are allocated to the with-profits policies through bonuses and the balance will be allocated to the shareholders of the firm. In a 100:0 fund, 100 per cent of the profits which the directors decide to distribute are allocated to the with-profits policies.

9.6.3 The old regime

There were a number of weaknesses in the regulatory regime prior to the introduction of the reforms in 2004. Perhaps the most significant was the lack of any requirement on a firm to explain publicly how it exercised its discretion in relation to, and accordingly managed, its with-profits business. Under the Insurance Companies Act 1982, which was repealed by FSMA 2000, the regulator was permitted to intervene in the management of a firm's business if it considered this to be desirable for protecting policyholders and potential policyholders against the risk that the firm may be unable to fulfil the reasonable expectations of policyholders or potential policyholders. As a result of this power of intervention, firms took account of what they considered to be "policyholders' reasonable expectations" in their management of their with-profits businesses.

Policyholders' reasonable expectations were generally considered to be shaped by the following factors:

(a) the terms of the contracts between the policyholders and the firm;
(b) statements made to policyholders by the firm;
(c) the firm's past practice; and
(d) practice in the industry.

However, it was left to the Appointed Actuary of the firm to decide what policyholders' reasonable expectations were— there were no objective standards by reference to which the views of the Appointed Actuary could be judged. It was also up to the Appointed Actuary to decide what amount of assets were required to meet the firm's liabilities and to sign off the regulatory returns filed each year with the regulator with no independent review or oversight.

A further weakness in the regulatory system was that the regulatory returns focused on the contractual liabilities of firms and not sufficiently on the non-guaranteed payouts that policyholders were entitled to expect. This, coupled with the gradual shift within with-profits businesses from the use of guaranteed reversionary bonus to unguaranteed terminal bonus, had resulted in the regulatory solvency position of with-profits firms becoming increasingly irrelevant. This in turn increased the risk of over-allocation of assets to particular groups and generations of policyholders to the detriment of other policyholders.

9.7   Current regulation of with-profits businesses

9.7.1   Overview

The current regulation of With-Profits businesses can be divided into the following categories:

(a)   rules that have direct implications for the management of With-Profits policies or With-Profits funds;
(b)   more specialist rules which deal with closed funds and inherited estates;
(c)   rules requiring publication of details relating to the management of the with-profits fund and communication with policyholders;
(d)   special rules dealing with the capital requirements for with-profits businesses; and
(e)   rules which impose requirements on the governance of with-profits businesses.

9.7.2   The management of with-profits policies and with-profits funds

9.7.2.1   Introduction

FSA regulation of with-profits policies and with-profits funds is intended to address specific situations where the risk of conflicts of interest giving rise to unfair treatment of policy-holders is considered to be particularly acute. However, as a general principle a firm should give careful consideration to any aspect of its operating practice that has a bearing on the interests of its with-profits policyholders to ensure that it does not lead to an undisclosed or unfair benefit to shareholders. In addition, neither the FSA's rules nor indeed Principle 6 relieve a firm of its obligation to deliver each policyholder's contractual entitlement.

9.7.2.2 *Amounts payable under with-profits policies (maturity and surrender payments)*

The basic requirement in relation to payouts on the maturity or the surrender of a with-profits policy is that the firm must have good reason to believe that its payouts are fair. This general requirement is supported by the following more specific requirements:

(a) Unless a firm cannot reasonably compare maturity payment with a calculated asset share, it must set a target range for maturity payouts which includes 100 per cent of unsmoothed asset share.

(b) A firm may make a maturity payment that falls outside the target range if it has a good reason to believe that at least 90 per cent of maturity payments on with-profits policies in the relevant group have fallen, or will fall, within the relevant target range.

(c) A firm must manage its with-profits business with the aim of paying on each with-profits policy a maturity payment that falls within the relevant target range.

For a surrender payment, the FSA's rules require a firm to calculate the payment as if it was a maturity payment. Deductions may then be made if necessary, in the reasonable opinion of the firm's governing body, to protect the interests of the firm's remaining with-profits policyholders. Deductions are therefore permitted for the firm's costs arising from effecting and administering the surrender.

9.7.2.3   *Market value reductions*

The FSA's rules state that a firm must not apply a market value reduction to the value of a with-profits policy unless:

(a)   the market value of the with-profits assets backing the policy is significantly less than the value of the policy; or
(b)   there has been, or there is expected to be, a high volume of surrenders.

9.7.2.4   *Distributions*

Under the FSA's rules, a firm must not make a distribution from a with-profits fund (in other words, pay a regular or final bonus) unless the whole of the cost of the distribution can be met without eliminating the regulatory surplus in the with-profits fund. In addition, the amount distributed to policyholders must not be less than the "required percentage" (the percentage attributable to policyholders) of the total amount distributed (in other words, at least 90 per cent of the amount distributed in a 90:10 fund).

9.7.2.5   *Charges and costs*

There are several of the FSA's rules which have implications for charges and costs which may be allocated to asset shares or with-profits funds as follows:

(a)   A firm may make deductions from asset share to meet the cost of guarantees or the cost of capital only under a plan approved by the firm's governing body and described in the Principles and Practices of Financial Management. Any such deductions must be proportionate to the costs they are intended to offset, and must not change unless justified by changes in the business or economic environment, or changes in the nature of the firm's liabilities as a result of policyholders exercising options under their policies. If charges for the cost of guarantees and capital are not sufficient to cover the actual cost, the firm has to fund the deficit otherwise than by making deductions from asset shares.

(b) Unless it is a mutual, a firm must not pay compensation or redress from a with-profits fund unless that compensation or redress is paid from assets which are attributable to shareholders, or unless the event which gave rise to the requirement for compensation or redress occurred prior to 31 July 2009. Assets attributable to shareholders in a with-profits fund would include assets which had been specifically injected into the with-profits fund by share-holders and also the shareholders' portion of any bonus distribution which has not yet been transferred to the shareholders' fund, but would not include the inherited estate of the with-profits fund except to the extent that part of it has been attributed to shareholders. A mutual may pay compensation or redress from a with-profits fund, but not from assets attributable to asset shares unless in the reasonable opinion of the governing body the compensa-tion or redress cannot be paid from any other assets in the with-profits fund. Rectification payments made to correct a previous error are not treated as compensation or redress.

(c) A firm may only charge costs to a with-profits fund which have been, or will be, incurred in operating the with-profits fund. This may include a fair proportion of the firm's overheads.

(d) A firm must not charge a contribution to corporation tax to a with-profits fund if that contribution exceeds the notional corporation tax liability that would be charged to that with-profits fund if it were assessed to tax as a separate body corporate.

9.7.2.6 New business

The FSA's rules state that if a firm proposes to effect new contracts of insurance in an existing with-profits fund, it must only do so on terms that are, in the reasonable opinion of the firm's governing body, unlikely to have a material adverse effect on the interests of its existing with-profits policyholders.

If it is difficult or impossible for a firm to mitigate the risk of a material adverse effect on its existing, or new, with-profits policyholders, it may be appropriate to establish a new bonus series or with-profits fund. Circumstances that might cause a firm to establish a new bonus series or with-profits fund include:

(a) where the firm has a high level of guarantees or options in its existing with-profits policies, which might place an excessive burden on new with-profits policies, or vice versa; and

(b) where the potential risks are likely to be so great that a single with-profits fund cannot provide adequately for the interests of new and existing policyholders. Such potential risks are likely to arise from significant differences in the terms and conditions of the new and existing with-profits policies, including the basis on which charges are levied and reviewed.

9.7.2.7 *Investment strategy*

FSA guidance states that when a firm determines its investment strategy, and the acceptable level of risk within that strategy, it should take into account:

(a) the extent of guarantees in its with-profits policies;

(b) any representation that it has made to its with-profits policyholders;

(c) its established practice; and

(d) the amount of capital support available.

There is also guidance in relation to specific investments which may be held in a with-profits fund:

(a) If a proprietary firm is considering using with-profits assets to finance the purchase of another business, or if a firm is considering whether it should retain such an investment, it should consider whether the purchase or retention would be, or will remain, fair to its with-profits policyholders. When a firm makes that assessment it should consider whether it would be more appropriate for the investment to be made using assets other than those in a with-profits fund.

(b) If a firm carries out non-profit insurance business in a with-profits fund, it should review the profitability of the non-profit insurance business regularly.

9.7.2.8 *Major changes in a with-profits fund*

A firm must not enter into a material transaction relating to a with-profits fund unless, in the reasonable opinion of the firm's governing body, the transaction is unlikely to have a material adverse effect on the interests of that fund's existing with-profits policyholders. A material transaction includes a series of related non-material transactions which, if taken together, are material. Examples of material transactions include:

(a) a significant bulk outwards reinsurance contract;

(b) inwards reinsurance of with-profits business from another insurance undertaking;

(c) a financial engineering transaction that would materially change the profile of any surplus expected to emerge on the with-profits fund's existing insurance business; and

(d) a significant restructuring of the with-profits fund, especially if it involves the creation of new sub-funds.

9.7.2.9 *Proposals for reform*

In February 2011 the FSA published its Consultation Paper CP 11/5 "Protecting with-profits policyholders" in which it made various proposals for amendments to the rules in COBS 20. At the time of writing, the FSA has not formally published the results of the consultation. Among the points of most significance are proposals regarding the interests of with-profits policyholders in with-profits funds, charges to with-profits funds (in particular, for services provided by companies in the insurer's own group), the writing of new business, strategic investments, market value reductions, reattributions and governance. If implemented, some of the proposals would have a significant effect on with-profits businesses. This will be the case in particular for mutual insurers (that is, insurers who are owned by their policyholders rather than by shareholders). For some time the FSA has been considering the extent to which mutual insurers should have to take into account the interests of their existing policyholders as owners of their businesses. Depending on the outcome of its review, its views about the precedence to be given to these interests may severely affect the ability of mutual insurers to write new business, meaning that many of them may be forced to close to new business.

9.7.3   Closed funds

The number of closed with-profits funds (or "zombie funds" as they are sometimes referred to) has increased significantly since 2000 (in many cases as a direct reaction to the sustained bear market which began in early 2000) to the point where they now represent a large proportion of the long-term insurance market. In September 2004, the FSA estimated that out of 110 with-profits funds, 66 were closed to new business. These closed funds had assets of around £191 billion representing approximately a fifth of the assets invested in the entire long-term savings market.[38] Further statistics published by the FSA in 2010 suggested that, as at the end of 2009, the value of assets held in closed funds had fallen to £110 billion, but represented one third of the total with-profits assets held in the UK.[39] Certainly until recently, the general perception of closed funds was that they delivered poor returns to policyholders (because of conservative investment strategies) who themselves were trapped in the funds by low surrender values.

Closed with-profits funds have therefore been an area of focus for the FSA over the last few years. The FSA's own review of the sector in 2004 drew the following conclusions:[40]

---

[38] These statistics were published by the FSA in an insurance sector briefing on closed funds which was released in September 2004.

[39] "With-profits regime review report", FSA, June 2010.

[40] These conclusions were published in the FSA's sector briefing on the regulation of closed with-profits funds released in September 2004.

(a) Funds do not close to new business only because of financial weakness. Other reasons for closure can include changes in business strategy, a desire to move away from capital-intensive lines of business such as with-profits, the viability of the fund in terms of size going forward and changes in the economic and regulatory environment.

(b) While some closed funds have performed poorly, others have performed well. It is therefore difficult to generalise in relation to the performance of closed funds. It may be perfectly sensible for a policyholder to hold a policy to maturity in a closed fund but for another policyholder in another closed fund to surrender his policy.

FSA rules for the regulation of with-profits business apply to closed funds just as much as they apply to open funds. However, closed funds pose particular issues which do not arise in relation to open funds, including the following:

(a) the need for an investment policy which meets the expectations of different groups of policyholders (in particular to ensure that investments can be realised during the lifetime of the policies), and at the same time safeguards the solvency of the fund as it runs off;

(b) the potential rise in costs charged to policies because of redundancy payments to staff and other up-front costs as a result of closure to new business and because of the loss of "economies of scale" as the fund runs off;

(c) whether outsourcing of administration and investment management represents a fair deal for policyholders. Outsourcing is a common feature of closed funds, often used to combat the rise in costs caused by the loss of economies of scale which would otherwise have to be charged to policies;

(d) the ability to smooth returns as the fund runs off;

(e) the availability of comprehensive and timely information for senior management;

(f) the retention of senior staff with the skills to manage the business.

As a result of these issues confronting closed funds, the FSA will normally refocus its attention in slightly different areas if a fund closes to new business or is nearing closure. Because of these issues, the FSA also expects firms to tell policyholders if a fund is closed to new business and the implications of closure.

Whether a fund is open or closed depends primarily on whether the firm is actively seeking to effect or actually effecting new contracts of insurance. However, a fund may be closed but still accepting premiums on existing policies. COBS 20.2.54 therefore states that a firm will be taken to have ceased to effect new contracts of insurance in a with-profits fund in the following circumstances:

(a) When any decision by the governing body to cease to effect new contracts of insurance takes effect.
(b) Where no such decision is made, when the firm is no longer:
(i) actively seeking to effect new contracts of insurance in that fund; or
(ii) effecting new contracts of insurance in that fund, except by increment.

In addition, COBS 20.2.55 states that a firm must contact the FSA to discuss whether it has, or should be taken to have, ceased to effect new contracts of insurance if:

(a) it is no longer effecting a material volume of new with-profits policies in a particular with-profits fund, other than by reinsurance; or
(b) it cedes by way of reinsurance most of the new with-profits policies which it continues to effect.

If a firm ceases to effect new contracts of insurance in a with-profits fund, it must:

(a) inform the FSA and its with-profits policyholders within 28 days; and

(b) submit a run-off plan to the FSA explaining how the run-off of the fund will be managed as soon as reasonably practicable and, in any event, within three months.

The run-off plan must demonstrate that the firm will ensure a fair distribution of the closed fund and its inherited estate (if any).

When a firm tells its with-profits policyholders that it has ceased to effect new contracts of insurance in a with-profits fund, the FSA expects the firm also to explain:

(a) why it has closed to new business;
(b) what changes it has made, or proposes to make, to the fund's investment strategy (if any);
(c) how closure may affect with-profits policyholders (including any reasonably foreseeable effect on future bonus prospects);
(d) the options available to with-profits policyholders and an indication of the potential costs associated with the exercise of each of those options; and
(e) any other material factors that a policyholder may reasonably need to be aware of before deciding how to respond to the closure of the fund.

9.7.4 Inherited estate

9.7.4.1 Identification and distribution of inherited estate

Almost all with-profits funds have assets in excess of liabilities known as "inherited estate". These assets are owned by the firm and can arise from a variety of sources (for example, shareholder contributions where the fund was first established or the prudent management of the fund). The sizes of inherited estates vary from fund to fund (in some cases up to several billions of pounds of assets). An inherited estate does not simply represent unutilised, surplus assets of a with-profits fund. An inherited estate supplies the working capital of a with-profits fund by providing reserves for smoothing and for the cost of guarantees as well as allowing the fund to invest a higher proportion of its assets than would otherwise be possible in equities and thereby giving policyholders the opportunity to receive better payouts. An inherited estate also provides a buffer against adverse market performance and therefore further financial security for policyholders. The amount of extra capital that a firm will aim to hold in a with-profits fund over and above regulatory capital requirements will depend on the risk appetite which the firm considers to be appropriate for the fund.

Under COBS 20.2.21, at least once a year, the firm's governing body must determine whether a with-profits fund has an "excess surplus". An excess surplus is defined as assets held in a with-profits fund which are in excess of the value required to cover liabilities (including future discretionary bonuses) and regulatory capital requirements and to support new business plans. If a with-profits fund has an excess surplus, and to retain that surplus would be a breach of its duty to treat its customers fairly under Principle 6, the firm should:

(a) make a distribution from the with-profits fund; or
(b) carry out a reattribution.

Any distribution of excess surplus would be made by way of policy bonus, by allocation in the normal proportion between policyholders and shareholders (i.e. 90:10 in a 90:10 fund).

9.7.4.2 Reattribution of inherited estate

A reattribution of inherited estate will normally involve a firm asking its with-profits policyholders to acknowledge that they have no interest in any possible future distribution of inherited estate in return for a payment. The benefit of a reattribution to the company is that the inherited estate can be transferred from the with-profits fund to a non-profit fund, which in turn allows the company to take greater credit for the inherited estate in its financial statements and to use the estate for a wider range of objectives. However, the estate will continue to support the with-profits fund after the reattribution by providing reserves for the cost of smoothing and guarantees, security and financial strength for the fund.

In 2005, the FSA introduced specific rules for reattributions of inherited estate for the first time. The most significant change was the introduction of a Policyholder Advocate to negotiate the terms of the reattribution with the firm on behalf of policyholders. This requirement arose from concerns that in previous reattributions there had been no one to represent the interests of policyholders and negotiate the terms of the reattribution with the firm.

The precise role of the Policyholder Advocate will depend on the nature of the firm and the reattribution proposed. However, the FSA expects the role of the Policyholder Advocate to include:

(a) negotiating with the firm, on behalf of the relevant with-profits policyholders, the benefits to be offered to them in exchange for the rights or interests they will be asked to give up;

(b) commenting to with-profits policyholders on aspects of the reattribution including the methodology used for the allocation of benefits amongst the relevant with-profits policyholders and the form of those benefits, the criteria used for determining the eligibility of the various with-profits policyholders and the terms and conditions of the proposals; and

(c) telling with-profits policyholders with reasons whether the firm's proposals are in their interests.

The FSA's role in relation to a reattribution is to facilitate negotiations between the firm and the Policyholder Advocate and to consider whether the reattribution proposals agreed between the firm and the Policyholder Advocate are fair to policyholders. If the FSA concludes that the proposals are unfair, it will challenge the firm, where necessary using its regulatory powers under the FSMA 2000, for example by imposing a requirement on the firm if it considers this is necessary to protect the interests of policyholders.

Recent statements made by the FSA reaffirm that its assessment of fairness starts with the principle set out in the Ministerial Statement of February 1995 that, in a 90:10 fund, the basis of distributions to policyholders and shareholders will be in the proportions of 90 per cent and 10 per cent respectively. If the reattribution proposal is to divide value between policyholders and shareholders on a basis that is different to the 90:10 starting point, the FSA will look at the basis for that proposed division and decide whether it is fair, compared with policyholders awaiting a potential future 90:10 distribution.

9.7.5 Principles and Practices of Financial Management ("PPFM")

9.7.5.1 Introduction

Firms are subject to a number of FSA rules requiring them to publish how they manage their with-profits businesses and to communicate with their policyholders. The most important of these is the requirement to publish information on the management of a with-profits business in a Principles and Practices of Financial Management or "PPFM".

9.7.5.2 Publicity and communication with policyholders

As the name suggests, PPFMs are divided into principles and practices. Principles must be enduring statements of the overarching standards which the firm adopts in managing its with-profits business, and must describe the business model used by the firm in meeting its duties to with-profits policyholders and in responding to longer-term changes in the business and economic environment. In contrast, practices should describe the firm's approach to managing its with-profits business and responding to changes in the business and economic environment in the shorter term. Practices are expected to change as the firm's circumstances and the business environment change every few years.

A firm must not change its PPFM unless, in the reasonable opinion of its governing body, that change is justified to:

(a) respond to changes in the business or economic environment;
(b) protect the interests of policyholders; or
(c) change the firm's practices in order to achieve its principles better.

A firm may also change its PPFM if that change is necessary to correct an error or omission, would improve clarity or presentation without materially affecting the PPFM's substance, or is immaterial. Any such change does not have to be notified to policyholders. Other changes to the PPFM must be notified to policyholders, in the case of a change to a principle, at least three months in advance, and in the case of a change to a practice, within a reasonable time either before or after the change is made.

Given the areas where firms have discretion in relation to with-profits business, it should be no surprise that PPFMs are required to cover investment and bonus policy, smoothing, charges and expenses, volumes of new business, the management of any inherited estate and how it is proposed to achieve a balance between the interests of with-profits policyholders and shareholders. Perhaps of greater significance are two specific but potentially wide-reaching requirements for the contents of the PPFM as follows:

(a) PPFMs are required to contain sufficient detail to enable a knowledgeable observer to understand the possible risks and rewards from effecting or maintaining a with-profits policy with the firm.
(b) PPFMs must cover the exposure of the firm's with-profits business to business risk. Business risk can include a number of exposures including exposure to risks from other investments, for example in investment management companies and service companies.

9.7.5.3 Consumer-friendly PPFM

FSA rules also require firms to produce a consumer-friendly PPFM or CFPPFM. This reflects the fact that PPFMs must be prepared with a knowledgeable observer in mind rather than the average policyholder whose understanding of with-profits is likely to be limited if not negligible. A consumer-friendly PPFM is therefore required to be expressed in clear and plain language that can be easily understood by a with-profits policyholder who does not possess any specialist or technical knowledge. The CFPPFM must describe the most important information set out under each heading in the PPFM and must be publicly available and prominently signposted on the firm's website.

The firm must also provide its CFPPFM free of charge with any:

(a) written notice sent to with-profits policyholders on proposed changes to its with-profits principles (where the firm must provide the version of the CFPPFM in use before the changes if this has not already been provided);
(b) annual statements sent to its with-profits policyholders (unless there has been no material change in the CFPPFM since it was last supplied); and
(c) key features document for a with-profits policy.

9.7.5.4 Annual report to with-profits policyholders

The FSA's rules require a firm to produce an annual report to its with-profits policyholders, and it must do the following:

(a) State whether, throughout the financial year to which the report relates, the firm believes it has complied with its obligations relating to its PPFM and setting out its reasons for that belief.
(b) Address all significant relevant issues, including the way in which the firm has:
    (i) exercised, or failed to exercise, any discretion that it has in the conduct of its with-profits business; and

    (ii) addressed any competing or conflicting rights, interests or expectations of its policyholders (or groups of policyholders) and, if applicable, shareholders (or groups of shareholders), including the competing interests of different classes and generations.

In preparing the annual report to with-profits policyholders, a firm should take advice from its With-Profits Actuary.

9.7.6 Prudential requirements for with-profits businesses

The FSA has made special prudential rules relating to the assets and capital required to be maintained in respect of with-profits business. These rules may be broken down into two categories:

(a) two rules relating to the amount of assets which must be maintained in each with-profits fund; and

(b) rules increasing the firm's capital requirement where, on a realistic measure of the assets, liabilities and risks relating to its with-profits business, the amount of capital actually required is greater than the regulatory capital requirement determined according to the ordinary regulatory rules.

9.7.6.1 Rules requiring minimum assets to be held in each with-profits fund

Under INSPRU 1.1.27, a firm must have admissible assets in each of its with-profits funds of a value sufficient to cover the technical provisions and other long-term insurance liabilities relating to all of the business in that fund. Under INSPRU 1.1.28, a realistic basis life firm[41] must ensure that the "realistic value of assets" for each of its with-profits funds is at least equal to the "realistic value of liabilities" of that fund.

---

[41] A "realistic basis life firm" is a firm which has with-profits liabilities in an amount equal to or exceeding £500 million, or which has at any time since 31 December 2004 had such an amount of with-profits liabilities unless it now has no with-profits liabilities, or which has, by notice to the FSA, made an election to be treated as a realistic basis life firm: *see* the definition in the FSA Glossary and GENPRU 2.1.19.

The concepts of "realistic value of assets" and "realistic value of liabilities" are defined at length in INSPRU 1.3. In overview, their purpose is, as their names suggest, to establish a realistic measure of the value of assets and liabilities, with the rules governing what may and may not be taken into account in measuring value being different in certain respects from those which would normally apply. For example, the realistic value of assets includes the value of admissible assets held in excess of asset and counterparty limits, the present value of future profits of non-profit insurance contracts and the value of inadmissible derivatives, all of which would normally be left out of account in valuing the assets of the insurer available to cover its liabilities. The realistic value of liabilities includes the cost of future actions which the firm, in the exercise of its discretion, may or may not decide to take, such as the payment of final bonuses and shareholder transfers out of the with-profits fund. Such liabilities are not taken into account in the determination of mathematical reserves.

Because of the overlap between the determination of mathematical reserves and the calculation of the realistic value of liabilities, realistic basis life firms are, in certain respects, allowed to calculate their mathematical reserves on a less onerous basis than other firms. For example, they do not have to take into account discretionary benefits, including annual bonuses.

9.7.6.2   *Rules increasing the firm's capital requirement*

As has been more fully explained in Chapter 4, UK insurers are required to hold a minimum level of capital resources equal to the applicable base capital resources requirement. The base capital resources requirement applies from the point of authorisation, irrespective of the amount of business written. When business has been written, the base capital resources requirement may be overridden by a higher requirement, the calculation of which differs depending on whether the insurer is a realistic basis life firm or a regulatory basis only life firm.[42]

---

[42] A "regulatory basis only life firm" is any firm carrying on long-term insurance business other than a realistic basis life firm.

For a regulatory basis only life firm, the capital requirement is the sum of the long-term insurance capital requirement and the resilience capital requirement. For a realistic basis life firm, it is the sum of the long-term insurance capital requirement and the with-profits insurance capital component. The rules are summarised broadly in Figure 9.1.

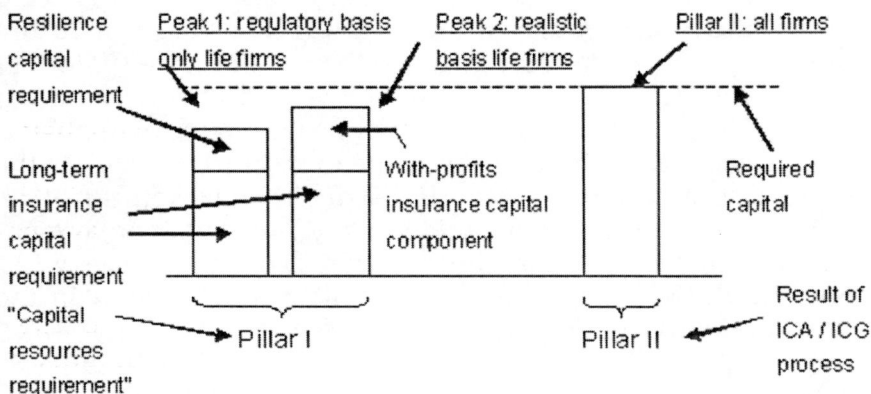

Figure 9.1 Rules increasing the firm's capital requirement

The resilience capital requirement has been described in Chapter 4. Its purpose is to require the insurer to hold additional capital to cover the shortfall in the value of its assets, as compared to the value of its liabilities, that might arise in certain prescribed hypothetical future scenarios.

The with-profits insurance capital component ("WPICC") performs a similar function, although it covers more than just the relative movements of assets and liabilities. It seeks to determine the full range and realistic value of a firm's assets and the full range and realistic value of a firm's liabilities. For each with-profits fund a calculation is made of the excess of (a) the assets over (b) the sum of the liabilities and capital requirement, each determined on an ordinary (or "regulatory") basis. This indicates the level of capital which each with-profits fund appears to contribute to the firm's overall resources under the ordinary regulatory valuation—referred to as the "regulatory excess capital" of the fund. A separate calculation is then made of the excess of (a) the assets over (b) the sum of the liabilities and capital requirement (or "risk capital margin"), this time determined on a "realistic" basis. This indicates the true (or "realistic") level of capital which the with-profits fund is actually contributing to the firm's overall resources— referred to as the "realistic excess capital".

If the regulatory excess capital of a with-profits fund exceeds the realistic excess capital of the fund then the difference is added to the with-profits insurance capital component. Otherwise no change is made to the with-profits insurance capital component—there is no reduction in respect of a with-profits fund whose realistic excess capital exceeds its regulatory excess capital.

The process is repeated for each with-profits fund, and the with-profits insurance capital component is then determined.

The principle underlying this process is that the ordinary ("regulatory") valuation of assets and liabilities may make it appear that an insurer has more capital than in fact it has. If, on a realistic valuation, the firm has less capital than is suggested by the regulatory valuation then some adjustment needs to be made to reflect this.

An intuitive adjustment would be to require the firm to make a deduction in the calculation of its capital resources, or simply to require it to report its level of capital resources on a realistic basis. However, this would create complications in the methodology for the calculation of capital resources and lead to inconsistency when comparing it with regulatory basis only life firms and other regulated entities.

Therefore, the preferable, though perhaps less intuitive, adjustment is to increase its capital requirement through the addition of the with-profits insurance capital component. The difference between the regulatory and realistic valuations is then reflected by the narrowing of the margin between the firm's capital resources (determined on a regulatory valuation) and its capital requirement, initially determined on the regulatory valuation but increased by the results of the realistic valuation. This margin will be narrowed by the same amount as it would have been if the capital resources had been reduced and the capital resources requirement had been left intact. If the firm's capital resources happened to be less than the amount of capital required on the realistic basis (the sum of the long-term insurance capital component and the with-profits insurance capital component) then it would have to hold more capital resources or it would be in breach of the FSA rules.

9.7.7 Governance for with-profits businesses

9.7.7.1 Introduction

Consistently with the Senior Management Arrangements, Systems and Controls ("SYSC") part of the FSA Handbook, the FSA's approach is that governance arrangements for with-profits businesses should "be appropriate to the scale and complexity of a firm's with-profits business" and should "involve some independent judgement in assessing compliance with its PPFM and addressing conflicting rights and interests of policyholders and, if applicable, shareholders". The main additional components for governance of with-profits businesses are provided by the With-Profits Actuary and the With-Profits Committee.

9.7.7.2 The With-Profits Actuary

The With-Profits Actuary focuses specifically on the with-profits business of the firm and advises the Board on areas where discretion is exercised in relation to with-profits, such as bonus policies.

The position of the With-Profits Actuary is bolstered by regulations which require a firm to keep the actuary informed of the firm's business and other plans, provide the actuary with sufficient resources, and hold such data and establish such systems as the actuary reasonably requires. The firm must also request the actuary's advice on the likely effect of a material change in the firm's business plans on with-profits policyholders and pay due regard to that advice.

9.7.7.3 The With-Profits Committee

As explained above, the governance arrangements expected by the FSA should involve some independent judgement to assess compliance with the firm's PPFM and address conflicting rights and interests of policyholders and, if applicable, shareholders. This may be (and frequently is) achieved by establishing a With-Profits Committee. A With-Profits Committee is simply a committee of the firm's governing body, including non-executive members of the governing body and possibly some external non-directors with appropriate skills and experience.

In the past the FSA has expressed concern that firms are not doing enough to provide independent input into the management of with-profits funds, and that some firms aim merely to comply with FSA guidance on independent judgement rather than considering the "bigger picture" in terms of the duties to treat customers fairly and manage conflicts of interest.[43]

9.7.7.4 Reporting requirements

In its annual FSA return (*see* Chapter 4), a firm is required to present its mathematical reserves and its realistic balance sheet, both of which are subject to audit. The auditor is required to appoint an independent reviewing actuary to advise him privately on the reasonableness of the valuation of policyholder liabilities. In addition, the directors must confirm that they have taken and had due regard to actuarial advice and that the with-profits business has been managed in accordance with the firm's PPFM.

---

[43] Press release issued by the FSA on 27 September 2007 relating to its thematic review of the management of with-profits funds. The issues identified by the review were explained in more detail in the FSA letter to CEOs of insurers dated 29 September 2007.

In respect of each financial year, the With-Profits Actuary is required to make a written report addressed to the relevant classes of the firm's with-profits policyholders as to whether, in his opinion, the annual report and the discretion exercised by the firm in respect of the period covered by the report may be regarded as taking, or having taken, the interests of the relevant classes of the firm's with-profits policyholders into account in a reasonable and proportionate manner.

Chapter 10

Sale and Administration of Life Assurance

Maria Ross,
Partner

Laura Hodgson,
Professional Support Lawyer: Norton Rose LLP

10.1　General

10.1.1　Overview

The Conduct of Business Sourcebook ("COBS") came into force on 1 November 2007 in order to implement the Markets in Financial Instruments Directive 2004/39/EC ("MiFID"). It replaced the previous COB rules. In introducing COBS the FSA took the opportunity to move towards a more principles-based system of regulation in the UK. COBS is therefore a high-level set of rules reflecting fundamental principles, and to a large extent removes the detailed rules and guidance previously found in COB and the other parts of the FSA Handbook. The COBS rules reflect the legislative requirements set out in several European directives relevant to the sale and marketing of insurance, namely the Distance Marketing Directive 2002/65/EC, the E-Commerce Directive 2000/31/EC, the Consolidated Life Directive 2002/83/EC and the Insurance Mediation Directive 2002/92/EC.

In relation to the sale of insurance contracts, COBS generally applies to intermediaries and to product providers carrying on insurance mediation activity in relation to investment (as opposed to pure protection) insurance products. *See* Chapter 7, Section 7.8 for information on the sale of non-investment insurance contracts. COBS also requires product providers to produce product information and imposes requirements in relation to financial promotions and other communications.

10.1.2   MiFID

MiFID does not apply to the sale of insurance contracts. However, the FSA rules apply the MiFID regime to the sale of mixed business (i.e. designated investment business and business classed as MiFID business). This Chapter considers only the sale of life assurance and does not cover those parts of COBS relevant to a firm carrying out mixed business. Where a firm is carrying out mixed business it should consider both the COBS requirements outlined in this Chapter and the specific additional MiFID requirements set out in COBS.

10.1.3   Application of COBS

COBS provides a consolidated set of rules to be followed by both advisers and insurers ("firms") in the sale of investment insurance products to clients. COBS applies to the sale of designated investment business, which includes the sale of life products but does not, in general, apply to pure protection contracts (i.e. term assurance contracts). However, where a firm is dealing with pure protection policies it may choose to comply with (the more onerous requirements of) COBS instead of the rules set out in the Insurance Conduct of Business Sourcebook ("ICOBS"). *See* Chapter 7, Section 7.8 for an explanation of the application of the ICOBS rules.

The COBS rules cover the whole process of selling designated investment products to clients, from the moment that a firm first deals with a client to the post-sale information and cancellation rights. COBS sets out how a client should be classified by a firm and the time and manner in which a firm may communicate with its client. COBS also covers product suitability, disclosure of product information and disclosure of information on the firm and its services. The main purpose of

COBS is to ensure that suitable and appropriate advice or information is given by a firm to its client.

10.1.4 The sale process for a life insurance product

An intermediary is required to classify a client or potential client into specified categories. The purpose of this categorisation is to determine the client's rights and the firm's obligations towards them under the regulatory regime (*see* point (c) below).

(a) A firm advertises its products or is introduced to a client. At this initial stage a firm will need to comply with the financial promotion rules set out in COBS 4 and disclose information about itself and its services to the client before it undertakes any work on their behalf (COBS 5 (Distance Communications) and COBS 6 (Information about the firm, its services and remuneration))).

(b) Classification of the client (COBS 3 (Client Categorisation)). The different types of client are:
(i)   a retail client;
(ii)   a professional client (either per se or elective); and
(iii) an eligible counterparty (either per se or elective).

(c) If advice is to be given, a firm will need the client to complete a fact find to ascertain the client's particular needs and circumstances. This information will enable the firm to discuss and recommend products to the client (COBS 9 (Suitability)). The firm will at this stage supply the client with a key facts document and key features illustration which explain the main features of the product that the firm is recommending (COBS 13 (Preparing product information) and COBS 14 (Providing product information to clients)).

(d) Underwriting. Once the client chooses a product which is suitable to its needs the requisite underwriting information on the client will be provided to the product provider and the contract will be concluded.

(e) Post sale. Once a life insurance product has been sold, post-sale information, including details on the right to cancellation (COBS 15 (Cancellation)) and details on the actual commission which is payable to the firm will be provided to the client.

10.2 COBS 2—Conduct of Business obligations

10.2.1 COBS 2.1—Acting in a client's best interests

COBS 2.1 sets out the high-level principles with which every firm must comply when dealing with its clients. A firm has an overriding duty to ensure that, when dealing with a retail client, it acts at all times in an honest, fair and professional way and in accordance with the best interests of that particular client. The importance attached to these overriding obligations is underlined by the exclusion of liability set out in COBS 2.1.2—a firm cannot seek to exclude or restrict any duty or liability which it may owe towards its retail clients under the FSA Handbook. The only circumstances in which a firm may seek to restrict or exclude its liabilities (other than those prescribed by the FSA) are where a firm can show that in the specific circumstances it was honest, fair and professional to do so.

10.2.2 COBS 2.2—Information disclosure before providing services

Basic information on the firm itself must be provided to any new client before a firm starts providing services (COBS 2.2). The firm must provide the client with information on the type of services it offers (i.e. is it an appointed representative, tied agent or independent firm) and the type of products which it sells together with generic information on its costs and other associated charges.

10.2.3 COBS 2.3—Inducements

The restriction on both paying and receiving inducements set out in COBS 2.3 is designed to ensure that when a firm is advising on the suitability of a particular insurance product, it is acting in its client's best interests and is not encouraging the sale of specific products to clients in return for benefits from that product provider. The most obvious way in which a firm accepts a benefit from the sale of an insurance product is through the receipt of commission from the product provider, although "inducements" cover non-monetary as well as monetary benefits.

10.2.3.1 *When inducements can be paid or accepted*

Firms may only pay or accept inducements (being fees, commission or non-monetary benefits) in accordance with the rules in COBS 2.3. A firm may receive or pay an inducement to its client or a person acting on behalf of its client. It may also pay or accept proper fees which enable the provision of services, for example legal, regulatory or settlement fees.

An inducement can only be given to or received from a third party where the receipt or payment of the inducement does not impair compliance with the firm's duty to act in the best interest of its client and, in relation to personal recommendations given in respect of packaged products, disclosure of the existence of the inducement is made to the client before the provision of services takes place.

Disclosure will not be required for what are considered reasonable non-monetary benefits (as set out in COBS 2.3.15).

Where the exact amount of the benefit cannot be ascertained, for example where the commission includes a proportion of trail commission, then the method for calculating the amount should be disclosed to the client in a clear and accurate way. A firm is obliged to disclose the receipt of a benefit prior to providing services to its clients. A firm will be deemed to be compliant with COBS 2.3 if it discloses the "essential arrangements" relating to the receipt of the benefit in a summary form to the client and provides further details to its clients where this is requested. Note that the obligation to disclose such benefits does not arise where a firm is providing "basic advice", as described in more detail at Section 10.9.7.

10.2.3.2   Small gifts and hospitality

The COBS guidance on inducements (COBS 2.3.3–2.3.8) suggests that a non-monetary benefit includes the referral of actual or potential designated investment business to a third party. The COBS rules on inducements apply to the firm itself and any person acting on its behalf. A firm should have in place a conflicts of interest policy which clearly sets out for its employees the type of items which will be regarded as inducements and any levels of monetary value which should be used to benchmark the receipt of gifts or hospitality from a product provider. The guidance states that where an individual receives minor hospitality or a small gift from a product provider, then as long as the value is below the level specified in the firm's own conflicts of interest policy, this will not be regarded by the FSA as an inducement.

10.2.3.3   Packaged products, volume overrides and bonus commission

FSA guidance also sets out the FSA's view that where a firm is required to disclose commission in relation to the sale of a packaged product, it should not enter into volume override commission arrangements (i.e. where the commission rate is increased by reference to the volume of business written) with the product provider. Terms relating to the repayment of indemnity commission should also not result in additional financial benefit to the intermediary if the commission becomes repayable (e.g. repayment should be on commercial terms). The guidance also suggests that unless additional commission becomes payable as a result of an increase in premium, then receipt of any additional commission may be regarded as breach of the disclosure requirements set out in COBS 6.4.

10.2.3.4   Indirect benefits

COBS 2.3 also restricts the way in which a product provider (or members of its group) can hold equity (whether directly or indirectly), exercise voting power or provide loans to a firm making personal recommendations to retail clients in relation to packaged products (basically, IFAs). In the UK a number of product providers have an equity interest in intermediaries and, to a lesser extent, provide loans to intermediaries. These equity investments and loans are only permitted if the following conditions are met:

(a) the transaction is entered into on arm's-length commercial terms;
(b) the firm has reliable written evidence that the transaction has been entered into on this basis;
(c) there are no arrangements in connection with the equity interest or provision of credit which provide for the channelling of business from the intermediary to the product provider; and
(d) neither the product provider nor any of its associates is able to exercise any influence over the personal recommendations made by the intermediary in relation to packaged products.

The rules regarding equity ownership of intermediaries may cause problems because of the requirement that any transaction of this kind is undertaken on a commercial arm's-length basis. A large proportion of the value in an intermediary, particularly a new firm, is often based on the value of its future goodwill. In valuing the intermediary it is often difficult to attribute a valuation price to the intermediary's goodwill which values the goodwill properly whilst reflecting that the transaction is on a truly commercial arm's-length basis.

10.2.3.5 *Reasonable non-monetary benefits*

The table in COBS 2.3.15 sets out a list of reasonable non-monetary benefits which a firm may receive from product providers without breaching the client's best interests rule. Whilst this table is only indicative guidance, in practice it is often relied upon by intermediaries and product providers. Where a firm is receiving a benefit it is important to consider its full implications, as there can often be a narrow distinction between a reasonable non-monetary benefit and a non-monetary benefit which conflicts with the best interest rules.

The guidance in the table does not apply to a product provider's own representatives or to intra-group arrangements. The matters which are classed as reasonable non-monetary benefits include:

(a) gifts, hospitality and promotional competition prizes of a reasonable value;

(b) assistance by a product provider to promote a packaged product (as long as the assistance given is not of a type or value which impairs an intermediary's ability to act in the best interests of its clients, i.e. the intermediary offers packaged products from its whole range and not just from that product provider);

(c) joint marketing exercises by an intermediary and a product provider using either generic or specific product literature;

(d) the product provider taking part in seminars and conferences organised by the intermediary and paying towards the cost;

(e) training provided by the product provider (attending lectures, written material or software); and

(f) the payment by a product provider of an intermediary's reasonable travel and accommodation expenses in limited circumstances (e.g. when attending training provided by the product provider or visiting the product provider's offices to attend a client meeting).

Where product literature is being distributed, if it is generic product literature then it must enhance the quality of the service provided to the client and not be primarily of promotional benefit to the product provider. The cost of distributing such literature must be borne by the intermediary, not the product provider. Where specific product literature is to be provided by a firm then either the literature should not include the name of any other firm or, if the intermediary's name is included, the literature should not itself be primarily of promotional benefit to the intermediary.

10.2.3.6   *Technical services and information technology*

Another area which is classed as a reasonable non-monetary benefit by the FSA, but which often creates the most difficulty in practice for both product providers and intermediaries, is the provision of technical services and information technology. The COBS guidance suggests that a product provider can supply intermediaries with free phone links, access to data-processing facilities, third-party electronic dealing or quotation systems and software providing information on the product provider's packaged products. However, the supply of these types of technological support is only permitted where it can be demonstrated that its provision has generated an equivalent cost saving to both the product provider and the client. This test is difficult to satisfy as it is hard to imagine how in quantitative terms it could be demonstrated that the provision of product information software to intermediaries, which may result in a cost saving to the product provider (i.e. more efficiency in back-office systems and the processing of applications) will offer an equivalent cost saving to the client (i.e. reduced annual management charges).

10.2.3.7   *Records keeping: Inducements*

A firm must keep records of (i) all inducements it discloses to clients and (ii) all reasonable non-monetary benefits which it receives and does not need to receive. The records must be kept for at least five years from the date the benefit is provided.

10.3   COBS 3—Client categorisation

The first step which a firm must take when it accepts a new client is to classify them. This is to ensure that in all of the firm's dealings with the client, the required level of regulatory protection is afforded to them. This is dealt with in COBS 3.

10.3.1   Who is the client?

A client of a firm is any person who is a potential, existing or previous client and to whom the firm may, is or has provided a service in relation to its regulated activities. COBS 3 does not apply to firms which only provide basic advice.

10.3.2   Classification of clients

The detail of the client classification rules is set out below but Figure 10.1 shows the basic principles:

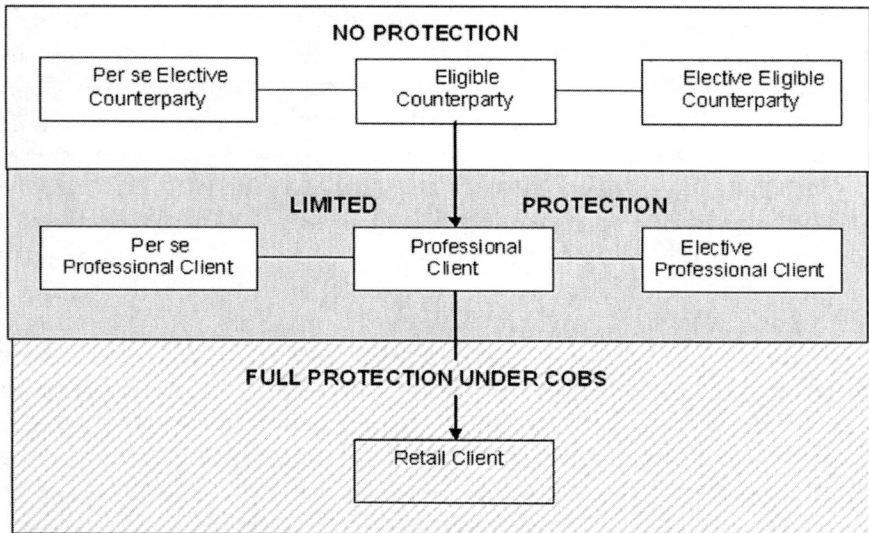

Figure 10.1 Client classification

10.3.3   Retail client

The definition of a retail client under COBS 3.4 is a client "who is not a professional client or an eligible counterparty". In the vast majority of circumstances a member of the general public will be regarded as a retail client and it is likely that most life insurance clients would be classified in this way.

In the case of appointed representatives or tied agents, a client is classified under COBS 3 as the client of the product provider rather than as a client of the intermediary.

10.3.4 *Professional client*

COBS 3.5 sets out who is regarded as a per se professional client. This list includes credit institutions, investment firms, pension funds, bodies corporate with either called-up share capital or net assets of at least £5 million and undertakings who meet two of the following three criteria: a balance sheet greater than €12.5 million; net turnover of €25 million; or who have, on average during the year, at least 250 employees.

The other type of professional client is an elective professional client. In order for a firm to treat a client as an elective professional client, an assessment must be made by a firm of the expertise, experience and knowledge of the client in light of the nature of the services and type of product which may be sold and that assessment must give the firm reasonable assurance that the client is capable of making its own investment decisions and understands the risks involved. For example, a sophisticated investor may fall into this category. Where a firm classifies a client as an elective professional client the client must agree in writing to be treated by the firm in this way, as they will be afforded less regulatory protection. The firm must notify an elective professional client of the protections and investor compensation rights it will lose as a result of being classified in this manner under COBS.

10.3.5 *Eligible counterparty*

COBS 3.6 sets out the criteria which are to be used in assessing whether a client is an eligible counterparty. It is highly unlikely that this categorisation would be applied to a client of a life insurance product provider. In order to be regarded as a per se eligible counterparty a client must fall into one of the following categories:

(a)   an investment firm;

(b)   a credit institution;
(c)   an insurance company;
(d)   a similar financial institution; or
(e)   a governmental, central bank or supranational organisa-
      tion.

Alternatively a client may be classified as an elective eligible counterparty. In order to be categorised as such a client must either be a per se professional client or an elective professional client and must be an undertaking rather than an individual. Where a client is classified as an eligible counterparty this will take them outside of the regulatory protections afforded by COBS. However, where the product being sold is a life product they would still be afforded regulatory protection under the Consolidated Life Directive. Due to the reduction in regulatory protection afforded to professional clients, it is very unusual for clients to be classified as non-retail clients or for the way in which a life assurance product is sold to reflect such classification.

10.3.6   *Providing a higher level of protection*

COBS requires the firm to allow both professional clients and eligible counterparties to request recategorisation in order that they might benefit from a greater degree of protection (COBS 3.7.1). The firm may, either on its own initiative or at the request of its client, treat as a professional client or a retail client, a client that would otherwise be a per se eligible counterparty. Similarly, a firm may treat a client who would otherwise be a professional client as a retail client.

Where a firm recategorises a client on its own initiative it should notify the client that it has done so.

10.3.7   *Record keeping*

A firm is obliged to notify a new client in writing of the classification which he has been given before services are provided to him by the firm. The firm must retain a record of the classification for a period of at least five years where the advice relates to a life policy, and in all other cases for three years.

10.4 COBS 4—Financial promotions

10.4.1 *Background to the financial promotion rules*

The Financial Services and Markets Act 2000 ("FSMA 2000") contains restrictions on the way in which investments may be advertised. Section 21 of the FSMA 2000 states that "a person must not, in the course of business, communicate an invitation or inducement to engage in investment activity" unless such person is an authorised person or the contents of that communication have been approved by an authorised person. The purpose of s.21 is to ensure that an authorised person is involved with any communications which are used by a firm for its clients or for consumers. Contravention of s.21 is a criminal offence which is punishable by either a fine and/or a maximum of two years in prison. It is an acceptable defence for a person to prove that they had reasonable grounds to believe that the communication had been prepared or approved by an authorised person or that they took all reasonable precautions and exercised all due diligence to avoid committing an offence under s.21. Certain exclusions to s.21 are set out in the Financial Services and Markets Act 2000 (Financial Promotion Order) 2005 ("FPO").

The legislation on financial promotions is embodied and expanded upon in COBS in relation to investment insurance contracts (*see* the remainder of this Section) and in ICOBS in relation to non-investment insurance contracts (*see* Chapter 7, Section 7.8). The use of advertising to market and sell insurance products is a major feature of the business of every product provider. Financial promotions can now be found in a wide range of media including the internet, television, text messaging, phone, radio and newspapers. The regulations now set out in COBS 4 have historically always been principles-based rules, and the move by the FSA to adopt principles-based regulation throughout COBS in November 2007 has not significantly changed the rules in this section. The overriding FSA principles of communicating information to clients in a way which is fair, clear and not misleading (PRIN 7) and treating customers fairly (PRIN 6) underpin the financial promotion rules set out in COBS 4. COBS applies to financial promotions made to clients in the UK, subject to exemptions in the FPO.

10.4.2 Application of the financial promotion rules

The financial promotion rules set out in COBS apply to every firm which communicates with a client in relation to designated investment business or communicates or approves a financial promotion. A firm is responsible for all financial promotions which are communicated by any of its appointed representatives, regardless of whether the financial promotion would otherwise fall within the exemption in Article 16 of the FPO for exempt persons. Where a firm is communicating with an eligible counterparty only the compensation provisions set out in COBS 4.4 will apply.

10.4.3 Jurisdiction of the financial promotion rules

The rules in COBS apply to any communication made to a client in the UK in respect of designated investment business. This includes where the communication is made by a "cold call" to a person outside of the UK unless the call is made from a place outside the UK and in relation to a business which is carried on outside of the UK. Guidance in COBS 4.1.10 states that the financial promotion rules will not apply to financial promotions which originate outside the UK and which are not capable of having an effect within the UK. In addition there are exemptions for overseas communicators if the financial promotion complies with the rules set out in COBS 4.9, as explained at Section 10.4.12.

10.4.4 Fair, clear and not misleading

A firm is obliged to ensure that any communication or financial promotion is fair, clear and not misleading (COBS 4.2.1). The rule applies to all communications by or approved by a firm to a client in relation to designated investment business, which are not a third-party prospectus, an excluded communication or a non-retail communication. Examples of the application of this rule by a firm include ensuring that the financial promotion clearly sets out whether a client's capital is at risk, explains clearly the charging structure which will be used, and names the FSA as the firm's regulator. The FSA guidance states that the fair, clear and not misleading rule should be applied in an appropriate and proportionate way taking into account the means of communication and the information that the communication is intended to convey. An example of this would be the difference in the information provided where a communication is being sent to a professional client as opposed to a retail client. COBS 4.2.4 sets out specific statements which must be made where a financial promotion relates to certain types of investment. If a firm is able to demonstrate that it took reasonable steps to ensure that a particular communication or financial promotion complied with the fair, clear and not misleading rule then this will be regarded as an adequate defence to any action for damages which may be brought by a client under s.150 of the FSMA 2000.

10.4.5 Financial promotion to be identifiable as such

Where a firm issues a financial promotion to a client then it must be clearly identifiable that the communication is to be regarded as a financial promotion. This rule applies to both the communication and approval of a financial promotion, but will not apply to the extent that the financial promotion is an excluded communication, image advertising or a non-retail communication or if it relates to a long-term care pure protection contract. Excluded communications are defined in the FSA glossary to include communications benefiting from an exemption under the FPO or FSMA 2000, personal quotes and one-off communications that are not "cold calls". Image advertising is a very simple, non-product specific advert which consists of one or more of the following features: the name of the firm, its logo, a contact point at the firm and a reference to the type of regulated activities provided by the firm or to its fees and commissions.

10.4.6   Communication with retail clients

Where a firm is providing information in relation to designated investment business which is likely to be received by a retail client, then the firm must comply with COBS 4.5. This rule states that the information provided to the retail client must:

(a)   include the name of the firm;
(b)   be accurate and not emphasise any potential benefits of the relevant business or investment without giving a fair and prominent indication of all relevant risks;
(c)   be sufficient for and presented in a way in which is likely to be understood by the person receiving it; and
(d)   not disguise, diminish or obscure important items, statements or warnings.

The FSA guidance states that where a firm is deciding how to communicate information to a client it should take into account the nature of the product or business, the risks involved and the likely information needs of the client. In addition the firm should consider whether the omission of any relevant fact will result in the information provided being insufficient, unclear, unfair or misleading.

10.4.7   Comparative information, referring to tax and consistency

Where comparative information is being provided to a retail client, then the firm must ensure the comparison is meaningful and presented in a fair and balanced manner.

If information is to be provided regarding a particular type of tax treatment in relation to a designated investment, then a prominent statement must be included that the tax treatment will be dependent upon the individual's circumstances and may be subject to change in the future. The information contained in a financial promotion must also be consistent with any other information that the firm has previously provided to a retail client. These obligations regarding tax references and consistency do not arise where the information provided relates to a long-term care pure protection contract (for further information *see* Chapter 7).

10.4.8 *Past performance information*

Where a firm wishes to provide information which contains an indication of past performance then the procedures set out in COBS 4.6 must be satisfied. Firstly, the past performance indication should not be the most prominent feature of the communication and the past performance information should cover the product's performance over at least the prior five years. If the product is less than five years old, then the period shown should cover the whole period in which the product has been sold. In all cases, the past performance must be based on and show complete 12-month periods (i.e. to avoid firms distorting performance by only showing one "peak"). The past performance information must also clearly state the reference period and the source of information as well as containing a prominent warning statement that past performance is not a reliable indicator of future results. Where the past performance indicator is based on gross performance figures, then the effect of commissions, fees and other charges must be disclosed. If the past performance indicator uses a foreign currency then this must be stated and a warning included that the investment return may increase or decrease dependant upon currency fluctuations. Where the life product is a unit-linked one, firms must present past performance information in accordance with the table set out in COBS 4.6.4A and the guidance set out in COBS 4.6.5.

If a firm decides to include an indication of simulated past performance then the information must relate to the investment or financial index in question and be based upon either the actual past performance of one or more investments or financial indices which are the same as, or underlie, the investment concerned. In respect of actual past performance, information should comply with the FSA requirements described in the paragraph above. In addition the information must contain a prominent warning that the figures refer to simulated past performance only and that past performance is not a reliable indicator of future performance.

10.4.9   Future performance

Where a firm's information contains an indicator of future performance it must satisfy the conditions laid out in COBS 4.6.7. The information should:

(a)   not be based on or referable to simulated past performance;
(b)   be based on reasonable assumptions supported by objective data;
(c)   disclose the effect of commission, fees and other charges; and
(d)   contain a prominent warning that forecasts are not a reliable indicator of future performance.

COBS 4.6.8 provides that firms should not provide information on future performance if they are not able to obtain the objective data required under (b) above. For example, objective data in relation to some types of investment may be difficult to obtain (COBS 4.6.8 gives the example of "EIS shares").

10.4.10   Direct offer financial promotions

Where a firm makes a direct offer financial promotion to a retail client it must comply with and contain any relevant disclosure information set out in COBS 6.1 (information about the firm, its services and remuneration) and 14.3 (information about designated investments). A direct offer financial promotion will normally be packaged with an application form or other means of applying for the product or services, but no advice should be given by the firm in relation to the product. As no advice will be offered on the product by the firm the financial promotion should include detailed product information (as well as information about the firm, its services and remuneration) to enable the client to make a decision on an informed basis. This rule will not apply where, in order to respond to the direct offer, the retail client must refer to another document containing the required information. The FSA guidance suggests that a firm may wish to also include: a summary of any taxation consequences for the average member of the group at whom the promotion is directed; a statement that the retail client should seek a personal recommendation if they are unsure about the suitability of the product for them; and a key features illustration (in which a generic projection can usually be used).

10.4.11 *Non-written communications—cold-calling retail clients*

Different rules apply in relation to financial promotions which are not in writing. This includes, for example, a financial promotion communication made via a telephone call, personal visit or other interactive dialogue where an invitation or inducement is made to a retail client.

Under COBS 4.8 certain restrictions are placed on "cold calling". A firm may only make a cold call where the retail client has an existing client relationship with the firm and that relationship is such that the client "envisages receiving cold calls"; or the cold call relates to a packaged product which is being generally marketed and which does not involve a higher-volatility fund (i.e. a fund which invests in warrants or derivatives, or is geared, such that price fluctuations are likely to be significantly amplified); or the cold call relates to safer investments and generally marketable non-geared packaged products. In addition COBS 4.8.3 states that the firm cannot initiate cold calls or other non-written financial promotions to its retail clients unless the call is made at an "appropriate" time of day (likely to be between 9:00 and 21:00) and the person identifies himself as calling on behalf of the firm, states at the outset the purpose of the communication, clarifies if the client would like to continue with or terminate the call and gives a contact point to a client with whom any appointment is made.

10.4.12   *Financial promotions with an overseas element*

COBS 4.9.3 states that a firm may not communicate or approve a financial promotion which relates to the activities of an overseas person (i.e. non-UK insurer) unless certain conditions are satisfied. A firm must not approve or communicate such a financial promotion unless the information explains that the rules made under the FSMA 2000 for the protection of retail clients will not apply. In addition the communication must state the extent and level to which any compensation scheme will be available and the protection and compensation which is available under any other system of regulation. A firm should only approve a financial promotion if it believes that the overseas person will deal with retail clients in the UK in an honest and reliable way. Further rules are set out in COBS 4.9.4 in relation to communicating or approving financial promotions which are being offered by overseas life insurers. A firm may only communicate or approve a financial promotion to enter into a life policy with the following categories of persons:

(a)   an authorised person;

(b)   an exempt person (who is exempt in relation to effecting or carrying out contracts of insurance of the class to which the financial promotion relates); or

(c)   an overseas long-term insurer entitled under the law of its home country to carry on insurance business of the class to which the financial promotion relates. In addition to EEA insurers and EEA insurance branches, this only covers insurers authorised in Jersey, Guernsey, the Isle of Man, Pennsylvania and Iowa. (See the FSA definition of "overseas long-term insurer").

Where the financial promotion relates to an overseas long-term insurer which has no establishment in the UK, the financial promotion must include:

(a)   the full name of the overseas long-term insurer;

(b)   the country where they are registered; and

(c)   if different, the country where the head office is situated.

A prominent statement must be included in the financial promotion that policies issued by the overseas insurer will not be protected by the Financial Services Compensation Scheme if the insurer is unable to meet its liabilities to policyholders, and that policyholders will not have the right to complain to the Financial Ombudsman Service.

10.4.13   *Systems and controls for the approval and communication of financial promotions*

The rules set out in SYSC 3 and 4 require a firm to have in place appropriate systems and controls, which should include those relating to the communication or approval of financial promotions. Under COBS 4.10.2 a firm must ensure that every financial promotion complies with the financial promotion rules before authorising such communication. If a firm subsequently becomes aware that a financial promotion no longer complies with these rules, then the firm must withdraw its approval to the communication and notify, as soon as reasonably practicable, any person that has relied upon the approval of the firm's decision. If a firm continues to communicate a financial promotion when it has ceased to be in compliance with the rules it will be in breach. However, where a financial promotion is clearly only relevant at a particular date then it will not cease to comply with the financial promotion rules because the passage of time has made it out of date. It should be noted that a firm cannot approve a financial promotion which is made in the course of a personal visit, phone conversation or other interactive dialogue. If a firm approves a financial promotion on the basis that an exception or exemption to the financial promotion rule applies, then the approval must be clearly caveated in this way. COBS 4.10.10 allows a firm (A) to rely on another authorised firm's (B's) confirmation that a financial promotion complies with the financial promotion rules provided A takes reasonable care to establish that B has given its approval and so far as A is, or ought reasonably to be, aware (i) the financial promotion remains clear, fair and not misleading and (ii) B has not withdrawn the financial promotion.

10.4.14   Record keeping

A firm is obliged to keep for five years an adequate record of any financial promotion which it communicates or approves in the case of a life or pension policy. Where a promotion has taken place using a telemarketing campaign, adequate records must be kept of scripts used.

10.5   COBS 5—Distance communications

COBS 5 implements, in relation to financial institutions, the European requirements regarding contracts that are concluded without face-to-face communication. These requirements derive from the Distance Marketing of Consumer Services Directive (2002/65/EC) ("DMD") and the E-Commerce Directive (2002/311/EC). The main provisions of the DMD were implemented in the UK in October 2004 and the E-Commerce Directive was implemented in the UK in 2002.

Where a firm deals with its clients on a distance basis, certain information must be provided by the firm to the client in good time before the client becomes bound by the distance contract or offer. There is no definition of what "in good time" means in the FSA Handbook and the timeframe for providing the information will be dependant upon the type of contract and who the client is. The distance marketing information which is provided to clients must be clear and comprehensible and in a durable medium. The purpose of the distance marketing information is to enable the client to fully understand the services which are being provided by the firm, how the firm will be remunerated and certain information in relation to the insurance product.

COBS 5 applies to all firms carrying on distance marketing from a UK establishment with or for a consumer in the UK or another EEA state.

10.5.1 *Provision of Information*

The type of information which a firm must disclose to its clients is set out in COBS 5 Annex 1R and includes the firm's name, a description of its main business and its address. In addition a firm must make an appropriate status disclosure statement to its client. This should include details on who the firm is regulated by and its FSA registration number. The firm must also disclose:

(a) information on the services the firm will provide;
(b) details on the total price which will be payable by the client to the firm (including all related fees, charges and expenses and taxes);
(c) arrangements for payment and performance;
(d) details of any specific additional costs which will arise as a result of using distance communication to conclude the contract;
(e) information on how to make a complaint about the firm;
(f) details on whether compensation will be available from the Financial Services Compensation Scheme; and
(g) information on the contract itself including details on the right of cancellation and the duration and conditions for exercising the client's cancellation rights (COBS 15 (Cancellation)) and the governing law and jurisdiction of the contract.

There are a number of exceptions to the disclosure requirements of the distance marketing rules. The first is where there is an initial service agreement which is followed by successive operations or a series of operations of the same nature over a course of time. In this case, the same information does not need to be provided to the client for each successive operation and the right of cancellation will only apply to the initial agreement. A second exception (which is much less likely to apply to life contracts) is where a distance contract is concluded merely as part of the provision of another service by the firm. A third exception is the sale of insurance over the telephone. Where a firm places a telephone call to a client it must inform the client of its identity and the purpose of the call at the beginning of the conversation. However, provided the client consents, only abbreviated distance marketing information (COBS 5, Annex 2R) need be provided during the communication, although the "standard" information must still be provided before the consumer becomes bound.

Where a distance contract has been concluded at a client's request prior to the distance marketing information being provided, a firm must disclose the required information to its client immediately after the contract has been entered into.

10.5.2 E-commerce

Where a firm wishes to conclude designated investment contracts through e-commerce it must comply with the rules set out in COBS 5.2. The usual way in which a contract will be concluded using e-commerce is through a website.

As with telephone sales, it is important that the client is provided with all of the requisite information in relation to the firm's services and the product itself to enable them to make an informed decision on whether to use the firm in question and to purchase the product before the contract is concluded. The E-commerce Directive requires a firm to explain to its clients in a clear and understandable way the different technical steps in the contract process which must be completed before the product is sold. Where a product will be sold over a firm's website it is important that it is clear from a contractual standpoint whether the firm is making an offer or invitation to treat to its clients. In most cases a firm's website will explicitly state that the information provided on the website is an invitation to treat so that a product will only be sold to a client and a binding contract entered into, on receipt by the client of an email confirmation to that effect.

COBS 5.2.2 sets out the specific information which must be provided to a client prior to the sale of a product using e-commerce and the requirements are very similar to those set out in the DMD. The firm must also state clearly on its website whether the concluded contract will be filed by the firm and will be accessible. In addition the firm's website must explain to clients how any input errors will be identified and corrected and the language in which the contract will be concluded. COBS 5.2.9 provides that where a contract is concluded between a firm and its client solely by email, the information requirements relating to technical errors, language of the contract etc. will not apply.

10.6   COBS 6—Information about the firm, its services and remuneration

Once a client has been categorised in accordance with COBS 3, then a firm must provide certain information about itself to its clients. This information is usually contained within a services and cost disclosure document ("SCDD"). Further disclosures will be required where a firm is selling packaged products to retail clients—*see* Section 10.6.8. In addition, where a firm is advising on a life insurance product, the information disclosure requirements set out in the Consolidated Life Directive must also be complied with. COBS 6 requires that such information disclosure is made to a retail client in good time before the firm provides designated investment business services for a client (COBS 6.1.11). However, where a firm is advising on a product using distance communication and the client expressly consents, the information disclosures required under COBS 6 may be supplied after the firm has started providing services. Where a firm is providing basic advice to a client in accordance with the rules set out in COBS 9, it does not need to comply with the disclosure rules in COBS 6.

COBS 6.1.4 requires a firm to provide the following basic information about itself to all of its retail clients:

(a)   its name, address and contact details;
(b)   the methods of communication which can be used between the firm and the retail client;
(c)   where the firm is acting through an appointed representative or tied agent then this must be stated;

(d) a statement that the firm is authorised and the name of its regulatory authority; and

(e) the nature, frequency and timing of the reports on the performance of the services to be provided by the firm to the client.

Additional disclosures in relation to any security interest the firm may have over client money, costs and associated charges, are also required under COBS 6.1.7 and 6.1.9.

If there is any material change to this information then the firm must inform its clients of these changes in writing.

10.6.1 Scope and range

One of the underlying principles of the COBS rules is to ensure that a firm provides to its clients full information on both its services and the products it can advise upon. COBS 6.2 sets out the information disclosure requirements which must be made by a firm to its retail clients on the scope and range of products which it offers where the firm is making a personal recommendation to such retail clients to buy a packaged product. A firm's "scope" of advice relates to the number of product providers' products which it can advise upon, and its "range" relates to which products from those providers it offers. The concepts of scope and range were introduced as a result of 'depolarisation' (i.e. removal of the former "polarisation" rule which had required advisers to be either independent or appointed representatives of a product provider or group). The rules on scope and range do not apply where a firm is giving basic advice in accordance with COBS 9.

10.6.2 Scope

A firm's scope will be dependant upon its regulatory status or the range of its permissions. If the firm is an appointed representative it will be limited to offering products from certain product providers (i.e. its principals). Where an authorised firm is independent it can offer products to retail clients from the whole of the market (COBS 6.2.6). In order to qualify as "independent" it is sufficient if a firm uses "panels" of product providers which are reviewed on a regular basis.

It should be noted that, as part of depolarisation and because of MiFID, the FSA had wanted to limit appointed representatives to one investment principal, but decided to retain an exception for long-term insurers within the same group and having the same holding company. However, this is subject to "the scope of each appointment not overlapping as to both activities and investments" (SUP 12.5.6A(2)).

10.6.3 *Independent firms—fees versus commissions and disclosure of relationships that may affect independence*

A firm must not hold itself out to a client as acting independently unless it meets the FSA requirements for determining independence. A firm will only be regarded by the FSA as independent if the selection of products that it offers to retail clients is sufficiently broad. In addition an independent firm must offer the client the option of paying a fee for the advice it provides, as an alternative to the firm receiving commission from the product provider whose product it sells (COBS 6.2.15). The product range must be sufficiently broad to ensure that the firm can satisfy the client's best interests before making a personal recommendation on a packaged product. This does not prevent a firm from using panels for this purpose, provided that it reviews them regularly.

Where a firm charges a retail client a fee for providing a personal recommendation on a packaged product, then any initial commission it also receives as a result of the sale of the packaged product must be passed on to the client. However, this does not prevent a firm from retaining an amount of trail or renewal commission which it receives in the future as a result of the sale of the packaged product, provided that such amount of commission is specified in advance and is so small, relative to the overall fees paid by the client, that it would be manifestly disproportionate for the firm to have to account for it to the client. A firm may choose to offer its clients the option of paying fees on a contingent basis, so that if the client decides not to purchase a product no fee will be payable by the client to the firm for the advice and services the client has received (COBS 6.2.18).

Where an intermediary holds itself out as independent, but (i) a product provider has an ownership interest in the intermediary (such as a shareholding), or (ii) the intermediary itself has such an ownership interest in a product provider, or (iii) the intermediary has a loan arrangement with a product provider, the intermediary should consider whether it should make an additional disclosure of this fact to its retail clients, in order to satisfy the fair, clear and not misleading rule (COBS 6.2.19).

10.6.4 Selling products within a firm's scope and range

COBS 6.2.11 sets out more detailed guidance on the rules relating to the scope of a firm's advice and the range of products it offers. A firm should not make a personal recommendation to a retail client on a packaged product unless the recommendation is within the firm's scope and range. A firm have systems and controls in place in relation to the sale of packaged products that ensure that its representatives have adequate knowledge of all of the products it offers across its scope and range before making a personal recommendation. If a firm's representative is advising on the sale of packaged products but is only able to recommend and sell products within a selective range, then the firm should ensure there is a referral mechanism in place so that a client can, if he wishes, receive additional advice from another representative of the firm who has the requisite knowledge to recommend products outside the selective range. The firm must not narrow the scope or range of products it provides to clients compared with the scope which was originally disclosed to those clients. Where an increase in the scope or range of products being offered to a retail client will materially alter the remuneration which a firm will receive, this must be disclosed to the retail client and appropriate information on the cost and charges which will apply must be provided (for example, a firm may supply the retail client with further details of fees and charges (*see* Sections 10.6.6 and 10.6.7)).

10.6.5   Records

A firm must keep a record of the scope and range of products which it will use and must keep a record of the particular scope and range on which its personal recommendations to each retail client is based. In addition, a list must be retained by the firm detailing those product providers whose packaged products it advises on so that it can be provided on request to clients. These records must be kept for five years.

10.6.6   Services and Costs Disclosure Document ("SCDD")

As mentioned above, the way in which a firm will usually provide the information disclosures required under COBS 6 is by supplying a retail client with a SCDD. The content requirements of the SCDD are set out in COBS 6.3. The SCDD satisfies the FSA requirements of both status disclosure and disclosure of a firm's charges. A firm must provide the information to its retail clients in good time and in a durable medium prior to:

(a)   a retail client being bound by an agreement for the provision of a personal recommendation on packaged product contracts;

(b)   the firm performing preparatory work for its personal recommendation in relation to a packaged product; or

(c)   a firm giving a personal recommendation in relation to a change to a life policy.

A SCDD may also contain the information disclosures required under COBS 2.2 regarding the firm, its services, status and charging basis, and compensation arrangements. Additionally a SCDD will often contain the information required under COBS 6.1.4 about the firm and its services and under the distance marketing rules (COBS 5). A firm must use the key facts logo, heading and text in the order set out in COBS 6

Annex 1G in its SCDD (COBS 6.3.7). The SCDD which is provided by the firm to a client must be appropriate and the firm must consider the type of service which is being provided to the specific client in compiling the SCDD.

A firm may also include in its SCDD any other information which needs to be disclosed by a firm to its client under the COBS rules but is not included in the template SCDD, as long as the information is displayed in a sufficiently prominent manner.

The template SCDD requires the following information to be contained in it:

(a) a statement that the firm is regulated by the FSA;
(b) information on the products offered by the firm;
(c) information on the services that will be provided by the firm;
(d) information on the firm's charges;
(e) the way in which payment should be made for the services provided by the firm;
(f) further information on who regulates the firm;
(g) any information required regarding any interest a product provider has in the firm (whether an equity interest, loan or otherwise);
(h) the action a retail client should take in the event that he has a complaint about the firm; and
(i) information on whether the firm is covered by the Financial Services Compensation Scheme.

A combined initial disclosure document ("combined IDD") (in lieu of a SCDD) should be sent by a firm to its client where combined products (i.e. COBS and ICOBS products) are being offered to the client. A combined IDD template is set out in COBS 6 Annex 2. This template includes the same information as the template SCDD but also provides for further information on the different types of products offered by the firm to be disclosed to the retail client.

A firm should consider the extent to which it is appropriate to provide a SCDD or a combined IDD if the appropriate information has been given to the client on a previous occasion and remains accurate.

10.6.7 *Disclosure of charges, remuneration and commission*

COBS 6.4.3 requires that when a firm sells, personally recommends or arranges the sale of a packaged product to a retail client and subsequently if the retail client requests it, the firm must disclose "in cash terms" any commission (or equivalents) which it or any of its associates will receive. Disclosure "in cash terms" in relation to commission does not include the value of any of the "reasonable non-monetary beliefs" in COBS 2.3.15.

10.6.8 *When should a firm disclose details of its commission?*

A firm should disclose the commission which it will receive from the sale of a packaged product to its retail client in a durable medium (COBS 6.4.5). The information which should be provided to the retail client by the firm on the commission payment is set out at COBS 6.4. A description of the amount or value of commission should be included, together with information on when and over what period the commission will be paid.

COBS 6.3.14 specifies that if a firm does not include expected commission arrangements in the SCDD or combined IDD it would be unlikely to be regarded as complying with either the client's best interest rule or the fair, clear and not misleading rule (COBS 2.1.1R and 4.2.1R). COBS 6.3.14 indicates that commission arrangements should therefore be set out in the SCDD or combined IDD. This is reiterated by COBS 6.4.5, which states that a firm must disclose its commission to a retail client as close as practicable to the time it sells, personally recommends or arranges the sale of a packaged product.

However, COBS 6.4.3(4) and 6.4.9 add some uncertainty over the timing of disclosure of commission information. COBS 6.4.3(4) states that the requirement to disclose commission will not apply where a firm provides a key features document to the retail client in accordance with the rules set out in COBS 14 and the firm discloses to the retail client the actual amount or value of commission it will receive within five business days of the sale of the packaged product. COBS 6.4.9 states that commission does not need to be disclosed before a firm makes a personal recommendation to a retail client.

Previously, under the old COB rules, commission disclosure was made pre-sale in the key features document. The key features document included a statement as to the amount that was likely to be payable as commission, and this was followed post-sale by a key features document setting out the actual commission which the firm would receive. It should be noted that COBS 13, which sets out the requirements for producing a key features document, does not now require commission details to be included in a key features document.

COBS 6.3.14 was added by the FSA in August 2008, presumably with the intention of removing this uncertainty over when commission should be disclosed to retail clients. It is current practice for life insurance product providers and firms dealing with long-term insurance products to insert commission details in a key features document.

10.6.9   *Calculating the commission equivalent*

Guidance is set out in COBS 6 Annex 6 on the receipt by a firm of a "commission equivalent", the types of items which will be regarded as commission equivalent and how a firm should calculate and attribute a figure to these items. A commission equivalent is where a firm receives cash payments, benefits or services from a product provider rather than a stated amount or percentage of commission from the sale of a packaged product. The receipt of commission equivalents will usually apply only where the intermediary is an appointed representative of the product provider. Cash payments will include any bonuses or over-rider commission sums which may be payable to the intermediary. Benefits received by a firm may include the use of a car, attendance at conferences or subsidised loans. Commission equivalent services which are received by a firm could include office accommodation, loans, computer hardware and software, business insurance cover and compliance monitoring.

10.6.10 *Telephone sales*

Where the firm makes initial contact with a client via the telephone it needs to bear in mind the rules in COBS 2.2.1R on information disclosure before providing services. It may, in addition, be required to comply with the requirements applicable to the conclusion of distance contracts (see COBS 5). Before providing a retail client with a personal recommendation on packaged products via the telephone, the following information (as set out in COBS 6.3.20) must be provided:

(a) the name of the firm and, if the call is initiated by or on behalf of a firm, the commercial purpose of the call;

(b) whether the firm offers packaged products from the whole market or from a limited number of companies or from a single company or a single group of companies;

(c) whether the firm will provide the client with a personal recommendation on packaged products;

(d) that the client can request a copy of the appropriate range of packaged products;

(e) whether the firm offers a fee-based service, a commission-based service, a service based on a combination of fee and commission, or a combination of these services, and the consequences for the client of proceeding with each type of service; and

(f) that information given under the above provisions will be subsequently confirmed in writing.

Where the initial contact with a retail client is via telephone in circumstances where the firm would otherwise have provided the customer with a SCDD or combined IDD the firm should consider sending either document as soon as possible following the call.

10.7   COBS 7—Insurance mediation

COBS 7 sets out the rules applying to a firm which carries on insurance mediation in relation to a life policy. This basically reiterates the rules set out in the Insurance Mediation Directive and will usually be satisfied by the provision of a SCDD to the retail client. COBS 7.2.1 requires that a firm provides a client with the following information prior to an initial life policy being concluded, amended or renewed:

(a)   the firm's name and address;
(b)   the firm's registration number and a statement that it is registered on the FSA Register;
(c)   information on whether it has a direct or indirect holding representing 10 per cent or more of the voting rights in an insurance undertaking;
(d)   information on whether a given insurance undertaking or its parent undertaking has a direct or indirect shareholding representing more than 10 per cent of the voting or capital rights of the firm; and
(e)   the procedures by which a client may register a complaint about the firm with the firm and the Financial Ombudsman Service.

All information referred to above must be communicated in a durable medium, in a clear and accurate manner and in the language of the place of residence of the policyholder. There is an exception to this rule where the client so requests, or where immediate cover is necessary, when such information may be provided orally. However, in such a case the information must be provided in a compliant manner immediately after the conclusion of the contract.

Additionally, a firm must inform the client whether the recommendation given to it has been based on a fair analysis of the whole of the market or if it is an appointed representative. Where no advice is given, COBS 7.2.4 requires a firm to provide a client with a letter outlining the client's demands and needs, modulated according to the complexity of the product, prior to a life policy being entered into by the client ("the demands and needs" letter). This is to ensure that the policy meets the demands and needs of that client and is the same as the requirement under COBS 9 for a firm to provide a "reason why" letter to a retail client before it purchases a product in the situation where advice *is* given.

10.8   COBS 8—Client agreements

COBS 8 sets out the requirements for client agreements. The rules in this chapter of COBS do not extend to firms effecting life contracts as principal (COBS 8.1.1(3)). A firm must enter into a written agreement with a new retail client if it carries on designated investment business (other than advising on investments) for that client. A firm must, before entering into any agreement relating to designated investment business, or before providing such services, provide a retail client with the terms of that agreement. The client agreement should set out the essential rights and obligations of the firm and the client, and contain information about the firm and its services, for example information on communications, conflicts of interest and authorised status. Where there is a material change to the information provided in relation to the firm then a firm must notify its clients of these changes. COBS 8.1.4 requires a firm to keep a record of any agreement entered into between itself and a client for the longer of five years and the duration of the relationship with the client. In the case of a pension transfer, a pension opt out or FSAVC the record should be retained indefinitely. It is standard practice that the requirements in COBS 8 will be satisfied by the provision of a SCDD.

10.9 COBS 9—Suitability

Where a firm is making a personal recommendation to a retail client in relation to designated investments it must assess whether the particular product is suitable for that client's specific demands and needs. Under COBS 9.1.5 if a firm makes a personal recommendation to a professional client in relation to a life policy then the recommendation must comply only with the requirements of the Insurance Mediation Directive, which requires the firm to provide information on whether it has conducted a fair analysis of the market and the range and scope used by the firm.

10.9.1 Fact find

In order for a firm to be acting in the best interests of its client, it must make an assessment of the client's needs before giving a personal recommendation to the client. To obtain this information a firm will ask its clients to complete an information sheet which is often referred to as a "fact find". The fact-find questionnaire seeks to extract the necessary information about a client's circumstances, financial situation and investment objectives. This information is then used by the firm to make an assessment of a client's specific demands and needs and in light of this to make a personal recommendation to the retail client of designated investment products which are suited to him.

The purpose of obtaining this information is to ensure that the firm both understands the particular needs of the retail client and has a reasonable basis to believe that its personal recommendations meet the client's investment objectives and that the client understands and is financially able to bear any risks involved in such a transaction. The type of information which a firm may need to obtain to assess the investment objectives of the retail client may include the length of time the client wishes to hold the investment, his risk appetite, risk profile and the purpose of the investment. The financial information provided by the retail client must include information on the source and extent of his regular income, his assets and regular financial commitments. A firm must encourage its clients to disclose any information which may be relevant to enable the firm to accurately assess a client's suitability to designated investments.

A firm is entitled to rely upon the information provided by its retail clients as long as it is not aware that the information provided is out of date, inaccurate or incomplete (COBS 9.2.5). If a firm does not obtain the requisite information to allow it to assess a retail client's suitability to a particular product then it should not make a personal recommendation to the retail client.

10.9.2   *Churning and switching*

When a firm is assessing a client's suitability for a particular designated investment it should also consider if the investment is part of a series of transactions which, when considered in isolation are suitable for a client, but when considered together are of a frequency which would not be in the client's best interests (COBS 9.3). This type of repeated switching in and out of investment products is called "churning". A firm should also consider whether it is acting in its client's best interests if recommendations are frequently made to a client to switch that client within or between packaged products. By ensuring that a firm considers the wider impact of its recommendations a firm should always be acting in the best interests of its client and treating them fairly in accordance with PRIN 6 of the FSA Handbook.

10.9.3   *Income withdrawals and short-term annuities*

Where a firm is making a personal recommendation to a retail client in relation to income withdrawal policies or the purchase of short-term annuities, a firm must also consider additional circumstances of the client. This requires a firm to have regard to the client's financial position. This might include for example, the investment objectives of the client, what his current and future income requirements are, his existing pension assets and the relative importance of the plan given his financial circumstances and his attitude to risk, as well as the client's need for short-term cash and his state of health (COBS 9.3.3).

10.9.4   *Suitability reports/"reason why" letters*

When a firm makes a personal recommendation to a retail client it must provide a "suitability report" or "reason why" letter to the retail client where the client intends to:

(a)   buy, sell, surrender, convert or cancel his rights or suspend his contributions to a personal or stakeholder pension scheme;

(b)   elect to make income withdrawals or purchase a short-term annuity; or

(c)   enter into a pension transfer or a pension opt out.

In addition, where a firm makes a personal recommendation in relation to a life policy a suitability report must be provided to the retail client before he purchases the life policy. The purpose of the suitability report is to explain to the retail client why the firm has made a personal recommendation in relation to the specific product after consideration of the client's demands, needs and circumstances.

There are certain instances when a firm will not need to provide a suitability report to a retail client. These include where a firm makes a personal recommendation to increase a regular premium on an existing contract or to invest additional single premiums to an existing packaged product to which a single premium has previously been paid (*see* COBS 9.4.3).

The rules set out in COBS 9.4.4 require a suitability report to be provided to a client at different times depending on the type of investment which is proposed. In the case of a life policy, the report must be provided before the contract is concluded (save where the information is provided orally or where immediate cover is necessary). Where the personal recommendation by a firm relates to either a personal or stakeholder pension scheme and the scheme has cancellation rights attached to it, then the report must be provided to the retail client no later than 14 days after the pension scheme has been entered into. In all other cases, the suitability report should be provided to the retail client as soon as possible after the investment transaction has been entered into. Where a life policy is sold over the telephone and this is the only form of communication between the firm and the retail client, then a suitability report must be provided immediately after the life policy has been purchased and it must comply with the distance marketing rules as set out in COBS 5.1 (COBS 9.4.6).

10.9.5 Contents of the suitability report or "reason why" letter

A suitability report is often referred to as a "reason why" letter and must include the following information:

(a) it must specify the client's demands and needs;
(b) it must explain why the firm has concluded that it can make a personal recommendation of the product to the client having considered the information provided in the client's fact find; and
(c) it must explain to the client any possible disadvantages of the product.

Where the personal recommendation relates to either an income withdrawal policy or the purchase of a short-term annuity, the suitability report should include an explanation of the possible disadvantages to the policy/annuity and the risk factors involved. Typical disadvantages which a firm may wish to disclose to its retail client include:

(a) a possible reduction in the capital value of the fund;
(b) the actual investment return being less than that demonstrated in the illustrations;
(c) the possible fluctuation of annuity or pension scheme rates where the maximum withdrawal is taken;
(d) an explanation that high levels of income may not be sustainable; and

(e)   a statement that the maximum income which can be withdrawn under an alternatively secured pension after the age of 75 is significantly less than the maximum that applies before the age of 75.

10.9.6   Record keeping

A firm must retain the suitability reports which it sends to its clients for at least three years from the date the report is produced. In the case of life policies, personal pension and stakeholder pensions, this time period is extended to five years and in the case of a pension transfer, pension opt out or FSAVC a firm must retain these records indefinitely.

10.9.7   Basic advice for stakeholder products

Where a firm provides stakeholder products, if it wishes it may provide only basic advice in relation to the sale of such stakeholder products to retail clients. If this is the case, the firm needs to comply with the rules set out in COBS 9.6 rather than the general COBS rules.

10.9.7.1   Basic advice initial disclosure document

Where a firm provides only basic advice to a retail client in relation to the purchase of stakeholder pension products it must not hold itself out to a retail client as providing independent advice. Under COBS 9.6.5 a firm must provide the retail client with basic advice initial disclosure information ("Basic IDD") prior to providing any basic advice. The Basic IDD explains how the basic advice which the firm will give will be remunerated and discloses any commission which the firm will receive.

The Basic IDD must contain the following information:

(a)   the name and address of the firm;
(b)   a statement that the firm is regulated and authorised by the FSA, details on how a complaint can be made (to the firm and the Financial Ombudsman Service) and a

description of the circumstances and extent to which the firm is covered by the Financial Services Compensation Scheme;

(c) information on whether the range of stakeholder products available are from a single product provider or a limited number of product providers; and

(d) a statement that the only service the firm is providing is basic advice on a limited range of stakeholder products and a statement that the firm will not make a full assessment of the retail client's demands and needs.

If a firm's first contact with a client, where it will be providing basic advice is not face to face, then the firm must inform the retail client of the firm's name and the purpose of the communication. In addition, the firm must inform its retail client whether the stakeholder products will be selected from one product provider or a select range of product providers and that the firm will not make a full assessment of the client's demands and needs. This information must all be confirmed to the client in writing before the client takes up a stakeholder pension product.

10.9.7.2   *Restrictions on product range*

The restrictions on the sales process of firms providing basic advice are set out in COBS 9.6.9 and 9.6.10. The sales process for basic advice is centred around providing scripted statements to the retail client, the completion by the retail client of a pre-scripted questionnaire and informing the retail client about the limited nature and scope of the advice provided. A firm cannot describe or recommend a stakeholder pension product which is outside the predetermined range or provide information on the fund choice of a product or the level of contributions which the retail client should make. However, a firm should explain to its retail client why it has chosen a particular stakeholder product provider. Where requested by its client, a firm must send him a list of its stakeholder product providers and the products in the range which the firm offers. Further guidance on the sales process is set out in COBS 9 Annex 2G.

10.9.7.3   Suitability of stakeholder product

A firm is only permitted to recommend a stakeholder pension product to a retail client if:

(a)   it has taken reasonable steps to assess the client's answers to the scripted questions and any other facts, circumstances or information which have been disclosed by the client;
(b)   on the basis of the information provided, the firm has reasonable grounds to believe the stakeholder product is suitable for the retail client; and
(c)   the firm reasonably believes that the retail client understands the firm's advice and the basis on which it is provided.

Before the contract is concluded, the firm must provide an explanation to the client of the nature of the stakeholder pension product and the aims, commitment and risks sections of the appropriate key features document. This information may be provided by a firm in a summary sheet format. Where this format is used the summary should set out the reasons for the firm's recommendation in light of the client's attitude to risk, any other information provided by the client on which the firm's recommendation is based and the specific amount the client wishes to pay into the product. An express warning statement must be included on the summary sheet that any complaint which the retail client may have against the firm will be reviewed by the Financial Ombudsman Scheme in light of the limited information on which the recommendation is based. A summary sheet should be provided to a retail client prior to the stakeholder pension contract being concluded if the firm and retail client have only dealt with each other using distance communication. In all other cases the summary sheet should be sent to the retail client as soon as reasonably practicable after the stakeholder pension product has been entered into.

10.9.7.4 Record keeping

A firm must retain a record of all basic advice given to its retail clients and the range of stakeholder pension products it has offered for at least five years from the date the advice is given.

10.10 COBS 13 and 14—Product disclosure

10.10.1 Product disclosure (COBS 13)

Prior to the sale of a designated investment product to a retail client a firm must provide its retail clients with a key features document ("KFD"), a key features illustration ("KFI") and, in the case of life products, comply with the product disclosure information requirements set out in the Consolidated Life Directive. Where the sale of a designated investment product is concluded on a distance basis the KFD and KFI may be provided to the retail client immediately after the product has been entered into. An explanation of the information which must be provided to clients who are entering into non-investment insurance contracts is set out in Chapter 7, Section 7.8.5.

A KFD must be produced to the same standard as other marketing literature which is used by the firm (COBS 13.2.2). KFD and KFI must include the key facts logo in a prominent position at the top of the document and, in the case of KFD, display the firm's brand at least as prominently as any other. In addition, both the KFD and KFI should include a statement that the FSA requires the information contained within it to be provided in order to help the retail client reach a decision on whether the specific product is the right product for the client. The mandatory wording of this statement is included in COBS 13.2.2(4). The information disclosure requirements of the Consolidated Life Directive can be included in either a KFD or a KFI or any other document which is provided to the client.

10.10.2 Content of key features

COBS 13.3 sets out the general requirements for the content of a KFD and the information to be included within it. A KFD should include information on the product, its nature and complexity and how it works. A KFD should also include information on the material benefits and risks of the product. The arrangements and procedures for making a complaint and information on the availability of compensation from the Financial Services Compensation Scheme should also be included in the KFD. In addition, a KFD should explain whether a right to cancel or withdraw from the product exists and if such a right does exist, its duration and conditions for exercising this right. Where a KFD is issued to a retail client in relation to a personal pension scheme, a statement must be included in the KFD that stakeholder pension schemes are generally available and may meet the client's needs as well as those of a personal pension scheme.

Additional disclosure requirements are required where a KFD is issued to a retail client in relation to a packaged product. The requirements are prescribed and the product must be described in the order shown in Table 10.1 and must provide the information under the headings shown in that Table.

Table 10.1 Additonal disclosure requirements

Heading	Information to be given
Its aim	A brief description of the product's aims
Your commitment/Your investment	What a retail client is committing to or investing in and any consequences of failing to maintain such commitment or investment

Risks	The material risks associated with the product including a description of the facts that may have an adverse effect on the performance of the product or which are deemed material to the decision on whether to invest
Questions and answers	(In the form of questions and answers.) The principal terms of the product, what it will do for a retail client, and any other information which will enable a retail client to make an informed decision

The additional disclosures required to comply with the Consolidated Life Directive are set out in COBS 13 Annex 1. These are usually covered by the KFD except for:

(a) general information on the tax arrangements applicable to the type of policy; and

(b) the law applicable to the contract where the parties do not have a choice of law or (where a choice of law exists), the law that the product provider proposes to choose.

10.10.3   KFI

The content requirements for KFIs are set out in COBS 13.4 and 13.5.A KFI must include the key facts logo, information on the charges which will be applied to the product and a statement that the FSA requires the information in the KFI to be provided to the retail client.

10.10.4   Appropriate charges information

The charges information to be included in a KFI is set out in COBS 13 Annex 3. A KFI must include a description of the nature and amount of expected charges and expenses to be borne by the client in relation to a product. The effect of the charges must also be specified but will of course be dependent on the type of product being sold. The effect of charges table displayed in a KFI should show the total amount that has been paid to date, any withdrawals, the total actual deductions to date, the effect of deductions to date and what the retail client might recover. It is of particular importance to note that the definition of "charges" does not include a disclosure of the commission received by an intermediary from the sale of the products; it relates only to fees or charges made in relation to the product.

10.10.5   Reduction in yield

A KFI must also include a reduction in yield table, and information on how a product provider should calculate yield is set out in COBS 13 Annex 3, para.3. The calculation for reduction in yield may include the cost of life cover and/or sickness benefits, commission remuneration, expenses, charges and surrender penalties or other similar adjustments. An explanation should be included on what the deductions are for, and information should be provided to the client on any actual deductions to date and the effect of these. A reduction in yield table is not required for certain products, for example a life policy which is sold with no surrender value (so long as a warning statement is made that the policy has no cash-in-value at any time), or a self-invested personal pension ("SIPP").

10.10.6   Projections

A KFI must also include certain projections in relation to the designated investment product. The purpose behind these projections is to ensure that the basis on which information is provided to the retail client is uniform and consistent regarding investment returns.

Projections should illustrate "the amount of any future benefit payable under a contract or policy, being a benefit the amount of which is not ascertainable under the terms of the contract or policy when a cancellation is made". Where a KFI is produced for packaged products then it must include a standardised deterministic projection ("SDP"). An SDP is a projection where an actuary has been able to accurately assess and predict certain sum values in relation to a particular product based on known variables. The SDP included in a KFI must be produced in accordance with the assumptions set out in COBS 13 Annex 2. Technically the SDP may be either generic or personalised. However, a generic projection may only be included in a KFI if there are reasonable grounds to believe that this type of projection will enable the retail client to make an informed decision on whether or not to invest in the specific product. The projection need not be included in a KFI if the product being sold is:

(a) a single-premium life policy which is being purchased as a pure investment product;
(b) a SIPP from which no income withdrawals are being taken; or
(c) a life policy which can be held in a child trust fund or sold with basic advice.

An SDP must include a projection of benefits at low, intermediate and high rates of return. These rates are set for packaged products as four per cent (lower), six per cent (intermediate) and eight per cent (higher). Because of the preferential tax treatment, the specified rates of return for pension products and other products subject to gross roll up differ slightly from those applied to packaged products and are five per cent (lower), seven per cent (intermediate) and nine per cent (higher). Details are also included in COBS 13 Annex 2 on the assumptions to be used when determining the rates of return on investment products and specified rates of inflation. There are additional requirements for calculating projections in relation to with-profits policies which are set out at Annex 2, para.2.8. An SDP must include risk warnings regarding volatility and the degree upon which a client may rely upon the figures (COBS 13 Annex 2, para.5).

Certain assumptions for contributions are made in calculating an SDP. For example, contributions are accumulated net of charges at an appropriate rate of return which is then compounded on an annual basis. The charges assumptions which are used to calculate an SDP must properly reflect all of the charges, expenses and deductions which a retail client will, or may be expected to pay, the tax relief which is available to a firm in respect of such payment and the fact that certain charges will be fully or partially offset. Where appropriate, mortality and morbidity should be included in the projection on a best-estimate basis and the basis for annuity should allow for future improvements in mortality. A projection should not assume that charges will fall over time to a rate that is lower than the current rate being charged. Where a projection of the surrender value, cash value or transfer value is made this should take into account any specific penalties which may be applied by the product provider.

An SDP for a pension scheme must also include, or be accompanied by, information on the impact of inflation (COBS 13 Annex 2, para.1.2(1)). For stakeholder pension products, the stakeholder pension decision tree may be used instead of providing a standardised deterministic approach if the decision tree shows initial monthly pension amounts and includes an explanation of the caveats and assumptions used.

10.11   COBS 15—Cancellation

The purpose of the cancellation period is to act as a standstill period for a retail client to consider whether or not they have made the correct investment decision. The list of contracts where a right to cancel exists is set out in COBS 15.2.1.

10.11.1   *Disclosure*

A firm must disclose to its retail client before they become bound by a designated investment product whether a right to cancel or withdraw from the contract exists. This information must be provided in a durable medium and in good time before the product is purchased. If it is not possible to give a retail client notification of his cancellation rights prior to entering into the contract, then this must be notified immediately after the contract has been entered into. The notification should include details on the duration of the right to cancel and the conditions for exercising it and whether or not the client will be required to pay anything to the firm if it decides to exercise its right of cancellation. In addition, practical instructions should be given to a client on how the right of cancellation should be exercised (i.e. the address to which the notice of cancellation should be sent).

10.11.2 Time period

The rules on cancellation for different types of designated investment products are set out in COBS 15. A cancellation period of 30 calendar days applies to the following designated investment products:

(a) life policies, including a pension annuity and a pension policy;
(b) a personal pension scheme or stakeholder pension scheme;
(c) a pension transfer; and
(d) exercising the income withdrawal option on an existing pension or stakeholder pension scheme.

Where a client purchases a unit in a collective investment scheme within a pension wrapper following a personal recommendation, a 14-calendar-day cancellation period will apply.

The cancellation period will start either from the date the contract is concluded or, where the client receives contractual terms and conditions or any other pre-contractual information required by COBS after the date the contract is completed, that later date. For life policies the cancellation time period begins from the date the client is informed that the contract has been concluded. If a right to cancel applies to a wrapper or a pension wrapper then the firm may offer its client the option of cancelling individual components of the wrapper separately.

As a result of the DMD, a 30-day minimum cancellation period applies to life policies. Prior to the DMD, pension transfers could (instead of cancellation rights), provide a 14-day cooling off period before the contract was issued. This is often referred to as the "cancellation substitute". The reasoning behind the cancellation substitute is that once a pension has been transferred out of an occupational scheme it may be very difficult to rejoin that scheme without losing some financial benefit. The cooling off period pre-transfer postpones the effective date of removal from a scheme to ensure that the client is happy with the transfer decision before the transfer is effected. The cancellation substitute must now effectively be 30 days.

10.11.3   *Exercising the right to cancel*

A client is not obliged to give any reason for exercising his right to cancel a contract for a designated investment product. If a client wishes to exercise his cancellation right he must notify the product provider of this before the expiry of the cancellation period. If written notification is despatched to the product provider before the end of the cancellation period then it is deemed served on the product provider (i.e. the policyholder gets the benefit of the postal rules).

10.11.4   *Effect of cancellation*

The exercise of the right of cancellation will automatically terminate the contract (COBS 15.4.1).

Where a client has exercised his right to cancel, a firm must repay any sums it has received from the retail client in relation to that contract without due delay, and in any event within 30 calendar days.

10.11.5   *Shortfall*

Under COBS 15.4.3, a firm will be entitled to recover any loss under a contract caused by market movements that the firm reasonably incurs as a result of a client cancelling his contract, provided the firm has complied with its obligations in relation to disclosure of cancellation rights. A firm's entitlement to recover a shortfall will not arise if the contract was a distance contract or a contract with regular or recurring premiums or payments. This shortfall rule allows a firm to recoup the difference between the actual premium paid and the amount which would have been paid if an equivalent contract was taken out at the time the cancellation is notified (i.e. any loss suffered as a result of market movement).

10.11.6 Record keeping

A firm must keep a record of the notifications it has sent to its retail clients of cancellation or withdrawal rights for a period of at least three years after the contract has been concluded. If the contract is a life policy, pension contract, personal pension scheme or stakeholder pension scheme the firm must retain these records for at least five years after the contract has been entered into.

10.11.7 The Retail Distribution Review

In June 2006, the FSA launched the Retail Distribution Review ("RDR") to address many of the persistent problems that it had observed whilst regulating the retail investment market. The RDR has been one of the core strands of the FSA's consumer protection strategy and its aim is to modernise the industry and give consumers greater confidence and trust in the retail investment market. The new rules will come into effect on 31 December 2012.

The RDR will impact all regulated firms involved in producing or distributing retail investment products and services, including insurers. The RDR rules are intended to improve the quality of advice and consumer trust and confidence in the industry by improving clarity for consumers about advice services, addressing the potential for remuneration bias and increasing the professional standards of advisers.

In *Consultation*Paper *09/18: Distribution of retail investments: Delivering the RDR*, the FSA proposed a new Handbook definition of retail investment products in order to more closely align its rules with European proposals on Packaged Retail Investment Products ("PRIPs"). In addition to packaged products including annuities, the new definition will include unregulated collective investment schemes, all investments in investment trusts and structured investment products, and other investments which offer exposure to underlying financial assets, but in a packaged form which modifies that exposure compared with a direct holding in the financial asset.

The proposed changes, as set out in the FSA *Policy Statement 10/6: Distribution of retail investments: Delivering the RDR—feedback to CP 09/18 and final rules*, are designed to help consumers distinguish between the different forms of investment advice on offer. Consumers will be entitled to know whether an adviser is searching out the best solution for him from all the products on the market or is advising on a more limited range of products. Under the RDR rules, firms will be required to clearly describe their services as either "independent advice" or "restricted advice". Independent advice constitutes advice which is unbiased, unrestricted and based on a comprehensive and fair analysis of the market whilst restricted advice is not independent and will be given on a limited range of products or providers.

Independent advisers will need to show that they have reviewed the market and selected products suitable for their client. The FSA does not expect a firm to review the market for a product which does not meet their client's needs and objectives. When the RDR rules come into effect the FSA's successor, the Financial Conduct Authority, will be tasked with ensuring that firms have adapted their business by supervising how advisers set and operate their charging structure, checking for key risks and identifying trends in product churning.

Upon implementation of the RDR rules firms will only be paid for advice and related services through adviser charges in accordance with the new rules and guidance to be included in

COBS. The RDR anticipates the initial conversation between the adviser and client to include a discussion about the cost of advice. The adviser should be paid by the client, as opposed to being paid commission set by the product providers.

The FSA wants to remove bias and the potential for bias which exists within the current commission system. The new rules will not allow advisers to receive commission from product providers, even if they intend to rebate these payments to the consumer. These rules are designed to prevent advisers from automatically recommending products which pay commission.

The RDR will also bring in significant changes in terms of professionalism. Advisers will have to hold a Statement of Professional Standing if they wish to give independent or restricted advice and must meet a minimum level of qualification, broadly equivalent to the first year of a university degree. A professional standards board will maintain and enforce an overarching code of ethics and the enhanced standards for continuing professional development.

In its Interim Report on the RDR, the FSA stated that there were no plans for a read-across of the RDR from the investment market to the general insurance market. However, specific rules have been developed which relate to the sale of pure protection products. The rules will only apply to firms that give investment advice and provide advised and non-advised services for pure protection products. Accordingly, they will not apply to firms who sell or advise on pure protection but do not give investment advice. Firms will continue to be able to elect to sell pure protection products under COBS, rather than ICOBS, after the RDR is implemented without having to apply the rules on adviser charging to their pure protection sales. This means that they will continue to be able to receive commission for such sales.

Chapter 11

The regulation of friendly societies

John Gilbert,
Consultant: Hogan Lovells International LLP

11.1 The nature and types of friendly societies

Although friendly societies resemble mutual insurance companies in many ways, they are a fundamentally different type of legal entity. Until the Financial Services and Markets Act 2000 ("FSMA 2000") came into force in December 2001, friendly societies were also regulated by different regulators (the Friendly Societies Commission in relation to prudential regulation, and the Chief Registrar of Friendly Societies in relation to the registration of rules), operating under different regulations and statutes. Despite the disappearance of the separate regulators, some aspects of the distinct regulatory regime for friendly societies remain. Furthermore, the constitutional differences which derive from the separate legal status of friendly societies still remain and the Financial Services Authority ("FSA"), as successor to the Friendly Societies Commission, has taken on the function of superintending their constitutional affairs. This means that the FSA has even wider responsibilities in relation to friendly societies than in relation to other insurers that it regulates.

The modern form of friendly society has been in existence for a little over 200 years. Until the advent of the Friendly Societies Act 1992, all friendly societies were unincorporated associations without a separate legal personality. Although the Friendly Societies Act 1992 prohibited the formation of new unincorporated friendly societies, it did not require existing societies to incorporate, and a number of smaller friendly societies therefore remain unincorporated. They are usually referred to as "registered societies" and this term will be used for them in this Chapter. As unincorporated associations, registered societies cannot themselves own property. The assets of registered societies are therefore held by trustees on behalf of the membership. Registered friendly societies are specifically included in the categories of legal entities which can meet the threshold conditions for the grant of permission under para.1(1) of Sch.6 to the FSMA 2000 and fall within the definition of "firms" for the purposes of the FSA's rules.

Registered societies may take the form of "orders", being societies with separately registered branches. Orders are relatively rare and their special regulatory position under the Friendly Societies Acts, the FSMA 2000 and the FSA's rules will not be considered further in this Chapter.

The FSA's rules distinguish between non-directive friendly societies (i.e. those which are exempt from EU Insurance Directives because of either the nature or scale of their business) and directive friendly societies. Although there are some non-directive friendly societies still in existence, they are, by definition, mostly small and their numbers will reduce further when the thresholds for directive status are lowered as a result of Solvency II. The special features of the regulatory regime that apply to them will not be considered in detail in this Chapter.

Under Part II of the Friendly Societies Act 1992 registered friendly societies may incorporate and all new friendly societies must be formed as incorporated societies. Most of the larger, more active, societies have incorporated and the largest remaining registered society, The Independent Order of Oddfellows, resolved at its 2011 AGM to move towards incorporation at the end of 2012.

Like all modern bodies corporate, incorporated friendly societies derive their legal existence from statute and their capacity and powers are defined by statute. In the case of incorporated friendly societies, the relevant statute is the Friendly Societies Act 1992. It is important to note that the Companies Acts have no relevance to incorporated friendly societies (except to the very limited extent that provisions of the Companies Acts are expressly incorporated into the Friendly Societies Act 1992 and to the extent that decisions of the courts on provisions of the Companies Acts may apply to analogous provisions in the Friendly Societies Act 1992).

It should also be mentioned that until 2001, the Chief Registrar of Friendly Societies was responsible for the registration not only of friendly societies but also of industrial and provident societies and certain working men's clubs as well as a miscellaneous collection of cattle insurance societies, benevolent societies and old people's home societies. This responsibility has also been taken over by the FSA under Part XXI of the FSMA 2000. Although the involvement of the Chief Registrar of Friendly Societies in their registration has often led to this hotchpotch of other societies being confused with friendly societies (and the confusion has not been helped by certain provisions of the Friendly Societies Act 1974 applying to some of these types of societies), these bodies are not friendly societies and any regulated activities they may undertake fall outside the scope of this Chapter.

11.2   Sources of law and regulation

The Friendly Societies Act 1974 was substantially repealed and amended by the Friendly Societies Act 1992. However, the remaining provisions contain the principal source of law on the constitution, powers and registration of registered friendly societies.

The Friendly Societies Act 1992 governs:

(a) the formation, constitution, capacity, powers and winding up of incorporated friendly societies (Part II);
(b) the internal management and administration of both incorporated and registered societies (Part III);

573

(c) accounting matters and audit (Part VI);
(d) the handling of disputes (Part VII); and
(e) amalgamations and portfolio transfers (Part VIII).

Other parts of the Friendly Societies Act 1992 formerly dealt with the prudential supervision of societies' insurance business and the powers of the regulator to investigate societies and to intervene in their affairs. Most, but not all, of these regulatory provisions were repealed in 2001, but there remains some overlap between sections of the Friendly Societies Act 1992 which relate to what may broadly be described as "regulatory" matters which have not been repealed on the one hand and provisions under the FSMA 2000 and the FSA's rules on the other hand (for example, those relating to investigatory powers under s.65 of the Friendly Societies Act 1992 and under s.166 of the FSMA).

In considering the regulation of friendly societies, it is therefore necessary not only to look at the FSMA 2000 and the FSA Handbook, but also to consider whether any provisions of the Friendly Societies Act 1992 (or any subordinate legislation made under the 1992 Act) are relevant either because of some constitutional limitation on friendly societies or because of some residual regulatory provision.

Friendly societies, as authorised persons under the FSMA 2000, are subject to the general rules of the FSA to the extent that they are relevant to friendly societies' business, in the same way as insurance companies. However, the regime for insurance business transfers under Part VII of the FSMA 2000 does not apply to friendly societies (Case 1 of s.105(3) of the FSMA). The regime for business transfers by friendly societies (known as "transfers of engagements") is dealt with in further detail at Section 11.8 below.

All directive friendly societies are subject to INSPRU and GENPRU in the same way as other insurers. Alongside INSPRU and GENPRU there is a separate interim prudential sourcebook for friendly societies ("IPRU-FSOC"). Despite the word "Interim" in its title, this sourcebook has continued in existence notwithstanding the introduction of GENPRU and INSPRU. IPRU-FSOC remains the principal source of prudential regulation for non-directive friendly societies. For these societies IPRU-FSOC reproduces, with some amendments, the repealed sections of the Friendly Societies Act 1992 which contained regulatory provisions and certain practice notes from the series of "Commission Practice Notes" issued by the Friendly Societies Commission under the Friendly Societies Act 1992 between 1992 and 2001. Certain high-level requirements under IPRU-FSOC relating to integrity, skill, care, diligence and to management and controls apply also to directive societies. Therefore, certain features of the separate regulatory regime for friendly societies, which distinguished the regulatory treatment of friendly societies from that of insurance companies, have been preserved under the FSA Handbook and overlap the integrated rules.

A further source of regulation is the Annotated Version for Mutual Insurers of the UK Corporate Governance Code published by the Association of Financial Mutuals. This is an updated version of the Annotated Combined Code for Mutual Insurers first produced in response to the Myners Report on the Governance of Mutual Life Offices which was commissioned by HM Treasury to investigate concerns about the governance of mutual insurers following the collapse of Equitable Life. Like the original UK Corporate Governance Code, the Annotated Version for Mutual Insurers recommends best practice but is not binding, although friendly societies are required in their annual reports to declare where they have deviated from it and explain why they have done so.

11.3 The constitution of friendly societies—general

An incorporated friendly society may only be established for the limited purposes ("purposes" being the friendly society equivalent to the "objects" of a company formed under the Companies Acts) set out or referred to in s.5 of the Friendly Societies Act 1992, and a registered society may only remain registered for the purposes referred to in s.7(1)(a) of the Friendly Societies Act 1974. The purposes of an incorporated friendly society are set out in its "memorandum" (the equivalent of a company's memorandum of association under pre-Companies Act 2006 company law) and the manner in which it is administered is set out in its "rules" (the equivalent of the pre-Companies Act 2006 articles of association). Registered friendly societies have a single constitutional document, known as the society's "rules", dealing with both purposes and administration.

The principal purposes for both incorporated and registered societies are the carrying out of the insurance and other activities set out in Sch.2 to the Friendly Societies Act 1992 (discussed at Section 11.4.1). In addition, incorporated friendly societies may:

(a)   include within their purposes social or benevolent activities under Section 10, Friendly Societies Act 1992 (see Section 11.4.2);
(b)   undertake group insurance business under Section 11, Friendly Societies Act 1992 (see Section 11.4.3);
(c)   undertake reinsurance under s.12of the Friendly Societies Act 1992 (see Section 11.4.4); and
(d)   control or jointly control bodies corporate under Section 13, Friendly Societies Act 1992 (see Section 11.4.5).

Although of rather less relevance to companies since the Companies Act 2006, the Friendly Societies Act 1992 still draws a distinction between the purposes for which an incorporated friendly society exists and the powers by which it may carry out its purposes. The powers available to incorporated friendly societies are considered at Section 11.5 below.

The memorandum and rules of an incorporated friendly society are binding on the members and officers of the society and on all persons claiming on account of members or under the society's rules, all of whom are deemed to have notice of the provisions of the memorandum and rules. Third parties are not bound by the permitted capacity of societies or by any limitation on the powers of the committee of management. Sections 8 and 9 of the Friendly Societies Act 1992 contain protections for third parties dealing with incorporated friendly societies in good faith analogous to the protections for third parties dealing with companies under ss.39 and 40 of the Companies Act 2006. The burden of proving that an act was beyond the capacity of the society or outside the powers of the committee of management lies with the person making the allegation. However, there is no provision equivalent to s.40(2)(b) of the Companies Act 2006 under which a person is not to be regarded as acting in bad faith by reason only of knowing that an act is beyond the powers of the directors of a company. Under s.9(7) of the Friendly Societies Act 1992 an act by the committee of management of a friendly society which is beyond its powers may be ratified by members in general meeting if the act was within the capacity of the society, but acts which are outside a society's purposes cannot be ratified. Thus, the law on the purposes and powers of an incorporated friendly society resembles the common law position on the objects and powers of companies prior to the amendments made by the Companies Act 1989 which have been consolidated into the Companies Act 2006.

11.4   The purposes of friendly societies

11.4.1   *Principal purposes*

Although they may carry out other activities, friendly societies must carry out at least one of the activities set out in Sch.2 to the Friendly Societies Act 1992. In the case of incorporated friendly societies, these activities must be "carried on by the society with a view to the provision, for its members and such persons connected with its members as may be prescribed by its rules, of insurance or other benefits" (s.5(2)(b)(i) of the Friendly Societies Act 1992). With the exception of group insurance business (which is discussed below), friendly societies are thus required only to insure members and persons connected with them (typically family members). Naturally, this does not prevent non-members receiving insurance and other benefits from subsidiaries of societies.

The principal activities set out in Sch.2 to the Friendly Societies Act 1992 include various classes of long-term and general insurance business. It should be noted that the classes of insurance business permitted for friendly societies are more restrictive than those permitted for insurance companies under Sch.1 to the Financial Services and Markets Act 2000 (Regulated Activities) Order 2001 (SI 2001/544). For long-term business (Head A in Sch.2 to the Friendly Societies Act 1992), the only classes omitted are classes VIII (collective insurance) and IX (social insurance), which are of scant relevance to the UK insurance market in any event. However, for general business (Head B in Sch.2 to the Friendly Societies Act 1992), most of the classes available to general insurance companies are unavailable to friendly societies, leaving only classes 1 (accident), 2 (sickness) and 3 (miscellaneous financial loss) available to friendly societies which carry out general business.

It should be noted that although the range of insurance business open to friendly societies themselves is limited, groups headed by incorporated friendly societies may carry out the full range of long-term and general business permitted under the Financial Services and Markets Act 2000 (Regulated Activities) Order 2001 (SI 2001/544) through subsidiaries which are insurance companies. Although the Friendly Societies Act 1992 speaks, somewhat curiously, of the purposes for which a friendly society may be *established*, the same limitations will apply to any amendments to the purposes of an existing friendly society.

Unlike the corresponding schedule to the Financial Services and Markets Act 2000 (Regulated Activities) Order 2001 (SI 2001/544) (Sch.1), Sch.2 to the Friendly Societies Act 1992 includes among the permitted purposes of friendly societies certain non-insurance activities. Head C of Sch.2 allows payments to be made "for the relief or maintenance of any person during sickness or when in distressed circumstances" and to meet funeral expenses whether or not a contract to provide these benefits constitutes insurance business. Head D of Sch.2 allows discretionary benefits to be paid for education, for relief and maintenance during sickness, unemployment or "distressed circumstances" and also for the payment of funeral expenses. Heads C and D of Sch.2 to the Friendly Societies Act 1992 also apply to registered societies by virtue of s.7(1)(a) of the Friendly Societies Act 1974 in the same way as they apply to incorporated friendly societies.

11.4.2 Social and benevolent activities

As well as having the capacity to engage in their principal purposes, incorporated friendly societies are also given the capacity under s.10 of the Friendly Societies Act 1992 to include among their purposes the carrying on of any "social or benevolent activity" which is not inconsistent with the other purposes of the society. "Benevolent activity" is widely defined to mean the making of donations, the raising of funds, or any other activity carried on for a charitable purpose or for any other benevolent purpose.

Section 10 of the Friendly Societies Act 1992 applies only to incorporated societies, although registered societies do commonly undertake social and benevolent activities. Indeed, such activities are a large part of the rationale of certain registered societies. Registered societies are unincorporated associations of natural persons and therefore do not need statutory powers to undertake each of their activities in order that those activities should be *intra vires*.

11.4.3 Group insurance business

Under s.11 of the Friendly Societies Act 1992, incorporated friendly societies are permitted to carry out group insurance business. Group business is an exception to the rule under s.5(2)(b)(i) of the Friendly Societies Act 1992 that friendly societies must carry out their insurance and other activities with a view to providing benefits to members and persons connected with members. Participants in a group scheme need not be members of the society but the society may (although it is not obliged to) allow for a representative of the group to be a member of the society. Friendly societies are subject to a rule prohibiting voting rights being weighted according to the amount of subscriptions (*see* para.5 of Sch.12 to the Friendly Societies Act 1992), which may be construed as preventing the representative of a group scheme having any more votes than ordinary members.

The parties for which group schemes can be established are employees of a particular employer and other groups pre-scribed in regulations made under s.11(7) of the Friendly Societies Act 1992. To date, the only groups prescribed in regulations (The Friendly Societies (Group Schemes) Regula-tions 1993 (SI 1993/59)) are sports clubs and clubs for the provision of recreation or other leisure activities.

Section 55 of the Friendly Societies Act 1992 gives the FSA powers of intervention if it believes that the group insurance business conducted by a friendly society is disproportionate to the other activities of the society.

Registered friendly societies are also able to undertake group business under s.65A of the Friendly Societies Act 1974, which is substantially the same as s.11 of the Friendly Societies Act 1992. Groups prescribed under s.11(7) of the Friendly Societies Act 1992 are valid for registered societies by virtue of s.65A(8) of the Friendly Societies Act 1974. Section 55 and para.5 in Sch.12 to the Friendly Societies Act 1992 apply to both registered and incorporated friendly societies.

11.4.4   *Reinsurance*

A further purpose of incorporated friendly societies is the reinsurance of risks insured by another friendly society. In order to conduct reinsurance business a friendly society must obtain the approval of its appropriate actuary and ensure that the risks reinsured are of a class or part of a class which the society itself carries on. Registered friendly societies are also permitted to reinsure risks underwritten by other friendly societies (whether registered or incorporated) under s.23A,

Friendly Societies Act 1974. It is important to note that in both cases inwards reinsurance may only be carried out for risks underwritten by another friendly society and not for risks underwritten by an insurance company. However, incorporated friendly societies are permitted under s.16 of the Friendly Societies Act 1992 to provide a wide range of services to their subsidiaries and jointly controlled bodies including "the use of services", "grants of money" and "guarantees for the discharge of their liabilities". These powers allow incorporated friendly societies to provide services to their subsidiaries with similar commercial effects to reinsurance services. However, for directive societies, INSPRU 1.5.13 would require any payment for these services not to be on a commercial footing.

11.4.5   *Control or joint control of bodies corporate*

Incorporated societies may also take part, as one of their purposes under s.13 of the Friendly Societies Act 1992, in forming, acquiring or holding "controlled bodies" (also referred to in the legislation as "subsidiaries") and "jointly controlled bodies" (i.e. joint ventures with other organisations). The purposes of forming, acquiring or holding subsidiaries or jointly controlled bodies must be specifically adopted by incorporated friendly societies in their memoranda. The adoption of (and any amendment to) the relevant purpose must be by special resolution as required by s.13(6) of the Friendly Societies Act 1992. All other amendments to a friendly society's constitution may be made in the manner set out in the society's constitution (i.e. usually by ordinary resolution—*see* Section 11.7). Until 2001 the Friendly Societies Act 1992 contained strict limitations on the activities of a subsidiary or jointly controlled body of an incorporated friendly society, the jurisdictions in which such bodies could be incorporated, the structure of a group headed by an incorporated friendly society and the persons with whom jointly controlled bodies could be held. These have now all been repealed.

The test of "control" in s.13(9) of the Friendly Societies Act 1992, as supplemented by Schedule 8, is the same as the test used in the definition of subsidiary in s.1159 of the Companies

Act 2006. A similar test applies to "joint control", which arises where an incorporated friendly society and any other person together have control "in pursuance of an agreement or other arrangement between them". This means that most joint venture agreements and any investment in a company subject to a shareholders' agreement will be caught as an investment in a "jointly controlled body". However, investments in limited partnerships would not normally be caught (even if the limited partnership itself is a body corporate) unless the friendly society invests through a corporate vehicle, or the friendly society or one of its subsidiaries controls the general partner.

The powers of the FSA in relation to groups consisting of incorporated friendly societies and their subsidiaries differ from the regulation of groups headed by a company formed under the Companies Acts, by virtue of the power of the FSA under s.54 of the Friendly Societies Act 1992 to intervene if it appears to the FSA that the activities of subsidiaries of the society (or of bodies jointly controlled by it) "are or may become disproportionate" to those of the friendly society group as a whole. In these circumstances, the FSA has power to direct the society to take steps to ensure that the activities cease to be or do not become disproportionate, or to dispose of the offending subsidiary or jointly controlled body or to wind it up. These apparently draconian powers, which were also vested in the Friendly Societies Commission before 2001, have never been used. The friendly societies movement did ask the government to consider repealing them under the FSMA 2000 at the same time that they requested the repeal of the other limitations on subsidiaries. However, the government declined to repeal s.54, which suggests that these powers are regarded as a useful tool for the regulation of friendly societies and that the FSA may consider invoking them at some point in the future.

A further distinguishing feature is that by virtue of s.68(10) of the Friendly Societies Act 1992, the requirements of s.68 with regard to accounting records apply equally to subsidiaries and jointly controlled bodies as they do to friendly societies themselves regardless of whether the subsidiaries carry on regulated activities. The requirements under Section 68 were significantly modified in 2001 by the removal of references to systems of business control and systems of inspection and report, and do not now impose significantly greater burdens with regard to the keeping of accounting records than apply to companies under the Companies Acts. The former s.68 requirements on systems of business control and inspection and report have been reimposed on both directive and non-directive friendly societies and registered branches under IPRU-FSOC 3.1, but not in relation to subsidiaries or jointly controlled bodies. Under IPRU-FSOC 3.1(7) non-directive friendly societies are required to send the FSA a statement of their own compliance with the requirements of IPRU-FSOC 3.1 (which includes the requirements under s.68). These statements must be submitted within six months of the beginning of each financial year. (Since friendly societies are required by s.118 of the Friendly Societies Act 1992 to have financial years which are coterminous with calendar years, this means by 30 June each year.)

11.5   The powers of friendly societies

While the purposes available to incorporated friendly societies may be restricted when compared with the objects available to companies incorporated under the Companies Acts, incorporated friendly societies may adopt wide-ranging powers. These powers fall into a number of distinct categories:

(a)   the power to undertake various miscellaneous activities set out in Sch.5 to the Friendly Societies Act 1992 (*see*Section 11.5.1);

(b)   the powers which incorporated friendly societies may adopt under s.7(3) of the Friendly Societies Act 1992 which are specifically referred to in Part II of that Act (*see*Section 11.5.2); and

(c)   the "catch all" power in s.7(4) of the Friendly Societies Act 1992 to do anything else which is "incidental or conducive" to the carrying out of the society's purposes or for doing anything falling within Sch.5—subject always to the other provisions of the Friendly Societies Act 1992 and the society's memorandum and rules. This "catch all" power does not have to be specifically adopted by a friendly society, but most incorporated friendly societies do refer to it in their memoranda and rules.

The specific powers which may be adopted under s.7(3) may only be exercised for the carrying out of the society's purposes and the "catch all" power also relates only to actions for carrying out the purposes of the society or for carrying out activities which fall within Sch.5.

There are no provisions equivalent to the powers of incorporated friendly societies in the Friendly Societies Act 1974 in relation to registered societies. Registered societies, as unincorporated associations of natural persons, have unlimited legal powers and therefore do not need powers to be granted to them by statute. However, it should be noted that the purposes of registered societies are limited (under s.7(1)(a) of the Friendly Societies Act 1974) to those set out in Sch.2 to the Friendly Societies Act 1992 and are therefore in practice more restrictive than the purposes available to incorporated societies.

11.5.1 *Power to undertake various miscellaneous activities*

Section 7(2) of the Friendly Societies Act 1992 gives incorporated friendly societies power to undertake a number of miscellaneous activities set out in Sch.5 to the Act. These consist of:

(a) the acceptance of contributions and deposits from members to establish a fund out of which loans can be made to members;
(b) the establishment of funds to purchase government securities on behalf of members;
(c) the investment of funds in housing associations;
(d) the accumulation of surplus contributions from members on which the society may pay interest; and

(e)   the making of subscriptions to hospitals, infirmaries and other charitable or provident institutions so that members of the society may enjoy the benefits provided by those institutions.

Finally, Sch.5 also permits incorporated friendly societies to contribute to the funds, and take part in the government, of any other friendly society (whether incorporated or not).

Although these activities might appear to be purposes, they are omitted from the list of purposes in s.7(2) of the Friendly Societies Act 1992 and are referred to in that section as "powers". This appears anomalous in that these activities cannot be undertaken in order to carry out the society's purposes as required for other powers by s.7(3). However, this appears to have been recognised by the reference to Sch.5 activities in s.7(4).

11.5.2   *Part II of the Friendly Societies Act 1992 powers*

Section 14 of the Friendly Societies Act 1992 confers general investment powers on incorporated friendly societies, including the power to invest in land, other securities or other investments which are permitted for trustees. These powers are conferred on all incorporated friendly societies and need not be specifically adopted in a society's memorandum or rules. In addition, any society which is subject to minimum solvency requirements under the FSA Handbook may adopt whatever wider investment powers it thinks fit.

Section 15 of the Friendly Societies Act 1992 confers on incorporated friendly societies the power (again, without specifically adopting the power in their memoranda or rules) to acquire and hold land for operational purposes or for the operational purposes of a subsidiary or jointly controlled body and also to dispose of such land or otherwise to deal with it.

Section 16 of the Friendly Societies Act 1992 allows incorporated friendly societies to provide services to subsidiaries or jointly controlled bodies and also to make payments towards the discharge of the liabilities of subsidiaries (but not those of jointly controlled bodies). The services permitted under s.16 are the making of loans of money (with or without security and whether or not at interest), the use of services or property (whether or not for payment), grants of money (whether or not repayable) and guarantees of the discharge of their liabilities. The Friendly Societies Commission accepted that the employment by an incorporated friendly society of staff engaged wholly or partly in the business of subsidiaries fell within the meaning of the use of services for the purposes of s.16. However, in relation to directive friendly societies this was on the basis that the services of staff (and any other services provided under s.16) had to be provided "at cost" or less and not at a profit to avoid a breach of what is now INSPRU 1.5.13 (*see*Section 11.6).

A further permitted activity for incorporated societies is the making of loans to members under Section 17 of the Friendly Societies Act 1992. Although this power applies only to incorporated societies, the language of s.17 betrays its nineteenth-century origins. The section permits an incorporated society to:

> "advance to a member of at least one full year's standing any sum not exceeding one half of the amount of an assurance on his life, on the written security of himself and two satisfactory sureties or, in Scotland, cautioners for repayment."

The requirement for two sureties makes this power difficult to use in practice and the need for it must be questionable since the amount advanced is limited to one half of the amount which would be payable to the member's estate on death under a contract of life assurance in any event. The ability to make advances to members is attractive to many societies and some societies have considered making advances through separate subsidiaries or setting up somewhat artificial arrangements, whereby the requirement to provide guarantees is satisfied by the members' entitlement to payment of life assurance proceeds being assigned to trustees who in turn provide guarantees to the society.

Like the "power" to undertake the various miscellaneous activities set out in Schedule 5, the power to make loans to members appears to be more a "purpose" than a "power". However, it does not appear in the list of purposes contained in s.7(2) and therefore would appear to be subject to the restriction in s.7(3), that it should only be exercised for the carrying out of the society's actual purposes. It is difficult to see how this might ever be achieved.

11.6   Combinations of business

Directive friendly societies, like other insurers, are subject to a restriction on the combination of their insurance business with other commercial business under what is now INSPRU 1.5.13.

This prohibition derives from the EU Life and Non-life Insurance Directives which were originally implemented more strictly for insurance companies than for friendly societies under Section 16 of the now repealed Insurance Companies Act 1982 which prohibited "any activities" other than insurance business. The prohibition for insurance companies has now been conformed with the "commercial business" prohibition which has always applied for friendly societies and permitted various activities for the benefit of members including:

(a)   the various social and benevolent activities permitted for incorporated friendly societies under s.10 of the Friendly Societies Act 1992;
(b)   the miscellaneous activities permitted for incorporated friendly societies under Sch.5 to the Friendly Societies Act 1992;
(c)   the provision by both incorporated and registered societies of contractual benefits under Head C and discretionary benefits under Head D of Sch.2 to the Friendly Societies Act 1992; and

(d) in the case of incorporated societies only, the provision of support services for subsidiaries either at cost or at a price less than cost and loans to members under s.17 of the Friendly Societies Act 1992.

The prohibition on the combination of long-term business with general business (except classes 1 and 2) under INSPRU 1.5.17 applies equally to directive friendly societies as it does to insurance companies.

11.7   The management and administration of friendly societies

The management and administration of a friendly society is entrusted to a committee of management which fulfils similar functions to the board of directors of a company. Indeed, a number of societies refer to their committee of management as a "board" and to the individual committee members as "directors". Section 27 of the Friendly Societies Act 1992 requires each society (registered as well as incorporated) to have a committee of management with at least two members. Guidance issued by the Friendly Societies Commission in CPN 1992/2 (para.12) suggested that the Commission would favour a maximum number of between five and 11 depending on the size of the society and the nature of its business. Although this particular guidance has not (unlike other Commission Practice Notes) been reissued as guidance in IPRU-FSOC and therefore ceased to apply in 2001, there is no reason to think that the FSA would depart from it.

Material relating to the regulation of committees of management is contained in s.27 and Sch.11 to the Friendly Societies Act 1992. The "approved persons" rules discussed in Chapter 3 also apply to committee members, subject to certain exemptions for "small friendly societies" discussed below. Although a detailed description of fiduciary duties is outside the scope of this Chapter, it should be noted that in addition to the statutory provisions and FSA's rules, the common-law rules on directors' fiduciary duties are thought to apply equally to members of the committee of management of a friendly society as they do to directors of a company, as the committee of management stands in the same fiduciary relationship to the members of a society as the directors of a company do to the members of the company. For companies, directors' fiduciary duties have now been replaced by statutory duties under ss.171–177 Companies Act 2006 but the previous common law will apply to friendly societies.

The requirements of s.27 and Sch.11 to the Friendly Societies Act 1992 contain a more restrictive regime for the appointment of committee members than applies to the directors of a company. A friendly society may regulate the appointment and retirement of committee members as it sees fit through its rules, subject to the general requirements of the FSA Handbook and the following additional overriding provisions, which have not been repealed by age-discrimination legislation:

(a) a committee member cannot be elected or re-elected if he has passed the age of 70 unless his election has been approved by resolution of the committee and the reasons for the committee's approval of his eligibility have been notified to members eligible to vote on his election;
(b) a person who is a member of the committee of management or is nominated for election or co-option onto the committee must give 28 days' notice to the society before he becomes 70 years old;
(c) committee members must retire no later than the fifth annual general meeting following the date of their election and, if over 70, at each annual general meeting;
(d) the committee of management may co-opt members, but they must pass a "fit and proper" test (this requirement remains as a separate statutory requirement for friendly societies in parallel with the requirements of the FSA Handbook) and cannot be co-opted if they have been proposed for election to the committee during the previous 12 months and the motion to elect them has been defeated. Co-opted members must stand down or offer themselves for election at the next occasion on which

elections are held for the committee (usually the next AGM following their appointment) or after 16 months, whichever is sooner.

Societies may adopt in their rules an age below 70 for the purposes of the tests described in paras (a)–(c) above but not a higher age. Persons retiring under these provisions may submit themselves for re-election.

The legislation on dealings between directors of building societies and their societies is applied to friendly societies under Part II of Sch.11 to the Friendly Societies Act 1992 with minor variations. This is broadly similar to the legislation on dealings between directors and companies under the now repealed Part X of the Companies Act 1985, but it does not reflect the current statutory duties of directors of companies under Part 10 of the Companies Act 2006. Where a friendly society has subsidiaries which are companies formed under the Companies Acts, directors who sit on the board of the society itself will find themselves subject to both regimes. However, somewhat confusingly, Part II of Sch.11 does incorporate into the Friendly Societies Act 1992 the provisions of s.217 of the Companies Act 2006, which require a payment to a director for loss of office to be approved by a resolution of members, subject to exceptions for payments in discharge of pre-existing legal obligations.

It should be noted that s.63 of the Building Societies Act 1986 on the disclosure of interests in contracts and other transactions (which applies to friendly societies by virtue of para.9(1)(b) of Sch.11 to the Friendly Societies Act 1992 and largely replicates the (now repealed) provisions of s.317 of the Companies Act 1985) does not prevent a director from forming part of the quorum or voting on a contract in which he is interested, as long as he declares his interest. It is commonplace for the articles of association of companies to give directors a specific power to do so in order to exonerate them from any breach of their fiduciary duties which may otherwise occur. The model memorandum and rules for friendly societies published by the Registry of Friendly Societies shortly after the enactment of the Friendly Societies Act 1992 contains prohibitions against committee members forming part of a quorum or voting on matters in which they are interested—a considerably stricter rule than that which applies to insurance companies.

The approved persons regime under the FSA Handbook applies to members of the committee of management who have "governing functions" for the purposes of SUP 10.4. SUP 10.6.26 recognises a separate "controlled function" for the members of the committee of management of a non-directive friendly society. SUP 10.6.28 allows the possibility for the committee of management of a non-directive friendly society to delegate responsibility for the society's regulated activities to a single individual to whom it is reasonable to delegate that responsibility, in which case the members of the committee of management will no longer have the responsibility themselves for the purposes of the FSA Handbook. The individual to whom the responsibility is delegated need not be a member of the committee of management but will, of course, himself need to be an approved person.

The only officers that an incorporated friendly society is required to have by statute are a chief executive and secretary (under s.28 of the Friendly Societies Act 1992) and these offices may be held by the same person. Section 28 of the Friendly Societies Act 1992 applies equally to registered societies, but registered societies are required, in addition, to have one or more trustees under s.24 of the Friendly Societies Act 1974. The trustees will hold the assets of a registered society and, typically, under the rules of the society they will be the persons entitled to sue, or liable or be sued, on behalf of the society.

Certain decisions may be reserved under the rules or by statute for the members of the society in general meeting. Friendly societies have unusually wide scope to determine for themselves under their rules which matters do require reference to a general meeting (e.g. friendly societies may amend their memoranda and rules by any procedure set out in the rules, although most do so by ordinary resolution requiring a simple majority of the votes cast at a general meeting). Some matters are required by statute to be approved by a special resolution (requiring a minimum notice period of 14 days and approval by not less than 75 per cent of the votes cast). The principal regulatory matters which require members' approval by special resolution are referred to in the relevant paragraphs of this Chapter.

The rules of most friendly societies allow all members to attend general meetings of the society and give each member one vote on resolutions at general meetings. Paragraph 5(1) of Sch.12 to the Friendly Societies Act 1992 prohibits voting rights from being conditional on the amount of subscriptions paid by members. However, a significant minority of friendly societies operate a "delegate" voting system under which groups of members appoint one or more delegates to represent them at general meetings. Where this system operates only delegates have the right to attend or vote at meetings. Friendly societies can, but are not obliged to, adopt proxy voting and para.8 of Sch.12 to the Friendly Societies Act 1992 also admits postal ballots as an alternative to resolutions passed at a general meeting of a friendly society. Those societies which have delegate voting systems generally do not allow either proxy voting or postal ballots. Since 12 April 2011, amendments to the Friendly Societies Act 1992 brought about under the Mutual Societies (Electronic Communications) Order (SI 2011/593) have permitted Friendly Societies to allow members to vote electronically on resolutions at general meetings.

11.8   Mergers and transfers of engagements

Friendly societies fall outside the regime for portfolio transfers under Part VII of the FSMA 2000 as described in Chapter 6. The procedure for portfolio transfers by friendly societies (known as "transfers of engagements") is set out in Part VIII of the Friendly Societies Act 1992 and Sch.15 to that Act. These provisions apply to both registered and incorporated societies. Broadly speaking, the procedure is similar to the procedure which applies to insurance companies with the preparation of an independent actuary's report (equivalent to the independent expert's report) and a circular to members, but there are important differences. It is beyond the scope of this Chapter to set out the full procedure for friendly society transfers, but the principal differences between the friendly society procedure and the procedure for insurance companies are as follows:

(a) Insurance business transfers under Part VII of the FSMA 2000 are required to be implemented by a court order. Transfers of engagements of friendly societies are implemented through the FSA confirming an "instrument of transfer of engagements" after considering any representations made to it by interested persons. The instrument of transfer then takes effect upon registration with the FSA. (*See* s.86 and Sch.15 to the Friendly Societies Act 1992.) The apparent duplication between confirmation and registration derives from the pre-2001 regime when the two processes were carried out by different bodies: confirmation by the Friendly Societies Commission and registration by the Chief Register of Friendly Societies.

(b) An insurance business transfer or transfer of engagements *to* a friendly society must be approved by the transferee friendly society by special resolution as well as by the transferor.

Where the transferor and the transferee are both friendly societies, the FSA has power under s.86(3)(b) of the Friendly Societies Act 1992 to waive the requirement for a special resolution of members of the transferee and to allow the transfer of engagements to proceed on the basis of a resolution of the transferee society's committee of management. Section 86(8) of the Friendly Societies Act 1992 requires inward transfers to a friendly society from a person which is not a friendly society to be approved by a special resolution of the transferee friendly society, but there is no power for the FSA to grant exemption from this provision. SUP 18.4.11G provides guidance on the circumstances in which the FSA proposes to use its discretion to allow a transferee friendly society to approve a transfer by resolution of the committee of management. The factors which the FSA will take into account are whether the transfer will be in the interests of the members of both societies and whether the transfer will require a "change of policy" by the transferee society. SUP 18.4.11G also states that the FSA is unlikely to exercise its discretion unless the transferee is significantly larger than the business to be transferred. In practice, the FSA has not exercised its discretion under s.86(3)(b) lightly but has shown some flexibility in borderline cases.

In addition to transfers of engagements, Part VIII of the Friendly Societies Act 1992 also provides a mechanism for friendly societies to amalgamate and to convert into companies. An amalgamation of two friendly societies (whether incorporated or registered) can take place under Section 85, Friendly Societies Act 1992 and requires a similar procedure of:

(a)   consultation with the FSA;
(b)   the preparation of an actuary's report;
(c)   a circular to members;
(d)   approval by special resolution;
(e)   confirmation of an instrument of transfer by the FSA after members and others concerned have had an opportunity to make representations; and
(f)   the registration of the successor society.

Any successor to two amalgamated societies, even if both were registered societies, must be an incorporated friendly society.

Section 90 of the Friendly Societies Act 1992 confers on the FSA power to direct a friendly society to transfer all or part of its engagements to another friendly society or to another body if the FSA considers that the transferor society is unable to manage its affairs satisfactorily in relation to the relevant business and the transfer would be expedient to protect the interests of members of the society. In the case of a compulsory transfer under Section 90, the proposed transferee is required, whether or not it is a friendly society, to approve the inward transfer by special resolution. However, s.90 also gives the FSA power to consent to approval being made by a resolution of the "committee of management of the transferee", which implies that the draftsman was thinking of friendly society transferees. How this might work with a non-friendly society transferee has never been tested in practice.

Section 91 of the Friendly Societies Act 1992 contains a mechanism for friendly societies to convert into companies. The mechanism again involves a circular to members, a special resolution of the society to convert and the process of confirmation by the FSA. HM Treasury has taken over the powers formally vested in the Friendly Societies Commission to make regulations in relation to the conversion of friendly societies into companies. To date, this power has not been exercised either by the Friendly Societies Commission or by the Treasury.

It should be noted that the FSA has considerable flexibility under s.89 of the Friendly Societies Act 1992 to modify the requirements for transfers of engagements *by* friendly societies (but not for transfers of engagements or insurance business transfers *to* friendly societies). The powers allow the FSA to waive the requirements for a special resolution by the transferor society under s.86(2)(b) and (c) of the Friendly Societies Act 1992 and to modify the requirements to circularise members under Sch.15. However, these powers may not be exercised so as to allow a friendly society to approve a transfer of engagements by less than a majority of those voting (or to require more than three-quarters of those voting to approve a transfer of engagements). The power may only be exercised upon application by at least 100 members of the society (or, if fewer, by 10 per cent of the entire membership).

Certain societies have adopted special rules in relation to transfers of engagement and conversions into companies. These rules include a minimum period of membership before members may vote on resolutions (including resolutions to approve transfers or conversions) and requirements for a minimum turn-out on resolutions to transfer engagements or to convert, analogous to the minimum turn-out requirements which automatically apply to building societies under Sch.2 to the Building Societies Act 1986.

11.9 Disputes and arbitration, disciplinary powers

Friendly societies are required under s.80 of the Friendly
Societies Act 1992 to include within their rules a mechanism
whereby disputes with members and certain other persons or
bodies can be referred to arbitration with the alternative, if all
parties to the dispute consent, to refer the dispute to the county
court (or to a sheriff in Scotland). This requirement has been
preserved notwithstanding the establishment of the Financial
Ombudsman under Part XVI of the FSMA 2000. Friendly
societies fall within the compulsory jurisdiction of the Financial
Ombudsman under DISP 2.1. Friendly societies are also
required to comply with the complaint-handling procedures
for firms under DISP 1. Section 80(1A) of the Friendly Societies
Act 1992 (inserted by the Financial Services and Markets Act
2000 (Mutual Societies) Order 2001 (SI 2001/2617)) states that
the arbitration mechanism is without prejudice to a complainant's right to refer complaints to the Financial Ombudsman.

The FSA has specific disciplinary and enforcement powers in
relation to friendly societies under the Friendly Societies Act
1992, in addition to the powers that it has under the
enforcement chapter of the FSA Handbook. These powers are:

(a) A power to apply to the High Court for the winding up of
     a friendly society under s.52 of the Friendly Societies Act
     1992 if the FSA has reason to believe:
     (i)   that the society is carrying out activities which are not
           permitted under the Friendly Societies Act 1992 or the
           Friendly Societies Act 1974;
     (ii) that the society is not carrying out any of the activities
           referred to in Sch.2 to the Friendly Societies Act 1992
           (as to which, *see* Section 11.4.1); or
     (iii) that it is failing to comply with the laws relating to
           insurance in any EEA Member State other than the
           UK.
(b) The power to issue directions in relation to disproportion-
     ate activities of subsidiaries under s.54 of the Friendly
     Societies Act 1992 referred to in Section 11.4.5 above.

(c) The power in relation to disproportionate group business under s.55 of the Friendly Societies Act 1992 referred to in Section 11.4.3 above.

(d) The power to direct a society to transfer its engagements to a third party under s.90 of the Friendly Societies Act 1992 referred to in Section 11.8 above.

Section 58A of the Friendly Societies Act 1992 (inserted by art.13(1), Financial Services and Markets Act 2000 (Mutual Societies) Order 2001 (SI 2001/2617)) applies the system of warning notices and decision notices under Part XXVI of the FSMA 2000, *mutatis mutandis*, to any actions taken by the FSA under ss.54, 55 or 90 of the Friendly Societies Act 1992. There is also a right to refer any decision notices issued by the FSA in respect of these matters to the Financial Services and Markets Tribunal under Part IX of the FSMA 2000. Parts IX and XXVI of the FSMA 2000 do not apply to applications for winding up under s.52 of the Friendly Societies Act 1992 as such applications must be made to the High Court.

11.10   Project Chrysalis

Since a significant number of friendly societies write with-profits business, no chapter on the FSA Regulation of Friendly Societies would be complete without a consideration of "Project Chrysalis", which was initiated by a group of friendly societies and other mutual insurers to seek a re-examination of how the FSA's rules on treating with-profit policyholders fairly operate for mutual insurers. The project arose out of a concern that the FSA's rules in COBS 20 had been drafted for proprietary with-profits insurers which, unlike mutuals, have a separate shareholders' fund alongside their with-profits funds. As is clear from COBS 20.2.1, the rules in COBS 20 seek to regulate the potential conflicts of interest between shareholders and with-profits policyholders in a proprietary insurer's with-profits fund. However, most mutual insurers (including friendly societies) writing with-profits business operate a single fund (often referred to as its "common fund") and inequitable results are likely to flow from applying rules designed for part of the funds of a proprietary insurer to the whole of the funds of a mutual insurer.

The FSA was not receptive to the arguments advanced in support of Project Chrysalis and published on 13 October 2009 a "Dear CEO letter" in which it stated its view that "the general position is that with-profits policyholders in their capacities as policyholders and as members of a mutual will be entitled ultimately to all or almost all of the assets in a mutual's long-term fund after the mutual's contractual obligations in respect of policies written into that fund have been satisfied". This conclusion was drawn from legal advice from Ian Glick QC and Richard Mott of 1 Essex Court. The Dear CEO letter invited mutual insurers to consider their own position in the light of the letter and legal advice, in response to which a substantial number of friendly societies and other mutual insurers wrote to the FSA disagreeing with both the FSA's position and the advice it had received. This resulted in a second Dear CEO letter, dated 28 September 2010 in which the FSA slightly modified its position, although the FSA has subsequently made further modifications in a paper entitled "Rights and expectations of with-profits policyholders in mutuals: the FSA's legal position" published in March 2011.

The FSA also published, in February 2011 its Consultation Paper CP 11/5 "Protecting with-profits policyholders" in which it made various proposals for amendments to the rules in COBS 20: these proposals have generally been seen as enhancing the position of with-profits policyholders as against other stakeholders in a mutual insurer. As at the date of writing (July 2011), the FSA is still considering responses to this consultation. To add to this uncertainty, the Bank of England and the FSA have published the proposed regulatory objectives for Prudential Regulation Authority (the "PRA") which is intended to become the lead regulator for with-profits insurance in place of the FSA with effect from the end of 2012. The PRA's objectives will be to secure an appropriate degree of protection for policyholders and, as needed, to minimise the adverse impact that the failure of an insurer or the way it carries out its business could have on the stability of the [financial] system. It is to be expected that the thinking underlying Project Chrysalis will remain very relevant to the industry's response to further developments both in relation to the FSA's CP 11/5 proposals and in relation to the PRA's new regulatory objectives.

Index

All indexing is to heading number